ON THE FRONT LINE

TRUE WORLD
WAR I STORIES

ON THE FRONT LINE
TRUE WORLD WAR I STORIES

Edited and Introduced by C. B. Purdom

Foreword by Malcolm Brown

Constable • London

Constable & Robinson Ltd
3 The Lanchesters
162 Fulham Palace Road
LondonW6 9ER
www.constablerobinson.com

First published in the UK by Robinson Publishing Ltd, 1997

This revised and updated edition published by Constable,
an imprint of Constable & Robinson, 2009.

Foreword © Malcolm Brown

A copy of the British Library Cataloguing in Publication data
is available from the British Library

978-1-84901-067-2

Printed and bound in the EU

3 5 7 9 10 8 6 4

CONTENTS

FOREWORD

This book was first published in 1930, appearing under the imprint of Messrs J. M. Dent, the originator of that illustrious, long honoured library of books bearing the name 'Everyman'. Also in that year there appeared on the scene that much consulted, much admired, magisterial work entitled *War Books: A Critical Guide*, written by Cyril Falls: professional soldier, noted historian and destined to become Chichele Professor of the History of War at the University of Oxford. This was, as we might now see it, an Ofsted report on works relating to the recent Great War published in the period from the Armistice of 1918 to the end of the 1920s. Falls was able to include, presumably as a last-minute entry, a comment on the present work. His verdict is worth quoting in full:

> This is a very striking book, throwing light upon almost every phase of the War. It contains sixty short narratives by writers of all ranks from private to lieutenant-colonel, but unfortunately only three from the Navy and the Royal Air Force. Practically every campaign is mentioned, though of course the vast majority of the incidents are from the Western Front. The narrators are in no case professional writers, and though some (but by no means all) lack literary skill, they are far more representative of the British Army, Navy, and Air Force, than any professional writer with his overcharged sensibilities and his inevitable reaction to literary influences and conventions.

That final sentence carries with it, surely, a clear if coded reference to the new style of writing about the recent war that was beginning at that time to make increasingly significant waves, a style of which, evidently, though not unexpectedly, Cyril Falls did not wholly approve. Heralded much earlier in the decade by C. E. Montague's grounding-breaking book,

Disenchantment, first published in 1922 – the message of which was clearly implied by its title – the books which now dominated the literary scene were to become the most famous and influential to emerge from the First World War, a conflict which to this day has never been allowed to slip quietly into the past, but remains a permanent focus of controversy. It is a conflict on which after almost a hundred years, (to borrow a key-note phrase from another area of continuing cultural disagreement), many still look back in anger.

To name some of the titles which appeared at this time: the year 1928 saw the publication of Edmund Blunden's *Undertones of War*, while 1929 produced a positive harvest including Richard Aldington's *Death of a Hero*, Robert Graves's *Goodbye to All That*, Charles Carrington's memoir *A Subaltern's War* (written under the pseudonym of Charles Edmonds), and the English translation of Erich Maria Remarque's *All Quiet on the Western Front*, a striking 'take' on the war from the point of view of the former enemy.

Falls's comments on the above were mixed. He had high praise for Edmund Blunden, claiming that his memoir was 'probably the only single book we have had in English which really reaches the stature of its subject'; he saw some virtue in Richard Aldington's offering, in spite of describing it as 'one of the bitterest war novels that has been written', but he was deeply critical of the works by Graves and Remarque. For the latter he had no time at all, blaming his book's runaway success on the massive publicity campaign that had preceded its arrival; and condemning it as 'frank propaganda' by an author who 'appears to know singularly little of certain of the details which he describes'. He praised Graves for his excellent war scenes, but found that overall his attitude 'left a disagreeable impression. One might gather that thousands of men instead of a few hundred were executed, and that suicides were as common as blackberries. He is in short an example of the "intellectual", whose intelligence with regard to the War penetrates a much shorter distance than that of the plain man.' He had highest praise of all for Charles Edmonds: 'The writer does not make war any prettier than its ugly self, but he shows that ordinary men endured it without becoming the shambling woebegone spectres so often depicted. These spectres would not have been victorious against the worst troops in the world. Mr Edmonds lets us see how and why the real men were victorious against the best.'

The following year, 1930, provided a further crop, including, as already stated, Cyril Falls's own *War Books*, which appeared late enough to catch *Everyman at War* but too soon for Siegfried Sassoon's *Memoirs of an Infantry Officer*, though he had warm praise for its already published predecessor, *Memoirs of a Fox-Hunting Man*, which, while mainly a paean for a lost peace, managed to include some brief war scenes which he found 'impressive'.

Another book of that year for which I think Falls would have not have found place even had it appeared in time, but which I see as a work of considerable significance in the present discussion, in that it enshrined a markedly different view of the world of the Western Front from that purveyed by the majority of the books mentioned above, was the collected reprint of the most famous of the trench magazines produced during the war, *The Wipers Times*.

The story of the founding of that magazine has been often told. In brief, two officers of the 12th Sherwood Foresters, Captain (later Colonel) F. J. Roberts and Lieutenant (later Major) J. H. Pearson, found an abandoned printing press somewhere in the ruins of Ypres, 'capital' of that infamous killing-ground known as the Ypres Salient, 'acquired' it, and turned their unofficial ownership of it to excellent effect by producing between February 1916 and December 1918 over twenty editions, which won such a reputation for good writing and wit that all but its last two issues were republished in Britain to considerable acclaim while the war was still in progress.

In 1930 it was thought timely to give the magazine a further airing, in a handsome collected edition, with a Foreword by a commander widely admired by the troops during the war, Field

Marshal Sir Herbert, now Lord, Plumer, and an Introduction by
the chief editor, F. J. Roberts. Roberts had mocked the military
hierarchy and joked about almost every aspect of the Western
Front war, but he had firmly believed in the justice of the cause
for which so many had suffered and died, and he had not been
pleased to find that the new wave of publications flooding the
nation's bookshops appeared to denigrate the values in which
he and his like had so firmly believed.

He declared his hand at once in the volume's dedication.
Whereas an earlier compilation had been dedicated to those
who had 'gone west'; this volume carried a more assertive
message, doubtless devised by Roberts himself:

TO THE SOLDIERS OF THE SALIENT
AND THE TRUTH ABOUT THE WAR

The 'truth about the war' was, clearly, *his* truth as he saw it,
not the new truth now being promulgated to the disadvantage
of the old.

He showed his hand even more pointedly in his Introduction
by resorting to a rousing foray in the house style of *The Wipers
Times* which had been its special hallmark, harking back to the
time of the great German offensive launched on 21 March 1918,
which, historically, had been the event that was most
responsible for taking his magazine off the presses for much of
the war's final year. Far from yielding ground to the best-selling
titles commanding the field in 1930, he took a deliberate,
brilliant lunge at them, as it so happened, very much in line
with the views expressed by Cyril Falls:

Hastily taking two aspirin and placing helmet, gas, in
position, I looked out of the door, only to find the
beautiful March morning obscured by what seemed to be
one of London's best old-style November fogs. Shouting
for batman, Adjutant, Sergeant, Sergeant-Major and the
Mess-Waiter, I emerged into the chilly air, which was
being torn and rent in the most alarming way. All was *not*

quiet on the Western Front, the Sub-Editor and I drank a case of whiskey, shot the Padre for cowardice and said "good–bye to all that". (The influence of these modern War Books is most insidious.)

Sadly, this was Roberts' last bow. He faded from the scene, wrote no more about the war or any other subject, emigrating to Canada to take up his pre-1914 profession as a mining engineer and dying in obscurity in the 1960s. The founder of *The Wipers Times* was not honoured as he surely should have been by an obituary in the newspaper whose title he had deliberately mimicked when founding his own publication, *The Times* of London.

The riches emanating from that highly productive year 1930, however, are not yet exhausted. For it also saw the first appearance of another remarkable book which has won a considerable reputation: *Soldiers' Songs and Slang*, collected and edited by John Brophy and Eric Partridge, both literary figures of considerable distinction, but, unlike Blunden, Graves, Aldington or Sassoon, former soldiers who had served not as officers but in the ranks. They offered a radically different perspective on the war of the Western Front, the viewpoint of the anonymous, unprivileged lower depths of the vast organisation that was the British Army, especially the shilling-a-day infantrymen who were at everybody else's beck and call, and who were frequently officially referred to not as soldiers but as 'rifles'; their status being defined less by the uniforms they wore or even the names they bore but by the weapons they carried. The new book added their hugely eloquent, ribald, funny, often world-weary voices to the rising clamour.

Soldiers' Songs and Slang was to go through several editions in the 1930s, re-emerge as *The Long Trail* in the 1960s, and it has now re-appeared in a new printing as *The Daily Telegraph Dictionary of Tommies' Songs and Slang* in 2008. (I confess to having been part of this process, having proposed its resurrection in the first place and contributed a new Introduction.)

But to return to the subject of *Everyman at War*, where does this book, also published in 1930, fit in this fascinating parabola of literary effusions?

Basically, I see it as firmly, and I would suggest proudly, occupying a substantial territory in the middle ground, between the high-octane literary works of the Graveses and the Sassoons of this world – to which the names of Wilfred Owen, Isaac Rosenberg and Ivor Gurney would be added in due course – and the writings and utterances of the 'warrior or warriors unknown' who devised the songs and the slang saved for posterity by Brophy and Partridge. The authors of the sixty pieces here reprinted were writing straightforwardly about what they knew, about what they saw, about what they experienced, and they clearly – as Falls swiftly realised – were untouched by any modish cult or trend in the literary circles of the time. They wrote as themselves, not in response to any school of thought or wind of change, and, in Falls's view, were all the better as chroniclers of the recent war on that account. As the reader will see, they were all were meticulously identified by the editor with details as to their service careers, so that friends and relatives would be aware of the fact of their contribution to the historical records, but their essential virtue is that collectively they constitute the 'Everyman' of the original title – the ordinary citizen, the unsung mass –and it is good to see this remarkable volume returned to its rightful place in the public domain with that title restored.

And there is, I should add, some quite outstanding writing here, writing that deserves to be remembered and not, as it were, allowed to be airbrushed out of historical memory. To name just one contribution, the terrifying plight of a fearful ordinary soldier caught up in a failed 'over the top' advance during a major battle has never been better evoked for me than in the account, only seven pages long, entitled 'Ordinary War on the Somme'. The author was former Private Fred Ball, who enlisted with the Liverpool Pals in January 1915, crossed to France in November that year and served continuously in France for the remainder of the war, then went to Germany with the Army of Occupation, finally being demobilised in March 1919, never having sought or received promotion. And he is just one of sixty.

The credit for all this must go to the editor of the book, C. B. Purdom. Essentially he wanted no fine writing, no show-off from his contributors, he wanted them to write in a clear, straightforward manner about what they had seen and experienced and to do so at minimal length. The result is a book which is of such overall quality that it cries out for a reprint. There is much talk these days of 'forgotten voices' when it comes to war subjects. Here we have sixty too-long-ignored voices which deserve to be remembered. I cannot recommend this book too highly. In fact, in view of its virtual disappearance for almost eighty years after its original printing, I believe it might fairly be described as a rediscovered classic, worthy of joining the rich ranks of books of permanent value in relation to the Great War of 1914–1918.

Who was C. B. Purdom? He was Charles Benjamin Purdom, born in 1883, died 1965. Perhaps his principal legacy relates to the founding of new towns such as, first, Letchworth Garden City and, subsequently, Welwyn Garden City, a subject in which was interested from 1902 onwards, championing the concept of this revolutionary style of communal living in a number of books written over several decades. Married in 1913, he appears not to have served in the First World War, though in the Second World War he held posts in the Ministry of Food, the Ministry of Supply and the Ministry of Information. He subsequently interested himself in the problems left by the Luftwaffe's bombing campaign, publishing in 1945 a book under the title *How Shall We Rebuild London?* A lifelong passion was the theatre. At one time he was general secretary of British Equity, at another he edited a magazine entitled *Theatregoer*, and over the years he poured out a spate of books on the subject, including such titles as *Producing Plays*, *The Pleasures of the Theatre*, *Producing Shakespeare*, a biography of the dramatist and producer Harley Granville Barker, and *A Guide to the Plays of Bernard Shaw*. It was his period as editor of the magazine *Everyman,* between 1928 and 1932, which led to the production of the present work. It was his idea, presumably launched in 1929, to invite readers of the magazine to send in brief personal accounts of their experiences in the war which had involved so many of his juniors and contemporaries, with a view to including the best of them in a new anthology.

But it is time for him to tell his own story, and I now hand the baton to him, inviting the reader to turn to his excellent and illuminating Introduction.

Malcolm Brown
January 2009

INTRODUCTION

These narratives of the War are not the work of practised writers but of soldiers telling their personal experiences. They have therefore an interest that War novels or stories or official records do not possess. A few of them are by sailors and by men in the Air Force, and by women; but the greater number are by men of various ranks who served on the different Fronts, most of them as privates in France and Flanders. They show what War is from the soldier's point of view. It is a restricted point of view, of course, but it is concerned with realities, and for that reason important.

The narratives came to be written in this way. A few months ago a friend was talking to me with admiration of Barbusse's *Le Feu*, and remarked incidentally that he had not yet written his own story of the War, though he intended to do so before he got too old. He served in the ranks in Flanders during practically the whole period of the War, and had, he thought, something to tell that had not yet been told. I urged him to sit down and write his account before it had gone from his mind, and he went away declaring that he would start upon it that very day. But he has not done it and *I* do not think he ever will.

There are many men in the same position. They have something to tell about the War, but have never been induced to put it on record. There is a deep reluctance in most men to write of things with which they were so closely concerned. To most of them the War was not an event: it was their lives stretched to the most painful degree of tension and desperate effort of which they were capable. Many men have never recovered from the numbing effect of the War upon their senses, and do not wish to recall all that happened in those dreadful years. Yet the world loses by the silence of those who have knowledge, and, for the full lesson of the War to be learned, as many as possible of those who know what it meant should put their experiences on record.

With that in mind I invited the readers of 'Everyman' to send me accounts of their actual War experiences, in not more than three thousand words, offering a small prize for the best narrative received. In the course of a few weeks I received over three hundred narratives, of which two hundred and eighty-nine were worth serious consideration. I did not expect so remarkable a result. At least half of them deserved to be printed, and I finally came to the conclusion that a selection of the very best should be made into a book.

The writers had been asked to relate their experiences straightforwardly and simply. 'Good writing' was not expected. The result was that the bulk of the manuscripts were plain statements of fact recording experiences that were deeply felt. The amount of 'literary' effort was remarkably small. A certain number adopted the short story form, but these were mostly rejected, and only a few are included in this volume. Most of the manuscripts were hand-written. Some of them were substantiated by diaries and other papers. On the whole the narratives did not seem to suffer from exaggeration. I ask the reader to judge that for himself from the selection in the following pages. Indeed, understatement was characteristic of many of them, they were very English in that respect. Some made comments on the War, deeply resenting its effects on themselves, or its social and political results. I have not included much comment of the sort. Here and there a tendency to overdo the 'horrors' was shown; but there was remarkably little bad language.

The narratives are of various kinds. Some relate to single incidents, others give a general impression of War experience. Some, as I have indicated, were written from diaries, others from deeply engraved memory. Some of them are human documents of the first order. Major events in the history of the War are referred to from time to time, but generally the narratives present personal experience. It is noticeable that hardly any feeling against the enemy is expressed. Only two writers referred to the Germans as 'Huns,' for 'Jerry' is the usual epithet. I have interfered with the narratives as little as possible in editing them, checking names of places as far as I could, and clearing up doubtful points, but the writers speak with their own natural rhythm and style.

The cumulative effect of these narratives is impressive. They seem to me to give a more convincing sense of the War than any War book that I have yet seen. They are best read, I venture to think, so as to get this cumulative effect. I have arranged them in the order of events as far as possible. I regret that there are so few from the Navy, but one of them by a seaman is an extremely vivid piece of writing.

The impression that I get from reading them is not that of suffering or horror, but of the senselessness of war. No one who served in it but was oppressed more or less constantly by its futility. Its political effects were far-reaching; but as a method of State action we discovered it to be without any redeeming features. In the narratives printed here the War is looked at from the point of view of individual men engaged in it. These men do not lose their human qualities, their courage, honesty, chivalry, and spirit of self-sacrifice, but those qualities themselves are seen to lose their value, for man surrenders himself to the machine, and all that makes life worth living is gone. The truth about war is that it is an evil, not only because men suffer and die in it, but because it destroys the meaning of life.

For that reason wars must be made to cease, and the lesson of the Great War is that war must be prevented in the future. War is not an adventure, but a disaster; it has no glamour or romance or nobility. But wars can be prevented only in times of peace, and if the lesson of the last War is learned now, we shall see that the relations between States make wars unnecessary.

When war comes there is nothing left but to do one's duty in it as these men did whose stories are printed here.

C. B. Purdom
London, February 1930

THE RETREAT FROM MONS

August 23rd–September 5th, 1914

Bernard John Denore

August 23rd – We had been marching since 2.30 a.m. and about 11.15 a.m., an order was passed down for 'A' Company (my company) to deploy to the right and dig in on the south bank of a railway cutting.

We deployed and started digging-in, but as the soil was mostly chalk, we were able to make only shallow holes. While we were digging the German artillery opened fire. The range was perfect, about six shells at a time bursting in line directly over our heads. All of us except the company commander fell flat on our faces, frightened, and surprised; but after a while we got up, and looked over the rough parapet we had thrown up; and could not see much. One or two men had been wounded, and one was killed.

There was a town about one mile away on our left front, and a lot of movement was going on round about it; and there was a small village called Binche on our right, where there was a lot of heavy firing going on – rifle and artillery.

We saw the Germans attack on our left in great masses, but they were beaten back by the Coldstream Guards.

A squadron of German cavalry crossed our front about 800 yards distant, and we opened fire on them. We hit a few and the fact that we were doing something definite improved our *moral* immensely, and took away a lot of our nervousness.

The artillery fire from the Germans was very heavy, but was dropping behind us on a British battery. The company officer, who had stayed in the open all the time, had taken a couple of men to help get the wounded away from the battery behind us. He returned about 6.30 p.m., when the firing had died down a bit, and told us the battery had been blown to bits.

I was then sent with four men on outpost to a signal box at a level crossing, and found it was being used as a clearing station for wounded. After dark more wounded were brought in from the 9th Battery R.F.A. (the battery that was cut up). One man was in a very bad way, and kept shrieking out for somebody to bring a razor and cut his throat, and two others died almost immediately.

I was going to move a bundle of hay when someone called out, 'Look out, chum. There's a bloke in there.' I saw a leg completely severed from its body, and suddenly felt very sick and tired.

The German rifle-fire started again and an artillery-man to whom I was talking was shot dead. I was sick then. Nothing much happened during the night, except that one man spent the time kissing a string of rosary beads, and another swore practically the whole night.

August 24th – Just about dawn a party of Germans came near and we opened fire on them and hit quite a number. We thought of following them up, but a corporal brought an order to retire. We joined the company again behind the trenches, and learnt that the town we could see was Mons.

After a while we joined up with the rest of the battalion on the road and went back the same route we covered coming up. All the time there was plenty of firing going on by Givry, and about midday we deployed, and opened fire on a regiment of German cavalry. They dismounted and returned our fire, which was all 'rapid') and was telling on them. Then suddenly they mounted and disappeared out of range. We continued marching back for about four hours. Then again we deployed and opened fire on more German cavalry, but this time they kept out of range and eventually moved off altogether.

My platoon was sent forward to a small village, where we stayed all night firing occasionally at what we hoped were German cavalry.

August 25th – We started off about 5 a.m., still retiring, and so far we had had no food since Sunday the 23rd. All day long we marched, and although a lot of firing was going on, we did none of it. About 6.30 p.m. we got to a place called Maroilles, and my platoon spent the night guarding a bridge over a stream. The Germans attacked about 9 p.m. and kept it up all night, but didn't get into Maroilles.

About forty-five of the company were killed or wounded, including the company officer. A voice had called out in English, 'Has anybody got a map?' and when our C.O. stood up with his map, a German walked up, and shot him with a revolver. The German was killed by a bayonet stab from a private.

August 26th – The Germans withdrew at dawn, and soon after we continued retiring, and had not been on the march very long before we saw a French regiment, which showed that all of them had not deserted us.

We marched all day long, miles and miles it seemed, probably owing to the fact that we had had no sleep at all since Saturday the 22nd, and had had very little food to eat, and. the marching discipline was not good. I myself frequently felt very sick.

We had a bit of a fight at night, and what made matters worse was that it happened at Venerolles, the village we were billeted in before we went up to Mons. Anyway, the Germans retired from the fight.

August 27th – At dawn we started on the march again. I noticed that the *curé* and one old fellow stayed in Venerolles, but all the other inhabitants went the previous night.

A lot of our men threw away their overcoats while we were on the road to-day, but I kept mine.

The marching was getting quite disorderly; numbers of men from other regiments were mixed up with us.

We reached St. Quentin, a nice town, just before dark, but marched straight through, and dug ourselves in on some high ground, with a battery of artillery in line with us. Although we saw plenty of movement in the town the Germans didn't attack us, neither did we fire on them. During the night a man near me quite suddenly started squealing like a pig, and then jumped out of the trench, ran straight down the hill towards the town, and shot himself through the foot. He was brought in by some artillery-men.

August 28th – Again at dawn we started on the march, and during the first halt another fellow shot himself through the foot.

The roads were in a terrible state, the heat was terrific; there seemed to be very little order about anything, and mixed up with us and wandering about all over the road were refugees, with all sorts of conveyances – prams, trucks, wheelbarrows, and tiny little carts drawn by dogs. They were piled up, with what looked like beds and bedding, and all of them asked us for food, which we could not give them, as we had none ourselves.

The men were discarding their equipment in a wholesale fashion, in spite of orders to the contrary; also many of them fell out, and rejoined again towards dusk. They had been riding on limbers and wagons, and officers' chargers, and generally looked worse than those of us who kept going all day. That night I went on outpost, but I did not know where exactly, as things were getting hazy in my mind. I tried to keep a diary, although it was against orders. Anyway, I couldn't realize all that was happening, and only knew that I was always tired, hungry, unshaven, and dirty. My feet were sore, water was scarce: in fact, it was issued in half-pints, as we were not allowed to touch the native water. The regulations were kept in force in that respect so much so that two men were put under arrest and sentenced to field punishment for stealing bread from an empty house.

Then, again, it wasn't straight marching. For every few hours we had to deploy, and beat off an attack, and every time somebody I knew was killed or wounded. And after we had beaten off the attacking force, on we went again retiring.

August 29th – A despatch was read to us, from General French, explaining that the B.E.F. was on the west of a sort of horseshoe, and that the retirement was to draw the Germans right into it, when they would be nipped off. That afternoon we went to a place called Chauny to guard the river while some R.E.'s blew up the bridges. It was a change from the everlasting marching, and we managed to get some vegetables out of the gardens and cook them. A few Uhlans appeared, but got away again in spite of our fire. So far as I could tell there wasn't a single civilian in the town, and all the houses were barricaded; while outside of them were buckets of wine-pink, blue, red, whitish, and other colours. We were not allowed to drink any.

August 30th – Just as we were leaving Chauny – about 4 a.m. – two girls were found and were taken along with us.

Although all the bridges were blown up, the Germans were after us almost immediately. God only knew how they got over so soon. Their fire was heavy but high; the few we saw were firing from their hips as they advanced. We fired for about half an hour. Then the artillery came into action, and we retired about two or three miles under cover of their fire. Then we waited till the Germans came up, and we began all over again, and then again, and then again, all day long. It was terribly tiring, heart-breaking work, as we seemed to have the measure of the Germans, and yet we retired.

During the evening the Guards Brigade took over the rearguard work while our Brigade went on to Castle Isoy, and bivouacked and slept for about six hours.

August 31st – Again we were rearguard, but did little fighting. We marched instead, staggering about the road like a crowd of gipsies. Some of the fellows had puttees wrapped round their feet instead of boots; others had soft shoes they had picked up somewhere; others walked in their socks, with their feet all bleeding. My own boots would have disgraced a tramp, but I was too frightened to take them off, and look at my feet. Yet they marched until they dropped, and then somehow got up and marched again.

One man (Ginger Gilmore) found a mouth-organ, and, despite the fact that his feet were bound in blood-soaked rags, he staggered along at the head of the company playing tunes all day. Mostly he played 'The Irish Emigrant,' which is a good marching tune. He reminded me of Captain Oates.

An officer asked me if I wanted a turn on his horse, but I looked at the fellow on it, and said, 'No thanks.'

The marching was getting on everyone's nerves, but, as I went I kept saying to myself, 'If you can, force your heart and nerve and sinew.' Just that, over and over again.

That night we spent the time looking for an Uhlan regiment, but didn't get in touch with them, and every time we stopped we fell asleep; in fact we slept while we were marching, and consequently kept falling over.

September 1st – We continued at the same game from dawn till dark, and dark till dawn – marching and fighting and marching. Every roll call there were fewer to answer – some were killed, some wounded, and some who had fallen out were missing.

During this afternoon we fought for about three hours near Villers-Cotterets I think it was, but I was getting very mixed about things, even mixed about the days of the week. Fifteen men in my company were killed, one in a rather peculiar fashion. He was bending down, handing me a piece of sausage, and a bullet ricochetted off a man's boot and went straight into his mouth and out of the top of his head.

We got on to the, road about 200 yards only in front of a German brigade, and then ran like hell for about a mile, until we passed through the South Staffs Regiment, who were entrenched each side of the road. I believe about six of the battalion were captured. Still we marched on until dusk, then on outpost again, and during the night the South Staffs passed through us.

September 2nd – At 2 a.m. we moved off, and marched all day long. It was hot and dusty and the roads were rotten, but, as we got mixed up with hundreds of refugees, we were obliged to keep better marching order. About 6 p.m., to 8 p.m. we reached Meaux – I believe we did about twenty-five miles that day, but no fighting. We bivouacked outside Meaux, but I went into the cathedral when we halted near it, and thought it was very beautiful. Also I saw some of the largest tomatoes I have ever seen in my life, growing in a garden. I was rounding up stragglers most of the night until 1 a.m. and at 3 a.m. we moved off again.

September 3rd – The first four or five hours we did without a single halt or rest, as we had to cross a bridge over the Aisne before the R.E.s blew it up. It was the most terrible march I have ever done. Men were falling down like ninepins. They would fall flat on their faces on the road, while the rest of us staggered round them, as we couldn't lift our feet high enough to step over them, and, as for picking them up, that was impossible, as to bend meant to fall. What happened to them, God only knows. An aeroplane was following us most of the time dropping iron darts: we fired at it a couple of times, but soon lost the strength required for that. About 9 a.m. we halted by a river, and immediately two fellows threw themselves into it. Nobody, from sheer fatigue, was able to save them, although one sergeant made an attempt, and was nearly drowned himself. I, like a fool, took my boots off, and found my feet were covered with blood. I could find no sores or cuts, so I thought I must have sweated blood.

As I couldn't get my boots on again I cut the sides away, and when we started marching again; my feet hurt like hell.

We marched till about 3 p.m. – nothing else, just march, march, march. I kept repeating my line, 'If you can, force, etc.' Why, I didn't know. A sergeant irritated everyone who could hear him by continually shouting out: 'Stick it, lads. We're making history.'

The Colonel offered me a ride on his horse, but I refused, and then wished I hadn't, as anything was preferable to the continuous marching.

We got right back that afternoon among the refugees again. They were even worse off than we were, or, at least, they looked it. We gave the kids our biscuits and "bully," hoping that would help them a little; but they looked so dazed and tired there did not seem to be much hope for them.

At 8 p.m. we bivouacked in a field and slept till dawn. Ye gods! what a relief.

September 4th – I was sent with six men on outpost to a small wood on our left front, and I had not posted the sentries more than half an hour, before an officer found two of them asleep. The poor fellows were afterwards tried by courts martial and shot.

About 3 p.m., we all moved off again, and came into action almost immediately, although I believe it was a food convoy that was mistaken for German artillery by our artillery.

Anyway no one I knew was hurt. It was said, however, that Jerry rushed his troops along after us in lorries.

All through the night we marched, rocking about on our feet from the want of sleep, and falling fast asleep even if the halt lasted only a minute. Towards dawn we turned into a farm, and for about two hours I slept in a pigsty. I noticed the same thing about that farm that I'd noticed about most French farms. That was, although they seemed more intensively cultivated than English, farms, the farm implements were very old-fashioned.

September 5th – Early on this morning reinforcements from England joined us, and the difference in their appearance and ours was amazing. They looked plump, clean, tidy, and very wide-awake. Whereas we were filthy, thin, and haggard. Most of us had beards; what equipment was left was torn; instead of boots we had puttees, rags, old shoes, field boots – anything and everything wrapped round our feet. Our hats were the same, women's hats, peasants' hats, caps, any old covering, while our trousers were mostly in ribbons. The officers were in a similar condition.

After the reserves joined we marched about twenty miles to a place called Chaumes, It was crowded with staff officers. We bivouacked in a park, and then had an order read to us that the men who had kept their overcoats were to dump them, as we were to advance at any moment. Strangely, a considerable amount of cheering took place then.

I discovered that the company I was in covered 251 miles in the Retreat from Mons, which finished on September 5th, 1914.

Corporal Bernard John Denore, 1st Royal Berks Regt., 6th Brigade, 2nd Division, 1 Army Corps. In Action at Battle of and Retreat from Mons; Battle of the Marne; the Aisne (about two months); First Battle of Ypres; in the Salient four weeks. Wounded at Zonnebeke (in seven places); in hospital at Boulogne, London and Reading.

AN OLD CONTEMPTIBLE AT LE CATEAU

R. G. Hill

On August 5th, 1914, I reported to my regimental depot, being an Army Reservist. What a meeting of old friends! All were eager to take part in the great scrap which every pre-war soldier had expected. At the depot all was bustle, but no confusion. In the mobilization stores, every reservist's arms and clothing were ticketed, and these were soon issued, with webbing equipment. About 300 men were then selected and warned to hold themselves in readiness to proceed to the South Coast to make up the war strength of the battalion stationed there. There was great competition to go with this draft, the writer being one of the lucky ones to be selected.

We entrained next morning. Then another meeting with old chums. That night, bully, biscuits, emergency rations, and ammunition, were issued. Surplus kit was handed in and next night the battalion entrained for an unknown destination. We eventually arrived in Yorkshire, and, after a fortnight's strenuous training, left for the South of England again, to join our division. By this time we had welded together, and were a really fine body of men, hard as nails, average age about twenty-five, and every man with the idea that he was equal to three Germans! Splendid men, enthusiastic, and brave, going to fight, they thought, for a righteous cause.

We embarked for France and landed at Boulogne on the morning of August 23rd. What a contrast between us and the slip-shod undersized French territorials who were guarding the docks. In their baggy red trousers and long blue coats, they looked like comic-opera soldiers. We looked smart in our new khaki, and training had made us broad-chested and clean-looking. We disembarked and marched through the narrow streets of Boulogne singing popular songs. The enthusiasm of the French people was unbounded. They broke our ranks to shower gifts upon us, and many a blushing Tommy was kissed by men and women. A few hours in camp, where we had to be guarded by gendarmes to save us from excited female admirers, and we entrained, leaving buttons and badges behind as souvenirs. A tedious journey in horse trucks followed. The line was littered with empty bully tins and Woodbine packets, showing that British troops had passed that way before.

We detrained just outside Le Cateau station. The town was in confusion, as Mons had just been fought; refugees, troops, and ammunition columns creating a dust that choked us. Civilians offered us foaming jugs of weak beer, but discipline was so strong that to accept it meant a court martial.

We marched out of the town along a typical French road. Just when we were about all in, a halt was called for dinner, which we never had as an outburst of artillery fire was heard.

It must have been miles away, but we had orders to open out to artillery formation and proceed. We saw no enemy that day, and at night bivouacked in a cornfield, where we enjoyed a long-delayed dinner. We marched off in column of fours next morning at dawn in a new direction. At noon we halted, piled arms, and rations were issued – the last for many days. Men were told off to dig trenches on rising ground to our left.

Whilst so engaged an aeroplane hovered over us. It had no distinguishing mark, and we thought it was French, but were soon disillusioned; as it scattered coloured lights over us. Too late, we opened fire. Soon large black shells were bursting in the beet field just in front of our improvised position. Rain then started, the shelling ceased, and a regiment of our cavalry came galloping up and jumped over us in our hastily constructed trench. We stayed there till nightfall, incidentally wiping out a small Uhlan patrol that blundered upon us. When we withdrew we could hear the jingle of accoutrements of many men approaching. That night we seemed to march round and round a burning farmhouse.

Day broke, and we were still dragging our weary limbs along in what seemed to us to be an everlasting circle. At last the word came to halt and fall out for a couple of hours' rest. We had been marching along a road with a high ridge on the right and cornfields on the left. High up the ridge ran a road parallel to ours, on which one of our regiments had been keeping pace with us. We had no sooner sunk down in the cornfield on our left than shrapnel began to burst over us. Our officers were fine leaders. 'Man the ditch on the road,' came the order.

In the meantime the battalion on the ridge had been caught napping by a squadron of Uhlans, who charged them while they were falling out for a rest. Our eager young officers went frantic with excitement. On their own initiative they led us up the hill to the rescue of our comrades. With wild shouts we dashed up. At first the ground was broken and afforded cover for our short sharp dashes. We then came to a hedge with a gap about four yards wide. A dozen youngsters made for the gap, unheeding the advice of older soldiers to break through the hedge. Soon that gap was a heap of dead and dying as a machine gun was trained on it. We reached an open field, where we were met with a hail of shrapnel. Officers were picked off by snipers. A subaltern rallied us and gave the order to fix bayonets. A piece of shrapnel carried half his jaw away. Upwards we went, but not a sign of a German. They had hidden themselves and waited for our mad rush. Officers and sergeants being wiped out and not knowing where the enemy really were, our attack fizzled out. A Staff officer came galloping amongst us, mounted on a big black charger. He bore a charmed life. He shouted something unintelligible, which someone said was the order to retire.

The survivors walked slowly down, puzzled and baffled. They had attained nothing, and had not even seen the men they set out to help. We lost half the battalion in that wild attack.

Then came our turn to do something better. The survivors, under the direction of a capable major, dug in and waited to get their own back. A battery of our eighteen-pounders started to shell the ridge. Suddenly shells started falling round the guns. One direct hit and a gunner's leg fell amongst us. The battery was wiped out. Tired and worn out, we waited. Towards afternoon shrapnel played on us, fortunately without serious result. Then it was our turn to laugh. German infantry were advancing in close formation. They broke at our first volley. Something seemed to sting my leg. I found a shrapnel bullet had ploughed a shallow groove down the fleshy part of my thigh. The enemy advanced. Another volley and they broke again. My leg began to pain me, so I hobbled along the road to a house which was being used as a dressing station. A long queue of wounded men were waiting to be dressed, whilst a crowd of thirst-maddened unwounded were crowding round a well in the garden. Despairing of medical aid, I begged a field dressing, and, catching sight of a sunken road, turned into it, and dressed my wound.

In this sunken road, I found battalion headquarters. At dusk they retired, I with them. I learnt afterwards that all our wounded were captured that night, and small bodies of our troops, trying to retire in the darkness, had fired on each other. This was our part in the Battle of Le Cateau.

Then began the retreat. I must have fainted, for I remember hobbling along with some chums, and next I found myself tied to the seat of an ammunition limber. We came to a village jammed with retiring troops, where an artillery officer bundled me off. Fortunately some of my own regiment passed, and, seeing me lying in the road, helped me along. My leg seemed easier and I was able to proceed at the pace my footsore companions were going. It was nightmare marching. Our party was now about 150 strong. Sleep was out of the question, and food was begged from villagers. Reaching St. Quentin, we had great hopes of rest, but were told that we were surrounded. We lay down to die through sheer weariness, but a Staff officer rounded us up, and got us out just as the enemy entered. Tramp, tramp, again. Engineers told us to hurry over the bridge at Ham, as they were just about to blow it up. A little scrap a bit further on, then Noyon, where we snatched a night's sleep.

One day we turned about; other parties joined us, and we were told we were now advancing. We hardly believed it until we came upon dead Germans. That put new life in us. Advancing! Hurrah! Our part was very small up to the Aisne.

We crossed the Marne without a scrap, and never met with opposition until we reached the heights the other side of that now famous river.

Some of our brigade were not so fortunate, and lost heavily from shell-fire while crossing. Our position on the Aisne was not so bad. We dug in on top of the ridge beyond the river. We were 1,100 yards from the enemy; and every four days we retired to a vast, evil-smelling cave, where we got hot meals and remained for two days. Most of our casualties were caused when fetching water and rations from the village below.

The battalion was made up with reserve men and the weather continued fine. The trenches on our left were not so fortunate, as they were attacked nearly every night, this causing us to stand to all night. After a few weeks of this we were relieved by French troops.

By forced marches and a train journey, we reached St. Omer. One night there, and we boarded French motorvans. We soon found ourselves scrapping after we had disembarked at a small village. The enemy had dashed down and seized the next village, Meteren, and our first task was to drive them out. The place was held by a rearguard of machine-gunners, and could have been encircled and captured, but we were ordered to take it by bayonet. We took it at a terrible cost, but found no enemy to bayonet. What few machine-gunners were there had done their work well and fled in time. Then through Bailleul and Armentières, which the enemy abandoned without a fight.

We were the first British troops in Armentières. As we marched through, the civilians went frantic with delight. The Germans had been there for a week, and had committed the usual excesses of troops flushed with victory. The Highlanders in our brigade caused much amusement, the female part of the population shrieking with laughter at the dress of the 'Mademoiselle Soldats.' Bread, beer, and tobacco were showered on us, and garlands of flowers hung on our necks and bayonets. However, a few hours only were our portion there, which we spent in a large flax factory wrecked by the enemy during their short stay.

Off again past a large lunatic asylum, on which shells were falling, the shrieks of the inmates sounding hideous. These poor devils were released, and some wandered into the firing line, and no doubt thought they had reached the infernal regions. The enemy took up a strong position at Houplines, where, after several minor attacks to straighten the line, we dug in, and then commenced the dreary trench warfare.

I have not enlarged on the hardships of war up to now, as, being, all healthy men and constantly on the move, we had not noticed them much. Settling down to inactive trench life, we soon discovered what a miserable state we were in. Most of the original men had left their spare kit and overcoats at Le Cateau, as we had received orders thereto attack in fighting kit. We were in the front line at Houplines twenty-nine days at one stretch. I for one had neither shirt nor overcoat. My shirt had been discarded at the Aisne, being alive with vermin. Beards were common, and our toilet generally consisted of rubbing our beards to clear them of dried mud. Our trenches were generally enlarged dry ditches, where we dug in when our advance was stopped. Sandbags were very scarce, and when it rained the sides of the ditches fell in. However, at Houplines we were better off than the majority of British troops at that time. It was a fairly quiet position and rations came up regularly and plentifully.

Fetching rations was our worst job, as the enemy's powerful searchlights played along the roads leading to the trenches each night. There were always plenty of volunteers, however, for this job, as they had first go at the rum, cigarettes, etc.

At the back of our trench was a large farmhouse. It had been shelled to pieces, but it proved a Godsend to us, as we discovered the wine cellar intact. Dozens of bottles of good wine were conveyed to the trench. The one officer in the trench (not popular enough to be told of our find) must have been struck with the cheery light-heartedness of the men at this period. We were at last relieved and proceeded to a large brewery at Nieppe, where four days' rest, a bath, and clean underclothing made new men of us. This was our first good wash since leaving England. I had not worn a shirt for six weeks. Whilst bathing (in large mash tubs), our khaki was fumigated. This seemed to send the lice to sleep for a couple of days, then they woke up and attacked with renewed vigour.

A draft of returned wounded men joined us and we left Nieppe to take up a position in front of Ploegsteert Wood. We spent the winter there doing good work, barbed wiring, and strengthening the position. The First Battle of Ypres was raging on our left. Four days front line, four reserve, and four in billets, until in April 1915 we were pitched into that awful hell, Ypres, when the battalion was wiped out time after time.

I lasted until Arras 1917, the only real victory I saw, when I received a longed-for Blighty one and got discharged.

Private R. G. Hill. Went to France on August 22nd, 1914, with the 1st Battalion Royal Warwickshire Regt., in the 10th Brigade of the 4th Division. Except for a few days in hospital in 1915, he served with this battalion until April 11th, 1917, when he was wounded in the face, and was discharged medically unfit in March 1918. In Action at Le Cateau, Marne, Aisne, Meteren (a little-known, but gallant fight), Armentières, Ploegsteert, Ypres (1915), the Somme, and Arras (1917).

THE FIRST BATTLE OF YPRES

October 1914

J. F. Bell

I bade farewell to my right leg, and to my career as a soldier, outside a trench at Gheluvelt, near Ypres, on October 29th, 1914. In the First Battle of Ypres the British were outnumbered by seven to one. On the previous evening we took over trenches – not deep or elaborate ones – from an English regiment. I cannot say which regiment we relieved. Our sergeant on entering the trench heard the last man, as he was doing a hurried exit, say, 'So long, Jock – not 'arf a nice place, Jack Johnson all bleeding day.'

On that night there was no sleep, as we had to dig and dig to improve the trench, and were being fired at all night. At 5 a.m. a group of us were standing in the open – everything had turned peaceful – admiring our now almost perfect trench when hell seemed let loose. All the guns in Flanders seemed to have suddenly concentrated on our particular sector of the British front. When the artillery fire subsided, Germans sprang from everywhere and attacked us. My platoon held fast; we lost some good comrades. Then we were ordered to evacuate the trench, and assist to hold a trench on the flank where the fighting was fiercest. I was a sergeant, and was told to take and hold a certain part of the trench where the occupants had just been driven out. On rushing the trench, and leaping into it, 1 found that the dead were lying three deep in it. After taking bearings, I told the men to keep under cover and detailed one man, Ginger Bain, as 'look out.' After what seemed ages Ginger excitedly asked, 'How strong is the German army?' I replied, 'Seven million.' 'Well,' said Ginger, 'here is the whole bloody lot of them making for us.'

We were driven from the trench, and those of us who were unscathed joined Lieutenant Brook, who had come up with cooks, transport men, and men who had been wounded but could still use a rifle. Lieutenant Brook was (outwardly) quite unperturbed, walking about the firing line issuing orders as if on the barrack square. I had served under him for nine years, and seeing him such a target for the enemy riflemen, I asked him to lie down as I felt if he was hit his loss at that particular time would be disastrous. He told me we must retake the trench I had been, driven from, and to pick twenty men to do so. All the men were alike to me – men I had known for years – so I told ten men on my right and ten on my left to get ready to rush the trench. We succeeded in this. No artist or poet can depict a trench after fighting in its stark hellishness.

If we could not be driven out of the trench, it seemed certain that we would be blown out of it. Shells kept landing near enough in front of or behind the trench to shake us almost out of it. Many got killed by rifle-fire, Ginger Bain being the first, then Big Bruce whom I boxed in a competition before going to France. I passed a message to Lieutenant Brook, informing him our numbers were so reduced that if attacked we could not hold the trench, and received back word that he had just been killed. (The V.C. was posthumously awarded him.) A message was then sent to me to retire and join a platoon entrenched near us. I gave instructions to the few men (eight I think) to retire along the communication trench, and I would join them at the head of it, and lead them to our new position. I slipped over the rear of the trench, to cut across and meet the lads as they emerged from the communication trench, but had only gone about six yards when I received what in the regiment was called the 'dull thud.' I thought I had been violently knocked on the head, but, feeling I was not running properly, I looked down and discovered that my right foot was missing. Somehow, I stood watching men running along the communication trench. My power of speech had left me, so I could speak to none of them, then I swooned into the trench. No one had seen me being wounded, but one of the men, 'Pipe' Adams, on missing me, returned to look for me.

On seeing me lying quite helpless, he prepared to lift and carry me out of the trench. I told him I was too heavy: that it was too dangerous, and that in time our regiment would retake all the ground lost, when I would be safe. When I think of the War comradeship, of unaffected and unknown bravery, I think of 'Pipe' Adams (killed later) telling me, 'Christ, Jerry [my nickname], I could not leave you here.' However, confident that our people would return, I persuaded him to go. I then put a field dressing and a shirt from my pack over my stump and lay down to wait further developments. In this trench there would be about sixty badly wounded British soldiers (mostly Gordons) of all ranks. The soldier nearest me was a sergeant of the Grenadiers who was severely wounded in both arms and both legs. I noticed a watch quite close to me; on looking at it I found the time was 9 a.m.

I must have dropped into a kind of stupor, and I woke suddenly with the noise of great shouting. I thought it was our fellows returned to their old position, imagined I heard voices I knew, also that of my company officer, Captain Burnett, shouting, 'Where are you, Sergeant Bell?' I tried to rise, failed, but kept shouting, 'Here I am, in this trench, sir.' Judge my surprise when two German infantrymen jumped into the trench. One of them got quite excited, raised his rifle, levelled at and within a yard of me, but the other knocked his mate's rifle up and asked me when and where I was wounded. I asked them to try and do something for the wounded Grenadier, but they seemed in great haste as they jumped out of the trench. It was then twelve noon. So ended one morning in Flanders.

I pass over the afternoon with its incessant artillery fire, and the long night. There were periods of heavy gun fire, periods of silence, periods when all the wounded – those still alive – were shouting for stretcher bearers, praying for death, moaning noisily and quietly with pain. Strange the thoughts that pass through one under such circumstances. I thought of a great-grandfather of mine who fought in the Peninsular War, and was badly wounded at the Battle of Waterloo. Then I would think of a picture I once saw of a trench during the Balkan War. I had considered the picture was overdrawn, and now I knew that it was not horrible enough for the real thing.

The Germans had taken a lot of ground, were busily consolidating their new position, and all morning (the 30th) groups of them and individuals kept looking into the trench.

Two German officers slowly and quietly walked along the trench, and when they saw me still alive they appeared greatly surprised. Each of them spoke to me in English, enquiring how long I had been lying there. They informed me that there were fifty-seven of my comrades dead in the trench, and that I was one of three still alive. One of them promised to send someone to pick me up, but I had doubts about him doing so. However, about an hour later, four German private soldiers arrived, bringing a waterproof sheet to carry me off.

They gave me a drink of cold coffee, and when I pointed out the Grenadier, one of them went back into the trench and gave the Grenadier a drink and made him comfortable before rejoining us. One of the Germans could speak English, and in his deep-spoken voice said, 'Ah! Scotlander, you lucky man. Get out of this damned war. It last long time. What we fight for? Ah! German Army and English Navy, both damned nuisance.' They carried me with great care to a barn about half a mile away that was being used as a dressing station. All the way from the trench to the barn I saw British dead, mostly Highlanders – Black Watch, Camerons, and Gordons – and as they lay there in their uniforms, I thought how young and lonely they looked.

My arrival at the barn caused a mild sensation, all the soldiers on duty near and in the 'barn coming to the door to see me being carried in. 'Scotlander!' 'Sarjant!' 'Nae Helmet!' (I was bareheaded) being remarks made to me. The officer in charge of the barn excitedly asked me, 'Knives and revolvers you got?' Replying, with a smile, in the negative, he gave me a cigarette and told some men to lift me and lay me on top of some straw. I asked for a drink and was given more cold coffee. I looked at a wristlet watch the man who gave me the drink was wearing, it was then 1 p.m., so another morning in Flanders had gone.

Sergeant J. F. Bell, 2nd Gordon Highlanders. Proceeded with 7th Division to Zeebrugge, took part in the fighting round Ypres in October 1914. Wounded and taken prisoner of war, October 29th, 1914. Leg amputated (below knee). Exchanged with disabled prisoner of war, February 1915. Discharged April 1st, 1915. Re-enlisted and commissioned as T. Officer in Labour Corps, 1917, and served till the Armistice.

A TERRITORIAL IN THE SALIENT

Frank L. Watson, M.C.

August 1914 found me turned forty, engaged in an engineering business, and a Captain of Territorial Infantry. I expected the War, but I did not expect it so soon. The Territorial Force was nominally for Home service only, our training was inadequate, and our armament obsolete. Yet we were more than half-way to being soldiers, and understood the position too well to hold back. Why did the twelve Territorial Divisions volunteer immediately for foreign service? The motive was quite simple: the Germans were in Belgium, their presence there threatened England, and no one suggested any other way of getting them out except by force.

Before mobilization, we were greatly below establishment. Leeds was a very unmilitary city, and we had to face a good deal of veiled hostility from various quarters: partly genuine pacifism – that is, opposition to war in any circumstances, partly an ancient prejudice connecting soldiers with immorality and drink, and partly, a strong objection felt by Trade Union leaders to their young members coming under the personal influence of the 'boss class' to which they conceived the officers to belong.

However, the first few days of August 1914 proved that we could have filled the battalion twice over with likely fellows, many who had served a short term with us and dropped out, many who had no previous thought of serving. Our headquarters were besieged by them.

So we completed our mobilization, which was done well and strictly according to plan, and we pushed off to Selby and York for war training.

From the first day our men were well fed, well billeted, and well looked after. We had none of those deplorable scenes of incompetence and neglect which disgraced the raising and training of the New Armies. We had the *esprit de corps* of a very old Volunteer battalion, with a long-established character for discipline, shooting, and good fellowship; and if some of us had not previously taken the question of war very seriously we had a high average of education and intelligence, and all a Yorkshireman's determination to make a job of anything he takes on.

All that winter there was an idea that they were going to send the New Armies to France before us – in fact, that was the official intention, although by Christmas our Division was equal to anything short of first-class regular troops.

However, the fight between G.H.Q. in France, who wanted us, and the 'dug-out' Staff in Whitehall, who wanted to keep us back, ended in our favour, and after two or three months on the Lincolnshire coast we actually went. That time on the coast was the most peaceful and interesting part of our training. At York, we had continual alarms and were constantly being ordered to stand by ready for a move. On the coast we were let alone, and we had priceless practice in occupying and relieving trenches and moving in the dark, and the companies, living and working independently, learnt to take care of themselves.

In April 1915 we concentrated at Gainsboro' and completed our war equipment, which did not include either up-to-date rifles or modem field guns. The new 18-pounders and the new rifles were reserved for the New Army, and in that respect the victory of G.H.Q. over Whitehall was incomplete.

We got into a train in the afternoon, neither knowing nor caring to which port we were going, and about midnight stepped out on Folkestone quay. Day was breaking as we landed at Boulogne and marched through the town and up the long hill to the rest camp, where we stayed until the following afternoon. I had some splendid whistlers, and between these and the usual songs we were never short of music on the march. Going down to La Brique station they whistled the 'Ça Ira' alternately with the 'Marseillaise' faultlessly, to the no small joy of the villagers.

All through the spring night we rumbled along in the wagons and, after stopping at every signal post in the Pas de Calais, we pulled up in Hazebrouck. Here a sergeant reported that one of my men had got up and dived out of the window somewhere *en-route*, and that the man was known to be an occasional sleepwalker. I wrote him down as our first casualty. The guns told us we were nearly there, at last.

About 2 a.m. we turned out at Merville, and the next day we moved into farms in the Forest of Nieppe, and here my somnambulist rejoined. He woke up to find himself on the line, somehow reached a British police post, and was passed on to his unit. He served creditably all through the War and when I met him the other day he told me he had never walked in his sleep since that night.

We went up in parties for trench experience, in the line between Armentieres and Neuve-Chapelle. La Gorgue, Estaires, and Laventie were still inhabited, but all frequently shelled. They had been looted by the Germans in 1914, and the Maire of Estaires had been shot for failing to produce the demanded ransom. The farms here were still cultivated, and old men, women, and children were at work in the fields within range not only of shells, but of stray bullets. The old breastworks below the Aubers Ridge have been often described; my fortune led me to the point where Fauquissart Church lay in ruins in the trench line, and my instructors were the best possible, the 1st Grenadier Guards.

In a week or so our Division took over a line between Neuve-Chapelle and Fleurbaix. A country of little fields, innumerable roads and water-courses, hedges, woods, and thickly dotted with farms and houses. A country of deep soil, with water a foot below the surface, where (on our side) trenches were non-existent, and we held a continuous sandbag breastwork with sand-bagged avenues leading up to it from the nearest hedge.

On the German side, a similar parapet in front, but behind it the long slope of the Aubers Ridge, dug all over with communication trenches, and looking into every inch of our positions. There was very little shelling, but continual rifle fire and sniping, day and night. More than one German sniper fell a victim to some of my crack shots, so they did not have it all their own way.

There was a shelter in the support line that we used as a mess. Its top was visible from the German lines, and they had a fixed rifle trained on it. Someone had put an iron plate up where the bullets struck, and regularly every two minutes a bullet rang on the plate.

This damnable and maddening iteration went on day and night, like the old torture of the regular drop of water on the victim's head. I was in this place when the usual 'ping' was replaced by a dull thud. I ran out to the front line, and found, as I expected, that someone had got in the way. A fine young fellow was lying in the trench with a hole in his forehead and the back blown out of his head. He must have died instantly, but he was making that awful throaty gurgle which follows brain wounds.

Shortly afterwards my second captain, a very promising young engineer, went the same way. These cases made one think of the damnable cry of 1914, 'Single men first.' Who would have been the greatest loss to England, a man like myself, with half his life's work done and a family growing up, or these splendid lads just starting their careers, whose unbegotten offspring was cut off with them and lost to the nation for ever?

Here also we took part in our first battle, the attack on the Aubers Ridge, on May 9th. We were to support by fire an attack straight up the Ridge, and afterwards to join in the advance. The usual notice was given by a feeble bombardment, the Germans were well wired in and quite ready, and the attack achieved nothing but the destruction of several good battalions and a very few Germans. Assembly trenches had been dug for a brigade in a ten-acre field just behind the line and in full sight from the Ridge. If you had not known they were assembly trenches, you would have thought the field had been ridged up for potatoes. This may have been an early effort at camouflage, or pure stupidity – the result was the same.

The next day I re-armed my company from those assembly trenches with short rifles and bayonets and handed our obsolete rifles into store. It was watching this tragic performance from the tower of Laventie Church which convinced Sir John French of the obvious fact that he had not enough guns or shells, and started that famous agitation which resulted in his losing his command, in the replacement of Asquith by Lloyd George, and in the all-too-successful search for some place to send Kitchener whence he would not come back.

In those days generals used to visit us on blood horses, with an orderly carrying a lance with a little flag, in case the troops should fail to appreciate the extreme salutability of these high personages. But Rawlinson, who was our Corps Commander, would go about with one A.D.C. for company, and have a friendly chat and pass on the latest news of the capture of three Germans, six yards of trench, and a sanitary bucket to any humble officer he might meet. He even came up into the front line, where his red hat stuck up over the breastwork. We believed that the Germans would never intentionally shoot a British general, for fear his successor might do something unexpected. But it was a good thing that they did not shoot 'Rawly.'

In June, we moved off northwards, and relieved, in the Ypres Salient, a Regular division which had been badly cut up in the Second or Gas Battle.

We took over the northern half of the Salient, with the 6th Division on our right and a French Territorial division on our left. Our line, as is well known, was a semicircle overlooked in every part by the foe, and fired into at close range from three sides. We held that line without divisional relief for six solid months. We went in with companies 250 strong, and were reduced by losses to less than fifty per company before we came out. The trenches were cut deep in the rich black soil.

This ground was full of corpses, mostly French, and when we dug any new work we resurrected bits of them. My first dug-out in the front line was adorned by a boot (with foot more or less complete) sticking out of the wall. It was unpleasing to the senses and unreliable as a clothes-peg, so I sacrificed one-sixth of my space by walling it up.

All reliefs, trench repairs, carrying, and general labour had to be done at night, but whilst the dry weather lasted we had communication trenches by which 'brass hats' could visit us in the day-time and wake the unfortunate officers to make suggestions for filling up our spare time and stimulating the fighting spirit of the troops. When the rain came in autumn, the trenches disappeared and the area became a lake of mud.

Our Divisional gunners had still the obsolete 15-pounders, for which no new ammunition was being made. They were restricted to three rounds per gun per day, which they saved up for emergencies. Day after day, we were shelled and shelled and shelled–whizz-bangs, gas shells, trench mortars, 9-inch and, occasionally, 17-inch 'heavies.' Our guns could only afford 'retaliation' when the shelling was exceptional; and if they pushed over twenty 15-pounders, we usually got about 100 'five point nines' back.

Steadily and surely, we filled up the cemeteries on the Canal bank, notably the large one at Essex Farm, where our Divisional Memorial now stands. The fewer the men, the heavier became the work, especially as the weather grew worse. Rations, trench grids, wire, etc., had to be carried up by night; the battalions in support had no more rest than those in the line, and wheeled transport stopped at the Canal, 1,000 to 1,500 yards in rear.

'Trench feet' made their appearance, and someone in our very energetic Division conceived the bright idea that this was due to want of exercise, and could be cured by imposing more labour on men worn out by overwork, exposure, and want of sleep. We got it down eventually by the aid of dry socks sent up nightly with the rations and 'gumboots, thigh.' We were several times seriously attacked, but they always found us wide awake, and we never lost a yard of ground.

I landed in France with four subalterns; when we had been a month in the Salient I had one, and my platoons were very well commanded by sergeants. The first time we got a real barrage, the one thing the company wanted was for the attack to develop and 'get it ovvered with.' The keynote of the whole business was hard labour and insufferable boredom. Something to shoot at was what we needed, but hardly ever did the Germans give even a sniper a target.

I honestly believe that no other troops in the world but British would have held the Salient, and no other generals but ours would have asked them to do it, or conceived such a line to be worth holding. It was a triumph of sentimental over military considerations. From the German point of view, the Salient was a spot where they could always depend on a regular supply of Englishmen to slaughter with the minimum of loss to themselves. They thought at first that it was also a place where they could break through when so disposed; and, by all the rules of commonsense, it was. There were good positions prepared in rear, but there were no troops to put in them. However, the Second Battle of Ypres taught them that no ordinary rules applied to that thin khaki line in its untenable and absurd positions.

In August the Brigadier took me out of the line to be Staff Captain of the Brigade, and my work and way of life entirely changed.

The War as a whole was a crime and a tragedy. But it was not the same from both sides. The Germans set out to achieve a purpose. They underestimated the task and failed. We set out to prevent that purpose, and to that extent we succeeded. The men on both sides were sacrificed, as they always have been, to retrieve the errors of the statesmen and the generals.

But sharing toil, exhaustion, hardship, and danger does not destroy a man's soul. The soldier is not the man who makes war – he is the man who offers his life to end it.

Major F. L. Watson was mobilized with his Territorial battalion in August 1914, in command of a company, proceeding to France in April 1915. From August 1915 until March 1917 he was Staff Captain of an infantry brigade in France, being recalled on the latter date at the instance of the Ministry of Munitions for technical service. He was subsequently sent to the Admiralty for similar service, and was demobilized in 1919. Mentioned in Despatches, July 1916. Military Cross, January 1917. Territorial Decoration, July 1920. Retired with rank of Major, November 1921.

THE FIRST GAS ATTACK

Anthony R. Hossack

It was Thursday evening, April 22nd, 1915. In a meadow off the Poperinghe-Ypres road, the men of the Queen Victoria Rifles were taking their ease. We had just fought our first big action in the fight for Hill 60. We had had a gruelling time, and had left many of our comrades on its slopes. We survivors were utterly spent and weary; but we felt in good heart, for only an hour ago we had been personally congratulated by Sir John French, also the Army Commander, General Smith-Dorrien.

Now some of us were stretched out asleep on the grass, others making preparations for a much-needed toilet. Our cooks were preparing a meal, and on our right a squad of Sappers were busily erecting huts in which we were to sleep. Alas! We never used them! As the sun was beginning to sink, this peaceful atmosphere was shattered by the noise of heavy shell-fire coming from the north-west, which increased every minute in volume, while a mile away on our right a 42-cm shell burst in the heart of the stricken city of Ypres.

As we gazed in the direction of the bombardment, where our line joined the French, six miles away, we could see in the failing light the flash of shrapnel with here and there the light of a rocket. But more curious than anything was a low cloud of yellow-grey smoke or vapour, and, underlying everything, a dull confused murmuring.

Suddenly down the road from the Yser Canal came a galloping team of horses, the riders goading on their mounts in a frenzied way; then another and another, till the road became a seething mass with a pall of dust over all.

Plainly something terrible was happening. What was it? Officers, and Staff officers too, stood gazing at the scene, awestruck and dumbfounded; for in the northerly breeze there came a pungent nauseating smell that tickled the throat and made our eyes smart. The horses and men were still pouring down the road, two or three men on a horse, I saw, while over the fields streamed mobs of infantry, the dusky warriors of French Africa; away went their rifles, equipment, even their tunics that they might run the faster. One man came stumbling through our lines.

An officer of ours held him up with levelled revolver, 'What's the matter, you bloody lot of cowards?' says he. The Zouave was frothing at the mouth, his eyes started from their sockets, and he – fell writhing at the officer's feet. 'Fall in!' Ah! we expected that cry; and soon we moved across the fields in the direction of the line for about a mile. The battalion is formed into line, and we dig ourselves in.

It is quite dark now, and water is being brought round, and we hear how the Germans have, by the use of poison gas, driven a French army corps out of the line, creating a huge gap which the Canadians have closed *pro tem.* A cheer goes up at this bald statement, though little we knew at what a cost those gallant souls were holding on.

About midnight we withdrew from our temporary trenches and marched about for the rest of the night, till at dawn we were permitted to snatch what sleep we could under a hedge. About the middle of the morning we were on the move again, to the north, and were soon swinging along through Vlamertinghe. About two miles out of that town we halted in a field. By this time we had joined up with the remainder of our Brigade, the 13th, and, after a meal had been served, we were ordered to dump our packs and fall in by companies. Here our company commander, Captain Flemming, addressed us. 'We are,' he said, 'tired and weary men who would like to rest; however, there are men more weary than we who need our help. We may not have to do much; we may have to do a great deal. Whatever happens, fight like hell. I shall at any rate.' A few moments more – then off we go again towards that incessant bombardment, which seemed to come closer every minute.

The Scottish Borderers led the Brigade, followed by the Royal West Kents, then ourselves – all with bayonets fixed, for we were told to be prepared to meet the Germans anywhere on the road.

We were now in the area of the ill-fated French Colonial Corps. Ambulances were everywhere, and the village of Brielen, through which we passed, was choked with wounded and gassed men. We were very mystified about this gas, and had no protection whatever against it.

Shortly after passing through Brielen we turned to the left down a road which led to the Canal, along the south side of which ran a steep spoil bank, and, as the head of our battalion reached this, we halted. We could see nothing of what went on on the other side, but knew by the rattle of musketry that there was something doing. So there was, for when we finally crossed the pontoon we found that the Jocks had met the Germans on the north bank and had bundled them helter-skelter up the slope to Pilckem, This saved us any dirty work for that day, so we spent the rest of it till midnight in carrying supplies and ammunition to the Jocks and Kents, and afterwards lay in reserve on the Canal bank. It froze hard that night, and after the sweating fatigue of carrying boxes of S.A.A. all night we were literally aching with cold.

All night there seemed to be a spasmodic bombardment all round the Salient.

Next morning about 12 o'clock the Adjutant, Captain Culme-Seymour, was chatting to Captain Flemming a few paces away from where I was lying, when up rushed a breathless despatch rider and handed him a message, which he read aloud to Flemming. I caught three words, 'Things are critical.' In about five minutes the Colonel had the battalion on the move. We moved off in double file by companies, our company leading; as we did so a big shell burst in the midst of 'D' Company, making a fearful mess. We moved on quickly, like a gigantic serpent, with short halts now and then. As we skirted Ypres there was a roar of swift moving thunder and a 17-inch shell, which seemed to be falling on top of us, burst a quarter of a mile away, covering us with dirt.

Over meadows and fields green with young crops which would never be harvested, past cows peacefully grazing that had had their last milking, we went, passing curiously unperturbed peasants, who watched us from the farms and cottages.

As we crossed the Roulers road a lone cavalryman came galloping down it, hatless and rolling in his saddle as though drunk. Some wag throws a ribald jest at him. He turns his ashy face towards us, and his saddle it seems is a mass of blood. Above us a Taube appears and, hovering over us, lets fall a cascade of glittering silver like petals. A few moments more and shells begin to fall about us in quantities, and gaps begin to appear in our snakelike line.

We pass a field battery; it is not firing, as it has nothing to fire, and its commander sits weeping on the trail of one of his useless guns. We quicken our pace, but the shelling gets heavier. It seems to be raining shrapnel. Captain Flemming falls, but struggles to his feet and waves us on with encouraging words. We double across a field, and in a few moments come on to the road again. Here was action indeed, for barely had we reached the road and started to work our way towards St. Julien, than we found ourselves amongst a crowd of Canadians of all regiments jumbled up anyhow, and apparently fighting a desperate rearguard action. They nearly all appeared to be wounded and were firing as hard as they could. A machine gun played down the road. Then comes an order: 'Dig in on the roadside.' We all scrambled into the ditch, which, like all Flanders ditches, was full of black, liquid mud, and started to work with entrenching tools – a hopeless job. A woman was bringing jugs of water from a cottage a few yards away; evidently she had just completed her week's washing, for a line of garments-fluttered in the garden.

'Dig! Dig, for your lives!' shouts an officer. But, dig! How can we? 'Tis balers we need.

A detonation like thunder, and I inhale the filthy fumes of 5.9 as I cringe against the muddy bank. The German heavies have got the road taped to an inch. Their last shell has pitched on our two M.G. teams, sheltering in the ditch on the other side of the road. They disappear, and all we can hear are groans so terrible they will haunt me for ever. Kennison, their officer, stares dazed, looking at a mass of blood and earth. Another crash and the woman and her cottage and water jars vanish and her pitiful washing hangs in a mocking way from her sagging clothes line. A bunch of telephone wires falls about us. To my bemused brain this is a catastrophe in itself, and I curse a Canadian Sapper beside me for not attempting to mend them. He eyes me vacantly, for he is dead. More and more of these huge shells, two of them right in our midst. Shrieks of agony and groans all round me. I am splashed with blood. Surely I am hit, for my head feels as though a battering-ram has struck it. But no, I appear not to be, though all about me are bits of men and ghastly mixtures of khaki and blood.

The road becomes a perfect shambles. For perhaps half a minute a panic ensues, and we start to retire down the road. But not for long. Colonel Shipley stands in the centre of the road, blood streaming down his face. The gallant Flemming lies at his feet, and the Adjutant, Culme-Seymour, stands in a gateway calmly lighting a cigarette.

'Steady, my lads!' says the Colonel. 'Steady, the Vics! Remember the regiment.' The panic is ended.

'This way,' says Seymour. 'Follow me through this gate here.' As we dash through the gate, I catch a glimpse of our M.O. working in an empty gun-pit like a butcher in his shop. Many were the lives he saved that day.

Once through the gate we charge madly across a field of young corn. Shrapnel and machine-gun bullets are cracking and hissing everywhere. Ahead of us is a large farm, and advancing upon it at almost right angles to ourselves is a dense mass of German infantry.

We are carrying four extra bandoliers of ammunition as well as the rest of our equipment. Shall I ever get there? My limbs ache with fatigue and my legs are like lead. But the inspiring figure of Seymour urges us on, yet even he cannot prevent the thinning of our line or the gaps being torn in it by the German field gunners, whom we can now plainly see.

At last we reach the farm, and we follow Culme-Seymour round to its further side. The roar of enemy machine guns rises to a crazy shrieking, but we are past caring about them, and with a sob of relief we fall into the farm's encircling trench. Not too soon either, for that grey mass is only a few hundred yards off, and 'Rapid fire! Let 'em have it, boys!' and don't we just. At last a target, and one that we cannot miss. The Germans fall in scores, and their batteries limber up and away. At last we have our revenge for the discomfort of the afternoon. But the enemy re-form and come on again, and we allow them to come a bit nearer, which they do. We fire till our rifles are almost too hot to hold, and the few survivors of our mad quarter of an hour stagger back. The attack has failed, and we have held them, and thank God that we have, for, as our next order tells us, 'This line must be held at all costs. Our next is the English Channel.' And hold it we did, through several more big attacks, though the enemy set fire to the farm and nearly roasted us, though our numbers dwindled and we were foodless and sleepless, till, thirty-six hours later, we were relieved in a misty dawn, and crept back through burning Ypres for a few hours' respite.

Anthony R. Hossack joined the Queen Victoria Rifles at the beginning of the War and served with them on the Western Front from early 1915 till after the Battle of Arras, where, in July 1917, he was wounded, returning to France at the end of February 1918, when he was attached to the M.G. Battalion of the 9th (Scottish) Division, and, after coming through the retreat from St. Quentin, was taken prisoner in the battle for Mt. Kemmel.

THE BATTLE OF LOOS

W. Walker

The 21st Division landed in France in the early part of September 1915.

In the dim light of a hurricane lantern, a few of us sat smoking and talking in an old wreck of a barn. It was full of evil-smelling hay on which, I suppose, thousands of our chaps had rested on their way up to the fight. We couldn't sleep for excitement, thinking we would be going up the line the next day, and wondering whether we would ever come down again. But the next day didn't take us up the line; for a solid fortnight we marched over many a dusty mile of white road and doubled over the green fields towards an imaginary foe. How the British Government and the War Office were cursed for keeping good soldiers rusting in the background!

We got on the move at last and of the places we passed through I have forgotten all but Nreux-les-Mines and Bethune. Never before had we seen a horse on the treadmill climbing an endless stairway as it threshed the corn. How incongruous, too, it seemed to see a giant Frenchman riding in a tiny cart drawn along by four galloping dogs. 'Lazy – ! Ger-r-r off!' someone shouted, but he, wise man, whether he understood or not, paid no heed. No one seemed to know where we were bound for. A push, we understood, was about to begin and we were going up to chase the enemy from the field, and a thousand other pieces of folly floated about.

Soldiers take little heed of times or places, general impressions alone are received. The march was an interesting round; the quaint villages; the large towns where we should have liked to stay a while; the nights spent in the open fields wrapped in our overcoats. Three of us slept together for warmth, taking turns who should sleep in the middle.

When I opened my eyes on Saturday morning, September 25th, I could see an aeroplane flying high. All about it round puffs of white smoke appeared, broke, and vanished into the blue. Whose it was I hadn't a notion. I felt glad that my body was not inside it. He didn't get the knock while I watched him, which was not for long, for we were routed out of our comfortable beds in the soft furrows of the ploughed land and, after a hurried meal, we hastened on.

We had not gone many kilometres when a new though distant sound could be heard, like far-away thunder with now and again a louder boom. The air seemed vibrant. It was a thrilling noise and it made my heart ache nervously as if it wanted to stop. Our lads had long since stopped singing on the march, and now, saving some braggart spirit, we had almost stopped talking and given ourselves over to thinking and listening.

The roadside gave evidence of our near approach to the battle. All the possible and impossible litter of war-old wrecked wagons, chairs, bedsteads, and mattresses, an old motor-bike and scraps of a machine gun, and in the ditch a dead mule lay, feet in the air, its belly torn out by shell-fire.

A Scots division had been heavily engaged with the enemy; they had suffered tremendous losses. For an hour or two a continuous stream of their wounded had trickled past us on their way to the rear. Most of them were hit about the arms. They looked grim and bloody. Mingling with these wounded troops were captured Germans who didn't look sorry; rather, one could see in their eyes a look of relief.

It began to grow dark. Vivid wicked flashes could be seen and bright dazzling balls of red, green, and yellow light illuminated the flattish land in front. We tramped on: the jingling of our equipment, the squelching of boots in mud, the laboured breathing of weary men, an occasional curse, was like an obbligato to the thunderous storm of war that surged around us.

After stumbling on for another half-hour, sometimes up to the knees in liquid mud, I could observe by the light of the sky signals the ruined outline of a village. It was Loos.

The moon now shone revealing the roofless walls of the houses, the open spaces where houses had once stood, marked by heaps of rubble. The village was slowly vanishing under the pounding of the guns. A German trench ran along the side of the street.

My company was halted in the village street. It began to rain. We stood talking and smoking and shivering. Suddenly, zip! 'What's that?' 'Some fool having a bang,' said a Newcastle lad. Again, zip. A bullet sang past us viciously and buried itself in the crumbling wall behind. 'Like a sniper,' someone ventured. At this we crowded together for moral support. Ping! there it was again; this time finding a billet in the thigh of a chap in No. 1 Platoon. He gave a howl of pain and was carried away. That was the first drop of blood shed by the 13th N.F.s, so far as I'm aware. It was not the last. Sure enough it was a sniper, and they weren't long in getting him. He had been concealed among the rafters of one of the higher houses, and had potted away at us by whatever light there was – moon, flares, and cigarettes. An officer and a man brought him down the road between them. He was a small white-faced man. I felt a pang of pity for him. He was brave. His comrades had gone on and left him to an almost certain fate. He would be thinking of his wife and bairns, maybe, in some quiet rustic village in the Fatherland. I heard later that they plugged him with lead.

We seemed to stand in that street for an eternity of time; actually, I suppose, not more than two or three hours. At last we got the order to move out, and we emerged into an open field, over which we walked, stumbling over little cocks of hay.

At this point we deployed and became hopelessly lost to one another. It was a cursed bad piece of work to be severed so soon from one's pals. It means a lot, that, in warfare. Friendship strengthens the heart.

Then there began to burst above us some kind of shell. We flopped on our stomachs when this began. The ground was a quagmire, but mud was better than blood, and we wallowed in the friendly filth.

After a while the cannonade quietened and word came along that we were to advance. We did not appear to have an officer anywhere near us. The fellows near me were strangers.

Hunger, thirst, and sleeplessness made me faint and weak. The mud on my greatcoat made it monstrously heavy, so that it flapped like lead against my legs, making the going utterly wearisome. I would willingly have died just then. The ground was so uneven that headway was difficult to make, not uneven by nature either, but by the huddled heaps of men's bodies. The ground had been bitterly contested.

Hill 70 rose above us darkly. It scarcely deserves the name of hill; quite a moderate rise, but that night it appeared intensely black and forbidding against the flaring lights that gleamed intermittently in the sullen sky beyond it. So far we had seen no enemy. They were over the hill. Would to God, I prayed, they would stop over. Never was I more out of love with war than that first night at the Front. Arrived at the foot of the hill we got orders to lie down. My watch said two o'clock.

Shall I attempt to hide my feelings as I lay there? Why should I? They were the common property of the whole host. How easy it is to sit in an armchair and scorn the coward who flees the conflict. I confess that I lay in that welter of mud devising schemes of escape; of getting back to the rear on some flimsy pretext or other. I even thought of going sick if I could have found a pain other than in my heart and nerve.

Bullets started dropping all around us like heavy thunder rain. The men on both sides of me lay snoring in exhausted slumber. I felt lonely and wretched. At last I fell asleep.

'The next b – I catch asleep I'll put a bullet through him.' By the flame light I could see the large face of an officer with the badge of the D.L.I.s in his cap. No one spoke, so he snarled again: 'The next. Do you hear?' he grated. 'Yes, sir,' someone muttered. No sooner had he walked off than we all dropped off to sleep again till the grey morning dawned.

It was Sunday, if it mattered. The sun peeped brightly over the hill. Except for a general murmuring from the serried and prostrate ranks, there was scarcely a sound. In the early light an appalling scene lay before us. The ground was strewn with dead and dying men. Pieces of horse and gun equipment and the motley gear of war lay everywhere. Behind the blackening cocks of hay lay men in the attitude of firing, now dead. One lay not two yards from my feet, a giant Scotsman stretched out in the posture of crucifixion. Leaning against a wall was a young fair lad of the Lincolnshires, kneeling as if in prayer; his hands clasped, his twisted face crimson from an ugly gash in his temple.

There was no food to be had – indeed food was far from my thoughts. I was thinking of the battle before us.

We got the order to advance up the hill. There was no officer near us, so an aged sergeant, who ought to have been at home with his wife, took charge of us. Our unreadiness to fight was obvious. Our greatcoats impeded our progress; we were still without ammunition in our rifles; our bayonets were still in the frogs. As we slowly advanced the Germans began sending over all kinds of stuff. The hill gave us fair cover and we weren't long in gaining the La Bassée road. Here we took off our greatcoats, loaded up, fixed bayonets, and made ready to advance.

At six o'clock, word came along that a general advance was to be attempted; already some had left the shelter of the roadway and were running over the open plateau. 'Come on, lads, we've got to do it,' cried stout-hearted old Sergeant J – . We braced ourselves and leapt on to the open field. Misery makes heroes of us all. The darkness of cowardice that had so clouded my mind and filled me with self-despair had fled. I marvelled at my carelessness. Possibly it was the reaction of exhaustion upon my brain. I neither know nor care, but there it was.

The shell-fire was deafening enough, but the clatter that commenced with our further advance was abominable. It was as if the enemy were attacking with a fleet of motorcycles – it was the hellish machine guns. I saw no foe. Where he was I couldn't gamble: somewhere in front, how distant or how near no one seemed to know. The firing was indescribably fierce; an invisible hail of lead winged past my ears unceasingly; one flicked my sleeve. How pitiful it is to recall. Our chaps fell like grass under the mower, mostly shot in the guts; so well had he got our range. Groans and shouting were added to the clamour.

A bullet hit me; I feel its sharp sting yet; it felled me to the ground. I imagined the shot was in the head at first, but I soon found out its position when I essayed to crawl back to the road: it had pierced a hole through my right elbow. There was nothing for it but to walk, and, although the fire was growing intense, I managed to dodge the rest.

How heavily we had suffered could be gauged by the bleeding mass of men that lay in the shelter of the roadside. One old man who used to play the pipes in my company was shot just above the belt and was sobbing hysterically for water. A stretcher bearer forbade anyone to give it to him. Poor old beggar, he should never have been there: he was sixty all but six months, so he used to say. How he raved for water. On my other side a young lad was attempting to staunch the blood which flowed from his opened cheek with a filthy rag. I fainted.

It took me a long time to get to the casualty clearing station. There appeared to be hundreds of wounded all making for the same place. As I passed along, a shell burst on a field-gun battery which had just galloped into a new position. There did not seem to be anything but brown dust and rubbish left. Flame and explosion surrounded me.

On arrival at the dressing station, came inoculation against tetanus; two delirious days spent in a ruined byre awaiting the ambulance. First I was taken to Arques, then to Rouen, and from thence to England, where, at Stratford-on-Avon, soft beds and kind hearts awaited me.

W. Walker joined the colours (13th Northumberland Fusiliers) September 9th, 1914. Went to France with 21st Division early September 1915. Was wounded at Battle of Loos, September 26th, 1915 (machine-gun bullet through elbow joint). Ten months' hospital treatment. Unfit for further active service. On staff of draft-finding battalion, Rugely Camp, Staffs. Promoted C.Q.M.S., March 1917. To Cologne, March 1919. Demobilized, July 1919.

A HIGHLAND BATTALION AT LOOS

Thos. McCall

For a whole week before the Battle of Loos, the artillery of our Division were bombarding the German trenches night and day, smashing up the barbed wire. On September 24th, 1915, my battalion, a Highland one, was moved up into covered-in trenches ready to attack on the morning of the 25th. At 3 a.m. we marched up the communication trenches under a heavy shell-fire from the enemy guns. Nearing the front line, we began to step over dead and wounded, and knew that it was no picnic, and that some of us would never return.

Arriving at the trench, it was over the top and the best of luck. Then we got our first taste of the real thing. Men of different battalions were lying about in hundreds, some blown to pieces lying mangled in shell holes. The platoon I belonged to arrived at a German trench, where about nineteen to twenty Jerries were shouting for mercy, after pinking some of us as we came forward. Someone shouted, 'Remember the *Lusitania*!' and it was all over with Jerry.

We moved on towards the village of Loos, where machine guns were raking the streets and bayonet-fighting was going on in full swing. Prisoners were being marshalled in batches to be sent under guard down the line. The most of the houses were blown in, but their cellars were strongly built, and it was in these cellars that many Germans were hiding.

Two other sergeants and myself ran down into a cellar. To our surprise we found an old fellow in a white jacket, apparently an officers' cook. The table was laid with plenty of eatables and wines. The officers had a pressing engagement elsewhere. As we were feeling rather hungry, and to guard against being poisoned, we forced the cook to eat and drink first, and then we all had a good tuck in and felt the better for it; and took old Jerry upstairs a prisoner.

Leaving the cellar, I kept well into the side of the street to escape the flying metal, and came to a little estaminet. By the noise going on inside I thought they were killing pigs. I went inside and opened a door where blood was running out from underneath. It was certainly a pig-sticking exhibition. I saw some Highlanders busy having it out with Jerry with the bayonet. My assistance was not required, so I set off for Hill 70, our objective,

Through some misunderstanding, about 500 of us went straight ahead towards Lens and passed a German redoubt, where they were all holding up their hands in surrender, but, as things were going well at the time we did not bother with them, as we were sure they were our prisoners, and we could take them any time. Making our way through gaps in the German barbed wire, we got into the outskirts of Lens, but were held up by machine gun and rifle-fire and had to lie down and take cover, and try and dig ourselves in with our entrenching tools, which is not an easy job when you are lying flat.

The ground was soft and muddy with the rain and seemed to have been a cornfield trampled well down. The soldier lying next me gave a shout, saying, 'My God! I'm done for.' His mate next to him asked where he was shot. I did not catch what was said, but he drew himself back and lifted his wounded pal's kilt, then gave a laugh, saying, 'Jock, ye'll no dee. Yer only shot through the fleshy part of the leg.'

Suddenly we got the order to retire and then saw the Germans sending forward strong reinforcements, and it is a wonder that any of us had the luck to get back, as the bullets were cutting the grass at our feet and flying round our heads like the sound of bees. I made for the gap in the wire I came through and found it piled with dead. However, I made a jump and landed on top and rolled over on the other side. I felt something hot pass my neck. Putting my hand up I found no blood; the bullet had cut the neck of my tunic – a near thing.

But worse was to come. When we again faced the redoubt on the return journey, the Jerries were working their machine guns on us, knocking us down like nine-pins – a lesson never to leave prisoners behind with arms and ammunition. Only about fifty returned out of the 500 that advanced too far over the hill. I got back to the hill, and there got a chance to get my breath again. After midnight, our Division was withdrawn gradually, to allow another to take its place.

Our battalion was taken to a little village not far behind the line. There we had breakfast and a wash-up, and expected that we were going further back for a rest and reinforcements, as our strength was down to about 160. But our hopes were dashed, as the Division (what was left) was ordered back to the trenches that night, as things were not going too well on the hill. We held the trenches until the next morning when the Guards arrived and helped to put things in a stronger position.

The following day our pipe band met us at Mazingarbe and played us down to Noeux-les-Mines, where we went into billets, and had quite a nice time visiting estaminets, eating *pomme-de-terres et ceufs*, and speaking broken French.

Two or three days later we were entrained for Lillers, and there received our reinforcements. The new arrivals were eager to get up to the fighting line. They had their wish, for in less than a week we were back again for a spell of four days in a front-line trench beyond the village of Loos. Before we got there we had to march up a communication trench half full of water and mud for a couple of miles, and looked like a lot of sewer rats when we reached the front trench, which had belonged to the Germans.

Then started the hard work cleaning up the muck and water, filling sand-bags and building up parts that had been blown in, and making snipers' posts, and all the time trench mortars were hurling over their shells, causing more muck and casualties.

Being the C.S.M. of my company, my duty was to take over trench stores, post guards, and detail ration parties to go down and meet the Q.M.S. at night, bring up the bully beef and biscuits and the most important of all, the rum. The men always got their tot about 4 a.m., and I can assure you they needed it. Standing about day and night wet and half-frozen, it always put new life into them.

Drinking-water was sometimes very difficult to get, and we had to bring it up in petrol tins. One day the water did not arrive. An officer's servant came to me and asked if he could get some to make the officer's tea. The only water, I told him, was that gathered in a waterproof sheet which was stretched above our heads in the dug-out to keep us dry. It was the colour of stout, and I was not very sure whether there were any dead Germans buried above us or not.

'Never mind; it will do fine. The officers will never know, as I will put plenty of tinned milk and sugar in it,' and off he went with his kettle filled. The following night he brought me a small mug of hot tea which I enjoyed very much, but suddenly I remembered the water had not arrived, and asked where he got it. 'Oh! just out of your sheet.' I flung the mug at his head and chased him along the trench.

One night I detailed a party of bombers to hold a sap. Later on I took a turn up the sap to see if all was well and found every man knocked out by a shell. Another lot had to be detailed at once, and a burial party to take the dead away and have them buried before daylight. This was our usual daily occurrence.

Early in the morning the snipers were at their posts, with telescopic rifles ready to put a bullet into any German that happened to look over the top. One morning I stood beside Sniper McDonald, and watched the enemy lines through my periscope. Suddenly opposite us a box periscope went up and, after a survey of our lines, was taken down and put up again further along.

I told Mac to put it out of action next time. But instead of the periscope a Staff officer put his head up and looked around. I heard the ping of the sniper's rifle and saw Herr Von throw up his hands and fall back into his trench. Immediately another officer sprang up and shook his fist. Another ping and that was two he bagged that morning. I am sorry to say that sniper was killed by a shell a week later. He was sitting with me and two or three others in a cover-in, down a support trench, when a shell hit the rear of our shack, nearly smothering us with muck. He darted to the opposite side to another shelter and the second shell, following hard on the first, got him.

One night in the front line the men were sitting about the fire-trench or wading about in the water, which was up to their knees, trying to keep themselves warm. It had been sleet and snow all day, and we had another two days to go before being relieved. I was walking along in the dark when I plumped into a hole full of water up to the hips. Some of the boys had dug it during the day to give them a drier place to stand on. I had just managed to pull myself out, when I heard a splashing and someone running towards me. shouting, 'Stand to, men! And, Sergeant-Major, come quick. The enemy are advancing in thousands on the right.' I immediately ran towards the direction the noise was coming from, and found it was a young officer running about with a revolver in his hand.

How he expected me to stop them I don't know. The men got up at once on the fire-step, getting their rifles ready and blowing on their hands. The officer still kept shouting to me for God's sake to come quick. I thought it was funny, if an attack was on, that the Germans still kept throwing up their Verey lights. I looked over the top and could see nothing. Neither could the sentries. The Captain came on the scene, gave him a telling off and ordered him back to his platoon, and passed the word along for the men to stand down. I think the young officer had got a touch of the 'jumps,' as it was his first spell in the front line.

C.S.M. Thomas McCall joined up at Inverness, September 1914, in the Queen's Own Cameron Highlanders. After training at Inverness, Aldershot, and Salisbury, sailed for France, July 4th, 1915, with 44th Highland Brigade, 15th Scottish Division, and was with them at Loos, Somme, Arras, and the Belgian Front. Held the rank of company sergeant-major from September 27th, 1915, until the end of the war. Was fortunate in never being wounded, or on the sick list, though he had many narrow escapes. Left France December 11th, 1918, and was demobilized January 11th, 1919.

AT A SAP-HEAD

David Phillips

A fellow named Kendall and I palled up the day after he joined our company. We were in a sugar factory at the time, where we were to spend the night before going into the line. I had found two planks and trestles, and thought, in my ignorance, to make a bed where the rats would not disturb me, and while I surveyed the available floor space the slinking form of a large rat, just discernible in the dimming light, made me turn sharply round. My planks struck Kendall's and, in trying to save them, he received the full weight of one on his foot.

'Clumsy swine!' he shouted, and hopped in a threatening attitude towards me. As I put up my fists, I appraised his ability. He was lean and lanky. I decided to punch him in the stomach and upper-cut him as he crumpled. But the platoon-sergeant intervened, warned us both for guard from two to four o'clock the following morning.

Kendall spat copiously after the retiring sergeant.

'Stop that!' I said in mock seriousness, 'or I'll have you up for dumb insolence.'

Kendall laughed outright.

'Well, if we've got to go on guard together we may as well kip together.' He had two planks but no trestles, so we jammed the four planks together on my trestles, and next morning on guard we got to know each other better.

Looking back, I am vaguely conscious that the human associations of those War years live more vividly in my memory than the horror and unspeakable realities of War, much as they tormented me.

Kendall and I did many duties together after that and we grew in each other's regard. Of course we never voiced it – at twenty years of age one does not, nor, I suppose, at sixty. I don't know! But how else can I explain why he cursed me more abusively than my fellows? Or that my references to his mode of travel along the trenches as being due to chronic 'wind-up' caused him to smile and make dumb signs with his fingers, yet when others said so he would rise in a flash to silence them with his clenched fists.

One night when Kendall and I, together with two others, were over the parados busily digging, the enemy's machine guns traversed in our direction. It was soon after nine o'clock when 'Jerry' started to strafe us pretty generally along the line with 'minnies,' 'coal-boxes,' 'flying pigs,' 'toffee apples, 'aerial torpedoes; 'flying fishes,' 'pip-squeaks,' – a very mixed assortment from his stock, to be recognized by whichever of their names you knew them.

Soon we heard the cry 'Stretcher bearers!' Again and again it was repeated as we crouched lower in our now deepening pit.

'Down Sap 26 – shouldn't wonder,' Kendall said, rising and plying his spade once more. ''D' Company's getting it good and heavy. Damned if I don't think we're better off out here over the – ' A 'pip-squeak' exploded near by and the sprayed earth tinkled on our steel helmets. The next minute our captain dropped into the pit. We stopped working and wondered what he wanted. He spoke to me:

'A 'minnie' has dropped plump into the middle of the support bay of Sap 26 and wiped all four of them out, poor chaps, and the two men at the sap-head have been sent down with shell-shock. I want you and someone else to man the sap-head and hang out as long as you possibly can, because the company is short of men and I can't spare any to remain in support. If you get into trouble you must send up a couple of Verey lights and make your way back to the front line. Now, who'll you take with you?'

'Me, sir!' Kendall answered quickly.

'Right! You others must come to the front line. This job must wait.'

We gathered our tools together and prepared to make our way back to the front line.

'Sergeant Popple and I will come with you as far as the support bay. Wait for us at the entrance to the sap.'

Arrived at the entrance, we waited for the captain and Sergeant Popple. They soon came up, bringing the Verey light pistol with them.

'All O.K.?' the captain asked.

We nodded.

'Then lead the way – you'll find it's knee deep in mud. Halt at the support bay, or where the bay was before the 'minnie' dropped. We're sure to straggle outgoing through the mud.'

For the first few yards of the sap – a roughly hewn trench leading forwards from our front line – the going was good and the desultory shelling ceased. Then the mud became thicker, almost knee high, and footholds none too easy. And the squelching as each foot was lifted out of the mud seemed deafening in contrast with the piercing quiet that had descended on our sector.

I floundered into a hole, loin high in the mud.

''Ware hole,' I whispered over my shoulder to Kendall and heard him pass the warning on to the captain, who in turn passed it on to Sergeant Popple. And in a few moments more I heard the captain's muffled curses as he floundered as I had done.

At last we arrived at the 'minnie' hole, where the support bay had been.

'Jerry could hear us a mile off,' Kendall whispered.

How much farther to the sap-head? ' the captain asked.

'Another 60 feet or so,' I replied.

'All right. We'll give you ten minutes by my watch, and unless you signal us before that we'll return to the front line. I'll have you relieved as soon as I can, but it won't be before morning. Don't make yourselves objectionable, because I can't spare any men to support you. Good luck!'

The mud was not so deep at the sap-head. Kendall made himself comfortable on the small fire-step close to the supply of Mills' bombs, having first put a couple handy beside him. He looked at his watch: 'Five minutes to ten,' he whispered. 'They'll be back in the front line by now. Say, Jerry's only a few yards away, isn't he?'

'Yes,' I answered.' No need to whisper, but don't shout. Jerry's sap-head is about 25 yards from here. Sometimes, when it's quiet, you can hear him knock a tin over. I believe they've got a little dug-out at their sap-head.'

'Seems damn silly, doesn't it,' Kendall remarked. 'Couple of Jerries, or so, 25 yards over there and us over here, sitting on our backsides doing nothing.'

'Shift farther up, then I can sit down and help you. When Jerry sends a couple of bombs over after he's had his supper we'll send one over just to let him know we're still awake.'

'We shan't have had any supper though. Have you anything to eat?' Kendall asked.

'No. Have you?'

'Not a thing, only these hard biscuits.'

Apart from two small explosions near by and our reply, the night was comparatively quiet. But a continuous booming as of distant thunder came from the direction of the Somme. Kendall noted it:

'Worse places than this, I suppose,' he said.

'Yes. Still you might have had a soft look-out job in the front line. What did you want to come down here for, anyway? Always thought you were windy,' I bantered.

'So I am,' he confessed; 'windy as hell.'

'So am I.'

'Then why did the captain call on – '

'Shut up! I haven't told him yet.'

Kendall became reminiscent as a rat scuttled up the bank to the side of us.

'Funny, that night in the sugar factory. Lord, how I cursed that sergeant sticking us on guard together! And here we are – snug as a couple of bugs in a rug.'

'Not so strange after all. Perhaps, if we knew Jerry better, there'd be none of this,' I ventured.

'Perhaps so. Yes. And here we sit, and over there Jerry sits, lousy as hell – platoons of 'em in column of route marching all over you: drink that's one part water and four parts chloride of lime and brought up from the well at Ecurie in 2-gallon petrol tins; a bath every eighteen days and a shave when you're lucky enough to find a puddle that hasn't been stirred for an hour or so. What the devil made you join up?'

'The papers talked me into it – and vanity, I suppose,' I answered.

And so we talked through the night, gathering our greatcoats around us in the chill of the morning before dawn. A night crammed full of self-revelation – interesting as nothing else – of intimacies conveyed half-banteringly, yet with a veneer of cynicism!

And at dawn we eyed each other, a little shamefacedly perhaps, with a new interest and greater understanding.

'Gets colder between stand-to and stand-down,' Kendall remarked. He jumped down from the fire-step, where he had been looking towards the German lines. 'The sun'll get stronger presently. Keep an eye on that poppy – it grew on the edge of the trench – ' watch it open. That'll help the time to pass.'

'Blimy!' he continued. 'We've done eight hours already. Must report to the union when we get back.'

Sergeant Popple crawled warily up to the sap-head, carrying two hunks of bread, two small pieces of bacon, and a dixie of cold tea. We welcomed him as uproariously as the proximity of the two sap-heads allowed.

'Well, Pop,' Kendall said, 'how are things?'

'Lost a lot of men in the bombardment last night – Jerry's got our range to an inch. Davies gone, poor fellow, and Wellshead; Ashton blown to pieces; and Wheeler, poor kid. Only seventeen too! Got out here by bluffing his age and now a shell's taken his head clean off while he was standing on the fire-step. Goodness knows how many have had 'Blighty ones.'' Sergeant Popple looked grave as he stood with bended back, biting the ends of his grey moustache, the mud dripping from his puttees.

We ate the breakfast he had brought, filled our water bottles with the cold tea that was over, and asked him when he thought we would be relieved.

'Can't say,' he replied. 'Won't be before this afternoon, anyway. And cookie's got a touch of nerves, so I'll bring you along some grub when I get the chance. Captain wants you to keep a sharp look-out from this sap-head, and you're not to leave it on any account.'

'Right-o! Pop. Kiss the captain for me,' Kendall answered, and we watched Sergeant Popple down the sap, his back bent low, and carrying the empty dixie.

'Some say, 'Good old Pop!'' I ventured.

'Some don't so say,' Kendall replied with gusto.

The afternoon turned in an hour from sunshine to rain. A wind sprang up, a regular gale, and from over the German lines heavy clouds rolled disgorging torrential rains. Dinnertime had long since passed and Sergeant Popple had not brought us any. We were hungry as we stood in the lee of the firing-plate, which, sand-bagged on the other side. except for the peep-hole, formed the sap-head. So we munched the few scraps of hard biscuits that were left and took draughts from our cold tea.

At six o'clock we tossed for sleeping. Kendall won, and, tucking himself well into the corner of the fire-step; with his waterproof sheet pegged to the sand-bags so that his head and body were completely covered, he tried to sleep. I heard him muttering to himself every now and then; he cursed the conditions, the rain, the lice and, above all, the relieving party that had not arrived. But it was evident he would not be able to sleep. He was already wet through from the thighs downwards as I was.

'Thank your lucky stars you're not out here,' I said, as I heard the scratching of his lighter and knew, although I could not see, that he was going to light a cigarette. He did not reply, but started cursing again.

The rain came down still heavier and the wind swept it across the open, washing the trunk of the tree on our right – such a tree; dead, shell-torn, barkless!

Night came. We continued to take turns at resting on the fire-step; one resting, the other standing at the far corner and looking out over the lines into the darkness, which was relieved now and again by a fizzing Verey light. At midnight our artillery made a show and the Germans replied vigorously. In No Man's

Land as we were, it was comparatively safe, though the shells screeching overhead in both directions were particularly nerve-racking in our exhausted state.

Kendall cursed the relieving party again and again for not coming. All that night he cursed them venomously; for no one had been to see us, to bring food, and our biscuits and cold tea were long since finished. We no longer attempted to rest. Drenched to the skin and painfully in need of sleep, we propped ourselves up on the fire-step or in the trench, now a quagmire. And Kendall's obsession, the relieving party, soon made it impossible for him to stay on the lookout. And as for me, every stake in No Man's Land turned into a stalking German after a momentary stare, and I would have to look away and blink before the Germans would revert to stakes once more.

After stand-to on the following morning we were relieved. Dog-tired and hungry, we returned to the front line, where only the minimum of sentries were on duty owing to the shortage of men. We were given hot tea, bread, and bacon, and we went down a dug-out to sleep.

Soon – it seemed about five minutes afterwards – we were roused again and placed on sentry duty in the front line. Perhaps our periscope was a little too high, for Jerry paid some invidious attention, so with the dirt showering all about us we lowered it for a while.

After two hours Corporal Simpson brought two men to relieve us. I was looking through the periscope at the time and Kendall, who sat cleaning his rifle, was the first to see them.

'What do you want? ' Kendall asked the corporal.

'Brought the relief, of course,' the corporal replied.

'Relief! We don't want a b – relief. We've held this position for 34 hours 27 minutes. Clear out or I'll plug you!'

Tired as I was, it was some seconds before I realized that this was no ordinary banter, that Kendall still imagined we were holding the sap-head. I turned round towards him.

'Clear out, you b – !' Kendall shouted, and with a quick movement slid the bolt of his rifle back and forced a bullet into the breach.

I fell on him, pinning his shoulders to the ground, and, with Corporal Simpson and the assistance of the two men, barely managed to restrain him. And as I sprawled across his chest I looked into his staring, glassy eyes and realized he was mad – stark, staring mad!

Private David Phillips enlisted September 4th, 1914. Served in England and France in the 23rd County of London Regiment. Graded C3 in 1917 and transferred to Brigade of Guards Section, Army Pay Corps.

TRENCHES AT VIMY RIDGE

Harold Saunders

As the War had to be, I shall always be glad I was able to play even a negligible part in it, or I should never have known with such certainty the madness of it. During training I was aware only of the glamour of War. I prepared myself for it with enthusiasm, and bayoneted and clubbed the stuffed sacks representing the enemy with a sort of exalted ferocity. I was as jealous of my regiment as I used to be of my school.

The journey from Southampton to Havre in an ancient paddle-boat and on from there by train in a cattle-truck to the mysterious destination called the Front seemed a fitting prelude to the adventure. It was tedious and uncomfortable, but we told each other this was War. We became better acquainted with tedium and discomfort later.

When I made my debut in the line I had a cheerful conviction that nothing would hit me. And I remember standing on the fire-step for the first time and saying to myself exultantly: 'You're in it at last! You're in it! The greatest thing that's ever happened!'

Lice and wind-up came into my life about the same time. At stand-to one morning a flight of whizz-bangs skimmed the top of the trench. The man next to me went down with a scream and half his face gone. The sand-bag in front of me was ripped open and I was blinded and half-choked with its contents.

This was in the summer of 1916. In the plain on our right the flash and rumble of guns was unceasing. It was the beginning of the Somme offensive we learnt afterwards, but even if we had known one of the big battles of the War was in progress at our elbows I doubt if we should have been deeply stirred. To every private in the line the War was confined to his own immediate front.

My first spell in the line lasted three weeks. Water was scarce, and even the tea ration was so short there was none left over for shaving. I had a nine days' growth of beard when we went down to rest. Some of us looked like Crimean veterans and we all began to feel like it. My socks were embedded in my feet with caked mud and filth and had to be removed with a knife.

Lack of rest became a torment. Undisturbed sleep seemed more desirable than heaven and much more remote. This is why two occasions stand out like beacons in my memory. One was when I found myself in bed in a field hospital for the first time. The other was when I dropped among the straw in a rat-ridden barn after a long march down the line, tired beyond words and exquisitely drunk on a bottle of Sauterne. As I dropped into forgetfulness I felt I had achieved bliss.

I have slept on the march like a somnambulist and I have slept standing up like a horse. Sleeping at the post was a court-martial affair, with death or field punishment and a long term of imprisonment as the penalty. But, try as I would not to fall asleep, I often woke from a delectable dream with a start to find myself confronted with No Man's Land.

Once I was caught. It happened soon after dawn near the end of my spell. I had been watching a spot in No Man's Land where we suspected a sniper was operating. Suddenly I became aware of a voice saying, 'The man's asleep,' and knew it referred to me. Giving myself up for lost I sniffed loudly and changed my position as a sort of despairing protest. Out of the tail of my eye I saw a Staff officer talking to the corporal. To my inexpressible relief, the corporal answered with one of the most ingenious lies I ever heard. 'He can't be, sir,' he said. 'He lent me this pencil only a second before you came.' The officer was rather disinclined to accept the pencil as proof of my wakefulness, but, as I was then manifestly quite alert, he presently went his way. The corporal's joy at having dished a brass-hat was unbounded. They were not popular in the line.

Stark terror got hold of me one night on outpost guard in the Neuville-St. Vaast neighbourhood. These outposts were beyond the front line, sometimes within fifty yards of Jerry's trench. The guard consisted of a corporal and four men. There were two sap-heads at the post in question. They communicated with each other by an underground passage as well as by a short trench. I did not realize there was an underground communication when I was posted at the sap-head nearest the line. The corporal and the other three men went on to the other entrance to the sap.

Jerry had been restless all the evening; and not long after we had taken over he opened out with every gun he possessed. One of the fellows from the other sap-head came by with a bloody rag round his face. The racket of crumps and crashes and shrieking shells was too great to hear what he said, but I guessed he was going down to the first-aid post.

A little later I saw a flickering light approaching me from the depths of the sap. My hair literally stood on end, notwithstanding the tin hat. In my panic I thought Jerry must have countermined or found some other way into the sap and had chosen this way of attacking. My first impulse was to fire and get a few shots in, anyway. Luckily, however, I was inspired to shout a challenge. It was answered by the corporal. He and another man, both wounded, were helping each other down to the dressing station. I envied them their luck and promised to go round occasionally to see how G., the only other survivor, was faring. G. and I had joined the same day and had been friends ever since. I felt anxious about him and I wanted company, so I went as soon as the others had gone.

At the end of the short trench I stumbled over something. A bank of cloud cleared for a moment from the moon, and I saw it was a headless body.

I went back to my post, frightened beyond anything that should be humanly possible. Twice I was blown off my feet by the concussion of bursting shells. The whine of falling shrapnel filled the air. I seemed to be all alone in a world tottering into ruin. If only the noise would stop I felt I might keep my reason. I think I prayed for a direct hit to end it all. By a miracle, however, I was not even touched.

I don't know how long after it was when my platoon officer crawled round the remains of a traverse. He had come to withdraw the guard. Back in the line I was told to take an hour's rest. In the dug-out, stretcher bearers, unable to get down to the dressing station, were doing what they could for a man who had been buried. The candles constantly went out with the concussion of explosions outside, and every time this happened the man screamed.

A year or two after the War I was told a curious sequel to that memorable night. It had occurred three nights before my birthday. My mother was living at Vancouver at the time. That night she roused the household in a panic because she said I had burst into her bedroom. I was wearing an old tweed suit in which she had last seen me in England. I looked ghastly, she said, and all I could say in reply to her questions was 'Oh...! Oh!... Oh!...' My sisters did their best to comfort her, but only the continuance of my letters, in which, of course, I said nothing about the outpost affair, at last convinced her that I had not gone West. I wonder if the essential part of me fled half across the world that night to a country I had never seen in search of the comfort and company I so badly needed?

We learnt next morning that Jerry had made an attack on our left. But it was all quiet then. Letters came up with the bacon. I had one from a woman friend who had always seemed intelligent and understanding. Yet she asked this singular question: 'Is it as bad as they say it is out there, or is it only the shortage of cigarettes that makes it seem so rotten?' The irony of it coming at that time made me giggle like a schoolgirl. The others wanted to know the joke so I read it aloud. The comments were unprintable.

One got used to many things, but I never overcame my horror of the rats. They abounded in some parts, great loathsome beasts gorged with flesh. I shall never forget a dug-out at the back of the line near Anzin. It was at the foot of rising ground, at the top of which was a French war cemetery. About the same time every night the dug-out was invaded by swarms of rats. They gnawed holes in our haversacks and devoured our iron rations. We hung haversacks and rations to the roof, but they went just the same. Once we drenched the place with creosote. It almost suffocated us, but did not keep the rats away. They pattered down the steps at the usual time, paused a moment and sneezed, and then got to work on our belongings.

A battalion of Jerrys would have terrified me less than the rats did sometimes. As a matter of fact, hatred of the enemy, so strenuously fostered in training days, largely faded away in the line. We somehow realized that individually they were very like ourselves, just as fed-up and as anxious to be done with it all. For the most part; the killing that was done and attempted was quite impersonal. I doubt if I ever killed or wounded anyone. If I did it was more by bad luck than good judgement when we took pot shots at little grey working parties scuttling about at daybreak in front of their line.

My closest contact with the enemy was on a night raid which ended disastrously. The engineers missed a strip of concealed wire when they made a gap for the raid. We failed to get through, and less than half the party returned.

The folly of it all struck us at the oddest times. There was a tall, oldish man in my platoon who had been fixed up at the base with a set of false teeth. Poor Mac was given to fits of sneezing and when this happened his Army teeth generally went flying. I was next to him on the fire-step at stand-to one night. Suddenly Mac made a queer half-strangled noise. Then I heard him mutter, 'Oh, hell!' and knew he'd lost his teeth. We fumbled among the sandbags, but it was quite a time before a Verey light revealed to me the lower set some distance over the parapet.

"Anks,' mumbled the toothless Mac, pocketing the dentures. Then, as a kind of afterthought: "Sall so dam' shilly, isn't it?'

There were many men it was good to have known. Soon after we got out one of our fellows found what looked like a bomb with a piece of fuse attached in the corner of the dug-out. He lit it with a cigarette end and then, getting frightened, threw it away. It sizzled venomously on the floor, but only one man of the half-dozen of us there had the pluck and presence of mind to do the obvious thing. While we all crouched where we sat, cursing the meddling fool, as we waited for the explosion, the clown of the platoon, a little Salvationist, threw his greatcoat over the smouldering thing and jumped on it. The bomb or whatever it was, proved to be harmless, but that made little B. none the less a hero.

A man next to me in hospital once had the most brutal looking face I think I ever saw. I learnt he was 'Young Alf,' or some such name, a professional heavyweight. I never expect to meet a man with a kindlier outlook on men and things. His boils got well, and he was marked for convalescent camp. When he said good-bye he insisted on giving me two English pennies, 'for remembrance,' as he said. I knew they were all he had in the world and I determined not to part with them. But I forgot. They were spent or lost when I got back to the regiment. I rather think 'Young Alf' would not have forgotten.

The most awesome and in some ways most dreadful thing I ever saw was a kind of ceremonial gas attack in the autumn of 1917. We withdrew from the front line to the support trench, so that the engineers could operate on the ground between. It was a still moonlight night, one of those nights when the guns on both sides were quiet and there was nothing to show there was a war on. The attack began with a firework display of golden rain. The fireworks petered out and a line of hissing cylinders sent a dense grey mist rolling over No Man's Land. What breeze there was must have been exactly right for the purpose. But the unusual silence, the serene moonlit sky, and that creeping cloud of death and torment made a nightmare scene I shall never forget.

It seemed ages before Jerry realized what was afoot. At last, however, the first gas alarm went and I think most of us were glad to think he would not be taken unawares. Presently the gongs and empty shell-cases and bars of steel were beating all along his front, almost as though he was welcoming in the New Year. But I was haunted for hours afterwards by the thought of what was happening over there. Sympathy was blown sky-high the next night, however. We were going out to rest and shortly before the relieving troops were due Jerry started one of the fiercest barrages I ever experienced. The relief could not come up. The trenches were crowded with men all packed up and unable to go, and it rained–heavens, how it rained! Hour after hour we stood there in the rising flood, helpless as sheep in the pen, while the guns did their worst.

It was six in the morning before we got back to the rest billets, more dead than alive. Even then there was no rest for me. I was detailed to parade for battalion guard in four hours. Battalion guard was a spit and polish business, and a full day would not have sufficed to remove nine days' mud from my uniform and clean my saturated equipment. A scarecrow guard of deadly tired men eventually paraded. We had done our best to get clean, but neither the sergeant-major nor the adjutant, both looking fresh and beautiful, applauded our efforts. Very much the contrary, in fact. But we were all past caring what they thought or said about our appearance.

The next time I went into the line a spot of gas sent me out of it for good. I did not know American troops were in France till I found myself in one of their hospitals at Etretat. The nurses and doctors were gentle beyond anything I ever experienced. I could only account for it by thinking they must regard my case as hopeless, and when I found a large white bow pinned on my bed there seemed no room for doubt. I got rather light-headed and fancied my obsequies had already begun in the hustling fashion of the Americans. But the white bow only meant that I was on milk diet.

A week later I was in Blighty, the soldier's Promised Land. Six months afterwards I appeared in the streets again as a civilian with a profound hatred for war and everything it implies.

Private Harold Saunders enlisted in the 14th London (London Scottish) in November 1915, and went to France with the 2nd Battalion in June 1916. When the 60th Division left France for Salonika he was left behind with a septic heel. He was transferred to the 1st Battalion, and was with them till a whiff of gas at Cambrai completed the wreck in October 1917. He was finally discharged April 1918.

IN A KITE BALLOON

W. Sylvanus Lewis

I am not what is termed a literary man, so I shall have a little difficulty in clearly expressing myself, but I have had some experiences as a flight sergeant in the Royal Air Force which may prove interesting. I will, therefore, do my best with a poor stock of words to give an accurate account of my experience in the Great War in a kite balloon on the Vimy Ridge sector of the line. I shall not give the name of the officer who was observing in the balloon with me, but I will give the first initial of his surname, so that if he reads this, he may recognize himself.

In the early part of May 1916, before the big Vimy Ridge battle, in the morning soon after sunrise the balloon ascended with Lieutenant H. and myself to about 5,000 feet. Everything was at peace except an anti-aircraft gun showing evident anger at an annoying mosquito that was buzzing over enemy country. That bark was the only sound that made one realize that a tragic war was on. For people with jaded nerves who are perplexed with the ceaseless hurry, bustle and noise of modern life, I recommend a few hours up aloft in a kite balloon as a tonic and respite from its cares and worries. There is a charming and attractive calm and quietness about the experience that is recuperative and restful.

Of course this is not recommended whilst there is a war on, because the clouds can harbour unseen, unknown terrors and instruments of destruction. For instance, the enemy developed an astonishing accuracy in shelling kite balloons with shrapnel, I have had some uncomfortable half-hours with this kind of attack. This morning in May one shell burst towards our balloon, only one, but it left us guessing as to when the next would be sent over, for the enemy rarely let us off with only one try, but this morning he did. He was kind to us that day.

Our object on this morning was to locate a very annoying gun that kept everybody in our sector of the front on tenterhooks by its back-area firing – a nasty irritating business.

We nicknamed the gun 'Ginger,' and its explosive crumps gave everyone the jumps. A hollow bang would faintly be heard in the distance, and, before you could count two, with a terrific whoop and crump, a high explosive shell would burst near.

I remember our sergeant-major getting terribly upset over this gun; we were at a part of the line, taken over from the French, called Bois de Ville, and our sleeping accommodation consisted of a lot of holes covered over with brushwood, mud and sandbags, and one went down three steps into it. One night 'Ginger' was particularly active; and 'Molly' M., our sergeant-major, could not sleep, but remained wandering about from one side of the small dug-out to the bottom step of the entrance, where he would fearfully look out. He did that once too often, for, with a roar and a crump, a shell exploded just outside our dug-out, and 'Molly,' with just his head showing, caught a drift of lyddite smoke from that shell that made him look like a nigger minstrel. He fled. We heard no more of him until our motor-cyclist reported having seen him running for dear life, with blazing and staring eyes, and a foaming and muttering mouth.

Poor old 'Molly'! It became particularly hard for him, after telling us all on parade at home, 'Now come on, you lazy lot of buzzers, lep, rite, lep, rite, faster, faster. When you get the other side and have a nine-point-two on your backsides, you'll hop it quick enough.'

Poor old 'Molly'! If he had gone to bed with Sergeant Tom B. and me he would have been all right; it was pure funk after all, for he never got a scratch otherwise.

We were out to locate this gun, but for a long time Lieutenant H. and I did not trouble much about guns. We were too enraptured with the glorious sunrise. It was wonderful, marvelous – words fail me to express what I felt. I felt very near to what some people call the infinite, whatever they may mean, or, as some may say, near to God, but whatever it was I was thinking and feeling, I began to realize in some dim way that to be absorbed in a vision of unutterable beauty is a fine experience. I was thinking that it was good to have been born, just to experience that one thing. I thought of many other things in a rambling sort of way...

Bang! like a big drum being struck. Swish-rip-a sighing whistle, a noise, or rather a shriek like the tearing of some gigantic piece of canvas. Christ! What's happened? Gee! the balloon has burst. It had collapsed about us, and we were coming down. I desperately struggled to push away the fabric of the balloon from the basket, and suddenly from underneath the mountain of fabric, I glimpsed the white face of Lieutenant H. 'We must jump,' he said. I agreed with him, and immediately dived over head first, and nearly dived through my harness. It had no shoulder straps, only a waistband and loops for one's legs. Never shall I forget that sickening horrible sensation when, in my first rush through the air, I felt my leg loops at the knees, and my waistband round my buttocks. I managed, however, to grab hold of the thick rope which is toggled on from the waistband to the parachute. Meanwhile, everything else seemed to go wrong; the cords of the parachute somehow in the struggle got entangled round my neck, so that as the parachute began to open with a deadly pull on my body, I was literally being strangled in mid-air.

The sensation was horrible and unforgettable; my face seemed to swell to twice its size, and my eyeballs to become too big for their sockets. Then I was suddenly freed, and could breathe again, but my neck was badly lacerated and raw. My bad luck was not over, however, because I was suddenly pulled up with a sharp jerk that jarred every bone in my body. I had fouled the cable which held the balloon to the winch, and my parachute had, in striking it, coiled itself round about three or four times. Suspended in mid-air! I remained in that helpless position for what seemed like hours, and I looked down, and saw Lieutenant H., his parachute getting smaller and smaller. Then I slowly began to unwind – round and round I went like a cork, and broke away with a rush, the silk of my parachute being torn almost across, and I began hurtling down at a great speed, with my damaged and useless parachute flap, flap, flapping above me. I thought it was all up with me. I had seen a couple of parachute accidents, and I knew what to expect. I could do nothing but curse at the damned bad luck I was having. I have read that face after face of one's friends and scenes of one's past haunt one when in danger. It is perfectly true, because I actually experienced it.

Crash! I had shut my eyes, I thought I had struck the ground. No; in a slanting, rushing dive, I had struck poor old H.'s parachute, and the force of my fall had caused his parachute to collapse. 'Sorry,' I shouted. One had to shout I remember, for the wind seemed to be blowing a gale, although actually it was a calm, sunny day. 'Sorry, but I couldn't help it.' 'It's all right, old man,' he shouted, 'but couldn't you find some other bloody patch to fall on? Millions of bloody acres about you, yet you must pick me to fall on.' 'It looks like finish,' he continued. It did.

Suddenly his parachute began to bellow out with a flapping roar, tumbling me off like a feather, but I was too inextricably bound up with his cords to shoot away altogether; incidentally, I was hanging like grim death to something or other. What it was I don't know, but I imagine it was about half a dozen of his parachute cords. And so we landed, two on one parachute. At least, I landed first, because I seemed to slip down just before we landed, and he landed full weight on top of me.

I know nothing of what happened immediately after, but I heard subsequently that we had landed almost on the support trenches, and scores of Canadians had rushed out and gathered round us, and that the enemy thought it was a fine opportunity to drop a few shells around.

Flight-Sergeant W. S. Lewis served with the R.F.C. and R.A.F. from June 1915 to March 1919. A good deal of that time was spent in France on the Vimy Ridge sector. He entered the Civil Service in May 1919 and is now an established civil servant.

A NIGHT COUNTER-ATTACK

F. W. Watts

On Sunday, May 21st, 1916, the battalion was in camp at Camblain-l'Abbe, behind Vimy Ridge. Recent spells in the line had been quiet, the weather was warm and sunny, and everyone was in good spirits. I was on camp-cleaning fatigue, but, the camp being in a good condition, there was nothing to do beyond picking up an odd piece of paper or two. After dinner most of the men settled down in the huts to sleep or write letters; it was all very pleasant and happy, something like Sunday at home.

During the afternoon, when I happened to be near the officers' hut, the company commander put his head out of a window (he was having a bath) and told me to let him know at once if any message came from Battalion Headquarters. I did not think much about the matter and, so far as I knew, no message came. About five o'clock we sat down to tea. In my hut we had just drawn our rations from the dixies when the company commander appeared at the door and said in a strange voice, 'Pack up immediately! Pack up immediately!' We swallowed our tea, put on our equipment and fell in outside. In half an hour the battalion was on the road, marching in the direction of the line. When we met the other companies it was obvious from the faces of officers and men that something serious was afoot. The old hands, I suppose, guessed what was coming, but to me it was all new.

We came to the hamlet of Villers-au-Bois, and there rested in a field for perhaps an hour in the evening sunlight. The officers went away to receive orders. When they came back we took the road once more, my company leading the battalion.

As we left the hamlet some Engineers ran across the road in front of us and climbed a bank on the side, apparently to get a better view of something. One of them shouted to his comrades as we passed, 'This way for the orchestra stalls!' Emerging from a belt of trees, we saw what they were looking at. Across a level stretch of country, two or three miles wide, we saw the Ridge. I do not suppose that it is much of a height as hills go, but it dominated the landscape at all times, and that evening it was as awful a sight as could be imagined. From end to end it was covered with a thick cloud of grey smoke, lit here and there by the twinkling flashes of shell-bursts. Seen across that peaceful-looking countryside it seemed unreal, fantastic, but there was no one so new to warfare that he did not know what it meant.

Before long the sun set, and in the twilight we left the road and began to make our way across country towards the Ridge. Half-way across we halted again and waited for some time for a guide who was being sent down by the battalion which was holding the line. He came at length, and in the fading light we set off again. Presently I began to notice a smell which reminded me of pear-drops, and a smarting of the eyes which became so painful that I had to shut them at frequent intervals. I soon found that everybody else was suffering in the same way, and we concluded that the cause of the trouble was tear-gas. The battalion had not experienced gas before, which accounted for our slowness in recognizing it. As soon as it was diagnosed we put on our goggles, but, what with the deepening gloom about us, the mist which gathered on the eye-pieces, and the roughness of the ground, we found that it was impossible to keep them on. After a while, when we had passed through the 'dosed' area, the symptoms passed off. Another stop, and a lot of argument in front. I heard the company commander say, with an intensity of feeling that only those who have been through such an experience will understand, 'The bloody b – of a guide has lost us!'

At length word was passed along to move on again. We entered a shallow communication-trench. Night had fallen; we had to go in single file and soon experienced the usual trials of men moving in single file in darkness. The trench climbed a gentle rise; then we ran into an obstacle, a high step or sort of stile made of earth. In daylight it would have been a trifle, no doubt, but that night it caused a great deal of anxiety and swearing.

By this time it was obvious that we were nearing the line. On the other side of the obstacle the ground fell away again, and ahead of us was another rise, the main Ridge, above which the enemy's flares rose every now and again and threw a sickly greenish light over the landscape for a few seconds. The night was as black as ink; it was impossible to see more than a yard or so, except when a flare went up.

Imagine a long line of hot and angry men stumbling along in utter blackness, everyone doing his best to keep up with the fellow in front yet not quite able to ignore the anxious cries from behind, 'Where are you? We're losing touch!' None of us was familiar with the country, and every man knew that on him rested responsibility for all those behind him. The man in front of me was a little fellow about fifteen years older than most of us and several degrees above us in social standing. He was said to be a First Division Civil Servant. Being short, he found even greater difficulty than the rest of us. I well remember seeing him climb the step and almost fall down the other side into the darkness. It may be said that that was my last sight of him, for he was killed that night. The valley between us and the front line was being bombarded pretty heavily. We could hear shell after shell hurtling down into it, the scream of its passage and the roar of its explosion magnified by the echoes. On the height a couple of machine guns kept up a rat-tat-tat-tat.

Somehow the company got across the valley at last, and found itself lined up under a rise which led away up into the darkness. Here we halted again, while the Company Commander went into a small hut made of sand-bags, which served, I suppose, as the headquarters of the battalion in the line. Shells thudded down and burst on the slope in front of us or shrieked over our heads. Presently word was passed along that every man was to take two bandoliers of ammunition in addition to the 120 rounds that were always carried. Boxes of ammunition appeared from somewhere and were opened; we each took a couple of bandoliers and hung the things round our necks. When all had been served word came along to fix bayonets. We fixed. Then the order 'Advance!' These orders were, of course, passed down from man to man in the good old Army fashion; we did not know from whom they came.

We were somewhat bunched up at the start, so someone gave the order, 'High Port!' The 'high port' is a way of carrying a rifle above one's head, so that the bayonet fixed on it shall not accidentally stab one's neighbour. It is used in drilling with bayonets fixed, but, of course, was not intended to be used under fire. The order may have come from anyone, a corporal or even some officious private, but we obeyed it. None of us, apart from the two officers and the sergeant-major, knew what was happening.

Opening out as we moved up the slope, we came to a trench, which I knew later was the British front line; to us it was simply an obstacle to be jumped into and scrambled out of in the dark. By this time we had come under machine-gun fire; the night seemed alive with bullets, whose crack, crack was almost deafening. As I got out of the trench I saw, by the light of a flare, our platoon-sergeant cursing some men who wanted to stop in it. He was threatening them with his bayonet and shouting, 'Get out, you b – s!'

In front of the trench the attacking party seemed to melt away, and I soon began to feel rather lost, and strongly disinclined to go any further.

I dropped into a shell hole with a half-hearted suggestion to myself that I only wanted to take stock of things for a minute. Another man got down into it at the same time who turned out to be my best chum. We exchanged some sort of greeting, and I soon discovered that he had no more desire to leave the hole than I had, which was some comfort for my conscience. We crouched against the forward lip. Another minute or so, and the night seemed to turn red. Looking up, I saw almost over our heads a rocket which had burst into three red lights. I knew what that meant. It was the German S.O.S. signal to the artillery at that period. I said 'Good God! we're for it now!' The barrage came down on us. This time the shells were not going over; but coming close to us, and their shrieks rose to an almost unbearable pitch before they burst. Around us the world seemed to be shattered by explosion after explosion; the hellish crack of bullets went on unabated, and in front the lights danced continually up and down. We cowered in our hole, our one object at the moment to take up as little space as possible. Bits of steel hummed over us, and dirt seemed to fall in showers. We heard afterwards that the enemy had a hundred batteries concentrated on a short bit of the line there; where the information came from I do not know, but I have never doubted it. During the bombardment something hit me in the back, and on putting my hand round to feel the place I found it damp. I thought I had been wounded, but found that the moisture was merely sweat, which was pouring down me as a result of excitement.

How long it went on I do not know – not many minutes, I suppose. When it had died down we peered out of our hole and discovered a few more fellows close by. It was necessary to decide what we were to do, for the darkness had begun to diminish. We held a consultation. You can imagine us lying there and looking anxiously at each other in the first dead light of dawn. Some were for staying where we were, most for going back. We crawled out in the direction of our own lines and soon fell in with a lance-corporal who, to everybody's relief, endorsed the decision. So back we went over the broad crest of the Ridge to our front line and got into it. There we found two or three more of our fellows, with another lance-corporal, a big Devonian who was quite cool after the events of the night. Under his encouragement we made a show of holding the line, though as far as we knew there were only thirteen of us. There were others away to right and left, but we did not see them until later in the morning.

When the sun rose I went exploring along the trench and found a short sap running forward from it; looking into this I saw another of my chums, a boy from Dublin, lying face downwards in the bottom and almost unconscious. He begged feebly for a drink. I believe I managed to moisten his lips, but I could not do much for him, because every time I tried to move him he groaned piteously. There was a large hole in the upper part of his back, which I tried to cover with one of my field dressings. What I did was not of much avail, I fear, but it was the best I could do, as he kept begging me to leave him alone, and I suspected that in moving him I was doing more harm than good. I took out his pocket-book and copied the address on one of his letters from home, with the purpose of writing to his people, as it did not seem likely that he would be able to write letters for a long while.

By this time the sun shone brightly and we were in comparative peace; only the occasional crack of a sniper's bullet reminded us that there was an enemy, and after what we had just been through, snipers' bullets did not seem worth worrying about. Later in the morning our little party was given permission to go down to the valley again. On the way we passed a number of wounded men whom we knew, waiting to be carried out. One of them, I was glad to see, was our platoon sergeant, a man I had always disliked. He had a wound in one of his feet. During the day we rested in holes and dug-outs under the lee of the hill and, apart from an hour's bombardment with high-explosive shells in the afternoon, the time passed pleasantly enough.

In the evening occurred two little incidents which have always puzzled me and will now, I suppose, never be explained. The first was a glimpse that I had of a headless corpse, or what appeared to be a headless corpse, sitting alone in a shallow dug-out. Looking for someone I knew, I put my head in and saw this thing; it gave me such a shock that I did not look again. How a headless corpse could be in that position and that place I cannot imagine. The other incident occurred after dark. I was sitting in a big dug-out when a few more of the company came in. They had been lying in a shell hole in 'No Man's Land' all day, expecting every moment to be blown to atoms by a trench-mortar. They did not dare to show a finger until nightfall, of course. One of them, who, though he had known me a long time, was not a chum of mine, was so moved at seeing me that he kissed me on the forehead. The same night the battalion was relieved and returned to Camblain-l'Abbe.

When the newspapers came up during the next few days, we looked eagerly for the official report of our adventure, but were bitterly disappointed, for the *communiqué* merely said that the situation on Vimy Ridge remained unchanged. It became known afterwards that when the company commander reported at the headquarters of the battalion holding the line on the fatal night he was told that the line of resistance and the support line had been captured by the enemy and that he was to deliver a counter-attack in half-an-hour. There was no time to make any reconnaissance, and no information was forthcoming as to the exact position of affairs. The company commander did his best, but it is not astonishing that the counter-attack was a failure. The commander and his only subaltern, their servants and the sergeant-major disappeared and were never heard of again. The company went into action 104 strong and came out with forty-eight.

My Dublin chum died in hospital in France about a month later, as I learnt from a letter sent by his brother.

Frank Wilfrid Watts enlisted June 1915 in 15th Battalion The London Regt. (Civil Service Rifles). Lance-Corporal, October 1915. Corporal, December 1915. Lance-Sergeant, March 1916. Wounded at High Wood on September 15th, 1916. Commissioned in the same battalion, October 1917. To Palestine, March 1918. Returned to Belgium, July 1918. Wounded at Messines in September and sent home again. Discharged from hospital, March 1919.

A GUNNER'S ADVENTURE

N. H. Bradbury

ONE of the most exciting experiences which befell me during the War happened on the Somme front on June 26th, 1916, four days before the great Allied offensive. Our battery, of which I was a signaller, was in action at Sailly-au-Bois, and was to support the attack on Gommecourt Wood on July 1st.

It was my turn to be on duty at the 'O.P.,' so off I started on my journey, accompanied by two other comrades, one acting as a runner.

We fully realized that a hot time was in store for us, his duty being to carry messages back to Headquarters, which were situated in Hébuterne village, should occasion arise in any emergency, such as telephonic communication breaking down or other unforeseen circumstances arising. My other comrade, Signaller Thompson, was to assist with the work that we were to do at the 'O.P.'

Leaving the battery at half-past seven, the three of us made our way over the plain, passing Hébuterne Wood and along the road, and through a winding of trenches known as 'Wood Street,' to a place called 'The Grotto ' and some more trenches known as 'The Keep,' well-known spots in this sector, where more often than not, one had to keep very alert of machine-gun fire, owing to the fine over-looking position the Hun had at his command.

The morning was fine and bright with the sun just breaking through. We leisurely made our way along the trench leading to our observation post, which was situated at a junction of the support and front-line trenches, arriving there about nine o'clock.

After testing our telephone lines and receiving the 'O.K.' from the stations in communication with us, we awaited the arrival of the major and Lieutenant Hasper, who took a very brave and active part, saving my life, of which I will give you further details later.

After we had been on the look out for some hours our infantry put over a smoke screen. Jerry had been on the alert for several weeks, knowing too well that we had been preparing for a big offensive. In fact more than once he had put notice boards on the top of his trenches, intimating that he was already aware of our intentions and suggesting a number of likely dates for the offensive to take place. Being in such readiness, he at once realized what we were at. His artillery opened fire on our front-line trenches, many shells getting direct hits on our 'O.P.' We at once made for our dug-out.

We had spent many days and long nights in making the place as secure as our means would allow. The stairs led down to a depth of 16 feet, the walls being held by corrugated iron. At the bottom there was a room 12 feet square. At the left-hand corner an airshaft had been cut, leading to the top of our trench, some 12 feet from the parapet. Unfortunately, this emergency exit had not been quite completed, having no support should the walls of earth cave in, which, as you will learn, was the cause of our major and my two comrades losing their lives.

By the time we had reached the bottom of the dug-out the trench outside had been destroyed by the continuous shelling, causing the entrance to our dug-out to collapse, thus cutting off our means of escape to the trench outside.

After some few moments, which seemed like hours, our major decided that Lieutenant Hasper should make an attempt to be lifted up the airshaft. We now began at once to pull out the timbers that had been blown into the dug-out to put under the feet of our comrade, in assisting him to make his escape, pushing the pieces of wood under each other, the higher he got up the shaft. After some considerable time Lieutenant Hasper reached the top. The bombardment was now at its height, but, thank the good Lord! He managed to get away without getting hit, to bring back a rescue party of half a dozen officers and men.

The time which elapsed between Lieutenant Hasper's escape and his return with the rescue party seemed endless. At last we heard shouts, and the next instant Lieutenant Hasper was being let down the airshaft. Unable to obtain a rope, our rescue party formed themselves into a human chain.

We now wondered who would be next to be got out. The major decided that he would make an attempt, but after many despairing efforts he was not able to get more than a few feet from the bottom: his figure was more robust than Lieutenant Hasper's, and our task of lifting him was much more difficult.

While all this had been going on I had been praying very quietly, asking the Almighty to save me. I shall never forget those moments of anxiety.

The major then said, 'Well, Bradbury, you have a go.' This was the last I heard or saw of him.

I began to claw my way up towards daylight. The German guns were now belching forth with more intensity than ever, and the work of the rescue party was becoming more difficult every moment. All this time I was working my way inch by inch, grappling the clay walls of the airshaft, and digging my fingers in as far as I could. I was now becoming very exhausted, and only the encouragement which I received from those up above made me go on.

Every moment, I kept on repeating the words, 'I cannot do it,' only to hear Lieutenant Hasper's voice calling, 'For God's sake, man, stick it!'

I now had worked myself half-way up, and the distance between myself and my rescuers still seemed a very long way. It was getting late in the evening and darkness was creeping upon us, the bursting of the enemy shells on top of the dug-out making a very vivid scene.

I could now see the outstretched fingers of another officer, Lieutenant Hibbins, who formed one of the rescue party and, try as I could, with all my strength, I was still unable to reach them. The exertion which I was putting into my efforts made the perspiration run down me, I felt that the veins in my hands were at bursting point.

At last I felt the tips of his fingers, and, after a couple of almost superhuman efforts on my part, he grabbed my wrists. The feeling that ran through me at this moment I cannot describe, realizing that I was now safe. At last I was landed safely at the top; each rescuer putting every ounce of energy behind his pull.

Shells were falling heavily as I lay in a semi-conscious and half-dazed condition on the ground.

Our corporal, Frierley, and some more men were now endeavouring to dig as hard as they could to widen the shaft to rescue Major Heard. After working many hours they had to give up, and the major and my other two comrades had to be abandoned in the collapsed dug-out.

Our infantry in the front-line trenches, which were only a few yards away, were depleted in number, the Boche attacking very heavily as I lay on the ground.

It was now eight o'clock in the evening and I made my way back along the shell-battered trenches, being assisted by Corporal Frierley, who was awarded the Military Medal in this action.

I was met by our captain, who afterwards took command of the battery. He congratulated me upon my escape. Eventually we arrived back at the gun-pits.

Lieutenant Hasper was awarded the Military Cross. I shall never forget him. This incident is only one of the many great deeds of heroism enacted during the Great War.

Gunner N. H. Bradbury enlisted in the Territorial service on May 6th, 1909, and was mobilized on August 4th, 1914, his unit then being the 3rd London Brigade, R.F.A., which stayed in England until October 4th, 1915, when it embarked for Prance, the first action being at Sailly-au-Bois, November 1915. January 27th, 1916, the Kaiser's birthday anniversary, he was in the front line at Loos, going from there to the Somme, where he took part in the Somme offensive of July 1st, 1916. After leaving there the brigade was in the Battle of the Somme. Afterwards took part in the capture of Vimy Ridge, April 10th, 1917, when, after doing good work there, the brigade was designated the 282nd Brigade, R.F.A., being Army field artillery; Other engagements were: Third Battle of Ypres, July 31st, 1917; Pilkem Ridge; St. Julien, August

3rd, 1917; Poelcappelle, August 19th, 1917; Passchendaele Ridge, November 6th, 1917; V Army retreat, March 21st, 1918. On the date of the Armistice at Cambrai.

THE CARNOY COWS

T. S. Williams

Both boots had been worn thin at the heel. They were also splashed heavily with mud. Slimy, grey, limestone mud. The puttees, too, were mudstained and the khaki pants, but it was the boots that fascinated me.

I had been watching those two boots moving up and down throughout the whole of a bleak winter's afternoon. There were hundreds of other boots – my own included – all moving up and down, but only the two directly in front really mattered. Left-right, left-right, on they went till the sun went down and the sticky surface of the road turned crisp with frost. The down-at-heel boots continued to plod onwards. Darkness came on apace and mercifully hid them from view.

Stars were shining in a clear sky when we halted, tired out and hungry, by the grey-stoned church of Bray-sur-Somme. At last we had arrived at our destination. The battalion had been marching for several days. We were about to experience our first taste of trench warfare in a 'quiet spot,' and Bray was to be our headquarters when out of the line.

We were to journey up to the trenches under cover of darkness on the following night. The orderly sergeant broke the news when he came to our billet with Battalion Orders. Nobody seemed to care. We were too weary and foot-sore to take much notice.

'Can anyone here milk a cow?' It was the sergeant speaking, but no reply to this strange question was forthcoming. If he had asked for a volunteer to kill a pig, the request could not have been more unexpected. The next moment, however, my elbow was nudged. 'Go on, chum. Speak up. There's a soft job for you!'

'Can you milk a cow?' said the sergeant, eyeing me suspiciously, I nodded my head. 'Then in future you will be attached to Headquarters' Company. To-morrow you will parade at 3.30 a.m. to march with the advance party for the trenches.' Without any further word of explanation, the sergeant turned and walked through the doorway, out into the darkness of the deserted village street.

What in the name of goodness had I let myself in for now? Weary with foot-slogging, I had hoped for at least a day's rest before going up the line, But, no. Long before dawn I was to be on the road once more. Cursing my luck, I turned in for a few hours' sleep before turning out again.

There is little need to dwell upon the discomforts of the following morning. The early rise in the dark and the parade of Headquarters' Company in the keen, frosty air. 'Is the cowman there? Right.' Off we trudged along the road to the trenches.

In the grey light of early dawn we found ourselves looking down on a few shell-shattered roof-taps – all that was left of Carnoy. Marching down hill, we halted amongst the ruins just as the rattle of a machine gun and desultory rifle-fire told us that it was 'stand-to' in the trenches.

Carnoy was Battalion Headquarters for the troops holding the line. On one side of the road was the colonel's dug-out. Opposite were the remains of a farmstead and near by a communication trench labelled Montauban Alley. Here amid the tumble-down debris of bricks and mortar I was to find a home. I was also to find my new job waiting for me.

'Is the cowman there?' asked a sleepy voice. 'Come on, chum. Follow me. I'll show you what kind of a job you've been let in for!' The speaker had evidently just emerged from beneath his blanket. I followed him between two buildings where once there had been a gateway.

The gateway had belonged to the farmyard which had been square in shape, a large midden in the centre and out-buildings all round. The midden was still there. No cows, no horses, no pigs were to be seen. Not even a barn-door fowl. The buildings were in ruins and a death-like silence seemed to brood over the whole place.

'Here we are,' said my sleepy companion as we clattered over the cobblestones and halted in front of the only building with any semblance of a roof. Somewhere in, the darkness beyond the open doorway there was a movement which produced a faint rustling noise. There was no mistaking that familiar sound. It was the swish of a cow's tail.

There were two cows – one dry and the other giving a bare quart of milk, I was told. The milk was to be taken to the colonel's dug-out. 'What do the poor beggars live on?' was my first question. 'I'll show you after breakfast,' was the reply. I was content to wait, for up the steps of a near-by dug-out came the savoury smell of fried bacon.

The dug-out was deep and down below it was comfortably warm and dry. Sore feet and aching shoulders were forgotten as we gathered round the fire to enjoy a drink of piping hot tea.

Breakfast finished, we returned to our charges once more. Undoing the tethering ropes, we led the cows out of the farmyard and along the roadway to a piece of waste land behind the colonel's dug-out. Here we fastened them to two long ropes which were pegged into the ground. 'That's all they get to eat,' said my companion, and he pointed to the withered, brown grass which grew between the shell holes. 'If it doesn't fatten it'll fill,' he remarked, and with that we left the poor beasts grazing peacefully.

Back once more in the farmyard we made our way across to the far side of the ruins, where a layer of ice glistened on the surface of a waterlogged shell hole. Here lay the main source of our water supply for the cows. But one had to be careful, for the spot was overlooked from the enemy's trenches. 'Keep your head down. That bloomin' sniper ain't a bad shot.' With these words I received final instructions for my newly acquired job as the colonel's cowman.

That night, while I lay snug and warm in the farmyard dug-out, my old platoon marched up Montauban Alley on their way to the front line. My thoughts went with them. I visualized the cold, clammy, trench mud, the lonely night-watch on the fire-step and all the discomforts of trench life. After all, that parade with Headquarters' Company at 3.30 a.m. had been worth while!

One morning, as I sat milking, a tabby cat wandered in through the doorway of the old cowshed. She mewed plaintively. The poor creature was nothing but a walking bag of bones. How on earth she got any food in this deserted place it was difficult to imagine. When I endeavoured to stroke her, she drew back, spitting savagely. However, a drop of milk in an old tin worked wonders and soon she became quite tame and confiding.

Often a skylark sang sweetly when I went to tether the cows on their scanty pasture amongst the shell holes. Apparently the birds were unaffected by the firing! At times a kestrel hawk could be seen hovering over the desolate wastes that had once been fields. Then there was a thrush that called from the shattered branch of a roadside tree. Men might die, cities, towns, and villages might fall in ruin, but still the birds sang on!

At night-time I discovered that the farmyard was by no means deserted. Standing; there in the bright moonlight, the scene was a grim one, with black ruins silhouetted against a starlit sky. In the centre of the yard the midden was alive with small, moving forms. Twin pairs of glittering eyes were watching in the shadows and high-pitched squeaky calls came from every corner. Rats. They were everywhere! They gambolled over the midden, fought with each other on the cobblestones, and went scavenging in parties through the gloom of the tumbledown buildings.

As I stood watching this strange spectacle a dark shadow passed over the moonlit ruins. This was followed by a sudden and shrill, scream of pain from the far side of the yard. Descending on silent wings, a great white barn owl had snatched up a victim. A wild scurry for cover and the yard was deserted. But not for long. In a very few minutes the hordes of rats were back once more at their nightly revels.

Looking back on those far-off days in the early spring of 1916 it seems difficult to realize that we used to keep cows in the trenches. Few survivors of those who were plunged into the terrible fighting on the Somme would find it possible to believe that the colonel in charge of the Carnoy sector had fresh milk for his breakfast every morning!

But then in those days the Somme was looked upon more or less as a picnic. Apart from one or two references in the papers to the leaning virgin of Albert, or the statement that another mine had gone up at Fricourt, there was little publicity given to these parts. Trones Wood, Delville Wood, Mametz, Guillemont and a hundred other historic place names were, of course, unheard of before the big push.

My job as colonel's cowman was a pleasant occupation compared to life in the front line. Once, when we attempted to increase the cows' milk yield and the C.O. demanded that hay should be sent up the line, I got into the Transport Officer's bad books for stealing his clover! Otherwise there were few happenings of note. A shell or two now and then and that damned sniper for ever trying to knock the last remaining scrap of plaster off the farm buildings. That was about all.

For nearly two months the battalion journeyed backwards and forwards between Bray and the Carnoy sector. But at length there came rumours of a move. We were going to take over another lot of trenches on the right. This meant, of course, that our headquarters would no longer be at Carnoy. It also meant that our colonel would no longer have fresh milk for his breakfast!

We are told that all good things come to an end sooner or later. I myself could not grumble, for the cowman's job had saved me many hours of tedious fire-step duty in the front line. We were resting at Bray when news of the move came through, and with it came orders for the colonel's cowman to be returned to his old company.

I saw no more of the Carnoy cows and can't even say what happened to them. It may be that the German sniper put an end to their precarious existence, or perhaps they were killed in that tornado of shell-fire which heralded the Somme attack. On the other hand, it is quite possible that they may have lived on to greet the astonished eyes of the old farmer when he returned to his ruined village.

Private T. S. Williams served in 19th Battalion King's Liverpool Regt., 89th Brigade, 30th Division, from 1914 to 1918, on the Western Front.

ORDINARY WAR ON THE SOMME

Fred Ball

I remember the first occasion when I was called upon to go over the top. It was during the Somme 'do,' where our battalion had already been in some nasty business near the Briqueterie and Trones Wood. I heard about the Third Company's experiences in Trones Wood during my recovery from an overdose of rum, and I was new enough a soldier to feel the strain on my heart-strings when I realized that rum stupor had saved me from participation.

The date was July 27th, 1916. We were bivouacked in a valley near Fricourt, a place of vast mine craters in virgin chalk. I remember clambering about them, trying to stop my imagination from recreating the sensations of the troops who once had occupied trenches there. Lying about were bits of equipment, clothing, *bodies.* God! imagination was not needed. The thing was reconstructed before my eyes.

I was in this frame of mind when we were told to be prepared to move into the line that night.

I was a signaller. Most old soldiers will know what this implies. Bayonet drill, bombing practice, in short, all those exercises which were supposed to make an efficient soldier, had been carefully and cunningly dodged. I began to regret this. Already I could see myself outclassed by some proficient German in a hand-to-hand encounter. To be sure, the blade of his bayonet would be saw-cut. Good Lord! What a fool I had been! Or I might be lying in a trench or shell hole, encumbered with rifle, flapper, telephone, and lamp, engaged in an unequal bombing duel with only the stone-throwing skill of my boyhood to help me against a highly trained adversary. I wondered what it might feel like to be wounded – to be killed!

All through that night I never had a wink of sleep. My stomach would insist on rising to my throat to choke me each time I thought of some lurid possibility. And so the night passed and we remained where we were.

In the morning we were told that our affair had been postponed twenty-four hours. Our C.O. kept us from a sleep of exhaustion, which is so easy in the morning, by choosing that time for his heroic lecture to us, in whose hands lay his reputation. How plainly I recollect trying to pierce beneath his brave words and to discover that horrible dread of death which was showing itself in the eyes of almost every one of us.

Slowly but surely that day, the 28th, passed. Last night we *thought* we were going over the top. To-night we *know*. Our C.O. himself has told us so. Back come all the bogies of the previous night. I find myself engaged in calculating the chances of escape. Surely a quarter of our number will remain unscathed. I have one chance in four of coming out none the worse. And the other chances, what are they? Maybe they are three to one against being killed. There is some comfort in that. One chance in four of being wounded, which means a respite, and one in four of being taken prisoner-almost as good as escaping scot free.

And so I tortured myself all through that second night. At times I would nod off to sleep. 'It's all off. It's all off,' something would say, and my whirling, maddening thoughts, becoming smoother, less insistent, more incoherent, would creep almost into the arms of sleep… '*Fool. Wake up, wake up. It's postponed one hour, two hours, that's all.*' I jump with a start. The whole mental anguish began all over again.

We did not go up that night; but on the night of the 29th we actually started for the front line. Where we had been lying in bivouac the noise of the guns had been an incessant thunder. We had found time to pity the poor devils who were already in the thick of it. Now we found ourselves approaching the monster. Gradually, as we moved, we were enwrapped in that almost homogeneous sea of sound, and shells burst nearer and nearer.

Stumbling along in the inky darkness, the intensity of which was preserved by frequent explosions, I can hardly attempt to describe my thoughts and feelings. There came a time when two horses dashed madly past us towards the rear. They had been released from their load by a shell which had killed their driver and shattered their wagon. With a crash, one of them collapsed within a yard of us, showing horribly plainly that even horse-flesh cannot be disembowelled and live. We continued going forward.

Then the darkness was temporarily relieved. A dump of Verey lights had been exploded, and a firework display, enough to confuse the most carefully contrived artillery signals, shed a fantastic light upon this hell on earth. Darkness may be awful, but when duty tells you to go and be killed and, in the going, to walk past wounded men, right and left, in the eerie light of military fireworks, the horror of it becomes almost unbearable.

Just before we arrived in our jumping-off trench something happened which I can never forget. A young soldier of my own section was struck by a shell fragment square between the eyes. His cries haunt me now. 'Mother of God! Mother of God!' he shrieked time and time again. We left him behind where he lay, whimpering 'Mother of God! Good God! I'm blind!' It got in my ears. 'Mother of God!' I reiterated, scarcely knowing what I was saying. Then I realized the meaning of the words. In a flash of violent emotion I denied Her there and then. If She existed, why were we here? She didn't exist. There was no such thing. My strength was in my three to one odds. It was all chance. Oh for a Blighty one. Even the fourth chance, death, was becoming less dreadful. It would take me out of it all, whatever else might happen. So, at last, we arrived in the front line.

Zero was 7.15 a.m. In a few minutes we should endure the supreme test. Furtive peeps over the parapet revealed nothing of the enemy trenches, for a mist lay over all. What if our artillery had failed to cut 'his' wire? Were his machine-gunners waiting to mow us down as we struggled to break a way through his entanglements? The monotonous hammering of these questions must have had different effects on different men.

In me, strangely enough, they induced feelings of utter weariness followed by spasms of fatalistic carelessness, which I could have wished to last the whole war through. But our emotions come and go like clouds in the sky, and my new-found peace of mind was short-lived.

Suddenly the noise of the guns eased off. For a second or two there was quiet. Then the fury of our barrage dropped like a wall of roaring sound before us. By some means the signal to advance was given and understood and we found ourselves walking forward into the mist, feeling utterly naked. Who can express the sensations of men brought up in trench warfare suddenly divested of every scrap of shelter?

Forward we stumbled into a mist that seemed to grow ever thicker. So great was the noise that the order to keep in touch with one another was passed only by means of shouting our hardest, and our voices sounded like flutes in a vast orchestra of fiends. All at once I became conscious of another sound. A noise like the crisp crackle of twigs and branches, burning in a bonfire just beyond my vision in the mist, made me think I must be approaching some burning building. I realized, when my neighbour on the right dropped with a bullet in the abdomen, that the noise was machine-gun and rifle-fire, and I felt the tiniest bit happier when I touched my entrenching tool which, contrary to regulations, was attached to the front of my equipment instead of the side.

Presently we came to the first enemy trench. How one's thoughts race at such a time! But the surge of apprehension dropped, the steeled muscles relaxed and our hearts ceased their frantic overtime – at least, mine did – when we saw that our artillery had done its work well and truly. We had to pass this trench, but there was no need to jump over it for it was almost filled in-blown in. Maybe the ground over which we walked already buried the enemy we had hoped to slay.

After scrambling over what remained of this trench, I found myself with another signaller, cut off completely from the rest by the mist. We had come close together in our scrambling and remained together. We were alone in a mist which we began to suspect was not altogether made by Nature. Here was a fine mess. Fryer (that was my companion's name) and myself cut off from our comrades, not knowing whither we were going nor how far we should go. What should we do? We did what irresponsible private soldiers could do – dropped into the nearest shell hole. Discussing our position over a Woodbine, shared by the simple and wasteful expedient of breaking it in two, we went to sleep!

An hour later I was nudged into wakefulness by Fryer. It was considerably quieter, but bullets were still zipping past. The mist had cleared a little and visibility was extended to about 400 or 500 yards. Together we raised our heads, cautiously, above the shell hole, and saw not a soul. Suddenly, from Fryer, 'Down! Keep down!' and he suited the action to the word, pulling me with him.

'What the hell are you playing at?' I asked. 'Keep down a bit,' he said; then, a moment or two later, 'Look *behind.*' Carefully I raised my head again and looked. Behind us, in a part of the trench we had crossed that had escaped the general smashing in of high explosives, was a German. A brave man, braver than either Fryer or I, was standing in that bit of trench. With a rifle to his shoulder he was firing steadily in the direction of our old front line, and by his side, keeping under what little cover there was, was another, busily loading a second rifle. I raised my own to shoot the first active German enemy I had seen, but Fryer pulled me back. 'Don't be a bloody fool,' he said. 'Don't you see we're surrounded?' I won't worry you with the argument I had with Fryer – nor with myself – about what was our duty. Enough that discretion won and, astonishing though it may seem, we lay down and went to sleep again.

We awoke a second time and fell to discussing plans to get back to our lines. If the worst came to the worst we considered how we might manage to be safely taken prisoners. Once more we carefully peeped over the lip of our shell hole, but the heroes of an hour ago were no longer there. Our inaction was getting on my nerves. I decided to look about me to see what had been happening, but Fryer wouldn't come. He, poor devil, had started to crack up.

Gingerly I climbed out of our friendly shelter. The attack was at that stage when one might walk about almost with impunity.

There were too many targets, I suppose, for one more to attract much attention. Besides, everyone was busy, either finding out where he was or digging himself in. Signal flares were going up half a mile away on our right front and I already began to imagine myself being court-martialled for shirking. What a contrast to my feelings of a short time before when we were 'surrounded.'

It was with real thankfulness that I found the captain of our company. He was sheltering in a shell hole just as Fryer and I had done. I grew positively superior when he insisted on telling me how his servant had saved his life. In tones as shaken as Fryer's, he described how a tin plate which his servant had put in his haversack had deflected a bullet which otherwise would most certainly have killed him. I fancied I knew where one Military Medal would go. Then he remembered his men. 'Go back,' he said to me, 'and tell the C.O. that we are absolutely lost; too much damned mist and smoke; and ask for orders. Is there anyone with you? Fryer? Take him with you.'

We went back, Fryer and I, reported to the adjutant of one of the battalions of our brigade who was acting brigadier, all his superiors having been killed or wounded, and received instructions to remain in the trench. Messages had already gone out, we were told, ordering a general withdrawal to our starting-point. The attack had failed. Pray God we should not have it to do all over again.

I am sorry I cannot finish this short account of a 'push' with some stirring deed of valour. Fritz soon became aware of our intention to abandon the attack and it was not long before his artillery was blowing our trench to pieces.

Fryer was killed at my side. I cannot describe the 'incident.' I saw about as much red as was left in the poor chap's face when he settled in a crouching posture – dead. From that time until we were relieved I waited every second for a similar end. I was buried, and got out. I trembled violently for ten solid minutes with shell-shock, but recovered and had to hang on. When the relief did come it was due more to sheer fatigue than self-control that we refrained from running out of the trenches.

Our whole brigade had suffered very heavy losses. We were taken behind the lines for a rest, addressed by our G.O.C., told how, through lack of information, we had valiantly attacked a force three times our number and, after being brought up to strength, we were sent in to do it again.

Private Fred Ball enlisted in the Liverpool 'Pals' in January 1915; crossed to France on November 7th, 1915; served in France continuously during the remainder of the War. Was wounded once – very slightly – near Arras in August or September 1918. After the Armistice went into Germany with the Army of Occupation, leaving there to be demobilized at the end of March 1919. He neither sought nor received promotion.

DELVILLE WOOD

Capt. S. J. Worsley, D.S.O., M.C.

Delville Wood is a name, even now, full of sadness and the suppressed agony of thousands who had to make its acquaintance. Probably nearly as many men remained in it as came out of it whole, and no one fortunate to escape from this hell can think of it without recalling hours of suffering and the names of many good comrades now no more.

Towards the end of September 1916 there seemed to be a lull in the Battle of the Somme. The glory of the first great achievements had somewhat faded with the realization of their cost and the doubtful value of their gains. One supposed that the High Command knew what they were doing, though even that is doubtful now. Most of us hoped that the lull meant a discontinuance of the battle, which seemed a hopeless hammering at a resourceful enemy in one of his strongest sectors. It was, however, not for us to argue why the strong rather than the weak positions were always to be attacked.

Anyhow our battalion, which had previously been in the line in front of Guillemont, moved into Delville Wood to take over the line on the eastern edge of the wood. The journey, as usual, began soon enough to bring us into the danger zone about dusk and was a nightmare. We were led by guides who had hardly been able to leave the front line and were hopeless, while landmarks had long ago been blown out of existence. Every semblance of a trench seemed full of dead-sodden, squelchy, swollen bodies. Fortunately the blackening faces were invisible except when Verey lights lit up the indescribable scene. Not a tree stood whole in that wood.

The weary tramp in single file went on for about three hours. Men carried heavy loads of equipment, bombs, rifle ammunition, Lewis guns, petrol tins of water, gas helmets, and so on. How they cursed as they one after the other collided with some obstacle or fell flat on a dead body. 'Pass it along when you're all up,' 'Mind the wire,' 'Mind the hole on the left' –

interspersed with humorous though trite remarks as to the first five years being the worst.

Eventually, after much searching, but without serious mishap, we found our sector. Two companies of the battalion were in front and two in support some distance back. Battalion Headquarters lay behind the wood. 'C' Company, in which I had charge of a platoon, was on the right flank in a shallow, incomplete depression shown on the map as Edge Trench, its name indicating its position skirting the wood.

By this time it was just after midnight and all was fairly quiet. As far as we knew there was no particular cause for alarm. The officers and senior N.C.O.s had got the hang of things and knew roughly the position of the other troops in the neighbourhood and of the enemy, who seemed quite a good distance away immediately in front, though away to the right he was considerably closer to the line.

I was at the time twenty-one years of age, my company commander twenty-two, but we had both had a good deal of experience – sufficient to realize that in case of anything like a bombardment a position on the edge of a very well known wood would be no fun. Hence we decided to push forward. Each platoon would send a strong section some fifty to one hundred yards ahead to dig itself in. If we were left in peace a night or two, our men, nearly all miners, would join up the posts and make a continuous and less clearly defined front line. So the detached posts went out.

The wished-for peace was not for us, unfortunately. At 2 a.m., the officers met the company commander in the one and only dug-out to discuss 'work done and work proposed' for the daily return, and to look at some preliminary orders for a rather big advance three days ahead. After that I was temporarily off duty, but I had no sooner settled myself in the dug-out for what I considered a well-earned 'shut-eye' till stand-to before dawn, when pandemonium broke out. It was soon apparent that something very unpleasant was about to happen, so we stood to arms, groused a good deal, and waited. The waiting was always the hardest part of it all. The hours till 6 a.m. seemed terribly long, but our casualties had not been more than fifteen all told. The worst of it was that the wounded and even the runners, stout fellows though they were, could not get away or reach Headquarters with our tale of woe.

Just about six o'clock the Germans came on. They never approached closer than 150 yards from our trench and they made an excellent target for Lewis guns and lost heavily. By 8.30 a.m. I heard that the company commander was out of action, though not seriously wounded. Then came the even more serious news that my fellow subaltern had been killed on the right, where the enemy had forced an entrance. The battalion on the right had also been forced to abandon their line. This left me very much alone, with between but fifty and sixty men who could use a rifle. Some of these were wounded, but any escape from the trench was out of the question.

By 9 a.m. there was comparative peace, except in our minds when we grasped the seriousness of the situation. It seemed that the left had also broken and that our two depleted companies were in the blue. The left company had fared better than we. On our right the Germans and we shared a trench – only a narrow barrier separating us from them. Moreover, this barrier was on the wrong side of Company Headquarters, which, with our greatcoats, food, and orders, was lost to us. The only thing to do was to strengthen the barrier as best we could and lie low. There would probably be dirty work at that barrier later on.

Conditions in the wood were now worse than ever. Most of us felt sick and ill even when unwounded. Food and water were very short and we had not the faintest idea when any more would be obtainable. By the end of the next day several, including myself, had dysentery, and that in a ghastly battered trench with no prospect of medical attention. After all, we stood and lay on putrefying bodies and the wonder was that the disease did not finish off what the shells of the enemy had started.

The day was, in fact, uneventful; but as evening drew on we again prepared for the fray. It was not to be supposed that the success of the enemy would not be pushed home, and, as far as we could tell, only two weak companies stood between them and the possession of Delville Wood. Sure enough, the attack began at dusk and again it lasted for three hours. This time it was no frontal attack across the open but a determined push down the shared trench and behind in the shelter of the stumps of trees. It is difficult, and even a week later it was difficult, to recall those three hours. It is only on Armistice Day that I can live them again; but I don't want to tell anyone about it. There was hand-to-hand fighting with knives, bombs, and bayonets; cursing and brutality on both, sides such as men, can be responsible for when it is a question of 'your life or mine'; mud and filthy stench; dysentery and unattended wounds; shortage of food and water and ammunition.

The fighting ceased and a curiously fitful peace settled over the scene. In some ways fighting was preferable – one's mind was distracted. Inactivity in such surroundings was harder than risking one's life. For an hour or two that night I lay on a board in a bay of the trench and slept. But an hour before dawn we were at it again, getting ready for the expected onslaught at daybreak. Why this did not come I have never been able to make out. There was no reason at all why the wood should not have been recaptured completely, especially as, on looking through our supplies, we could not muster more than 500 rounds of rifle-ammunition and thirty bombs.

By this time I was getting beyond effective command, but my senior sergeant was still very much alive and as aggressive as ever. His suggestion was that we should take a big risk as no attack appeared to be developing and have a shot at regaining Company Headquarters. I am afraid that the object of the projected operation was food rather than secret orders. Four others volunteered to see what could be done, and before dawn was far advanced we peeped carefully over the barrier half-expecting something unpleasant. One German was asleep on a fire-step five or six yards from us, and there was not a sign of activity. In these circumstances we agreed to risk it. I, being armed with a revolver, was to act as a sort of advanced guard while the others were to trail behind with bombs and bayonets to deal with any opposition. The essential factor for success was quietness – no bomb throwing or shooting except as a last resource. Nothing but a bayonet was in fact necessary, much to our amazement. Some half-dozen weary and comatose Germans were quietly and expeditiously removed from the active list, and Company Headquarters was gained in safety.

Yet there were no reprisals. Apparently no German officer or N.C.O. came round, and to our joy we were able unmolested to move the best part of our barrier to a point 50 yards beyond the Headquarters dug-out. We found all the officers' kit, food, and orders intact, but neatly packed up as though for removal. The mystery of this non-interference is unexplained and I can only surmise that a few tired troops had got left behind, although the main forces of the enemy had for some reason or other been withdrawn. All that day not a shot was fired, though our nerves had gone almost to pieces and we were sure we should be amply repaid for our early morning escapade.

But no word came from the outside world, which seemed very remote, until about four o'clock in the afternoon. At that hour a British aeroplane appeared flying low and calling for signals. With great joy we sent up our flares to indicate our position. I have always wanted to thank that airman. He must have taped us out with great accuracy, because when an hour later our own guns opened fire and put a box barrage round us, not a single shell fell in our lines.

This bombardment meant that an attack was being launched in order to get us out and at dusk the attack came. A whole brigade of infantry, well supported by artillery, had been put in to restore the line, and they did it splendidly despite the heavy shelling of the enemy, especially on the back areas through which they had advanced. Gradually we were able to slip away. I had now pronounced dysentery and was helped by two men. We were all so far gone and so tired that we never hesitated to rest when and where we felt inclined, shelling or no shelling. I called at Battalion Headquarters and reported as best I could what had happened. The 'powers-that-be' were most complimentary on the work of the company and the adjutant's 'Well done, 'C' Company!' made up for a good deal.

After a wretched night in a dug-out in Montauban I went down sick, glad to be out of things for a bit, but rather conscience-stricken at such an inglorious departure; a wound would have been much more satisfying.

Some weeks later I received a chatty letter from the adjutant, who told me a touching story. He asked if I remembered the posts we had sent out in front the night we occupied Edge Trench. It came as rather a shock to find that I had, indeed, in all that confusion and scrapping forgotten them. He went on to say that two days after we had been relieved the new people had discovered a section of my platoon still doing the job they had been sent out to do. The corporal and his men had been out there for four days with no food other than emergency rations, but they had remained interested spectators of a good deal of the fighting, though in their exposed position they dared not move much. The relieving company commander told them about the relief, and said they had better clear out. To this the corporal replied that he had no intention of moving without a personal or written order from one of his own officers. This order the adjutant had supplied.

Captain S. J. Worsley. Gazetted, aged nineteen, North Staffordshire Regt., August 1914. Served with 1st Battalion North Staffordshire Regt., 1915, and most of 1916, in France. Awarded Military Cross, 1916,. Bar to Cross, 1916, for incident contained in narrative. Served 4th Battalion North Staffordshire Regt., 1917, and up to end of September 1918, in France. Awarded second Bar to M.C. after great retreat, March 1918. Awarded D.S.O., and mentioned in despatches in respect of advance round Hill 60 and the Bluff, September 1918, when was wounded by bullet through both lungs.

IN A BILLET

Harry Drake

There are many Tommies who will tell you that the average French peasant would not move a hand's turn to ease the lot of the British soldier, but this is what happened to me.

I had a workable knowledge of French, and so it became my job to go on ahead of the battalion and help to find billets. We were coming out of the line to a small village called Famechon in the winter of 1916–17. The billeting party of one officer and five more cc other ranks arrived at the village, and set out in parties to find the possibilities of the place. I knocked at the door of one cottage that stood in the corner of a small field, and an old woman came to the door.

It would be very hard to describe her, for she was bent, wrinkled, and her tousled hair and toothless gums gave her the appearance of a witch. She was more like one of Macbeth's witches than any that I have ever seen on the stage. Her appearance almost repelled me, and more out of custom than from any other motive I asked if she had any accommodation.

She looked at me very keenly for a moment and then said, 'I have a spare bed.'

'For an officer?'

'An officer, ah no! My son used to sleep on straw. You can have his bed, but no officer shall ever sleep in it.'

I thought she must have some bee in her bonnet on the matter of officers, so I bade her adieu and went on with the rest of my job. I found that we had beds enough without troubling the old woman, so I wangled that particular bed for myself. Any bed before a barn was a working motto in those bitter days.

The first evening I was there she asked me all the particulars she could think of. She wanted to know my name, age, next of kin, and so on, until I thought her the limit in being inquisitive. Then she took me into the family, for she addressed me as 'mon garcon' and used the familiar 'tu' in place of 'vous.' To carry on the comedy, I often called her, 'ma mère,' and she seemed to like that mode of address.

She had one peculiar habit. She often opened a black snuff-box and took a very liberal pinch. When I teased her about it, she merely shrugged her shoulders and said it was 'Bon pour la tête.'

The second night, as I sat near the stove, I shivered ever so slightly. Her quick black eyes saw it.

'Thou art chilled, my son,' she said.

'It's nothing,' I remarked.

'Nothing? I can see by thy eyes that thou art ill. Get thee to bed.'

'Not yet,' I mumbled.

'Not yet? Do as I bid thee,' and she turned on me like a fury. She knew I was ill. She thought so at first, and she was sure now. I was a fool to sit up near the stove. My place was in bed, and so on. More to humour her, I went to bed.

It did not seem more than two minutes after I was in bed before she came into the bedroom with a great bowl full of boiled milk.

'It is for thee,' she said, by way of explanation. 'Drink it.'

Protests were useless, and I had to drink it whilst she stood over me, looking like a veritable witch. I slept that night bathed in perspiration, and woke to find that she had sent word to the M.O., and he was standing over me, feeling my pulse. I was ill and had to stay in bed. Pills were sent round per the orderly.

'Didn't I tell thee?' said the old crone. 'Now stay where thou art and do as I tell thee.'

Bowl after bowl of boiled milk she brought to me, until I seemed to be drinking all the yield of her solitary cow. I loathed the sight of her milk. She busied herself on my behalf, and I could hear the patter of her wooden sabots on the tiled floor as she went about some household tasks.

Often I would see her looking at me with a very strange look on her old wrinkled face, and on the last day of our 'rest' I was allowed to get up. It was then that the M.O. told me how ill I had been. I had just missed pneumonia. If I had not had a bed I should have been sent to the Field Ambulance, and I remembered a pneumonia case that died two cots from mine in the Field Ambulance.

'Ma mère,' I said to the old woman, 'I have been very grateful for all that you have done for me. How much shall I give you to repay you for your work and worry?'

She took my great rough hand in both of hers, and with a look of inestimable charm that her wrinkles could not efface, she looked up into my face and smiled.

'My boy,' she said, 'thou art such another as the son I had, but whom the good God thought fit to take from me. Thou art of his form and almost of his face. Thou art of his age, too. Sometimes I have prayed that the Blessed Virgin might send him back to me, but that thou knowest is impossible. She sent thee to me when thou hadst most need of a mother, and for these last few days I have been with a son of my own again.

'Talk not to me of repayment.

'I will tell thee what thou mayst do for me. Buy no more than *quatre sous*' worth of snuff, for a pinch is good for the head.'

I listened with tears in my eyes as she told me this, and I do not think I shamed my manhood by them. I felt ashamed to think that I, as big as a bull compared with her, should not have a heart as big as a pea, whilst in her poor, shrunken form was a heart as big as a drum.

C.Q.M.S. Harry Drake enlisted September 9th, 1914, in the 16th West Yorks Regt. (Bradford 'Pals' Battalion). Served with the battalion as corporal, sergeant, C.Q.M.S., and A/R.Q.M.S. in Egypt and France. Upon the reorganization of brigades in 1918, he was posted as A/R.Q.M.S. to the 3rd Entrenching Battalion. In March of 1918 he was reposted as C.Q.M.S. in the 15th West Yorkshire Regt.; he was demobilized in February 1919.

George F. Wear

I landed in France with a medical unit attached to the 7th Division in November 1914.

I was a boy just turned seventeen, straight from school, and all the thrill of romance and adventure was on me. The story-books were coming true, and by an extraordinary piece of luck I was privileged to be a participator. How enviously my school friends had written to me when they heard that we were definitely under orders to proceed, after a bare three months' training, on active service.

There was a wonderful march through the streets of Southampton at midnight, amid crowds of cheering and delirious people. A woman had thrown her arms round me and kissed me, thrusting cigarettes into my pocket. We were inundated with gifts. No knight of old went to war with a more exalted heart or a purer enthusiasm. I was only seventeen, and many who might have known better were just the same.

At Poperinghe and other places we were soon hard at work with the wounded from Ypres. As I had already done duty on an ambulance train in England, this was nothing new to me, except that now the casualties poured into the clearing hospital day and night; there was no rest; the smell of blood, gangrened wounds, iodine, and chloroform filled the twenty-four hours. Sights that made older men sick with horror served only to harden my determination, and, though often terrified and worn out by the unaccustomed heavy labour, I grew more and more anxious to play my part.

As the fighting died down, and our work grew less, a group of us, similar in age and station, gradually became dissatisfied with what we thought our inglorious share in the War. We felt we were not soldiering. The glamour was wearing off.

Winter came and went, and in the big building, an old convent, where the hospital was, we spent our spare time devising schemes for getting into a combatant branch of the Army. Strange as it may seem, we were not dismayed by what we had seen of the pain and suffering, the groans and agonies of the sick, wounded, and dying. We were used to all this, but we were not callous.

It was, indeed, a dull monotonous time, scrubbing floors, washing windows, cleaning latrines, doing a hundred odd jobs with compensations of a sort in the cafés of the town near by. I learned to drink, I could already swear as fluently as any other Tommy, and occasionally grew bold enough to kiss a Flemish girl at the cottage where we took our washing. The sudden rush of work and the excitement that accompanied the Battle of Neuve-Chapelle and the disastrous attack on Aubers Ridge did not change our minds. Several of us applied for commissions, and we counted the days till they came through, and, one by one, the lucky ones of us returned to England in the early summer of 1915.

I joined a Territorial reserve brigade of R.F.A. just being formed, and before my eighteenth birthday appeared at home resplendent in a second lieutenant's uniform. There were several of us in the brigade mess, and, having little to do, we spent the time ragging about like the schoolboys we were, boasting of our female acquaintances picked up easily enough in the large town where we were quartered, teaching one another how to drink and still retain a semblance of sobriety, doing anything, in fact, which youthful exuberance could suggest, sometimes going even further than that.

A few horses arrived and we learned to ride. We did gun-drill on wooden guns, and took imaginary batteries into action on hillsides outside the town. We went on courses of gunnery, signalling, and other things, and in a few months were pronounced trained and fit to go abroad. The little we knew, and mostly theory at that, was just enough to give us boundless confidence in our ability. Certificates of proficiency were as easy to obtain as autumn apples.

It was a mad merry time while it lasted, but the second winter of the War came on, and the time came near for going out again. The majority of us, I think, were anxious to go, though our reasons were no doubt selfish and vainglorious.

The time came soon enough, and after a cold February journey of several days, three of us joined our first-line brigade in France. The division was at rest, which meant that we spent our time exercising horses, slipping and squelching in muddy fields all day, playing bridge in the evening, while it rained and rained. Orders came in a week or so that we were going into action, but we newly joined subalterns found it politic to keep our jubilation to ourselves.

The battery left the village one morning at two o'clock. It was still dark, of course, and raining. Riding in the wet at a walk all day long is by no means pleasant, but even now I can remember the feeling of exultation that filled me. At last I was going to see some real war.

Three days later we were in action near Albert. I soon found my hastily learned theories of very little use. For one thing, our training had been for open warfare; for another, there was a great scarcity of ammunition. We were allowed twenty-one rounds a week; our reply to an infantry S.O.S. signal was to fire three rounds! I was up at the battery for some days before I heard an enemy shell. It was all so quiet I couldn't believe that this was being under fire. I don't think any shells came near our battery all the time we were in, which was not very long, as it happened, for we were withdrawn to undergo intensive training for the big offensive.

I still felt as though the War was eluding me, especially during some weeks I spent in hospital as the result of a slight wound received, not in action, but in playing football against a rival battery. When the training became really intensive, even the hardest bitten veterans began to grumble and express desires to get back into the line for a quiet life.

Rumours regarding the 'push' were thick for a long time. Before we left our rest billets we knew the front our division was to attack, what our objectives were and the rest of it. In those days there was little secrecy, and the constant postponements must have given plenty of scope to German spies. Numbers of human lives were to pay for this later, but at the time the feelings of optimism everywhere rivalled those of 1914.

One June night in 1916 we occupied our allotted gun-pits opposite Thiepval, and began firing in real earnest. No more limits, no more peace and quiet. Batteries were scattered all over the white scarred slopes beyond the Ancre, firing day and night. We were engaged chiefly on wire-cutting. We had a new O.C., an unpleasant touchy man who knew very little about his job. To be in the observation post with him was an experience that few of the younger officers or any of the men could endure for long. He cursed continually, swore that he hadn't an efficient man in the battery, declared that the observers were blind, the gunners unable to shoot, and so on. As a matter of fact, the gunners, though inexperienced, were a splendid lot, full of enthusiasm.

The pounding that the Boche trenches received in that last week of June was unprecedented. Everyone confidently expected that no one could live under it. Orders were sent to the wagon lines to have the gun teams ready for the advance. The infantry were to go straight through when zero hour came, and our advance position was clearly marked on the map. As the bombardment grew, so did the retaliation. We had several casualties; the one which most affected me was the death of our senior lieutenant. He was literally blown to pieces by a shell on the battery position, bits of flesh besmearing one of the gun-pits and covering the gun in blood. The remains were collected in a sandbag and buried.

July 1st came, but Thiepval was not captured. Division after division went in and came out, but a few lines of trenches were all that many thousands of casualties had been able to buy. The expected orders to lift the barrage never came to the battery, and it was soon obvious that the attack was a failure. Rumours of success in other places filled the air, but as the days went by it became clear that a frontal assault on such a place was doomed to defeat. We took turns up at the O.P., on the battery, and down at the wagon lines. German shelling increased on the roads and the battery position, until it became a dangerous journey that the ammunition teams had to make daily.

It was a long time before I felt any fear. At first I had, like many others, been afraid of being afraid, but I soon learned there was no danger of that. The excitement and thrill of battle were on me. I was too young to think of anything else.

As the weeks passed and we did not advance, the unpleasant relations between the O.C. and some two or three of us increased. Many times I prayed heartily for a wound as the only means of escaping from him. This second reason for welcoming danger soon outweighed the first. There is pettiness in war, as in all other human activities.

Some time later I was fortunate enough to get myself transferred to a trench mortar battery, then popularly known as 'The Suicide Club.' Here I found myself in as jolly a crowd as I ever met in the War, and amongst whom I spent my happiest times. For they were happy times, in spite of the greater discomfort and undoubtedly greater danger than I had experienced in a field battery.

The small guns fired a 60-lb. bomb for a maximum distance of 500 yards, and consequently were usually in or near the front-line trench. The bombs did great damage to wire and trenches and naturally enemy retaliation was prompt and heavy whenever we fired.

The first time I was in action with them, we were at a quiet spot on the Front, and lived in a broken-down house a mile from the front line. One evening, just after supper, a 4-2 shell came through the wall into the room, bursting at once. We were thrown on the ground, the candles extinguished, and bits of plaster and falling brick showered on us. The door and window of the room, frames and all, were blown out, but, marvellously, no one was hurt. It was from this time that I began to experience what fear was. This sudden shock (I trembled for an hour afterwards) gave me a completely new outlook on life, life and War being, of course, synonymous terms. I crouched at the sound of a shell, found myself on a dark, quiet night in the trenches shivering with terror at what might happen. A distant machine-gun rattle would make me jump, and I often found it impossible to suppress such starts when not alone. I began to wonder if I was becoming a coward.

Soon after this, we were wire-cutting opposite Beaumont-Hamel. The trench conditions here in late October were appalling. Long communication trenches, full of thick sticky mud often waist deep and constantly shelled, led up to a similar front line. Good dug-outs were few, and the heavy rain made things about as bad as they could be. During the day we fired at the German wire and in the evenings returned to our billets in the smashed-up village of Mailly-Maillet. A 9-2 howitzer was in our back garden, and the whole dilapidated house shook to its foundations every time it fired. In spite of this, and the shelling of the village, we led a seemingly care-free life, spending most of the night playing poker and *vingt-et-un,* drinking enormous quantities of whisky, cursing the War, and wondering if we should ever go on leave.

Beaumont-Hamel was taken on November 13th, and, as we had nothing to do, we volunteered to take stretcher-bearing parties over to the captured trenches. We crossed the old No Man's Land in daylight, and, in spite of our being unarmed and carrying stretchers, were heavily fired on, and lost several men. It grew wetter and more misty, and just as we reached the newly won trenches, a German counter-attack started. We cumbered the trench rather uselessly until some of us were able to get hold of rifles from the killed and join in repelling the attack. There was little to be seen in the inferno of bursting shells ahead, though a few shadows in the mist were undoubtedly the advancing Boches. They never came any nearer, and gradually it became apparent that they had been kept off. Even so it was dusk before we could get away with our burdens, the number of whom had been vastly increased during the day. During the attack shells had come into the trench every minute, and it was completely blocked with dead and wounded. We removed as many as possible during the night, having more casualties ourselves on the way back from a raking machine-gun fire.

It was not till four days before Christmas that we came out of the line definitely for a real rest, the first since early June. Six months of action! The crowning moment came when my turn for leave arrived at last. It was on the first day of the New Year, 1917. There are some things about the War one can never tell, and this is one. It is enough to say that it was a very different young officer who came home from the one who had gone out eleven months before. Mentally, physically, morally, I was changed, and I felt it myself very strongly.

Further periods of action followed in various places, but my diary entries for this time record little beyond the cold, frosty weather, an occasional casualty, a note of a trip to Amiens. For the rest, there was nothing but the deadly monotony of trench warfare. None of us could understand why – just as the year before – the spring and early summer came and went without any resumption of the offensive. Not that we worried. We were one and all only too pleased to be in a quiet place, with nothing beyond a raid or two now and then to disturb us.

In July, however, there was a recrudescence of activity. We took over from the Belgians at Nieuport, but the projected attack was prevented by the German capture of our jumping-off ground beyond the Yser Canal. It was here that we first met the new 'mustard' gas. Our division suffered heavily; men dropped in the streets, on the roads, in billets, often many hours afterwards. New respirators had to be served out.

Meanwhile the Third Battle of Ypres was continuing. We came into the Salient in the autumn, and, there being no scope for trench mortars, we were scattered among field batteries, on ammunition dumps, and other jobs mostly as inglorious as they were necessary. Not that I personally had any longer any illusions about glory. In common with most others, I considered going up the line little more than a horrible necessity, the odd periods of rest in uncomfortable cold tents or huts surrounded by seas of mud a heavenly respite almost too good to be true.

I doubt if anyone who has not experienced it can really have any idea of what the Salient was like during those 'victories' of 1917. The bombardments of the Somme the year before were nothing to those round Ypres. Batteries jostled each other in the shell-marked waste of mud, barking and crashing night and day. There were no trees, no houses, no countryside, no shelter, no sun. Wet, grey skies hung over the blasted land, and in the mind a gloomy depression grew and spread. Trenches had disappeared. 'Pill-boxes' and shell holes took their place. We never went up the line with a working party with any real expectation of returning, and there was no longer any sustaining feeling that all this slaughter was leading us to anything. No one could see any purpose in it.

I remember watching a company of infantry marching up the greasy duckboard track one evening. A young subaltern with them recognized me. We had been in the same sector once south of Arras.

'Our turn now,' he said, without a smile. 'Bye-bye.'

They marched on, bowed, hopeless.

I had all sorts of escapes; in fact they were so frequent that I got into a strange frame of mind, and became careless. It seemed as if I couldn't bother to try and avoid unnecessary danger. The only matters of importance were whether the rations would come up promptly and if the bottle of whisky I had ordered would be there. It was for me the worst part of the War. Even now it looms like a gigantic nightmare in the back of my mind.

Rest came again, and my third leave. I did not enjoy it. I was bitterly unwilling to go back. How I envied those who had never gone out or had never joined the Army!

In February 1918 we were in the Salient again, this time with new 6-inch mortars. Attacks and raids were fairly frequent, but our work was mechanical and had no interest for any of us. We hated our turns in the trenches, and thought only of when we should come out. Most of my friends had left, some for the Flying Corps, the majority for ever. Gas, death, and wounds had accounted for them. New officers and men came out, the proceeds of conscription, but, whatever their quality, they were not like the old lot. How could they be? I began to feel like one who had outlived his time, and grew more and more depressed, I certainly had no hope of surviving much longer. The odds were heavily against it.

After the big attack on the Somme in March, we evacuated the Salient. It presented a strange empty and quiet appearance as we marched out. I think many of us could have sat down on the duckboards and wept that April day. All the fruits of the appalling struggle of the year before were given up in a night. We were sent to field batteries again, and there was some excitement in the new open fighting. We would trot calmly into action in full view of the Boches as steadily as on parade. But we were never left long in peace, and had to endure a great deal of heavy shelling and gas bombardment.

At last, one early morning, at the beginning of the last German attack south of Ypres (as I learned later), in the middle of an S.O.S. a perfect deluge of 4-2s rained on the unsheltered battery. I was one of the first to be hit, and, despite the pain of the wound and the terror that I should bleed to death before I was attended to, I kept on repeating to myself, 'It's over now. It's over now.'

And so it was, for me at any rate. When I came out of hospital many months later the Armistice had been signed. I was just twenty-one years of age, but I was an old man – cynical, irreligious, bitter, disillusioned. I have been trying to grow young ever since.

George F. Wear enlisted in the R.A.M.C. on August 9th, 1914; went to France with the 7th, Clearing Hospital at the end of October, and returned to take up a commission in the R.F.A. in July 1915. In February 1916 he returned to France, joining the 49th Division. He served with them till April 1918, when he was wounded near Kemmel, and he was afterwards in hospital in London and Newcastle till August 1919. The chief engagements he took part in were the Somme, 1916; Ypres, 1917; and Ypres 1918.

A WIRELESS OPERATOR

B. Neyland

At the age of eighteen I crossed to France early in 1917, a sapper in the Royal Engineers Wireless Section. We operators had only a vague idea of our likely duties, for the Wireless Section was only then becoming of use in the trenches.

I was sent via St. Pol to Arras, and with a fellow-operator was led into the trenches at Roclincourt. There I first experienced the bursting of a shell near me, and I laughed at the frightened manner in which our guide flung himself down when the shell fell about thirty yards away. It was not long before I took to flinging myself down on such occasions. When our guide led me into a trench filled waist deep with muddy water, I could not believe he was serious – and I hesitated – I was wearing brand-new riding-breeches, puttees, and boots. However, I waded in, and it was seventeen days before my boots touched dry soil again.

We were left in a muddy dug-out at Roclincourt with an officer and his batman, waiting for the attack. We spent our time experimenting with a small British Field set – the Trench set – and we still had no idea of our purpose.

Then, on April 5th, we were called into Arras where a R.E. officer 'put us wise.' The attack was to be made within the next few days, the infantry waves were to advance under cover of a formidable barrage, and each wave was to be provided with a wireless station. The Roclincourt station was to go over with the first infantry wave. The Roclincourt station! That was Hewitt and I and an officer! Four infantrymen were to assist us in carrying our weighty apparatus, the set, accumulators, dry cells, coils of wire, earth mats, ropes, and other details.

We returned to Roclincourt and sent many practice messages to our Directing Station at Arras. That night one of our aerial masts was shattered and we were instructed to erect another. We had no reserve mast, but, fortunately, we found a large crucifix nearby.

'That's it,' said the officer. 'Hewitt, climb up there and attach the aerial as high as possible.'

Hewitt clambered up over the figure of Christ just as a German machine gun swept the line, the Verey lights revealing Hewitt distinctly. He soon fell into a depth of slime, frightened, but unhurt. It was our first experience of enemy machine-gun fire.

'You try,' the officer pointed to me.

It is an eerie sensation to climb over an effigy of Jesus, to dig your feet into any parts of the figure offering foothold, to hold on to the outstretched arms, and breathe on to the downcast face, to fix a rope somewhere on the Cross and to hear the German machine gun tat-tatting all around. Failing to secure the rope, I slid down and we returned to the dug-out with our officer extremely annoyed. Early the next morning we secured the aerial to the ruins of a building.

On April 7th our officer laid a plan of the German sector opposite us on the table, and he detailed our instructions. At a particular tree-stump far over in the enemy's Blue Line we were to erect a station as rapidly as possible and transmit any messages handed in by the officers engaged in the attack.

I felt intensely relieved that I was to be given an opportunity of doing something useful, and of feeling that at last I was to play a real part in the Great War. I found that Hewitt, too, experienced this sense of relief.

On the evening of the 7th some letters came up. There was one from my father telling me he had bought a new bicycle, a Raleigh, for 'when I came home.' It affected me strangely, and when I mentioned the new cycle in the dug-out, our officer grunted 'some hopes!' When I considered our immediate future I must have echoed the sentiment.

Our officer's nerves were rather frayed that evening. Perhaps in the infantry he had led many attacks, perhaps he had been badly knocked about before he came to us. We didn't know; nobody seemed to know much about him.

Through the night we waited for the signal. One o'clock, two, three, four (or was it five?)...the barrage started! A roar all along the line. Then suddenly, with a similar 'snap' to that with which it started, the barrage stopped. Sunday, April 8th, dawned and passed without the attack having been made. Had a change of plans taken place?

Sunday night – further infantry poured into the trenches, slowly, nervously, pressing along. All was tense…no laughter, no jesting, no conversation. There was no doubt that the attack would take place on the morrow.

All night the muddied figures stood outside our dug-out; inside we sat, each with his load close at hand. Apart from wireless material we carried ground sheets, rifles (unloaded!), bandoliers, each holding fifty rounds, gas masks, iron rations, and our clothes.

At 3.30 a.m., we went out into the trenches, eight in all: the officer, his batman, two operators, and four infantry carriers. We threaded our way along the crowded trenches as best we could until we reached a company of Tyneside Scottish. There we waited.

The silence remained tense, more awful than ever. Everyone 'standing to' awaiting the barrage and the signal!

4 a.m. The barrage opened with a mighty roar and there it fell incessantly just across the waste. 'Go!'

Over the top we clambered, over the stricken wilderness we stumbled. We wireless 'merchants' mixed with the infantry, hoping for some protection. We carried no bayonets, our unloaded rifles were strapped across our backs and our only means of defence was apparently fists. Why wireless operators were not allowed to load their rifles we never learned.

We attained the enemy lines. Jerry was engaged in peaceful domestic functions! Some washing, others making coffee, and many had to be awakened to be taken captive. The blow had fallen before they expected it.

It was not long, however, before the German defences, the colossal barrage tearing into their supports, were roused to a fierce retaliation. Heroic and desperate Germans mounted machine guns, and knowing they could not withstand our onslaught they exacted a heavy toll for their own lives. One enemy sergeant I saw shot twenty of ours before he was bayoneted in his back. Then a rain of spluttering ferocious shrapnel fire came over from the German artillery and 'heavy stuff' crashed into us. The waves of our infantry became somewhat disorganized owing to the difficulty of moving over the heavy, pitted land and to the congestion of the German prisoners, who were dazed by their good fortune in being taken.

The second wave passed – the third – the fourth, and soon the well-defined waves were indistinguishable.

We wireless 'blokes' struggled on with our burdens, aiming, of course, for the tree-stump by the Blue Line. When daylight came we found we were only seven – our officer, carrying no burden, had hurried on with the leading infantrymen.

Through the hours we continued stumbling, sinking, slipping, into old trenches, shell holes, all the time in the midst of a scattered but advancing infantry.

Noon – we still struggled, overburdened with wireless parts. The wounded were limping or being carried in, the thousands of prisoners formed long, straggling processions, the dead lay unnoticed.

At 12.30 we reached the tree-stump. Our officer stood in a deep trench scowling at us.

'Get into communication at once, I have messages here.' He waved a sheaf of papers in his hand.

Hewitt and I immediately set about erecting a 60-yard aerial on 18-foot masts. It was an uneasy task erecting this fully exposed to the vicious enemy fire. Actually I counted afterwards ten men who had been killed outright by shrapnel near us, as we secured the masts. Presently we dropped into the dug-out allotted us and we tuned in for our D.S. I was told to operate. At length I heard D.S. 'Wait,' he said. He was dealing with early morning codes from other corps. At length I seized my turn and transmitted as many messages as I could before I lost my priority. I continued sending messages at intervals (but listening-in all the time) until 8 p.m., when our work died down, land-line communication having been established.

But the officer forbade me to get up.

'Continue listening-in. Hewitt will relieve you at midnight.'

So I sat huddled on a box in a narrow tunnel with the candle-lit set before me and the telephones tightly gripping my ears. In the dug-out the officer, his batman, and Hewitt sat, while in a stifling den underneath the dug-out the four infantrymen rested. On this part of the Hindenburg line the trenches were 'double-deckers.' Sometimes my back touched the clay wall behind me, and my eyes; when turned from the set, blinked into clay – clay everywhere. Two candles flickered above the set, resting on bayonets stabbed into the clay.

Just on the side of the set, away from the dug-out, the tunnel had been shelled, and it opened into the yawning shell hole. Deep in this a young, handsome Tyneside Scottish soldier lay dead. His feet pointed upwards, his body lay on his back with his face upturned. He was not more than five yards from me.

The night air became chill and the rain drizzled.

I asked Hewitt to string up some sacking. I wanted it for two reasons – to reduce the draught and to help me forget the dead soldier lying there. Presently the others curled themselves up, and their snores soon assured me that they were asleep. I remained listening-in for a possible emergency call.

10.30 p.m. An eerie silence on the ether, pierced only by atmospherics crackling in my ears. As the time went on the strange quietude became ghastly, and; all the time, the Tyneside soldier lay there, just the other side of the sack, his eyes probably still gazing blindly to the darkened skies.

A wind sprang up, blowing the sacking in towards me, as though some enfeebled soul pressed against it. Sometimes the wind lifted a corner of the sack, and I peered through into the darkened shell hole.

The rain became sleet, and it turned to snow. I knew because the snow soon attained sufficient weight to bear down lumps of earth, and fugitive flakes drifted into the tunnel.

12 o'clock. Hewitt's turn! Was it worth his listening-in? Perhaps I would get instructions to close down any minute...pity to wake him! I decided to continue the watch

myself. (I should have stated before that Hewitt suffered from cramp in his right elbow and our officer had no confidence in his operating, hence the long watch that fell to me.)

1 o'clock. I was really cold now. Snow and mad rolled into the tunnel from the shell hole, and the sacking became insecure. And then D.S. told me to close down.

I tried to sleep, but my weird imprisonment in the tunnel had disturbed me. I could not sleep...perhaps the Tyneside soldier prevented it.

I suppose I dozed, for I awoke to find faint gleams of daylight peeping down the stairway. The others were soundly asleep. I got up and went outside.

A snow-covered wilderness!

All was still. Not a gun shot, not a voice, not a living person in sight.

The sun was about to rise, and I watched fascinated.

As the yellow sun became flushed so the disappearing snow revealed the toll – the countless black lumps lying everywhere in the mud. The snow soon thawed on the Tyneside soldier, and he seemed as tragically beautiful as he had appeared the previous day.

The silence continued. The silence of a winter morning in the fields of Gloucestershire. Where the war of yesterday?

The sun soon sipped up all traces of the snow, and all was naked again – shambles, mud, desolation!

Silence, profound, unreal.

Then suddenly as though from nowhere a faint, lazy, approaching whistle – bang! A big German shell burst at my back.

The spell was ended, the silent drama wrecked, for, taking up the challenge, our artillery renewed its articulation. I was once more back in the Great War.

I saw terrible sights subsequently, endured cruel hardships. I saw the bones of snipers hanging freakishly from ruined trees, headless bodies, bodyless heads, a pair of soldiers, one British, one German, who had each bayoneted the other, standing, dead, and other gruesome things.

But the experience that stands out most vividly in my memory is that of the night when I sat in a tunnel near a Tyneside Scottish corpse, and the miraculous dawn of the following day.

B. Neyland served from September 1916 to December 1919: Sapper, Royal Engineers (Signals), Wireless Section. In France, January to June 1917, all this time in the Arras district. As wireless operator, took part in several attacks, wounded by shell splinter and home to Blighty, June 1917. On recovery sent to Ireland to help in the erection and maintenance of an almost unused wireless (military) service.

AT MESSINES RIDGE IN 1917

E. N. Gladden

Working Party – Early in the spring of 1917 the 11th Northumberland Fusiliers, to which I belonged, were taking their share in the final preparations for the assault on the Messines Ridge. Our divisional front was in the Salient, and nightly working parties up to the Bund at Zillebeke, Jackson's Dump, or Sanctuary Wood were both hazardous and fatiguing. Casualties were heavy, for the enemy knew that a storm was brewing, and his dominating positions on the low heights around the shattered remains of Ypres made it easy for him to turn the Salient into a shambles. The trenches on Hill 60 were not many yards apart, but conditions were so hellish that both sides had reduced their garrisons to a string of strong posts and held only the support lines in force.

There was, under the hill on the British side, a wonderful system of saps and dug-outs, a veritable underground settlement. The concreted and sand-bagged posts above were joined by wooden stairways to the narrow bunk-lined sleeping quarters of the forward troops. Further down, passages lined with wooden planks led to larger barracks, and here were the headquarters offices and dressing station, so far below the level of the ground that the heaviest shell bursting above caused but a distant tremor through the galleries. The whole place was illuminated by electric light and the chug-chug of the pumps keeping the water out of the galleries continued day and night.

The company had come down from the front line into deep support as it was called. We occupied one of these billets, a cavern divided into two stories by a wooden shelf some four feet from the ground and large enough to house a whole platoon. We slept, when we had the chance, in two layers, and there was a passage leading along one side right through the chamber. On the morning of June 5th I was awakened from a deep sleep – I had been out carrying bombs until the early hours of the morning – and ordered to join the party detailed to assist the Australian Tunnelling Company, who were working day and night in six-hour shifts.

The sergeant in charge of the party conducted us down a labyrinth of passages more marvellous at every step, until we came to an opening to the outer world. Just where it was I could not make out: it did not seem to be under direct observation. A high and considerable breastwork of sandbags zigzagged away to the right (this had been the method of disposing of the earth brought out of the workings), and the ground beyond, which rose quickly to a low ridge not far away, was absolutely desolate. We moved around a corner in the breastwork and formed a continuous chain to transport the bags back into the galleries where they were wanted for tamping – that is, for building a barrier against the backward force of the explosion.

I was the last man in the chain and consequently the farthest from safety, a position for which I had in no way manoeuvred, and I stood in the corner of a traverse where the breastwork turned sharply to the left and gradually petered out in the waste. We worked with a will, for our task was light and the fresh air – a welcome change from the stuffy atmosphere of the saps. An observation balloon on the far horizon attracted our attention, but whether friend or foe we could not decide. Shortly after, a battery began to fire and the shells burst on the ridge about a hundred yards away; another salvo passed over and crashed on the hill behind. 'No need to worry'; we thought. 'They were not intended for us.' We had progressed so well that the N.C.O. thought it would be a good idea to lengthen the chain. Three of us moved round the corner and the work continued. Suddenly the gun fired again and something in the scream of the first shell foretold that it was for us. I ducked as it burst opposite the corner of the breastwork. We ran like rabbits for the sap. I was turning the last bend when a man a few yards in front crashed to the ground. He was a youngster just out from England who had taken up the position I had recently vacated. Aided by the man in front I attempted to lift him, but we were now alone, some 50 yards from the entrance, and an approaching salvo urged us forward again. I reached the sap opening, panting and frightened, and hung on to the timber baulk at the side to regain my breath. It was safe there, and we waited while the sergeant went to Headquarters for instructions.

At that moment Corporal B. of our company arrived on the scene, and, on learning what had happened, demanded why we had left the casualty out there. We were certain he was dead, but the corporal would not be satisfied. 'Come on, one of you men.' he said. 'We must fetch him in.' No one moved. We had all been thoroughly shaken. I felt ashamed. Why wouldn't someone go? A last appeal and Corporal B. started alone. Something for the moment overcame my terror and impelled me to follow him. We raced along the breastwork. All was still. We bent to raise the prostrate figure at the corner, but the hand of Death had made the task too much for our strength, weakened by the stress and excitement. Shelling recommenced and the bags above began to scatter around us. '*Run!*' screamed the corporal, and with my remaining energies I ran as I had never run before, as a regular tornado of shells smashed down the breastwork behind us. The stretcher bearers who fetched him in later, when all was again quiet, reported that he had pieces of shrapnel through the brain and the heart and therefore must have died instantly. How he had managed to run a dozen yards and turn the corner I could never understand.

The Attack – The afternoon of June 6th found us back at the Bund dug-outs preparing for the advance. It had been rumoured for some days that the long-expected offensive was imminent, but the actual orders came suddenly, as they usually did to the men in the ranks. The battalion was to attack on the morrow. 'B' Company was to be in close support, and this was generally thought preferable to 'going over the top'; though memories of a similar position before the Butte de Warlencourt on the Somme, when the supporting company was severely punished, did not reassure me.

The sun shone brightly and the Bund dug-outs had thrown off the lethargic appearance usual at that time of the day. We were not under observation, and could go about our preparations unmolested. All was quiet. In the little stream that trickled down the embankment from the lake we were able to wash ourselves-perhaps for the last time. Some whose steel helmets lacked the regulation canvas cover were daubing them with mud; officers were trying on their rankers' tunics, which would make them less conspicuous to the enemy; while stretcher bearers, runners, and others were sewing distinctive badges to their sleeves.

On the embankment above a notice board, relic of a more leisurely type of warfare, forbade us to catch fish with Mills' bombs – a sport in which we were very unlikely to indulge just then. Below lay the flats dividing us from Ypres, which filled the middle distance and stood out clearly, a tooth edge of jagged ruins, in the afternoon sun. Tea was served and those fortunates detailed to go back to the transport field as reinforcements were preparing to leave. Those last bright hours passed slowly. When at last night began to fall tractors hauling heavy guns crawled out from Ypres and took up positions on the flats in front. At certain points guns were placed wheel to wheel and no attempt was made to hide them. Gun after gun left the town, and now with the thickening dusk there followed streams of men: small groups at first, followed later by long files reaching out like tentacles into the Salient. Lastly, throwing caution to the winds, the field guns galloped up the roads, followed closely by their ammunition trains. Surely never through all its vicissitudes had the Salient witnessed such a furious activity.

At midnight the company moved off and followed the duckboard track towards Hill 60 once again. Lying by the route at the corner of the Bund, I saw two shapes, roughly covered by a piece of old sacking. The blackness of their exposed features told me that they had long lain thus: in the bustle of preparing for a push the small services due to the dead were often overlooked. I felt sad; there was no peace here even in death. Suddenly the raucous blast of a Strombus horn came from near at hand, and the terrifying cry of '*Gas!*' passed down the file.

The enemy were 'strafing' with gas shells, which whined over and struck the ground with their peculiar undecided thud, while a sickly smell came to my nostrils. The fear of gas was the greatest fear of all, and we sighed with relief when we had passed through the danger zone, and could take off our box respirators. The remainder of the journey to the jumping-off trench was accomplished without mishap.

The trench was newly dug somewhere' on the hill and nowhere more than $4^1/_2$ feet deep. We looked like getting a thrashing when the show commenced. The attack was to be preceded by the explosion of the mine. There in the bowels of the earth after many months of preparation, tunnelling, and counter-tunnelling by the enemy, an unprecedented amount of explosive had been buried and the effects of the detonation of such an immense charge were uncertain. We might all be involved. In any case our trenches might close in, and, to evade that possibility, we were ordered to lay out on top for the event.

The night was clear; the guns were silent. Ever and anon an enemy Verey light went up from his line and spread a lurid glare over the scene. Those hours of waiting were hardly bearable. At last the first streaks of dawn showed in the sky, and whispered orders sent us to our positions a few yards in front of the trench. The last few minutes dragged with relentless slowness; each second seemed an hour, each minute an eternity.

The greyness of a new day now suffused the sky. I felt a tremor of fear run through my body; the silence of the grave seemed to enfold the whole world. With a sharp report an enemy rocket began to mount towards the heavens. A voice behind cried 'Now!' It was the hour, and that last enemy light never burst upon the day. The ground began to rock and I felt my body carried up and down as by the waves of the sea. In front the earth opened and a large black mass was carried to the sky on pillars of fire, and there seemed to remain suspended for some seconds while the awful red glare lit up the surrounding desolation. No sound came. I had been expecting a noise from the mine so tremendous as to be unbearable. For a brief space all was silent, as though we had been too close to hear and the sound had leapt over us like some immense wave. A line of men rose from the ground a few yards in front and advanced towards the upheaval, their helmets silhouetted and bayonets glinting in the redness of that unearthly dawn. I saw no more.

We hurled ourselves back to the trench. And then there was a tremendous roar and a tearing across the skies above us, as the barrage commenced with unerring accuracy. It was as though a door had been suddenly flung open. The skies behind our lines were lit by the flashes of many thousand guns, and above the booming din of the artillery came the rasping rattle of the Vickers guns pouring a continuous stream of lead over into the enemy's lines. Never before, surely, had there been such a bombardment, and I shuddered for those unfortunates caught in that storm of death.

Yet the German gunners were not slow to answer their S.O.S. call, for before I had crossed the few yards back to the trench their shells were already bursting around. I saw the trench before me and in my excitement I slipped upon the edge and fell headforemost amidst a rain of loose earth. My helmet slipped off and I was just able to drag out my Lewis gun buckets before a stream of humanity striving to reach the deeper parts of the trench carried me before it. I had lost my steel helmet and could think of little else during the whole bombardment. The shells lashed the ground with fury. Each piece of flying shrapnel seemed to be searching for my unprotected head and as I pushed it into the parapet the loose grains of earth matted my hair and trickled into the collar of my tunic. The rest of the section crouched near.

Our corporal, Regular soldier and veteran of the First Battle of Ypres, sat crouched in the corner, his knees almost to his chin, and, except for an occasional blasphemy or laconic: 'The next one'll get us,' he remained motionless. My pal leaned against the parapet, his eyes closed as though death had already come to him, and a little further along another youngster cried audibly. From right and left came cries of pain and the stretcher bearers, risking all in their devotion, pushed backwards and forwards to dress the wounded. Our casualties were heavy, but fortunately the enemy batteries were disorganized and the shooting somewhat haphazard, otherwise few of us would have escaped that morning.

News came back of the success of the first advance with comparatively light casualties, and, after a lull, our guns increased again to tremendous fury while the attack was further developed. The crack of rifles and rattle of machine guns came through the din. Casualties this time were much heavier, as was to be expected. Then the bombardment slowly died away and it was obvious that the time for consolidation had arrived. Orders came for us to lead along the trench, and I soon found a helmet for which the owner no longer had any use. I appropriated it thankfully.

We got mixed up with a carrying party coming from the opposite direction, and the enemy, who could see into the lower parts of the trench, began sniping with 'whizz-bangs.' Those small, swiftly travelling shells came without warning and spread a greater feeling of 'wind-up' than did the larger varieties. Something had gone wrong and we were turned about. A shell hit the parapet near by and a second burst on the inside of the parados, but 2 or 3 yards away. The man in front was killed, while I, who was lifted from my feet by the explosion and enveloped in a thick suffocating cloud of yellow fumes, remained unscratched. Such were the fortunes of war.

For the next hour or so I was suffering from shell-shock and only half-conscious of the withering fire that the enemy directed against us from the left sector of the old line behind us. The shelling was measured and nerve-racking. Each shell was intended for the trench and did not fall far away. The casualty list lengthened, and it seemed that endurance could stand little more. Our inactivity was deadly. At last the enemy got tired, and towards the late afternoon all became quiet.

Then came the order for us to reinforce the troops in Battle Wood. We left the trench and crossed the shell-torn hill by the railway cutting. The crater, which I expected to see as an immense jagged hole in the ground, was actually a large flat-bottomed depression like a frying-pan, clear and clean from debris except at the further edge, where vestiges of one of the enemy's trenches showed through its side. The poor devils caught in that terrible cataclysm had no chance. Yet what chance was there for anyone in that war of guns and mathematics?

On the nearer lip of the crater lay the body of a German still clutching his rifle. He was a tremendous fellow well over 6 feet in height, I should think, and seems to have made a single-handed effort to hold up the advancing British line. How he got there is difficult to imagine. He was probably out on advance post between the mine and our lines and had retreated to the crater to make his last brave stand. A murmur of admiration passed down the file at the recognition of such courage. Here and there black fountains of earth were thrown up as heavy enemy shells burst in the wilderness and put a finishing touch to that scene of desolation. I could survey the whole of the famous hill and, away in front, the tree stumps of Battle Wood; and it occurred to me that until that day no man had, during those many months since the first battles, stood on that same ground in daylight and lived.

Private E. N. Gladden, at the end of 1915, when eighteen years of age, attested under the Derby Scheme. Called up in the following May. Passed for home service and posted to the 2nd/1st Hertfordshires. Left England on August 30th, 1916, and joined the 7th Battalion Northumberland Fusiliers on the Somme. Badly handled both by the enemy and the weather in the October-November battles about Le Sars and Warlencourt. Contracted trench feet and crossed to Blighty in the ill-fated 'Glenart Castle' at the end of December. Early March back at the Depot at Catterick and to France May 2nd, 1917, and posted to the 11th Battalion in the Salient. Then followed Messines, the Third Battle, and Passchendaele. Italy (23rd Division) in November. Xmas in the trenches on the Piave-Montello front. Transferred to the mountains in March 1918. The battalion took a leading part in

both the Austrian offensive on the Asiago Plateau on June 15th,
and the final crossing of the Piave on October 27th, 1918.

A JULY DAY AT ST. JULIEN

Alfred Willcox

We had waited a long time for nine o'clock on that July night of 1917, and now that we were nearing the hour to be off we wanted sleep. Yet, through the nervous excitement which weeks of preparation had engendered we could doze but fitfully. On the rat-eaten boards of a dug-out on the canal bank we sprawled, pinned down by our battle clobber. A curtain hung at the door to keep out gas. It also kept out the twilight.

'Can't someone get a blasted light?' Private Smith suddenly exclaimed, and as an answer a match was struck, applied to a piece of four-by-two, which in turn was stuck in the middle of a tin of dubbin. This acted as a candle, and threw a strange eerie light that turned the faces of the twenty of us who were huddled there a pale green, with dark shadows that made holes for eyes.

Smith, who stared vacantly across to my side, broke the silence again.

'God, this makes you think,' he said, in a voice which wasn't quite like his own.

'Put a sock in it, Smith,' was the solitary answer he received to his philosophy, and once more silence descended upon the dug-out, and shadows jumped over the domed roof as the green light bobbed up and down.

I reflected idly on the happenings of the past month. Right back, where we could sleep in tolerably clean straw and pinch the eggs and cherries of an old French farmer, we had also crushed down his growing wheat and had cut trenches across his fields.

We were told that these trenches followed the line of those we were to attack later, and, having cut them out, we rushed over them every day for a fortnight, always, at the end, capturing the little village of St. Jullen at the bayonet. Only it was rather different there. You see we had a breathing space half-way across the fields, and from nowhere French girls came with baskets of oranges and chocolates for heroes – only the heroes had to pay through the nose for the dry or gritty delicacies.

It was a great holiday, that – when we put one foot in paradise, experienced the unregretted loss of lousy shirts, stole eggs for breakfast, got fruit for tea and generally were fattened up. For what end?

Then we marched back again. But we were still fairly well behind the line. There the sergeant, whom we hated because he snarled every time he spoke, was unlucky, for a flying piece of iron caught him in the liver. Somehow we found we were sorry when he died because when he had gone we discovered there were a lot of things he had done for his platoon that weren't done for anyone else.

Then there was the working party that went out to carry 'footballs' up to the front line and, cutting across the field between the two lines of trenches by way of the light railway, was suddenly swept by German guns, and turned back, with gas-masks fixed, into a dug-out to lay panting. But eleven of the twenty-four were left huddled up by the railway line. And the colonel had told Brigade Headquarters, so the rumour ran, that he wasn't going to have his bloody battalion cut up before they began. (At any rate, there were no more working parties.) And as the movements in the back area increased, the padre rigged up a cross on a sugar box one morning, and we had communion, though the beer parade collided with this. What memories! It seemed so long ago: we were much nearer to death now...

There was a tap on the curtain which was lifted as the colonel came in. I don't know where we had picked up the old man, but he was a decent old buck.

'Now, my boys,' – something like that he began – 'you've been practising and waiting for this moment for a long time. Try to remember what you have learnt, and keep up the name of the regiment. I've just come to wish you all the best of luck. There'll be some porridge up soon. Fill your bellies. And God bless you.'

I hadn't the heart to eat much of the porridge. I stuffed down two or three spoonfuls and dozed off again...

I awoke with a start. The light had burnt out. My mate, George, gave me a kick because I wasn't moving.

'Come on,' he said; 'they're falling in.'

'Here, give me a hand. This blasted clobber's weighing me down.'

He pulled me up, and with a good deal of clatter we struggled through the little door. There was still a bit of light in the sky, which was reflected in the muddy water of the canal. There was also a suggestion of rain in the wind.

We fell in. The roll was called: we were all there.

Then, in single file, we turned left to the communication trench and the enemy's lines. We reached our positions and waited, sprawling in the Flanders mud on a summer's night. George and I sprawled together to keep warm; for even a summer's night, with the rain in the wind which comes across the plain, Flanders can be chilly.

George, always a voluble member of the platoon, had still a little to say, though now in whispers. He could see no outcome of the War in its present form. In the evening platoon discussions he had been in favour of a general armistice. But he pronounced it 'ar-mis-tik,' with the accent on the second syllable.

'If only we could have an armistik,' he began, as Fritz started a devil's tattoo on his machine guns. Ta-t-t t-ta! How well he played it. Then from our own lines came the finishing notes, Ta-ta. We laughed at this exchange of courtesies, in spite of our discomfort. They kept it up till the thing got on my nerves. Then the guns which had been growling in the background suddenly burst out in a screaming tornado of lead, and heavy stuff dropped just behind us. There was some suppressed commotion.

'Stretcher bearers,' came a voice.

'Coming up,' was the reply.

'Someone hit,' muttered George.

'Ay.'

'Lucky sod. He's saved a lot of trouble.'

I never knew who it was. The poor devil called out for his mother.

'Oh, put a sock in his blasted mouth,' came another nerve-racked voice.

The stretcher bearers got the chap away and there was quiet again. Every few minutes the officers came round to see if we were all right. I was more thankful to see the cooks. They had struggled up with hot tea, strengthened with rum. It was the most liberal treatment we had had during the War. By the way the liquor burned, I should say it was fifty-fifty. The youngest lad in the platoon – he must have lied to get into the Army, poor fool – crawled on his belly and would insist on shaking hands with every one of us. He was thoroughly drunk.

It was still dark, and my illuminated watch said 3.30. That meant half an hour more. Then we became very silent, and even the guns seemed to be still. It seemed like the calm that comes before the thunderstorm...

An officer came round once more.

'Five minutes more, boys,' he said; 'get ready.'

We fixed our bayonets. We gripped each other's hands. And waited. My heart seemed to take up that devil's tattoo and thumped against my ribs...

Suddenly it came. I can still hear those three sharp staccato cannon shots which seemed to split the darkness, for there followed a tremendous roar and crash which sent the first light of dawn trembling along the distant horizon above the mist, suddenly to burst into miles of flames. And from No Man's Land shot up a myriad of distress lights, trembling. And 'express trains' roared overhead.

It was a wonderful moment. Some magic force drew us up from our crouching positions, and in the blue mist which still clung to the hollows in the battlefield we looked like ghosts wreathed by smoke. Eighty thousand of us. Then we swept forward as if caught by the wind. The spreading light of dawn caught the glint of bayonets as they moved on and on...

I met Ira by the side of a shell hole. He had pulled out his leg from the squelchy mud which had dragged him down to the knee. Months we had campaigned together. The happiness which we had managed to squeeze out of those dreary months we shared; the sorrows we shared; the parcels from home we shared. On those blessed days of rest we had flung bits of poetry to each other and had teased to say what we had quoted. We thought that after the War we would quit the monotonous life at home and would go adventuring. We had mapped out what we would do, where we would go – this country and that. They knew us as the twins. Before we went over we had been told to press on: if a man dropped down he must be left – others would follow to patch him up.

'If you fall I shall stop,' said Ira to me a day before. 'Hell to them all! I shall stop.' But we were separated before we began. He was attached to another platoon. I saw him as I went over. He was well.

He laughed as he swore, 'What a bloody mess!' We said good-bye – 'God be with you.' I never saw him again. Later I wrote to him. The letter was returned – undelivered. The mark of a rubber stamp was on the envelope, 'Killed in action.' Just that. A country's regrets to me that my friend was dead...

Most of the firing had been on our side. We did not know it at the time. There was such a screaming in the air that lead seemed to be flying everywhere. Something whipped by and one swore that his ear had been missed by a hair's breadth. In front our barrage fell like a curtain and the earth vomited up mud and dirt. Then the fun began.

A rattle, with that well-known crescendo and diminuendo as the machine gun swept from east to west, cracked out. In front of me I saw a pair of arms go up and a rifle drop and six feet of khaki crumple up. I saw George hurrying to get behind a scrap of a hedge. He never got there. But he got his 'armistik' all right; he got it in the guts. I dropped on my knees and crawled to that little bit of shelter. I saw stretched at full length, with his face towards heaven, a boy in grey with the down of youth upon his chin.

We were off our track. We turned left and reached a road. It was strange to see abandoned guns and parapets turned the wrong way. Down the road came two other figures in grey. One was leaning heavily upon the other. His shirt was torn off his back and there was a great gash in his flesh. We looked at each other in passing. We spoke to each other only with our eyes and went our ways.

Then a frightened group with hands in the air came towards us. Old Tom placed his bayonet on the grey tunic of one and sent the fear of God through his body. Tom laughed at the young boy's squeal, then quickly went through his pockets, jerked his thumb towards our lines, kicked his backside and went on.

The devil had a busy morning raking out his furnaces, but left us quiet for an hour in the churchyard of St. Julien in the afternoon. I tried to make some tea in a shell hole with the remains of my water, some old tea leaves and solidified methylated spirit. There were too many snipers about to be very comfortable, but those of us who kept our heads low survived the hour. Our platoon was like a spearhead in the line. In the early evening the enemy opened out on us; in mistake our own guns opened, too.

'Better fall back a few yards,' said the officer, and even as we were doing so something jabbed my hand. It dropped down and blood spurted out.

The others had gone. I was alone. The fire was not continuous. It came in fits and starts. In an interval my good hand helped me out. I dashed out and dropped in the shadow of a grave. I was seen. From the pillbox, hidden somewhere about, which had given us trouble all the day, a couple of bits of lead whistled. I crawled into an enormous shell hole and began to sink into mud. With the slime clinging to me I got away, through the bottom of a hedge which, by the grace of God, had remained there.

No one to be seen now and my head facing I knew not where. A great, livid waste, the light of day going, and the way might be to the north or the south. I had lost my bearings. Not far away a tank, half embedded, was getting it full tilt. The sweat stood on my dirty face. And then in that great expanse of mud and wire I spotted a little red cross on a little flag, sticking eighteen inches out of the ground. I felt safe again.

It was at the entrance to a cellar. The cellar was filled to overflowing. Men and bits of men were huddled there or stretched at full length.

'Better get on,' said the doctor, noticing that my legs were whole. So, duly labelled, I turned to home again. I passed my mates with waterproofs on their shoulders, standing to. I tried to run, but felt weak. Suddenly a barrage fell in front of me. I turned into the remains of a cottage by the side of the road, found a seat on an empty petrol tin in the corner, pulled down my tin hat to cover my face. But, like some venomous beast, the barrage crept nearer and soon bits of the brick wall began to fall. I was shaking with fright. I decided to bolt the moment the barrage lifted. My arm was throbbing with pain. My leg had gone to sleep. I thumped it with my other hand – and life came back again and with it hope. There came a flash. I shut my eyes. A deafening crash and tumble of mortar. The firing stopped. I bolted. Down the road zigzag, zigzag, to dodge the snipers, on and on nearer home. Soon I saw the white tapes. I followed. My throat was burning with thirst. I saw a watercart in a ditch and soon water was running down a long throat that asked for more and more.

In the early hours of the morning I tumbled into an electrically lighted dug-out dressing station two miles from the front line where there were clean bandages and steaming tea. I fell at full length, motionless. Someone pressed drink to my lips.

The journey was not ended. Soon they came to carry me on again.

'Got a couple of Jerries here. Do you mind if they go with you?'

Mind? Not if it was the whole German Army. They bundled us in together and we were off. The rain was falling piteously. At the field ambulance we were taken out. The place was full. Hope and despair lived there side by side. There were screams as the broken bodies were lifted on to the tables for the surgeons' knives. There was a great light on dirty faces of men as they sat on wooden forms, their arms bared to the doctor who pricked the flesh with his inoculating needle to carry its serum to attack the tetanus germ.

They took us to a tent on which the rain beat down ceaselessly and mercilessly. I fell on a stretcher and pulled the damp blanket on top of me. What did it matter? Rain – rain – rain. Far away the guns growled. Rain – rain – rain. It splashed on to the canvas and dripped into the tent. Drip – drip – drip. Each drip seemed to fashion itself into a word – sleep. Sleep – sleep – sleep. Nearly twenty-four hours after the attack. To-morrow the hospital train – and Blighty. But now sleep. Sleep. Sleep. Sleep. S–l–e–e–p. Oh, thank God! Thank God, s–l–e–e–p.

Alfred Willcox, a private in the Royal Sussex Regiment (various battalions), always on the Western Front, chiefly in the Salient. For a very brief period was a cook, but poisoned himself with coke fumes, to the relief of his comrades. In the 13th Sussex (Lowther's Lambs) when they took the village of St. Julien in the Third Battle of Ypres. The incidents in the narrative took place that day, when he was wounded.

A LABOUR COMPANY AT YPRES

J. Cumming Morgan

The delusion existed, and probably still exists, that no labour companies were ever nearer the line than twenty miles. But when I tell you that the company to which I belonged originally half of a Scottish labour battalion – was for the last seventeen months of the War never at any moment out of range of Jerry's guns, and that when he did get us he got us with his biggest guns and with his high-velocities, from which there was no dodging, and that during the struggle for Passchendaele in the autumn of 1917 our company were awarded a Military Cross, a D.C.M., and eight M.M.'s – well, we must have been within *hearing* distance, anyway.

The word 'labour' also gave people the impression that we were an uneducated, uncivilized, unwashed lot of beings, whereas we were composed of exactly the same sort of men as every other branch of the service, except that most of us were short-sighted, and some of us wanted a finger, or possessed varicose veins, or suffered from some other stroke of luck. In my own section alone (I was a corporal), I had all types of men, from Bill Barnes, whose ideas of conjugal felicity had caused his wife to throw herself from a high tenement window in Edinburgh, with the result that Bill served his country for seven arduous years in a northern institution, to the man (I forget his name, but I honour his memory) who, wounded on the roads at Ypres, went to hospital, and in whose kit, to make an inventory of which was part of my duties, I found a volume of the *Golden Treasury*, a copy of *As You Like It*, and Hume's *Treatise on Human Nature*.

I confine my narrative to these few months in the fall of 1917. We had been billeted at Dickebusch, a ruined village south of Ypres, and at that time about five miles behind the line. On July 30th, the day before the Third Battle of Ypres began, we moved up to a spot about a couple of miles behind Hill 60, and just in front of Scottish Wood. Here we dumped our kit-bags, immediately in front of an East of Scotland battery of 6-inch guns, placed just within the edge of the wood, and there we remained for three solid weeks with no other protection than canvas bivouacs in a region where everybody else lived underground. These 'bivvies' were merely canvas sheets hung over poles and stretched out at each side and pegged down. To get inside one had to crawl on all fours, and into each of them crawled every night to sleep eight weary and generally wet men and a large and varied assortment of other creatures which, though they crawled, did *not* sleep.

I can feel the guns of that battery in my ears yet. Every time a gun went off it felt like hitting your head against a stone wall. I am reminded here of our sergeant-major. While the rank and file slept in 'bivvies,' the officers and the sergeant-major were allowed to put up tents, both bivvies and tents being camouflaged with leafy branches. Being at that time company clerk, I had the privilege of sleeping in the sergeant-major's tent. Nobby was an old Regular, a bluff Yorkshireman of the 'Ole Bill' breed.

Although not a thing of beauty, he was to me a joy for ever. He wore a body-belt. I think he had to, he was so stout. And a flannel body-belt on a fat man acts exactly like the small flower-pot a gardener inverts on top of a dahlia stake to trap earwigs. They crawl up the stake into the flower-pot at night, and are caught there in the morning. Nobby didn't wait till morning. He lit his candle, took off his body-belt, and set to work. He got on famously for a minute or two, then when on the point of making a particularly valuable capture, one of the guns went off, out went the candle and Nobby lost his prey. He found his tongue, however, and his matches, relit his candle, and proceeded on his quest.

How we weren't all splashed out over and over again while in that camp, I do not know. Between us and the battery a railway ran straight up towards Messines Ridge. It was used by one of those big railway guns, which used to slip quietly up during the night, fire a few rounds and slip down again. On our other side was a light railway on which ran small cars conveying men or ammunition. In front and crossed by both railways ran the main road from Ypres to Lille. Just behind us was one of our captive observation balloons; and Jerry was always having tries for one or other of these. He smashed up a battery of guns on the other side of the main road; he cleared out another labour company on the other side of the light railway; he blew holes in the road and blew up the railway; and one day he came across in one of our own planes, fired explosive bullets into the balloon, setting it ablaze, and calmly flew back again to his own lines.

During those five months of fighting for Passchendaele our company worked on the forward roads in front of Ypres, advancing as our line advanced, working parties being sometimes in front of the field guns. On one occasion a party were working exceptionally far forward, and from a recently captured pillbox in the vicinity of Westhoek Ridge were watching our shells bursting over the German trenches. Some line men came down past, clearing out as far as they could. 'Come on, Jock,' they shouted to one of our men. 'What the 'ell are you hanging about here for? If Jerry spots you, he won't half give you gippo.' 'Och, its a' richt, chum – sanriy-fairy-an. We're workin' here.' 'Working! My Gawd!' and they stayed not upon the order of their going.

It was certainly no joke working on these roads when there was a stunt on. Jerry had them taped off to an inch and was shelling them unmercifully.

The traffic on such a road was a wonderful sight. It is a steady, continuous stream, a stream often temporarily checked when a block occurs perhaps miles further up. A shell has landed in the road and knocked a hole in it and, as likely as not, put out of action a lorry or a man or two. The traffic stops dead, perhaps both ways, and the danger of destruction is greatly intensified. Forward the 'Labour Corps!' A squad of men is quickly on the spot with pick and shovel, and the hole is filled up with any mortal thing that can be found – stones, beams, bricks, railway lines, sleepers, bits of cars or lorries, wheels, cases of bully, tombstones, dead horses – anything that will occupy space, and in a few minutes the traffic moves on once more, and the War goes on!

After it had become evident that our hopes of an immediate advance were doomed to disappointment, our company was taken back to Dickebusch. There we built a camp for ourselves, where we spent the winter before moving up to Shrapnel Corner near Ypres in the spring-time. The C.Q.M.S. and myself built a little hut of corrugated iron with a good sound 3-foot-high parapet all round. Our Quarter-bloke at that time was a big, black-moustached, clear-to-hell-out-of-it, sort of chap, just the very man for a company of 500 skrimshankers like ours. While he was a Q.M.S. and I only a lance-jack, in civil life I was a schoolmaster and he a school janitor. However, we worked and lived together in great harmony and friendship for a year. I did the work and he took the responsibility. He was a beadle (church officer) in the Auld Kirk, and a teetotaller. I was a deacon in the, Free Kirk, and drank his nightly tot of rum at bedtime as well as my own.

Our hut was about 8 feet by 6 feet, and just so high that if the Q.M.S. wanted to stretch himself he had either to lie down or go outside. He slept under the duckboard table-shelf-desk on which the rations were kept during the day, and I on a stretcher, with a little 'Queen' stove between us. In the morning at Reveillé – perhaps – I rose, lit a fire in the stove, on the top of which I put a petrol tin full of water for shaving and washing purposes. If the chimney smoked, as it usually did, I. went outside, mounted the parapet and cleaned it out with drain-rods.

Then I drew my breakfast at the cookhouse. When the petrol tin began to steam, the Quarter-bloke rose, shaved and washed, and I, having breakfasted, partly on what I got at the cookhouse, which generally consisted of a square inch of ham fat and a mug of ham tea, but chiefly on bread, butter, cheese, and jam (strawberry) that had never seen the cookhouse, proceeded to do the same, washing contentedly in Sandy's second-hand warm water. He then went for break, fast to the Sergeants' Mess, and I sat down by the stove to rest and smoke.

In this job there was not much to be done during the day. Perhaps one went for the rations, or to the A.O.C. dump for clothing or shovels or gum-boots, or to Pop for beer for the canteen, but our busy time was at night when the boys returned to camp. There was clothing of all sorts to be issued, allotments of pay had to be adjusted, remittances to be sent home, and all sorts of correspondence to be conducted between the men and the pay office with regard to their domestic relations. The number and nature of the family secrets I got to know would have made my fortune were I a blackmailer.

I used to have quite a number of unofficial visitors when the Q.B. went to dinner. A head would pop in at the door, and there would be a hoarse whisper: 'Could ye spare us a candle, corporal? I want to write hame, an' Jock McGreegor's usin' oor ane to heat a Maconochie wi.'

'Anything to read, Jimmy?' inquires a pal. I used to keep a small circulating library of magazines and books.

'Are ye in, sorr?' from an Irishman. 'Could yez give us a house-wife? My threid's all done.'

'Hello, dominie.' (Another pal.) 'Any buckshee fags?' 'The answer is in the negative.' 'Get out! Here's some oatcakes I got in a parcel to-day.' The fags are forthcoming ('Flags' this week).

A platoon officer: 'You might give this man a new shirt, Morgan. The one he had has just walked across to the incinerator.'

Then when the Last Post had sounded, and I had drunk my tot of rum, and the little tin hut was vibrating like a French cattle truck in sympathy with the continuous bombardment of the guns, I drank the Quarter-bloke's tot, and I laid myself down on the stretcher, the handle of which had been accidentally broken in order to make it useless for its proper purpose, and, with my feet against a sack of bread and my head in aromatic proximity to half a cheese, I fell asleep.

Corporal J. C. Morgan was on the National Reserve of Officers before the War, but was rejected for service owing to eyesight, until accepted in Class B2 under the Derby Scheme. Being a schoolmaster, he was not called up for 'Labour Abroad,' but enlisted as a private in July 1916, and was posted to 9th Cameron Highlanders (Labour Battalion). Landed at Havre in September, and until the formation of the Labour Corps in 1917 was employed at various jobs in the back area of the Western Front. In April 1917 the battalion became the 8th Labour Company, and in June were sent up to Dickebusch; remained working on the forward roads till the Armistice, Corps Troops, II Army. Then followed the Army into Germany, marching on foot all the way – the halt, the maimed, and the almost blind. 'Our platoon,' he says, 'whistling (of all things) the Russian National Anthem practically the whole way.' Reached Cologne on December 30th and were billeted at Ohligs. Sent home for demobilization in January 1919.

TWO NIGHTS

P. Hoole Jackson

The year 1917 gave our battalion the last of a series of changes in the war areas to which it had gone. The ravages made by Gallipoli had been repaired by drafts of recruits and the return of recovered wounded men to their various platoons. Reorganization in Egypt, coupled with intensive training, had welded the new blood and the old together; and a tip-and-run campaign with the Turks in Sinai, the worst features of which were thirst, flies, and forced marches, had given the new men a slight foretaste of shell and machine-gun fire.

We came to France as a tried division, and, after a little allowance of time for acclimatization, were tested on various fronts before being given a gradually worsening front to hold.

The end of May and the beginning of June 1917 were wonderful months. In shattered villages behind the lines the ruins were being hidden by tall grass; garden-flowers, seeding themselves, spread swiftly and mingled with their wild kind. Everywhere the waste of war was softened by the prolific growth of unchecked crops and uncut hay. The birds mated and nested within a stone's throw of the gun emplacements, and their songs filled the woods and even reached to the front-line trenches.

We took over our new area at night; passing over a log track through Havrincourt Wood. It was thick, extensive, full of tangled growth and beautiful 'rides.' The trenches lay forward of it just over a rise, whence a gentle declivity descended to the German lines. Our own trenches were newly formed; much of the front line remained to be dug, for the division we relieved had followed up a German retreat that left ground to be entrenched. Everything was new; even the distance to the German lines unknown. Bullet wounds were plentiful, but shelling light.

That night a number of us lay 200 yards in front of our own line while the rest of the battalion dug the trenches under cover of our screen. Everything was quiet; there were no casualties, and, after the colonel's inspection of the lines just prior to dawn, the screen was withdrawn and ordinary trench routine installed.

Four of us who had been with the battalion since the beginning of the War, and only known the separation due to light wounds that had allowed us to return to the battalion after a flying glimpse of Blighty, were engaged as scouts. The duty, hitherto, had been light enough: sniping from advanced positions, an occasional patrol on a very quiet front.

Now we were to know a new phase of our task. On the second night the colonel sent for us, and we gathered round the table of boxes that occupied the centre of his dug-out. After going carefully over the ground on the map, we were ordered to go out and inspect the German lines. A thousand yards was named as being the possible distance of their front line. Our own quarters were in a small dug-out that we had dug on the previous day; well inside the wood and about 500 yards behind the trenches. This was our privilege for undertaking scout work – that we did not occupy the front line, where we could not get the rest necessary to the nightly work of going out in front of the trenches.

We worked in groups of three; one man remaining in the dug-out to prepare tea and food for us on our return just before dawn the following day. We left our own front-line trench at ten o'clock at night and remained out as long as was necessary. The rum ration was issued to us before leaving, but we never took it, preferring to have it in our tea when we returned, soaked from crawling in the long, dew-wet grass. Also, the task required quick ears and eyes, undeadened by liquor.

Two sunken roads bounded the left and right of our lines; these were convenient places for getting away from our trenches, though too dangerous to use further than that, being places obviously doubly watched.

After a few preliminary trial outings, we arrived in the front line one quiet evening just before dusk, waiting in the open trench until our eyes had got their night sight. Then we set off, this night four of us working in twos. We worked from left to right, reaching the German wire about twelve o'clock midnight. Then we lay listening.

The guns were silent; now and then a minenwerfer would soar up into the air from the German lines, and we would take rough bearings of the position of the mortar that fired it. We could hear the clack of talk in their front line, only 10 or 15 yards away; from behind we could hear the rumble of their transport bringing up rations under cover of darkness. Now and then a sniper's bullet would ping towards our lines. Sometimes, when our own line had a working party out, we could hear the strident tones of a particularly noted-voiced serjeant-major, 'Come on, get them spades crackin'. A set of old women ud dig quicker.' Then one of us would touch the other and we would grin in the darkness at the little touch of humour that relieved our tension. Often we could hear the clink of German picks as they dug or mended trenches; once a working-party of fifty of them marched past where we lay in the grass and began to work about 100 yards away. We had to lie there until within an hour of dawn before they ceased, and the crawl back to our lines in the slowly increasing light was one that we patted ourselves on the back for as equalling any Red Indian's stalking in its noiselessness.

We left everything behind us in the trench that was likely to identify us if we had the ill-luck to be captured or 'scuppered' while scouting-pay books, identity discs, and letters; and we discarded steel helmets because they clanged like a bell if they hit a branch or were accidentally knocked by our rifles, substituting forage caps. We wore no equipment except a bandolier of ammunition; and our bayonets were, of course, always fixed except on bright, moonlight nights.

Men whose luck it was not to have worked in this manner thought our job a dangerous one compared with ordinary trench-life, but this was not correct. Once between the lines the War became a personal affair. Each side had its men out, therefore No Man's Land was untouched by gun-fire. Snipers and enemy scouts and patrols were our enemies, and our lives depended on our own eyes and ears and sense of direction. The life, we considered, was far better than sitting in a trench waiting for shells or digging new trenches. We were exempt from fatigues and onerous duties, and we had our own little dug-out near to Battalion Headquarters, and drew and cooked our own rations. In the daytime we rested. Every third night was followed by a period of a full twenty-four hours' rest, and the following day we took a turn of duty on a day observation-post that was concealed amongst fallen logs on a rise overlooking the German lines, which we watched by telescope. At this post we took turns with the other headquarters' scouts; they worked between the lines on the nights when we rested.

On the night already mentioned we lay for some time making notes and then began to crawl slowly along the German wire, parallel with it. There was a moon due up, but the clouds had so far obscured it. Just as we came to a small hillock it burst from behind the clouds and flooded the country with light. We lay still and waited; a German's bayonet gleamed from the trench, where his rifle lay pointed over the parapet – a sentry post. But the most thrilling thing of all was the sight we had of a road through a gap between two low hills behind the enemy lines. We could see guns and transports passing across the moonlit stretch; we could see men moving up and down, groups of them stopping and talking just as we did when moving behind our own lines. It was a glimpse of a forbidden land.

Suddenly my pal touched my arm; we wriggled close together; he stretched his hand on the ground and slowly turned it to the right. Following it with a slow movement of the head, I saw shadowy figures between us and the moon – ten, fifteen, twenty, thirty, forty, fifty – we counted. They moved slowly towards our trenches.

There was only one thing to do safely; we followed them, hoping that we could send some kind of warning to our own line. Crawling in their wake was exciting, though quite safe. When they were 50 yards from their own line they dropped to the grass and began to crawl.

We followed them to within 100 yards of our trenches, and were almost on the bank of the sunken road flanking us on the left when a Verey light sent up by some troops on our left threw us into silhouette on top of the bank; to descend into the road was to choose Scylla instead of Charybdis, for it was traversed by machine-gun fire. We flattened ourselves as soon as the light allowed us to change from our 'frozen' attitudes by dying out. But we had been seen, not by the patrol, but by a covering party to the patrol, who opened fire wildly on the spot we occupied. They must have formed the opinion that we were a large force attempting to cut off the big patrol; a signal sounded and the patrol retreated away to the right. Then, for some minutes we lay, our hearts panting wildly while bullets thudded into the opposite bank of the sunken road, which was raised about 3 feet above our bank. They sang over us in a continuous volley, and we gauged the numbers of rifles as being about twenty. There was nothing for it but absolute stillness; if we as much as moved a hand to thrust our rifles into firing position, or raised our heads an inch to try and find out by the flashes where the enemy was, a volley was the result. This was due to the fact that we were lying in long grass, uncut hay, which waved every time we stirred. The movement was obvious to the enemy because of the brilliant moonlight.

To make matters worse, our own line practically gave us up and began machine-gun fire on the German lines. The night woke to pandemonium. Fortunately this saved us and we crawled and slithered back to our own trenches with a delightful amount of information.

In three months we never lost a man on patrol, though a few German prisoners were collected, mostly snipers caught between the lines. This period of warfare concluded by an advance which lost us more men in a day than we had lost in the previous months, and we came out on rest. Sports were organized; a shooting competition was arranged. One of the prizes was carried off by a chum and myself, though there was little credit in this seeing that we had been using our rifles in sniping and scouting work for months, whereas the average

Tommy rarely fired his unless an attack matured. The prize was sixty francs, and we repaired to a favourite estaminet and treated our pals after the time-honoured manner. That was the night my pal saw most distinctly *two* sentries on the gateway of the ruined chateau that lodged us. We had great difficulty in drawing him past before he was thrown into the guard-room. The single sentry became almost annoyed...

After a few weeks' rest and intensive training, we went to Ypres, bound for the Passchendaele Ridge. We were to be the second brigade in, another brigade preceding us to the line. We knew the place by repute only. Its reputation was similar to that of Verdnn to the poilus – hell on earth. Every part of the line was shelled hourly; the roads behind were shelled; the camps were shelled by huge guns.

A full-strength brigade went in. About a week later they came down again, not much more than the strength of a battalion. They were ragged, muddy, unshaven, the remnants of a glorious attack that had taken a few more yards of that contested bit of muddy, pock-holed earth.

For the only time in my experience I saw a whole camp of Tommies turn out to cheer others returning from a line they themselves were bound for. As that draggled little mob slithered down the road to their rest they were cheered every bit of the way. One of them turned a haggard face to the door of a hut where a group of the others were cheering. 'You won't blasted well cheer when you gets up there, mate,' he said grimly.

The same night we went 'up there.' We went in little groups of five, with intervals of more than 100 yards between each two. The Menin road was a river of mud in which our boots sucked and slipped. Down one side of it came horses, limbers, wagons, ambulance cars, guns – all at full speed. The horses seemed to know they were coming from danger; their hoofs thrashed the mud about us as they flew down to the rear, their drivers sitting stolidly, using the whip now and then, and smoking as they drove. There were no restrictions needed there. Up the other side the road a slow procession of vehicles crawled, one behind the other: new guns going up to the positions, ammunition wagons full of shells, ambulances bound for the clearing stations, ration carts for the troops in the line. Piccadilly could not have been more crowded, and over all these the German shells moaned and whined. Now and then a cart would have to pull round a heap of wreckage that had once been men, horses, and wagons. By the side of the road lay the stiffening carcasses of horses and mules, and around, on every hand; the big guns crashed.

On three sides was the arching Salient, marked out as though on a mighty map by the ring of flaming flashes from the German guns. A peninsula of death and terror. As we drew nearer to the Ridge, the howling in the sky grew more fierce. We had to pause while a shell dropped before us; rush on as one hurled down almost on top of us; dive for cover in the slimy ditch. All along the road were the skeletons of shattered trees; some shivered off at the base of the bole, others with a grotesque branch left; and over all was the livid light of the gun-flashes, which rose and fell like a fiery, ceaseless tide.

By Cambridge Road we were halted. Here were the field-guns, wheel to wheel, the guns which provided the barrage fire – behind which flaming wall all advances were now made. The gunners were working stripped almost to the waist. The pound and crash of the noisy little guns was terrific, deafening. If a gun failed or was knocked out another was soon in its place.

Mud and slime; a night in a shell hole that was little better than a hollow of ooze. There were no proper shell holes, no communication trenches. All around was the most desolate landscape of shell-harrowed land. Shell hole merged with shell hole; many were death traps in which the wounded slipped and died. The only safe approaches to the line were over the duckboard tracks thrown over the mud loosely, which were trodden in and replaced often. Up these we had slipped and stumbled, while shells burst and smothered us with slimy liquid. I think we almost prayed for the attack and the consequent death, wound, or relief. It came on the zero hour with a crash of artillery fire that I heard as a stretcher bore me down to the dressing station. Within two hours I was lying between blankets, somewhere behind Ypres, in a large, comfortable marquee.

All I remember is pain and then dullness. I recollect lying in a huge corrugated-iron elephant-hut, where four doctors, stripped to their trouser-tops, worked like butchers on mangled men; the sweat streaming from them as they amputated some hopelessly shell-shattered limb; and, as fast as they worked, the ambulances rolled up that shelled road for their loads. I remember being jolted up and down on the stretcher to which I was strapped, hearing shells rushing over, and then the smoothness of a quiet road after the shell-torn *pavé* of Ypres.

P. Hoole Jackson joined the 6th Battalion Manchester Regt. (T.F.) in September 1914. Served in the Dardanelles campaign as a private soldier from May until October 1915. Invalided to Malta with slight wound and dysentery. 2nd Eastern General Hospital, Brighton, from November until January 1916. Rejoined Division in Egypt in May 1916. Served in the Sinai campaign as private soldier and scout. Took part in battle of Romani, when the Turkish second attempt on the Suez Canal was defeated with heavy loss to the enemy. Forced marches and desert fighting. In February sent to France. Served as scout to the brigade. Wounded and gassed in the Battle of Ypres of September to October 1917. Returned to battalion and served again as sniper and scout. Granted commission as second lieutenant in 1918, and attached to the Lancashire Fusiliers.

ON THE BELGIAN COAST

George Brame

I had not been in France more than a few weeks before I was detailed off with a permanent working party. My friend H. was also put into this section, and our acquaintance soon developed into the richest friendship. We were constantly together until he met his death.

About a dozen of us were eventually attached to the Royal Engineers' trench store dumps. Our activities began at Fresnoy. For the next three months we were kept fully occupied. No short time on this job! For the whole period I was there, I had only one half-day holiday.

It was easy to see where the money was going and why we were spending so many millions a day. The amount of hurdles, duckboards, barbed wire, etc., we turned out of that dump was enormous. I remember asking Sergeant M. how much we went through in a week, and he put the sum at £30,000.

Taken on the whole, my sojourn at this 'park' was fairly pleasant. I had a good billet, good food, and some good friends.

Orders at last arrived that we had to leave this place and take over a dump right on the Belgian coast. We soon realized the difference between Le Fresnoy and Nieuport-Baines. Instead of being able to work in the daytime, we had now to rush things through at night.

Well do I remember one incident which occurred shortly after we had taken over. My duty was to get materials ready for the troops in the trenches. A runner would be sent from the trenches with a chit for duckboards, hurdles, barbed wire, etc. This particular afternoon an orderly had brought a chit asking for a certain number of feet of timber 7 inches by 2l inches to be called for later, and I set out to get it ready for the fatigue party, which would call for it at night. This timber was kept in one of the shell-shattered villas on the front, in what had formerly been a bedroom. I measured the timber and instead of carrying the lengths down the stairs, I thought it would be easier to throw it out of the bedroom window. After sending three or four lengths out, and just as I was in the act of throwing another, I was almost blinded by a blast of lightning. I knew it was the bursting of a shell.

I had often heard it said that the shell which was meant for you always went about it quietly.

As soon as I was able to pick myself up I rushed from that unhealthy place like one possessed, and never stopped until I reached the safety of the subterranean passage running through the cellars of the house. I was certain that Jerry would follow the first up with another, but he did not.

When I was able to take my bearings, I noticed a man running towards me who seemed to be saying something, for his lips were moving as if in speech, but I could not hear a sound.

The explosion had deafened me.

'Cannot hear,' I said.

He came towards me, making a megaphone of his hands, and shouted, 'I thought of picking you up in bits.'

'Not yet,' said I; 'but it's been a near thing.'

We went out together and found the nose-cap of the shell on the ground underneath the window. I went back to the sergeant and reported the incident, still trembling through the shock, and he advised me to rest a few minutes and then carry on. I carried on.

It was the intention to make a big advance here, and if possible to drive the German Army out of Ostend. The enemy was not asleep, however, and just as we had got everything ready for the push, he opened out with a vengeance.

I shall never forget that terrific bombardment. I never experienced anything like it before or since. The shells were flying in all directions, heavies, lights, high explosives, armour-piercing shells of all calibres, some whistling overhead, to burst as far away as La Panne, others dropping in the village with a roar that shook the foundations of the earth.

Our only refuge was our billet, a most horrible and loathsome place – a cellar alive with cockroaches and other vermin. And there we were, cooped up like rats in a trap, waiting for we knew not what.

Hour after hour the awful bombardment raged. To venture out was certain death, for the enemy aircraft were dropping bombs and training their machine guns on to the cellars. And we were without ammunition.

Evening came, and still the shells were dropping as fiercely as ever. Midnight arrived without the slightest cessation in his devilish artillery fire. The cry rang out, 'Will it never end?' One soldier cried 'Can't we run for it?'

'Where can we run to?' asked Sergeant M. 'There must be no running or moving until we receive orders to that effect' – a thing that was impossible, for we learnt afterwards that all lines of communication had been cut.

The tempest raged all through the night. No one slept; every man was waiting to be captured or slaughtered by the foe. The enemy now changed his tactics, and, in place of his high explosives, he turned upon us his new and diabolical mustard gas. The order went through the dungeons, 'Gas! All men put on your masks.' For four hours we had to keep them on.

As day was beginning to dawn, the twenty-four hours' awful tornado ceased. What a transformation met my eyes when I went out for a breath of air. Houses, theatre, Casino, the Church were levelled to the ground. During the day we learnt that two thousand of our lads had been slaughtered or taken prisoners. In fact, every soldier on the other side of the Yser Canal, excepting one or two, was rendered *hors de combat.*

The result of Jerry's attack drove us out of the village, and we attempted to establish a dump at Laitre Royale.

Every night a train of five trucks, loaded up with trees, pit-props, hurdles, elephant shelters, etc., came to the dump.

It was whilst engaged on the task of unloading the train that I lost my pal H. We were carrying the pickets, etc., into the dump, a matter of some 20 or 30 yards, and were making good progress with the work, for so far there had been little shelling. We were congratulating ourselves that we were going to have a quiet night when Jerry opened out.

I heard a shell coming, and before I had time to fall, the shell burst with a terrifying crash. The concussion sent me headlong over the rails. In an instant I was on my feet, and rushed off to the gable end of Laitre Royale for cover. When I got there I found that H. and a few more of the working party were already there.

The shelling soon became violent, and it was obvious that Jerry was after the dump.. for the shells were gradually closing in upon us.

I turned to H. and told him that I was going to make for the covered communication trench, which was about 100 yards away, as I thought it would be safer there than where we were.

'I think we are better here,' said H. 'He will have to blow this house over before he can get us.'

'If you think you are safer here you had better stay, but I'm off for the tunnel,' and, after waiting until the next shell burst, I made for the trench. I had just got about a third of the way when I heard another shell coming which exploded some yards distant. I flung myself to the ground before it burst. Thinking I might gain the trench before another arrived, I picked myself up and made a spurt, but before I reached that harbour of refuge, another was on me, and such was the effect of the concussion that it lifted me clean off my feet and pitched me over a stack of wire some 3 feet from the ground. I again attempted to reach the tunnel, when I heard H. calling me.

Retracing my steps, I found my friend lying on the ground in great pain.

'What's the matter, H.?' I enquired.

'The square-headed b – has got me this time, George.'

'Where are you hit?'

'Right in my back.'

'Do you think you can manage to get to the trench if I help you?'

'I'll try, George.'

Stooping down, I put his arm round my neck and assisted him into the trench. How we got there I never knew, for the shelling became intense, and the shells dropped round us like hailstones. Having got him under some semblance of cover, I asked him how he felt.

'George, I am done.'

I tried to' comfort him by telling him they would soon put him right when he got to hospital.

'No, Jerry's done me this time.'

Stretching out his hand and placing it into mine, he said, 'George, you have been the best pal I've had. I want you to write to my wife and mother and tell them that I died doing my duty.'

'No, no,' said I. 'But I'll write and tell them that you are wounded and that you are in hospital.'

'But what's your address?' I asked him.

He motioned to me to feel in his tunic pocket. I did so and took some of the letters he had there.

I could see that he was mortally wounded. Every time he spoke blood spurted out of his mouth.

'One more thing I want you to do for me,' he said.

'What's that, H.?'

'Pray for me now.'

'I am not much used to praying, H.,' I replied, 'but I'll do my best.'

I knelt down and offered up a simple prayer, and I was conscious that the prayer was received. My friend again seized my hand and thanked and blessed me. The stretcher bearers arrived, placed him upon it, took him to the dressing station, and I saw him no more.

After three months there, with never a rest, I was ordered to rejoin my battalion, which was about to go over at Passchendaele.

When I reported to the sergeant-major, he said, 'You'll see some *soldiering* now.' I smiled, for I considered I had received my baptism of fire.

When we went over the top the sergeant-major was miles behind the line *soldiering* at forming an echelon.

We had scarcely got there before we were making ready for the grand assault. Our officer came to make an inspection of us. In my section there were ten soldiers, differing in many respects: some taking it as an adventure; one or two were developing nerves – none more so than the lance-corporal who was supposed to be in charge of us.

The officer asked us if there was anything we required.

I replied asking if we might be allowed to give our rifles a 'pull through.' We had constantly been falling into the mud during the twelve hours' march, owing to the terrible state of the roads, with the result that our rifles were covered with dirt.

'Oh, no,' said he. 'You have no time to do that. You must be up and over at once.'

'But who's going to lead us?' asked one of the squad. 'Surely you do not expect us to go over with W. in charge. Look at him; he's frightened to death.'

True, poor W. was in a bad way; his face was the picture of death. I felt sorry for him, for it was evident that he was feeling his responsibility. In the section was a soldier who had recently been reduced from corporal. The officer turned to him and asked him if he would take charge of the section. He replied that he did not wish to go over the head of the lance-corporal.

And there we stood, arguing the point as to who should lead. The situation appeared so ludicrous to me that, in spite of the awful carnage that was going on around, I burst out laughing. The ex-corporal noticed me, and immediately struck a dramatic pose. Brandishing his rifle in the air, he cried, 'Follow me, boys, I'll pull you through. This is no laughing matter – it's the real thing!'

The situation was so funny, I could not help laughing louder still. Here we were, in the midst of our own barrage and the German barrage. Shells were falling round us and taking their toll of human lives. And we were being entreated to look upon it as the 'real thing.'

The officer came to us once more, and, taking the matter into his own hands, cried out in an heroic tone, 'Follow me.' He rushed off, pointing his revolver into the air, shouting, 'There is your objective; take it.' He then began to fire into the clouds and it struck me he must be trying to kill skylarks. Had it not been so tragical, it would have been a farce.

We followed as best we could. We had not gone far before we had to plunge into the sodden ground. Someone gave the alarm 'Gas!' and we struggled into our gas-masks. No sooner had we got them on than the officer ordered us to take them off as there was no gas.

We advanced in rushes, and on looking round I found we were mixed up with men of another battalion. An officer approached me and asked who I belonged to. I told him the 5th East Lancs. 'Come on,' says he, 'follow this sergeant; you will be all right.'

I kept up with my fresh non-com. until, passing over a shell hole, I felt something like a red-hot needle go through my shin. It dropped me into that hole, one foot resting on the other, and I realized that I was wounded.

The sergeant asked me what was the matter. I told him I was hit, but advised him to go on as I thought I could manage.

It was not until I tried to liberate myself that I found out what a trap I was in. The shell hole was full of mud, slime, and barbed wire, and for three hours I was held there as if in a vice. I felt myself gradually being sucked under. The slime was rising higher and higher, until I found it above my waist. My cries for help were unheeded. I suppose every man had as much as he could do to look after himself.

When I was giving myself up for lost, a lad from the 4th East Lancs saw the plight I was in, and came and rescued me from that awful death.

If he did not win the V.C. that day, he won the eternal gratitude of the soldier he had liberated.

Whilst in that hole, I heard a heavy thud, and, looking up, I saw a soldier crouching on the top. I told him not to stay there, as Jerry had got me there. Then I noticed that he had been hit behind the ear. He must have been killed instantly.

This soldier, who was a sergeant wearing a green flash, was of the same battalion as the soldier who came to my rescue. I pointed him out to my friend and told him that he was killed and fell like an ox. He looked up and recognized the sergeant, then turned to me and said, 'It's Sergeant R. It serves the b – right.' I knew what he meant. I had had some myself.

The wound which I received got me back to Blighty, and, among thousands of others that day, I counted myself very fortunate.

Private George Brame joined up under the Derby Scheme in 1916. Drafted to Colchester in the 2/5th Battalion East Lancashire (Territorial) Regt., 66th Division. The Division arrived in France early in March 1917. They took over the line on the Givenchy and Festubert front. In April became attached to the Royal Engineers and served in the dump at Le Fresnoy. A few weeks afterwards, transferred to Nieuport-Baines. Rejoined battalion in the autumn of 1917. Went over the top with them in the Passchendaele attack, and was rather badly wounded. Remained in hospital until April 1918, having undergone two operations. Again in France, November 1918, in 1/5th East Lancashires. After the Armistice was billeted at Gilley, Charleroi, and worked in the demobilization office until April 1919.

A NIGHTMARE

Alan F. Hyder

Lark, a weazened, foul-mouthed, little lump of unconscious Cockney heroism, nicknamed under the usual order of such things 'Sparrer,' lies o' nights untroubled, I suspect, by any nightmares occasioned by his part in the blood-spewing earthquake of eleven years ago that made his Whitechapel of to-day fit for heroes to live in. His job done, it is forgotten, except perhaps for periodical arguments in the public bar of his 'Local' as to the exact position in Étaples of a certain Red Lamp. Lucky man, may his shadow, always attenuated, never grow less.

A fair enough bricklayer by trade, he preferred the hawking of rags and bones, getting thereby more scope for his genius in winning unconsidered trifles from areas and back entrances. During the War, as a member of His Majesty's Corps of Royal Engineers, he was very much in demand. Was there a shortage of rum, Sparrer would casually stroll into the blue, and reappear shortly, clasping to his meagre person a large stone jar of S.R.D., won from some Army Service Corps quarter-master, preferably a very stout Q.M., who was actually in the act of sitting upon the said stone jar. Was there a sap-head made uninhabitable by cannily aimed stick bombs for its sniper inhabitant, Sparrer, using his skill as a bricklayer, feverishly, in the blue mist caused by perspiration and his carefully whispered comments on stick bombs, Jerry, and the world in general, rapidly rendered it safe again.

This goes to explain why, on a November night during the latter part of the War, he was detailed off with me for a job of work that left Sparrer's ensuing nights serenely untroubled, but mine...!

A minor operation close to 'Plug Street' had pushed our line forward, and we held a patch of land, horse-shoe-shaped, upon which alighted many screaming messengers of death despatched from all points of the compass except that directly behind us. Altogether, during its frequent spasms of playfulness it was as nice a little slaughtering place as any on the Western Front.

In the midst of this plot, but nearer our lines than the German, half buried by indescribable debris, lay a captured Jerry pillbox. This massive structure, its walls 4 or 5 feet in thickness, consisted of a room some 9 feet square, loop-holed for a machine gun, with a single door that, by the thickness of the walls, was actually a small tunnel, perhaps 18 inches wide by 4 feet high. It had its loop-hole peering towards the British lines, whilst its exit stared Berlin-wards. The desirable residence having been acquired by us, this lay-out had to be reversed before the place could be occupied without nasty things arriving through the front door.

So, behold Sparrer and I on the spot with instructions from the original of all 'Mad Majors' to cut an exit facing our lines, a loop-hole facing Fritz, and using the concrete therefrom to block up the existing apertures.

It was a beautiful night when (after making sure the word was passed along the trench that we were out in front, and the sentries were to greet us as friends on our return) Sparrer and I crawled over the top, under our barbed wire, and proceeded through No Man's Land towards our pillbox.

Half a dozen yards from our front line we were alone – two specks in a vast dark void, its unseen horizon an encircling flitter of light from the distant guns. In our sector things were extraordinarily quiet, except for the occasional 'Phut!' from the rifle of a bored sentry on either side. Yet it was a curious night, in which the major sounds, the throb and rumble of far-off artillery, the stuttering of a Lewis gun, seemed muffled and deadened, whilst the minor noises, the thin chinkle of an empty beef tin carelessly tossed into barbed wire, the faint squelch of stench rising in slow bubbles from the noisome pool in an old shell hole, were magnified into weird whisperings and stifled sighs.

A night for spirits to be abroad, and Sparrer and I could have done with some, the genii for preference that rises from out a jar (S.R.D.) and bestows cheer and courage as its magic potion. Later that night when the admirable Sparrer supplied our needs out of a mud-encrusted tin mug I needed that rum, I tell you.

The ground having been recently fought over, going was hard, but eventually we reached our objective. The pillbox, with its chattering machine gun mowing down approaching troops, had attracted the attention of many shells, and evidently a German doctor had shared the room with its gun crew, rendering first aid; whilst many wounded sheltering in the lee of its concrete walls had been caught by our guns. The place inside and out was a shambles. Outside, a churned-up mixture of limbs, trenching tools, rapidly decaying bodies, fragments of accoutrements, mud, and foul slime. Inside, a welter of what had been, perhaps, six men, lying disjointedly in a foot of discoloured water.

With the aid of a carefully shielded electric torch I discovered that the place could be drained of water by clearing around the entrance and through the tunnel; so with a couple of long-handled German shovels Sparrer and I set to work, throwing the filth on each side of a low bank, using both our shovels to lift a rotting body, pushing it as far over the bank as possible, balancing a severed arm, dimly phosphorescent in the dark, on the shovel blade and hurling it away in the manner of a lacrosse player, Sparrer humming gently a song of his own,

I am a lavatory attendant,

I live in a W.C.

'For God's sake, Sparrer!' I chide him, and we work on in silence. The entrance cleared we start on the tunnel and, as the water gradually flows out, guide, and ease the floating remains of the gun crew through the exit, and heave them over the bank.

The slime on the floor scraped together and flung out through the doorway, the stench visibly abates, and I sit down on an unsmashed case of first-aid appliances and gratefully light a cigarette from Sparrer's proffered glowing fag-end.

'A mucking fine war,' says Sparrer, 'living in – dying in – and becoming – arter yer blinking well dead. Why, one of them blokes we just flung art 'ad an 'andful of white maggots in 'is trarser pockets. 'Ho, yus,' says some beggaring Brigadier back in 'eadquarters, 'anding 'is shampine glass to 'is servant hand putting 'is lilywhite finger on the map, 'a pillbox! 'Ow nace! We really must secure that, what!' An' 'ere's you an' me smothered in – finking abart cutting froo 6 foot of reinforced concrete wiv an 'ammer as wouldn't crack a louse on the sergeant-major's neck an' a cold chisel wot I dropped coming along that – communication trench.'

'Good Lord! Sparrer, haven't you got the chisel?' I asked in dismay. 'How the hell are we going to try to do something? Still the work we've just done is sufficient for me, and if the major happens along we can spruce him clearing the place was a long job.'

'Is that old grass'opper coming arahnd?''

'He didn't actually say so, but you know how he likes springing the unexpected. So it will be advisable for us to stop here until just before dawn in case he does, even though we can't do anything. But, tell you what, Sparrer, it wouldn't be a bad scheme if you slid off back to the line and scrounged a couple of tots of rum. If the major should flash his monocle round the corner I'll be able to explain your absence.'

'I'll bring some back, corp, even if I 'ave ter wham the Quarter-bloke over the ead wiv a pick 'elve, an' I won't be mor'n ten minutes.'

And with a 'Cheerio!' Sparrer slipped into his equipment, picked up his gun, and departed.

Squatting on the case of medical stuff, I leant my back against the concrete wall and prepared myself for a dreary wait in the darkness, pitch black in the pillbox, until my confederate returned.

Perhaps fifteen minutes after Sparrer's departure, things suddenly happened. Without the slightest warning Jerry dropped a box barrage on that part of the line exactly behind my pillbox! The lay of land at this point made it easier for Jerry to raid our line than for us to reach his.

Sitting there in the darkness; listening to the screaming,

crashing inferno that had so suddenly shattered the night, I reasoned that it was unlikely for the Germans to visit the pillbox, though they probably would pass within a few yards of it on their way to and from our line. Gradually, our artillery thundered into retaliation in response, no doubt, to urgent appeals from our front line. The bombardment swelled, roared, and then, nearly as suddenly as it had begun, died out. The crackle of rifle and machine gun faded away, and peace in this sector reigned again. Verey lights, fired every few minutes, showing that, although the cannonade had stopped, the line was still alert, hung high in the air, lighting the landscape in a pale glimmer, sank and died away.

But for knowing that Sparrer was sure to return, I'd have gone back to the line, for I was pretty windy, and even then I was in two minds about it, when a peculiar noise outside brought me to my feet, tense and listening. Someone undoubtedly approaching the pillbox. Stealthily, almost silently, as though creeping! Sparrer? No! He would have returned carefully, it is true, but not in this slow fashion. Besides, he would have whispered a greeting! Closer and closer he, it, or whatever the thing was, came, silently crawling.

I was in a quandary. Leaving the pillbox might mean running into a party of Jerries – then Good-night! Lying doggo was all right if whatever it was passed by, but if my presence was suspected then also Good-night! A bomb tossed in that pillbox would have turned me into pictures on the wall!

Little icy-cold drops of sweat ran down my spine, as, with rather a shaky hand, fumbling in the darkness, I silently slid back the safety catch of my rifle and, drawing the bolt, saw to it that a cartridge was in the breach.

Challenging was not to be risked, for I was like a rat in a trap, and the eerie sound came nearer, a rustling sliding as of someone crawling belly-to-earth for a yard or two, then silence, as though he had stopped to listen. Tiptoeing slowly across the room to the corner opposite the entrance, I flattened against the wall, rifle covering the entrance.

The Verey lights fired now and then shone down the tunnel,

cutting a shaft of white light through the pillbox, leaving the rest in pitch blackness.

With beating heart and dry lips, I listened... He was outside the entrance... Then, as I strove to pierce the darkness, I realized that someone was creeping down the tunnel... Silence; though it seemed to me my beating heart must tell the world I was there and in a hell of a funk.

A Verey light glared, grew brighter, and there down on the floor, peering into the pillbox, was a white face, the top portion black under the shadow from the grim German steel helmet. Crack! Clang! I put two shots through it. Then, my ears ringing from the shots in that confined space, the Verey light died down. Silence and darkness! Were there any more out there? I sweated and waited for the expected bomb to arrive. But no! Another Verey light shone, and there was that ghastly head, peering up from the floor.

Stepping forward to get out in the open again, I was halted by the sound of someone else approaching, but walking, not creeping.

'Rum up, corp,' said a cheery voice at the entrance, and Sparrer stepped down the tunnel to stumble over the dead Fritz.

'Blimy! Wot's this?'

'It's all right, Sparrer. Did you see any Jerries out there?'

'No, but the blighters came over on a raid. Never 'ad no luck, though, and went 'ome again. Wot's that bloke in the passidge?'

'He's one that didn't go home, Sparrer. Let's pull him in and have a look at him.'

We pull the body into the pillbox and I switch the torch on him. One bullet hole through his temple and another through his jaw under the ear. Then, as I throw the pencil of light down his body, I understand.

His left leg is badly smashed, half covered by a bloodsoaked bandage with the white of bone protruding from hanging lumps of flesh. He had come over with his raiding party, stopped a piece of shell and crawled into the pillbox, perhaps to die; perhaps for safety.

I had shot him.

'Well, yer might 'a' shot 'im art in the open, corp. We've only got ter fling the poor sod art again.'

'Sparrer' I cut in... 'Did you manage to scrounge any rum?'

'Me nime being what hit is, I not only got some Nelson's blood, but I got a water-bottle full of 'ot tea aswell.'

'You can have the hot tea, Sparrer. For Christ's sake give me a swig at that rum, and then we'll get to hell out of this.'

'An' s'posing the major comes, corp?'

'And to hell with him as well, Sparrer!'

Twelve years ago, and still at night sometimes comes a sweat that wakes me by its deathly chill to hear again that creeping, creeping.

Alan F. Hyder, an 'Old Contemptible.' War service in France 1914 to 1918.

A CAVALRY BRIGADE AT CAMBRAI

November 1917

Chris Knight

Our cavalry brigade arrived in Peronne in November 1917, after a long trek up from billets. We had had a fairly easy time during the summer of that year. For a few months we had been dismounted and had been up at Vimy Ridge doing all sorts of work: digging reserve trenches, reinforcing communication trenches and digging new ones – in fact, doing real navvy work, which, on the whole, was enjoyable, as far as anything could be enjoyable in France during the War. The weather was good, rations were plentiful, though the water had a wicked taste.

The front line was far enough away then to allow us to have concert parties in the evening, when we could stretch out on the grass and have our beer brought to us from the canteen. We sang songs, told yarns, and played cards. In the words of Flynn Mitchell, we were having a 'hell of a time.' Although there was plenty of work, life was bearable.

There are doubtless plenty of men still living who will remember Roclincourt and Ecurie Camp during the summer of 1917. Those of you who know that sector will remember Essex Walk – the duckboard track – and Ouse Alley, Tired Alley, and the Oppy Switch. It was along these that we trekked to our nightly tasks, at which we sweated and grumbled; and it was along these that we trekked back after we had finished, at two, three, and four o'clock in the morning. We had to get away before daybreak, under the ever-friendly cover of Ouse Alley. Where this communication emerged there was a water tank, our welcome half-way rest.

This sojourn at Vimy ended only too soon. One evening dozens of lorries lined up at Labyrinth Avenue, and we returned to our horses. At last the cavalry was to be used in its proper capacity. Great preparations were going on for the Passchendaele stunt. We-trekked up to Dickebusch, stayed there for a couple of days, and came back to the very billets we had deserted. Then we heard that we were to take Cambrai. We arrived in Peronne, as I have said, in November 1917.

The great offensive was to begin on the 20th, Meanwhile, officers and N.C.O.s were being given instructions. New maps were issued to section leaders; the types of aeroplanes that were going to work with us were explained, and the streamers and the colour of the Verey lights. On the night of the 19th we moved off at a walk. It was pitch dark and approaching midnight. 'March at ease, but no smoking' was the order, and later on, 'No talking.' All that could be heard was the clip-clop of horses' feet, creaking of saddlery and champing of bits. Now and again the sound of a muffled cough. Fins was the rendezvous. We got there about 3 a.m., and off-saddled.

Zero hour was 6 a.m.

I was detailed for fodder fatigue. To get to the limbers we had to go through the lines of several regiments, and here I saw men with whom I had been training in 1914 in barracks in England. All our cavalry in France was concentrated at this rendezvous. I had never seen so many horses and men together at one parade. It was an awe-inspiring sight. Dragoons, Lancers, Hussars – they were all there, as well as Indian mounted troops. The 'saddle-up' went for an Indian brigade first. By this time the bombardment was heavy. Tanks and infantry were well on their way to the Hindenburg Line, the supposed impregnable trench. Rumours had already reached us that this trench was taken. The Indian brigade disappeared over the Ridge in column of troop. Prisoners were coming towards us. A good sign. Everybody seemed in high spirits.

Saddle-up came for our brigade next. We moved off in column of troop. We crossed the Hindenburg Line fairly early in the morning. Many tanks had got across, but several had been put out of action and were lying derelict.

Seemingly we marched for hours, without a sign of the enemy, except for prisoners. We went through captured villages two abreast. In the afternoon we received a check, but no Germans were in sight. Only their artillery was in evidence. We took cover behind a battered hedge. Our troop lost a couple of horses there. They had to be destroyed after being wounded.

All the afternoon we moved about, trotting here, galloping there, scarcely knowing in what direction the enemy was by this time. Towards dusk we halted and dismounted on the borders of a village. There were many prisoners here, looking at us with fixed gaze. Some had a cynical smile upon their faces, some looked dejected, while others simply grinned. Later, we moved off at a walk, and, coming to an open field by the roadside, we again dismounted. It was raining. A dismal rain. Real November stuff that gradually wetted us through until eventually we could feel it trickling through our puttees. For hours we stood by our horses. Then, at midnight, we were told to off-saddle and peg down for the night. The prospect was by no means a cheerful one, but we lay down behind the horses to get what little sleep we could.

Two or three hours later I was aroused by a savage dig in the ribs. My section corporal had been told to get in some ammunition that had been dumped by the roadside, so, with several others, I was kicked into a state of somnambulism, and we trudged down the road for about half a mile in one of the blackest nights that I can remember. We sweated, we grumbled, and we cursed. But the job had to be done. Our Hotchkiss gun team would need this ammunition tomorrow. Tomorrow came. It was still raining.

At daybreak we went on fodder fatigue, replenished nosebags, had a bully-beef and biscuit breakfast, and went forward once more. Early in the afternoon our regiment lined up in a sunken road in front of a small village. The enemy was there. We were to drive him out. Enemy 'planes had spotted us though. Enemy shells were plentiful. Lieutenant T. galloped along the rear, at the same time shouting, 'See that your swords are loose.'

We sat tense in our saddles, waiting for the order to go forward. Everybody was 'keyed up.' Would the order ever come? Now, after the lapse of a dozen years, I try to recall some of my thoughts and emotions during those moments. I was young then, very young indeed to be a cavalryman. Barely twenty, and there were men in my troop who had campaigned in South Africa. There I sat astride a powerful bay, wondering whether he would keep his feet in the plunge that was to come, or whether he would fall in the morass; whether we should both come back triumphant or whether I should come back carrying my saddle. It never occurred to me that I should not come back.

At last the orders came: 'Half-sections right, walk march! Form sections! Head, left wheel! Draw swords! Trot! Form troop! Form column of half squadron! Gallop!'

The village lay about three-quarters of a mile away. We galloped fiercely to the outskirts, rapidly formed sections and got on to the road, numbers 1 and 2 troops cantering into the village first. Donelly, the Irishman, went, raving mad, cutting and thrusting wildly at retreating Germans.

Indescribable scenes followed.

The order came to dismount. Germans emerged from dug-outs in all directions, some giving themselves up, others making a fight of it with a few bombs. No. 1 troop received the bombs in its midst. The bomb-throwers were accounted for with rifle and revolver.

We took many prisoners, but the major portion of the garrison holding, the village had cleared out before we arrived. Very soon their machine guns were in action again, and shells were dropping in and behind the village. I, being No. 3 of a section, was a horse-holder and had to take four horses to the rear. All except No. 3s manned the trenches. Then followed a night of anguish. A week in the front-line trenches is better than one night as a horse-holder under shell-fire. What can one man do with four terrified horses? Nothing, except keep them together as much as possible. If shells burst behind they lunge forward. If shells burst ahead they go back on their haunches, nearly pulling your arms out of their sockets.

It is a constant worry of body and mind to keep them in some sort of order. Towards midnight the shelling died down. Said our shoeing-smith corporal, 'We'd better give 'em a feed.'

And we did – after a struggle. These horses were hungry and thirsty. Neither horses nor men had had anything to eat since early morning. The 'shoey' said 'Don't let 'em eat it all.' But to stop them was the thing. Once the nosebags were on they took good care we didn't take them off again until they were empty! No. 2 of my section, a noted glutton, finished his corn first. Not being content with his feed, he had licked all the paint from a bully-beef tin that his owner had placed in the nosebag for safety. Two candles also fell victims to his voracity.

Just before daybreak orders came to take the horses further back. We retreated out of gun-fire range and hung about all that day. Late that night our comrades in the trenches were relieved. They joined us about midnight. There were many empty saddles. I led Corporal Smith's horse. Smith, the lucky devil, had received a 'Blighty' wound. His horse would have a new owner with the next draft.

We got back to Metz at 3 a.m., watered and fed, and then got down behind the horse-lines in a drizzling rain. Réveillé at 6 a.m. Rations came up for a full regiment. It worked out at two to a loaf, instead of three or four. Full stomachs improved our spirits. But what mud! Up to our knees at the water troughs. No attempt was made at grooming. 'Leave the mud on,' the squadron leader said, 'help to keep them warm.'

Rumours were now flying about that we were to move up, dismounted. At dusk, orders came to be in readiness at a moment's notice – one man to a troop of horses to stay behind. Eight, nine, ten o'clock came, but no order to 'fall in.' 'Let's get down to it,' said Nobby Clarke, and we were just dozing off when 'Fall in' sounded. We grumbled and cursed at the fates that had beguiled us. If we had kept awake the situation would not have been so bad. As it was, we could barely rouse ourselves.

It was about 11 p.m. and inky black. Our blankets, rolled in ground-sheets, were worn bandolier-fashion over our ammunition bandoliers. (A cavalryman working as an infantryman is an awkward-looking creature. He has to wear kit which would otherwise be worn by the horse.) We fell in, numbered off, and started on a night trek up to the line. We travelled along a very rough road, stumbling and slithering for hours. Then after a time we left the road and started across country in single file. Many times the rear files would lose contact with the front files, only to get into touch again in the most unexpected places. It was a night of blasphemous utterances. Our thoughts dwelt too much on comfortable beds – beds at home, beds in barracks, and even beds of straw in barns behind the line.

In quiet retrospect, one does not regret the experience, but at the time!…

At 6 a.m., or perhaps a little later (for I remember the dawn coming shortly afterwards), we arrived in a sunken road near some old trenches, where we rested awhile. The rain increased, and after the sweating on the march, we were becoming clammy and cold.

Later in the morning we moved into an old trench, quite habitable, but within nice range for the enemy artillery. Still, he did not worry us overmuch. Our worst trouble was no water. There was a well down in the village on our right front, but not until dusk would we venture out. Rudge and I took several water bottles with us, as well as a couple of petrol tins. At the well we had to get on the end of a long queue of infantrymen. One of these wished to God he could get another 'Blighty one,' and he already wore three wound stripes!

The well was deep, and the windlass was not all that could be desired. A petrol tin served at the end of a wire rope – one of our canvas buckets would have served much better. Still, a couple of hours' wait in France was neither here nor there.

Orders now came that we were to take over a part of the front line. Our headquarters were made in a sugar refinery by the side of the main Bapaume-Cambrai road, which was being pounded by heavy artillery fire. There was a putrid smell of dead horses and mules.

Leaving the road in sections at intervals, we entered a field where gas shells were dropping. (To the uninitiated they had a sound like 'duds.' I had learned my lesson earlier.) By keeping well to the right, we were quite safe, for a north-easterly breeze carried the gas away from us.

After reaching the line in safety, our men were deposited in pot-holes, there being no continuous trench. We appeared to be in a deep salient, for the enemy flares seemed to form a semicircle.

When our men had been posted, I returned to headquarters with Captain K. 'Keep your eyes skinned,' he said. 'The Boche will be sure to have patrols out to-night.'

There was machine-gun fire and desultory rifle-fire. Dead men lay all round. Yet we managed to get back to the sugar refinery. 'Get under your blanket for the night,' said Captain K. I eagerly obeyed. In less than half an hour I was shaken by the shoulder. 'Come on. Message for front line.' I went along the road to a dug-out for orders. Letter for Lieutenant H. 'Tell men to eat emergency ration. Use ammunition sparingly.'

I once more began a weary tramp to the line, with Bourlon Wood on my right front. I found Lieutenant H. and delivered my message. He gave me a drink from his flask and said, 'I don't suppose it will take you long to get back.' 'No, sir,' I replied. 'It ought not to take long.' I retraced my steps, glad at the thought that I should now at long last be able to get some sleep. I had not had any worth speaking of for four days.

Trudging along with rifle slung over shoulder, I suddenly saw looming ahead of me five or six dim figures. Captain K.'s words flashed through my mind: 'Keep your eyes skinned.'

A cold shudder chilled me to the bone. They were Germans!

Now, as I think of those moments, my heart beats harder. When faced with death, man's mind instinctively escapes from the scene and dwells in other realms. For one brief moment I was home on leave from Cambrai. I saw my mother's face. Then I was being stripped of rifle, bayonet, and ammunition. Soon I was in the German front-line trench. An officer was informed that a prisoner had been brought in. He came out from a covered-in shelf that was cut in the trench. In his hand he held what appeared to be a revolver, and was loading it. He was going to finish me? He fired. It was a Verey light pistol!

I was sent back with an escort, but not before being relieved of a precious packet of cigarettes.

The reserve trenches were well made, but the smell in the dug-out was horrid. The stink of flesh – sweating flesh of men who had not washed for weeks. Some snored on wire mattresses. Some sat up smoking. Others were killing lice.

I was taken, in fear and dread, to the officers' quarters. At a rough table a typical German officer sat writing. For a few moments I awaited my fate. Suddenly the officer looked up and, to my amazement, flashed at me the greeting: 'Good evening, Lloyd George.' He smiled at my astonishment. I knew then. I was safe.

A close cross-examination followed. Finding this of little avail, he next examined my pay-book. But even this did not reveal a lot, except that I was acting as an infantryman.

Being sent farther back, I arrived with an escort – two youngsters about my own age – at divisional headquarters. I flopped down, dead beat, on a dug-out floor. The telephone operator would not let me sleep. He began eagerly to enlighten me as to his past. He had been a waiter in London for years, and he now greatly missed the English breakfasts – porridge, bacon and eggs, marmalade and rolls. 'Yes, Tommy, English breakfasts good. Ach! this bloody war.' Another escort arrived. I went on to Germany.

Private Chris Knight, joined 6th Dragoon Guards (Carabineers) September 3rd, 1914. Sent to 3rd Reserve Cavalry Regt. at Canterbury. After training, employed in remount depot. In 1915 sent to 2nd Reserve Cavalry Regt. at Aldershot. 1916, transferred to King's Shropshire Light Infantry. Went to France. Passed through infantry training on Bull-Ring, but was transferred back to cavalry (2nd Dragoon Guards) as a specialist. Served on several parts of Western Front until taken prisoner at the Cambrai battle, November 1917. In Germany for thirteen months: Munster, Westphalia, Parchim, Mecklenberg, Springhirsch, Schleswig-Holstein. Returned home two months after Armistice.

LA VACQUERIE

December 3rd, 1917

W. R. Dick

We are marching up the line, 500 strong, trudging past the chalk mounds of the great mine crater at Trescault. Directly ahead the enemy gun flashes flare against the eastern night; our own guns answer without strength.

We pass a huge German howitzer, its heavy underframe incredibly twisted by a direct hit; beyond lies a derelict ambulance car. I am chiefly conscious of many feet squelching and splashing, of mud ruts and shell holes, the dark figures of the men in front, of wind-swept darkness and the quick red flashes of the German gun-fire. Shells drone over right and left and fall with heavy crashes, but they are well clear of our road.

We plough our dreary path onward at a steady pace. The water-laden petrol tin I am carrying pulls down my arm till the sinews ache. I change it frequently, but it drags like a lead weight. I wish fervently I could dump it.

We halt for a breather and squat on the low bank of this churned mud track. From the direction of the line we hear footsteps approaching – heavy labouring feet – and, as they splash slowly nearer, a man groaning at intervals marks their progress. The party of stretcher bearers looms level, shoulders bowed, we see four recumbent figures borne aloft, and against the flashes of the guns and the distant glow of the flares, I see a figure twisting and turning and the swaying, stumbling bearers striving to hold him still. We move on again. The road gradually slopes down between high banks. Here the darkness is acute; in the inky pit only the water and mud underfoot seem tangible, and we grope and slip and curse. Our eyes grow more accustomed to this denser gloom, the forward movement becomes faster, only to slow down in response to warning shouts from the front. 'Keep to the left!'

The file closes in to the left bank, and I see that the centre of the road is blocked by a dark mass. A sickly reek pervades the air as we skirt a trail of wreckage, a couple of splintered limbers, the black rounded heaps that are dead mules, and some of the passing feet ring against a steel helmet half crushed in the mud. I am thankful for the merciful darkness.

Piles of stretchers, cheerful chinks of light, litters of discarded dressings trampled underfoot, and the sharp odour of iodine mark the advanced dressing station. Further on, a long stream of walking wounded splash by us, while the night resounds to the heavy crashes of the shells.

At last we move out of the ruts and soft mud on to the battered stony surface of a road that slopes easily upward. A dead pannier mule lies athwart our track; a few yards beyond a man is sprawled in the gutter, his head, a dark ball, lies two or three feet away.

Directly in front I see a trail of red sparks soar above the ridge, a radiant star appears, which sinks slowly out of sight and leaves in black silhouette the ragged sprawl of ruins on the crest. By the glow of the flares we avoid tripping over the stretcher with its officer occupant, a khaki handkerchief spread over his face held in position by his helmet, a grim note of refinement in contrast to the other forms we have passed. On through the flickering shadows of La Vacquerie, to plunge again into gloomy depths of a sunken road. It is deep with treacherous mud, water sodden; a foot-wide squelching track presses us to the left bank.

There is a block. We are crushed together in single file in pitch darkness. A man behind growls anxiously, 'Get a move on in front.'

'Shut up,' is the retort. 'A man is sunk in the mud here.'

'Pull him out, or tread the blighter in then, but let's get out of here.'

An officer is calling anxiously from the far bank, 'Come along, men, don't lose touch, for Heaven's sake!'

The deeply bogged man is plucked out by two men heaving on an extended rifle. We escape from the foul pit and rush frantically over shell-churned ground to regain contact. A wide trench yawns darkly below our feet.

It is a deep trench, lately German – a trench in which the air is heavy with a peculiar odour, not only of earth or rotting sand-bags, but a clinging sickly taint.

At irregular intervals in the deep shadow of the trench bottom lie the dead, some sitting with rigid legs sprawled out, some crouching into the trench wall, some huddled together in pairs. We step carefully, then, without warning, a series of fierce shrieks springs from the night, a mad tattoo of ringing crashes hammers about the trench top. The living crouch down with the dead, and showers of earth and stones rain upon us.

A handful of weary men start to edge by us, but another storm bursts along the parapet. Again we cower in dread companionship. Again and again the savage crashes drum viciously just above our heads.

One of the remnants of the company we have relieved mutters grimly, 'You'll have worse than that before morning, mates.'

Double sentries mount the fire-steps, and the night wears on to the constant hissing of the German flares, rising and falling, flooding the trench top with a cold white light. Occasionally a burst of machine-gun fire screams harshly along the parapet.

About four o'clock, stiff and weary, I rear up on the fire-step.

For some time the machine guns opposite have ceased fire, the flares have dwindled, until a heavy darkness broods over the sector, and I peer into a black void.

It is the cold lifeless hour before the dawn; the night presses solidly down. An uncanny quiet pervades the enemy trenches.

I hear footsteps in the trench below me, and the company officer's voice: 'Too quiet altogether, sergeant-major. Something brewing over there. Get the men roused out. 'Stand to' in twenty minutes, in any case.'

The men emerge from the shafts and corners, cold and cramped, and line along the trench, gradually sensing the mysterious stillness of the German front line.

Eastward a vague diffused greyness has appeared, spreading imperceptibly. My neighbour leans more comfortably on the parapet. 'Roll on, daylight,' he mutters. 'It's – What the hell's that?'

Well along to our right a rifle cracks sharply, and immediately a couple of heavy crashes reverberate. Involuntarily I crouch. I hear a shout swiftly drowned in a roar of rifle-fire, the fierce stammer of a Lewis gun; above all the heavy crashing of bombs. The eastern sky is now a spread of dirty grey, in front the rusted tangle of wire is taking dim outline. We are crouching tensely, expecting to see a rush of grey figures loom up against the streaks of the pallid dawn.

On the right the rifle-fire swells into a furious roar, intermingled with prolonged Lewis-gun bursts, the deep crashes of 'stick' bombs, and the heavy ringing explosions of Mills grenades.

Suddenly the bomb explosions cease, though the rifles still crackle strongly. A short silence, another stinging spatter of fire that trails off into desultory cracks.

A minute or two later there comes the sound of footsteps stumbling down the trench, and a bloody-faced boy reels into view. 'The aid post?' he asks in a high hysterical voice. His forehead is gashed and blood is streaming into his eyes. Closely follows a stolid individual with a spreading stain on his shoulder, a wincing man whose hand drips a crimson trail. Others follow rapidly, and last an unconscious form sagging in a stretcher.

We waylay the returning stretcher bearers. They confirm our suspicion that the Germans occupy trenches to our flank, as well as in front. This trench is part of the Hindenburg system, and forms a small salient. The stretcher bearers are nervous. Saps and trenches, apparently heavily manned, hem in the right of our battalion.

In the early daylight the trench appears appallingly grim – high yellow walls, debris-littered floor, and everywhere, up and down, the dead lie in all postures, some squatting with heads resting on drawn-up knees, some face downwards, full length, a few stretched on the fire-step. I look at two men huddled below me, mud-encrusted, blood-soaked, brutally mutilated. My fear of shell-fire is acutely sharpened. The fire-step opposite bears another, sand-bag covered, but his tunic and leg are darkly saturated. His arm protrudes from the filthy covering and the muddy hand seems to clutch at passing men.

My comrade on the fire-step lights a cigarette and nods in the direction of the fallen. 'Good job their wives or parents can't see 'em, or ours see us, either.'

I escape from the presence of the dreadful dead; the stairs of the shafts are crowded with dozing men.

As the morning progresses the enemy activity increases; machine guns thrash the parapet, sudden whizz-bang storms lash the trench tops, so that we move in constant apprehension. Overhead heavy shells howl continuously, and quick blasts of gun-fire come from the east. The men are anxious; everything portends a storm.

Gradually the German gun-fire increases; the 'stand to' order brings us out below the parapet, while an enemy plane methodically surveys the position.

Around and above is a turmoil of noise; the mighty roar of dropping shells, the incessant rending crashes of the explosions, the scream and thud of whizz-bangs, and permeating all, the booming thunder of the guns. In this battering inferno of sound, we have to shout to make ourselves heard. The earth quivers continuously under the metallic flail.

Across the shattered soil behind our position, a barrage is falling, a vast unbroken curtain of spouting bursts, spraying up earth, smoke, and steel in a dark and furious barrier, half veiled by dense black fumes that writhe, heave, and trail upward in a mist of dirty grey. Heavy black shrapnel, storms of whizz-bangs add to the deafening tumult. Earth, mud, and metal shower into the trench, the parapet rains little avalanches of dirt with each vicious impact, the air, shrill with flying metal, screeches with the added burden of intense bursts of machine-gun fire.

We strain fiercely into the mud of the trench wall, half deafened, mute. The Lewis-gun team beside me crouch below their deadly charge; it is tilted up ready to heave on the parapet; a drum is fixed for immediate firing.

For a few awful minutes the racking inferno swells to a frantic intensity; the air vibrates to the battering hurricane behind. It is as if trench and sky are rocking and reeling. The stench of shell fumes is heavy in the air. A stinging musty odour permeates the trench; the men around make swift motions, and peer like hideous goblins through the wide flat eyes of their gas-masks. Gradually the taint passes and with relief we rip off the heated rubber.

A minute later the man at the periscope gesticulates wildly and gives a high-pitched yell, and we scramble swiftly on to the fire-step.

I see the wide waste of shell-churned soil, the tattered wire, and, well over, a dark and far-flung line of grey-clad stormers; behind them others rising fast, apparently springing from the drab earth in knots and groups, spreading out, surging forward.

Simultaneously from our trench bursts a great roar of fire. I fire with fiercely jerking bolt, round after round merged into the immense noise. The squat Lewis gun is thrust over the parapet by my right shoulder, it leaps into stabbing bursts of sound, that makes my deafened ears ring again and again. The rifles spurt hotly, the Lewis gun ejects whirling streams of cartridge cases that heap thickly by my feet. I breathe whiffs of expended gases escaping from the gun.

I see the first line of attack appear to wither, men reeling, stumbling, disappearing into the blasted contour of the earth. Others, in loose formation, springing swiftly erect, coming grimly forward. With each short rush the rapid rifle-fire rises to a crescendo of savage concentration. From the right, but now hardly audible in the stupendous noise, comes the crashing of bombs.

In front, before the furious fire, the German rush has died into the earth again.

We subside quickly below the parapet as some flanking machine guns commence to sweep the trench top. My rifle is hot to the touch. Above the parapet is flayed by a constant stream of bullets.

A surge of wounded presses down our section of the trench, limping, staggering in a steady stream, dazed, mud-fouled, bloodstained, faces blackened with cordite fumes.

An officer, gripping his Webley, appears amid another bunch of wounded. He bellows hastily for bombs, and returns again to the right. A few of us are told off to collect all the bombs we can, and we gather armfuls of captured German egg bombs, mixed with the heavy Mills; they are passed up, and we hastily search for more.

Suddenly, I hear faintly a medley of confused shouts. I see the men on the fire-step firing fast again, and up the trench they are firing both to front and flank. I am swiftly immersed in another rush of wounded, that pours along in urgent haste, despite their wounds. Another group rushes down, some men hoisting along badly hit pals, a volley of bomb explosions bursts closer to us.

A shrill alarm yell comes from the parapet, a few more wounded push swiftly past, half crouching. I see bomb smoke above the parapet to the right, I see men leap back from the fire-step and merge with another little rush of confused wounded. The platoon sergeant waves his arm urgently, 'Down the trench!'

Beyond him I see others leaping hurriedly and climbing over the parades, two officers scrambling on the mound above a shaft, and I see the Company Officer's revolver spurt twice.

Four or five smashing explosions disrupt the earth of the parapet, one bomb flies over and bursts on the parados. We crouch, wounded and unwounded, and run the gauntlet of the final volley of bombs. Where the trench curves sharply to the left I catch another haunting impression – a shaft crowded with the helpless wounded, pale, anxious faces looking upward, a man trying to crawl out, guarded by a stooping stretcher bearer. The trench divides, we plunge into an opening, pass a side trench, turn traverses. The air above is swept by machine-gun fire, the shell fall is still in thundering flood.

The man in front has a bomb splinter in his back, the small rent is surrounded by a red stain. His boot heel is torn, too, and blood oozes out with every step. We turn another traverse and come into a wide and empty trench in which long pools of water gleam dully.

We do not know where we are. Two men only are behind me, the sergeant and the three men following him have disappeared. We plough through the mud of this deserted line. At a block we must perforce cross a few yards of open ground; we do it at intervals, leaping prodigiously, to the accompaniment of severe machine-gun fire. The barrage fire has died away, but outside our narrow route shells still crash. We finally emerge into a trench fully manned by a strange battalion.

A day or so later the remnants are gathered together, and we line up again in Havrincourt Wood. Two short lines only, for 'A' Company is about twenty-five strong, and the battalion musters 100.

A few yards away, under the dripping trees, lies a heap of opened parcels, and a sergeant is apportioning the litter of home-made cakes, cigarettes, and sweets that have no owners.

Private William Reginald Dick joined Army February 7th, 1917. Posted to 3rd Battalion Gloucestershire Regt. France, September 1917, 2/6th Gloucestershire Regt., 61st Division, at Arras. Cambrai December 1917. January 1918 St. Quentin, February 1918 transferred to 2/5th Battalion of the same Division; held outposts in front of St. Quentin until March 21st. German offensive, March 21st. In action throughout the whole of the second Battle of the Somme; survivors relieved near Amiens. Battle of the Lys, April 12th, 1918, invalided from infantry June 1918. Posted to forward area Labour Company, and attached to Australian Tunnelling Company, and Engineers in the Loos and La Bassée sectors.

A BOY'S EXPERIENCES

C. J. Arthur

I was born in November 1898, so that when war was declared I was at school. I joined the School Cadet Battalion in 1914 and was appointed corporal.

At Whitsun, 1915, I told the O.C. cadets I was going to join up. 'Good,' he said. 'How old do you want to be?'

We fixed things between us, and armed with a letter from him, I presented myself, after attestation, to the colonel of an infantry battalion which was just being formed, and on the strength of the letter I was appointed a lance-corporal and told to get my hair cut. I did so and afterwards saw the regimental sergeant-major, who put me through my paces and told me to get my hair cut. In ten weeks I had been made sergeant.

We did the usual training in England until May 1916, then went to France as a complete division. Some of the N.C.O.s were sent up the line for instruction with a Scottish battalion at Ploegsteert. What a lovely war that was! In complete daylight we marched up to and through the wood to find a network of trenches and sand-bags. Still in daylight, but now through the trenches, one was able to wander up to the front line.

During instruction with the Scottish, I was sent out on a wiring party. We were subjected to machine-gun fire, but oh, blissful ignorance, I kept upright, a perfectly good 6 feet of human target!

'Git doon, ye fool!', and, crash! my legs were knocked from under me and I fell flat on my face with a good coil of barbed wire in my stomach. The Scot explained and marvelled at my ignorance.

Our time in the line was occupied with patrols, wiring parties, and minor offences. The minor offences consisted of sending over a few rifle grenades, sniping with periscope rifles, and generally asking for trouble. We were not to rest too long, however. Time and 'Intelligence' decreed that a raid had to be made on the German line. Volunteers were asked for and I asked the company commander if I could go as the N.C.O. The major had seen service in Gallipoli, and was not nearly so bloodthirsty as we new soldiers, and he promptly asked me if I wanted to end my young life. Being facetious, I answered that I thought there was a war on. I had my wish and the raiding party was sent back from the line to prepare.

The right of the raid was perfect so far as weather was concerned, but something went wrong. Either the wire had not been cut in front of the enemy trench, or it had not been cut in the right place, or the Germans had been successful in filling the gap. In any case, we did not get through and luckily enough the raiding party suffered but few casualties, although there was quite a number in the company from the barrage put down by the enemy. One of the casualties was the company sergeant-major, whose place I had to take before I was eighteen.

From 'Plug Street' we went slightly north to Messines Ridge, and spent about thirty days in the line and in supports without getting a change of clothing. This was a little more like the war we had read about at home and less like a rather dangerous picnic.

About this time the great Somme attack started, and we were chafing because we could not get there. We were still joyfully ignorant of the real conditions, but we were soon to experience them. The Division was moved to the shambles.

On the first day the tanks went into action, the Division went over and this was our real baptism. We had marched all one afternoon and part of the night to reach the front line, which consisted of a tape along the shell holes. What a contrast! From the comparative quiet of a proper line and minor shelling, to come to this shell-torn tape line, absolute din, rain of shells and machine-gun bullets. We had had our instructions, however, which were, to attack at zero hour. We composed ourselves as best we could for the rest of the night and at dawn the attack began.

During our transit from Messines to the Somme the major had impressed upon me the necessity for removing all maps and documents from his person as soon as he was hit. I endeavoured to 'pooh-pooh' the idea; but he knew. How he knew only God can tell; within two minutes of the start he was hit, and badly. I heard later he lost a leg, and I expect he was thankful to get away with that.

To carry on with the attack. I took the maps, etc., and looked round for another of the company officers, but could see none. There were only two, and I found out that one of those had gone out about the same time as the major. I had to keep the papers and carry on.

The tanks were at once a delight and a disappointment. They were fairly easily ditched, but at the same time they were impregnable. I saw a party of the enemy clamber on to one in motion and endeavour to put it out of action, after firing at it point blank with a machine gun and throwing bombs from about 5 yards range. I saw another run along a thick belt of wire in a sunken road, and so clear the way for us. Yet another spotted a machine gun in a house in Flers; this fellow wandered up the road, did a sharp turn, and ambled through the house.

Shortly afterwards I had one of the best meals I can remember. We had been attacking since dawn; it was now about 1 p.m. I produced a hunk of cheese and some biscuits. Another fellow scrounged a huge Spanish onion. That onion made the meal.

By this time we had secured a couple of miles of enemy territory, and while going through the doorway of a building I was hit. It was only a shrapnel bullet but it felt as though half the house had fallen on me. I was bowled over and, on trying to get up, found my leg would not move. I had by now lost at least half my bravado, and was sent back, having to hop and crawl as best I could; but eventually I did get there, and in due course arrived at a base hospital. Our losses must have been fairly heavy, but those of the Germans were at least three times as great. We seemed to take hordes of prisoners, and numbers were left behind waiting burial, either proper or accidental.

In due course I arrived back in England to experience the joys of hospital life. The men in blue were well looked after.

Even towards the end of 1916, after two years, the hospitality of the general public was astounding.

Until the end of June 1917 I was convalescent at the regimental depot and at reserve battalion. The application for a commission, which I had made in the early part of 1916, before going to France, was then entertained, and I was sent to an officers' cadet battalion at Oxford. Four months were spent there preparing for the examination, at which I was successful. I was granted a commission in my old regiment and returned to the same reserve battalion.

After a short time at the depot, I was sent to France to join a very depleted battalion, in the early days of January 1918. This battalion was temporarily under the command of a major from another regiment, and I regret to say he was not at all popular. Being fed-up with him, another subaltern and myself applied for transfer to the Flying Corps.

The first part of our time was spent in the line in the northern part of France. When we took over, it was deep in snow and we held a string of outposts on the eastern side of a stream. The first trench patrol I did, I spent most of my time in the stream. There was only one way to get to the sentries and if one deviated from the narrow path by so much as a foot, it usually meant one had to remove one's waders to empty out the water.

In January, in this part of the line, the war was not waged very furiously. The trench mortar batteries used to come up and let off a few rounds, then go back. We were left to patch up the trenches after the usual replies from the 'Minnie' brigade. Those Minenwerfers! I shall never forget their soul-destroying qualities.

To be hit by something you could not see was not too bad, but to see something coming, sufficient to blow a crater of 15 feet diameter and not to know which way to go to avoid it, was enough to destroy the nerve of a suit of armour. You can imagine, therefore, how decidedly unpopular the trench mortar batteries became. The daily 'strafe' too, was far more intense than in my earlier days. I have already said that my bravado had been reduced, and this did not improve it. In various ways one was able to forget, but I nearly gave out.

It was in the early days of March. The Germans were raiding; we were counter-raiding. Each company had only three officers in the line, and it usually meant two patrols in No Man's Land each night. In addition to this we were subjected to intermittent gun-fire and 'Minnies' during the day. Luckily, the colonel, who had returned by this time and who was one of the best men I have ever met, talked to me very severely and made me pull myself together. It was an effort, but, thank God! I succeeded.

About March 20th we were relieved from the line and started rest. I lost eighteen men the first day on a working party.

Next day came news of the great enemy attack. We received orders to dump all surplus kit and pack up to go south again. We started early in the morning, and reached a village towards evening. We were shown our billets and the cooks prepared a meal. Just as we were sitting down the 'Fall in at the double' was sounded. Good-bye dinner. Throughout the night we rode in lorries and chars-a-bancs, and towards noon we reached some deserted huts, had a short rest and a shave. Then we started to march on to a position between Bazentin-le-Grand and Bazentin-le-Petit. We never arrived. The Germans were first. From there we changed direction and retired through Pozières, where we managed to set fire to the place. It burned for three days and nights, so we did that job well. We eventually took up a position along the railway line in Aveluy Wood.

On the first night, the enemy marched through on the left of us in column of fours, blowing bugles and singing. He was beaten back and next afternoon we were attacked from the right flank, and the Germans were again behind us. Again we rallied beat them back and retook our position along the railway. We were attacked again that night, and next morning found ourselves very short of ammunition. The colonel wandered along the line carrying over 2,000 rounds in bandoliers round his shoulders.

That night we were relieved, but simply took up another position at dawn on the top of a hill. In the evening we were attacked again, and the colonel was wounded once more, making the seventh time.

We were relieved next day and got back to rest, a sadly depleted battalion. When we got back to rest I think every man slept the clock round. The men were falling asleep during the march back and after every halt it took us nearly ten minutes to wake them up.

During the time we were in the wood, five of our aeroplanes went over and were shot down in flames, making me begin to wish I had never applied for transfer. But after two days rest our transfer to the Flying Corps came through, and my chum and I promptly hurried back to England, arriving there the first week in April.

On July 21st I was back in France, this time with the Air Force, wherein life was great. One had only a nominal amount of work to do compared with the P.B.I. In fact, if you had to work more than four hours a day, you were decidedly unlucky.

After about six weeks with the squadron I was third senior observer. This rapid change of personnel was a serious drawback, but otherwise everything was much more comfortable.

One morning, taking off at dawn, we hit the top of a hangar in which were sleeping several mechanics. Their language was an education in itself. The machine was written off, but the flight commander and myself escaped with a shaking. We did no more work that day.

On another occasion, while taking a new pilot over the line, we were closely shelled. I smacked him on the head and told him to get back, as he appeared quite unconcerned. When we returned to the aerodrome, the bus badly riddled with shrapnel holes, which I pointed out to my pilot, he said he thought the shell bursts were small clouds. I thought of my first wiring party and said no more.

Our job was to do contact work in machines that were designed for artillery observation. Contact, of course, had to be kept with people working, on the ground, and, in the particular kind of machine we were using, was an unenviable task.

About this time we were beginning to win the War, and one night the Squadron Commander outlined our job in an advance for next day. It was very ambitious, and was met with some facetious remarks. From the squadron point of view, the first job was for all machines but one to go over and drop smoke bombs at dawn. The other machine, containing my pilot, aged seventeen and a half, and myself, had to take off about an hour and a half later and watch the Canal du Nord, which at this particular spot emerged from underground and was supposed to house large numbers of the enemy. Whether it did or not I never knew. We got over the line, flying just below 1,000 feet, to find that the usual late September ground mist and the effects of the squadron's smoke bombs were such that the ground was obscured. We could not see the line but apparently could ourselves be seen, for a machine gun was firing at us and I, as observer, was firing in the direction of the sound, with my back to the pilot. Suddenly the nose of the machine went down and we started to spin. I turned round to ask what the – . Imagine my consternation at finding the pilot shot through the head and leaning forward on the joy-stick. I had no visions of my past life; I merely clutched at the straw. In other words, in a fraction of a second I had the spare stick out of its place on the fuselage and into its socket for dual control. With the other hand, I stopped the spin by hauling on to the rudder wire alongside my seat, then I pulled at the stick, and can dimly remember the nose of the plane rising.

The next thing I remember is being offered a drink by a German officer. This I refused, so he drank it himself and offered me another from the same bottle, I could only have been semi-conscious, for I again refused, Once more I lapsed into unconsciousness and returned to find somebody taking a souvenir in the shape of my wrist-watch. I was then told to sit at the foot of the steps of the dug-out, as our attack was expected. I was to call up that there was a British officer there. Having myself dropped bombs into dug-outs first and asked questions afterwards, I suggested going to the top of the steps. This did not meet with approval, so I was left below to nurse a cracked chin, a bleeding head and a very sore body, the only ill-effects to myself. Our attack was not successful, so I was not rescued, but was sent behind the German lines.

During my short stay in Germany, I was in many camps, the chief of which were at Karlsruhe, Kamstigall, near Munich, and Landshut, near Konigsberg, From Munich to Konigsberg we travelled through Berlin, where I bartered half a bar of Sunlight Soap for five shillings' worth of cigarettes.

I arrived back in England before Christmas 1918, thus creating what appears to be a record of every Christmas at home during the War. In 1915 I was lucky in a ballot at Aldershot; 1916, being convalescent at Epsom, I was allowed out a certain amount and plead guilty to taking a little more without being found out; 1917, I was on draft leave; and 1918 I have just recounted.

C. J. Arthur enlisted in May 1915, after Whitsun week-end in camp with Boy Scouts, and within ten weeks was promoted to Sergeant. Went to France May 1916. Wounded September same year, and awarded M.M. In hospital until December, then convalescent until February 1917. Thence to depot until gazetted in November 1917. To France again, January 1st, 1918, until April 5th, when he was sent home for transfer to R.A.F. On July 21st again went to France and was shot down on September 29th, and taken prisoner, returning to England December 20th, 1918, and demobilized March 1919. Whilst in the infantry he served with the (Queen's Own) Royal West Kent Regt., both in the ranks and when gazetted.

VARIETIES OF TRENCH LIFE

A. A. Dickson

August 4th, 1914, in a little country bank: 'Broad's gone with the Terriers: you'll have to take charge.'

It was 1915 before wire-pulling brought a strange, lame man to the office. 'I've come to let you get away,' he said.

'To let me go?'

It was as if a spring that had been wound up and up all these months was suddenly released. That made the bump against a brick wall all the more dumbfounding. To be rejected by the doctor, turned down as physically unfit after all manner of sports and specializing in gymnasium work it was staggering. But there was no doubt: 'danger of rupture: operation and a month's rest.'

The day did come at last to be sworn in. It wasn't quite so thrilling as I'd expected because the last words before the Bible was passed round were words of advice from the captain:

'I should advise some of you – I mention it now because after you have sworn I shall have to order, not advise – to get your hair cut rather more à la military; at present some of you have it decidedly not à la military.'

Still, we were soldiers, even if we weren't soldierly enough in forming fours to please the corporal. And we took his word that it wasn't any use thinking we were soldiers until we could jump to it better. No one argued that we shouldn't be fighting the Germans from the formation of 'At the halt, facing left, form close column of – platoons!'

It wasn't until months later, after a tenth successive two-hour wait on the same patch of snowy bog-holes for an attack the never came, that the frozen silence of dismissal was broken by Johnson's acid comment – he was a schoolmaster from the north, so his critical faculty was not quite tame: 'I may be obtuse, but I really can not see what earthly good anyone has got out of this night's battalion training' – and oh! the world of scorn in that word 'training.' 'Learning to follow each other about in the dark? I'm afraid, Dickie, if you can think of that, you've got the making of a better soldier in you than I have.'

But there was still enthusiasm, even though only of the sticking-it order: we wouldn't *let* it be damped quite out: keenness enough to bring stripes and their load of care, stripes that evoked cynical ribaldry from pals, hostility from the fed-up and, the jealous, and that lynx-like antagonistic vigilance that noncom and private mutually felt.

And then a commission and a new world to conquer. One would be able to do so much more.

Could one, though? When we asked about the men: 'Are they old soldiers? Do they need much training?' and got the answer: 'Training? They've been getting all the training they want this last year and more,' it became apparent that fed-upness was not confined to the ranks.

It wasn't to be wondered at, really: a few Zep scares, a few entrainment orders that turned out to be only practice, did make us wonder whether the duration of the War was to be spent in English billets. Then, Easter 1916, at 2 a.m. came another entrainment order.

Half the battalion didn't believe it: many a one had no razor in his kit when the next chance to shave came. For the trains that we really did entrain into sped off not south-westward for the Plain or France, but away and away up the 'North Western,' and it wasn't until they disgorged us on Liverpool Docks that rumours could be swopped about 'Sinn Fein gentry – broken bottles and shillelaghs.'

It was a baptism of fire all right, with flintlocks, shotguns, and elephant rifles, as well as more orthodox weapons. And 100 casualties in two days' street fighting was a horrible loss to one battalion: the more so since my one friend from the ranks, commissioned same day, was shot through the head leading a rush on a fortified corner house; first day on active service, and it was my job to write and tell his mother, who thought him still safe in England.

A hateful task: so was another duty of one misty dawn soon after, when four young officers had to command four firing parties, and four rebel leaders stood in turn blindfold against a wall.

After that, more training – a repetition of the training so wearisome in England, till the Irish winter made even trench-digging impossible; but we could always have 'Lecture by Company Officers on March Discipline.'

We did get to France at last, though; and into the trenches, too. The memory of that is mainly – mud. There was the ominous donning of 'gum-boots, thigh'; the shell holes and slithery duckboards (dear old Johnson and his 'following each other about in the dark'); the front line, where, by constant baling, liquid slime could just be kept from lipping over the dug-out door-sills. And there in that nightmare of mud and wire, by the deathly light of occasional star-shells from over the way, we learned the landmarks to guide us: 'Left by the coil of wire, right by French legs.' 'French legs?' 'Yes, we took over from the French; the legs of one they buried in the side of the trench stick out a bit, you can't miss it.' It was rather startling, but didn't seem to merit a second thought.

Sniping, shelling, and the Sisyphean labour of trench maintenance were endured until relief, and even that was nightmare, too. Climbing out of the river of sludge called 'C.T.' we trudged along the top, caring for nothing but those wicked ankle-high strands of wire across the track – oh! the concentrated loathing in that warning growl of 'Woy-er' from each man to his follower. And so we bundled on until the guide-poor lad, he'd only been up once before – confessed he'd lost his way, for the duckboard track we'd struck led up to the line again, to the sector on our right.

Despair? There was pale grey dawn behind us by the time compass bearings, verified by a periodic 'ploomp ah' from one of our own kindly howitzers, led to the double line of shattered tree stumps along the great straight Amiens road; and we held off utter exhaustion until dug-outs, black, boiling tea, and sleeping like logs, ended the first turn in the line.

Then suddenly, those trenches were abandoned: on we pushed for the Hindenburg Line. But though company after company was flung on a mass of wire with machine guns sweeping its face, the Hindenburg Line was proof against little local attacks like these; mortifying thought after hell let loose with rifle and machine gun, artillery and trench mortar, that the pandemonium whose only visible result was those corpses on the wire – men we had never known till a year ago and since then had known as brothers – was nothing but a demonstration to pin the enemy down, unworthy even of mention in the report of activity on the Western Front.

Still, we saw a real big push later on. How many trucks from those mazes of sidings at St. Pol and Hazebrouck are needed to move a battalion? How many trains to move a division? And how many divisions poured into that never-ending assault – a division a day, we heard – beyond the Menin Gate, a one-way road for thousands in the British Army?

Fancy going on leave from the Ypres Salient to England! It seemed unreal all the way; at Poperinghe rail-head, at Boulogne rest camp. Even when Grisnez at last faded into the sea and Folkestone rose nearer, one could hardly believe it – until the barrier at Victoria.

It *must* have been in a different world.

Lifted out of the mud of the Salient to derelict seaside villas; taking up a new lot of men to a section of front made up of town, canal, and dyke-edged polder, with a foot of water rippling around the earth-works; fetid fluid in the dykes around the ruined town; inky-black, icy river swishing under flimsy duckboard bridges: no wonder that trench-foot sent more men down the line than wounds. Add the ever-present shelling of the town that brought tottering brickwork crashing down on us; add the machine-gunning of the straight right-angled streets; add dysentery; add utter exhaustion from hurrying in sodden, heavy clothing around those slimy tenacious 'boyaus,' and realize that relief from the Nieuport sector, wherever it might mean we were going, seemed a blessed release from purgatory.

A ten-mile canal voyage and three days' march on good roads through inhabited country might have been a glorious rest cure, but for feet rendered soft and agonizing by standing and sleeping in sopping boots and socks.

Down among the tunnels and brick-stacks of La Bassée, trench mortars on both sides rained down their 12 lb, 50 lb, 112 lb of high explosive: and such lumps of death as that can't be thrown about without the casualty returns growing sadly. It was all in the day's work, but none the less it meant the loss of pals, when one after another went west through a direct hit, or a premature burst, or an unlucky shell clean into the ammunition store.

So all the spring of 1918, ever feebler reinforcements came, slim boys and weary crippled men; and ever rumours grew of the great push coming.

It was a certain satisfaction to the wiring parties of those nights – every available man – that this sector was one of the few points invulnerable to the German rush of March 21st: so that Collishan, the little cook's mate who had been a Manchester coster and showed a magic skill in coaxing barbed wire around those terrible screw-pickets, had accomplished something before the machine gun got him down south. Down south again – oh, the pitiful irony of it – on that same old battlefield where the Somme advance had started nearly two years before; and after all that measureless slaughter men were to fight again over that same blood-soaked ground.

And the weary, wearing hopelessness of it joined with the fearful intensity of the shelling to make this such a culmination as even previous experience had never made us dream of. Shelled continuously through the night; dashing out to tie up and replace the sentry hit by shrapnel; floundering with the dead weight of a wounded man along the collapsing makeshift trench, and then back again, lurking in a flimsy brick cellar that shook with every blast. And in the morning the rims of five great shell holes around the dome of our tiny shelter.

Blazing away with the dawn at massed attacks in full view. One gun blown up; dragging back the other to reserve positions, while every pair of men who could walk, or stagger, loaded up with boxes of ammunition, and tramped up the open road with that frightful barrage spouting up cascades of earth on right and left. What was in everybody's mind? What was in the mind of old Private Jim Black, a road labourer by trade, when the man carrying with him got a splinter in the leg, and Black tied him up and then humped the 2-cwt. box on his own rheumaticky shoulder and trudged on?

So it went on for days, with 'wounded' and 'killed' appearing against name after name. It never crossed my mind to wonder whether I'd ever get hit – too busy to think of such a thing, and that is a literal fact.

That was why it was such a surprise. Up the long valley north of Gommecourt, where bits of line changed hands every few hours, I tramped choosing gun positions: passed a rough trench cutting across the track, and reconnoitred the shoulder of the hill. 'Smack!' 'Smack! ' at intervals went the sound of bullets at medium range. But one had grown to disregard them: till it struck me, 'They're sniping from across the valley: they've pushed us off that nearest ridge; and I'm in No Man's Land.'

That moment he got me: a terrific 'Bung-g-g' on the jaw, and down in the ditch by the track I spun, face and neck streaming blood. Field dressing was pulled out in a moment, but it was no place to stay: back to that trench I must creep, dragging flat along the ditch. Too slow, though; bleeding at that rate I'd never cover 200 yards: up on all fours and crawl. But then 'Smack-k!' came the vicious spit again: was I to crawl and be potted at? Up and run for it; and 'Smack-k-k!' came again as I tottered forward, half the field dressing in its waterproof cover still clenched in each hand. One hundred and fifty yards to go: 'Smack-k-k!' again before half-way, and a spurt of earth just behind.

How long – how long, to get into that trench? And how long does it take to reload and fire? I know that perfectly well, and I see time for one more shot before I can reach it. Slacken speed, to make a final effort, and 'Smack-k-k!' into the ditch a yard ahead. 'Ah! Safe!' and I tumble into that trench on top of a knot of mud-caked Fusiliers.

'My Gawd! Field dressin', sir?' and the two bits are ripped open and clapped on, and the word goes along for stretcher bearers.

Memories after that? A kindly efficient American M.O. bandaging cases by the dozen. Then another figure emerged out of the mist: the dearest old silver-haired padre, who didn't waste any silly words, but brought a luscious sponge and hot water, and tenderly bathed face and forehead clear of mud and blood. Then they took my boots off: that meant rest for a while, anyway. And when the ambulance pulled in to a chateau marked 'C.C.S.,' I heard the voice of an English nurse; and at the sound there came a most wonderful feeling that now everything would be perfectly all right: there was no need to worry any more.

Hospital in Rouen, where at length the M.O. took down the card from my bed, and at that mystic sign the next man – oldest inhabitant of the ward, he had seen dozens pass through while his leg refused to mend, but still he enjoyed their good luck – turned to me and whispered, 'Blighty, Dickie.'

Captain A. A. Dickson, Inns of Court O.T.C., September to December 1915. Commissioned to Sherwood Foresters. Dublin Rebellion. France, January 1917: Somme, Ypres, Nieuport. Commanding trench mortar battery. Wounded, November 1917; again in April 1918, during German attack. Hospital until September 1918. Demobilized unfit, January 1919.

A RUNNER'S STORY

1916–18

R. W. Iley, M.M.

In November 1915 I was one of those accepted by Colonel Lord Feversham to be enlisted in the Yeoman Rifles being formed at Helmsley Park.

In January 1916 the battalion was transferred to Aldershot, where we became fit for our great adventure. Runners were asked for, and I volunteered for the job.

After a terrific route march (from the effects of which some died) and an inspection by H.M. the King, our ammunition and identity discs were issued and we sailed for France on May 4th, 1916.

We received our final training in the Meteren area before taking over the line at Ploegsteert.

In our first day in the reserve line we received our baptism of fire: a platoon of 'A' Company was nearly wiped out during rifle inspection, and I helped to carry one of our first dead to the dressing station. That night we totalled up our casualties and divided the number into the strength of the battalion, so as to estimate our expectation of life; not in a spirit of despair, but that we might face the facts as we saw them on that miserable night.

We soon settled down to trench warfare as an existence to be made the best of and joked about whenever possible. One night the deathly quiet of our sector was disturbed by one of our 18-pounder batteries shelling at regular intervals; we wanted rest, and cursed the gunners. The enemy replied by shelling, not the battery, but our Battalion Headquarters. We were ordered to withdraw, but four of us were imprisoned by a shell blocking up our dug-out. Every other dug-out was wrecked. Ours was covered with earth and filled with fumes. In the morning we were disinterred for burial, but were found unharmed, a dud shell had half buried itself in a tree which supported our dug-out. Three of us played cards all night; the fourth prayed.

One day two of us were cycling along a duckboard track when we heard the approach of a shell. My companion dived into a trench. I foolishly cycled on quickly and was blown into a tree, but got off with scratches. My pal was not so lucky, the trench being full of water.

In August we were relieved to take our part in the Somme offensive. The incoming runners asked us if we'd been on the Somme, and on our replying that our only experience was at Ploegsteert they looked at us with scorn, saying, 'And you think you're soldiers. They kill more therein a day than up here in one year.'

Despite our numerous casualties we realized that Ploegsteert had been but an apprenticeship for sterner events. Notwithstanding shells and machine-gun bullets, Ploegsteert had, at the hour of dawn, been stirred by the songs of the birds, while the Somme was one black, evil-smelling waste.

On the morning of September 15th, 1916, our Division, accompanied by the Tanks, which were being used for the first time, attacked on the Somme. I was left behind at Brigade Headquarters. Shortly after the attack opened, I accompanied the Brigadier-General through Delville Wood to our battalion. He pointed out a German well within our lines who seemed badly wounded and helpless.

After reaching our colonel, the general gave me an urgent despatch for Brigade Headquarters, with instructions to go quickly, stop for no one, and return to the same spot, whatever I heard to the contrary. These instructions gave me a very exciting time, for, on re-entering Delville Wood a wounded Tommy shouted, 'For God's sake, drop!' I dropped and found that the wounded German had shot this man and some others. The Tommy wanted me to hunt the Jerry, but, remembering instructions, I ran for it. On my return journey I found the German dead.

On nearing the trench where I had left the general, I was told to stop as the trench had been recaptured. But I was too keen to carry out my orders, and thought those fellows mistaken, so I jumped confidently into the trench amongst some Germans.

I was too surprised to do anything, but the Jerries more so, as all but one ran away. The remaining one raised his hands, saying, 'Mercy! Kamerad!' and came back with me. I handed over my prisoner and found the general, and heard that Lord Feversham had been killed. Our gallant colonel's body was recovered a month later by a small party including myself.

On October 7th we again attacked on the Somme, and I was continually on duty as runner. Our front line was a very hastily dug, shallow trench, and the Commanding Officer gave me a message to the battalion on our right, saying, 'There is no room to pass along the trench, so you must run along the top. You'll probably be killed, but you must go.' I returned safely and was greeted with 'Hullo, Iley, still alive,' and was sent with a similar message to the left. Again I was lucky, but had wind-up all the time.

We suffered heavily during the attack, one new draft of thirty men straight from England being almost wiped out within a day or two of leaving home.

When we were due to leave this sector I guided the incoming C.O. to our battalion. He asked me about the line and I told him it was quiet, but that we'd filled one cemetery and got well on with another, and various other true but unnecessary things. The adjutant told me later how amused he'd been at my efforts to put his wind up. The colonel had won the D.S.O. at Gallipoli and seen a lot of hard fighting.

One dark night two of us runners had to leave our usual track owing to shell fire, and were suddenly ordered to drop by an artillery sentry. Some guns fired immediately over our heads. In Seaham Hospital months later I heard a gunner relating how two infantrymen nearly had their heads blown off, and how he, as sentry, had not observed them until almost too late, owing to the intense darkness. I questioned him as to time and place, and surprised him by telling him that I was one of the men.

During the Messines advance on June 7th, 1917, when all the mines were exploded I pointed out to an officer that he and

I were advancing too fast and were losing touch with the colonel, so we sat in a shell hole until Headquarters caught us up. A sergeant seeing us sitting there and apparently not noticing the officer, rushed at me with fixed sword, shouting, 'Move on, you bloody coward.' The officer's revolver held him up and he passed on swearing.

When moving up for the Third Battle of Ypres on July 31st, 1917, I had to guide a party into the line, and had a fearful journey. The enemy evidently expected an attack, as he shelled all roads heavily with gas shells and shrapnel.

My party was the last to leave, and I took them by a route not taken by the other parties. The officer was alarmed, thinking I was lost, but we reached our position first. Wearing gas masks, we doubled most of the way, dropping into ditches here and there and always finding a shelter when most necessary. We galloped over the Ypres Canal, a heavy shell just missing our rear, but reached our destination without casualties. I felt handsomely rewarded when the officer and each man shook hands with me. Most of the parties going up had suffered heavily, many being gassed.

At 5 a.m. on September 20th, 1917, our Division attacked Tower Hamlets Ridge, Passchendaele.

I lay next to our commanding officer waiting for zero. Watch in hand, he counted the seconds – fifty, forty, and down to ten, five, four, three, two – and off we moved to meet a very stubborn resistance from the pillboxes which had not been touched by our barrage.

Their machine guns swept us with bullets, and some of our new men wavered; this was their first experience in the War. The colonel rallied them and ordered the section I was in charge of to rush a pillbox that was holding us up. We rushed straight at it. The Huns threw a flare bomb in our midst and mowed us down with machine-gun bullets. Of my section of ten, five were killed and four wounded.

I felt as if a stone had hit my leg and spun round. Two bullets had gone through my thigh, but they were not dangerous. Other bullets passed through my clothes without touching me. As I lay I heard that the colonel was badly wounded, and another section had captured the pillbox while we drew the fire.

I made my way back, and, resting awhile, fell asleep, to be wakened by a German touching my shoulder. For the moment I thought I was captured, but found that he was the prisoner. He helped me back about three miles to the main road, and assisted me into a passing lorry. I turned to thank him, but he was gone.

After passing through the base hospital and Whalley Range Hospital I was sent to Seaham Hall, one mile from home. I mended very quickly, had a jolly two weeks' leave, and was sent to the King's Royal Rifle Corps Command Depot at Tipperary, where I found the Southern Irish very bitter against the British troops.

After a short spell there, I was passed A1 and transferred to Sheerness, where, after a severe course of training, I left for active service again, rejoining the Yeoman Rifles in January 1918. We went to Italy, which was very quiet, our chief casualties being caused by vino.

Early in March we arrived back in France, and, to the sorrow of all ranks, the Yeoman Rifles were disbanded. As the various detachments marched away to other battalions veterans of many actions wept. They marched away with heads erect and smiling faces as we shouted our 'Good-byes,' but the tears were showing through their smiles. A few of us were transferred to the Machine Gun Corps.

On March 21st, 1918, the German offensive commenced and we were rushed up the line to Achiet-le-Grand.

I retained my job as runner, and was with Battalion Headquarters. News came through that all in front had perished, and I was detailed with another runner to go forward and discover the position of the enemy. Our commanding officer gave each of us a revolver and instructions that if necessary we had each to shoot five Germans and then ourselves. He gave us each a drink of whisky, and as we left our chaps shook hands with us and looked as if they thought us doomed.

Our journey was uneventful for a while. Shells fell occasionally; then we saw hazy figures, then a tank, and found them to be British troops. The tank officer suspected us as spies and would give us no information. We reached a wood and found some of our machine-gun companies. Things had been very bad, but were now quiet. The troops in the line had suffered heavily, and Brigade Headquarters were manning the trenches.

We got such information as we could and were shelled freely on our return journey, having found our big adventure as tame as a Sunday-school treat.

We found our camp deserted and our equipment left. Our headquarters had evidently left hurriedly, as a half-bottle of whisky and some rum were left in the mess. We soon disposed of this, donned our packs and left to find our headquarters. We found them in a trench. The C.O. was pleased with our report and sent us to rest.

We were soon disturbed and sent to Divisional Headquarters with a message. As we returned we met the British Army in retreat. Moving forward keeping to the side of the road we were passed by galloping artillery, staff cars, and infantry, swearing and shouting as they rushed backward. The retirement was 'according to plan,' but we had a feeling that we were losing the War.

When we got back to our trench everything was quiet. The returning troops had all passed and the enemy had not yet reached us. We just stayed there, knowing we had no reinforcements and that for some miles back the country was deserted, that the Huns were feeling their way towards us, and that we might expect some trouble that night. While we were awaiting the attack, the regimental sergeant-major sent me back for some water. I found water and a store of whisky. I returned with some of each.

Just then we observed the enemy approaching over a ridge some 700 yards away. They advanced in open formation and appeared to be assembling in the hollow where our camp had been. We kept up a steady fire and took things comfortably as their shells passed over us.

Quite suddenly German cavalry, which had assembled behind a wood about 300 yards away, charged us. This was a new experience, and my heart jumped. We fired rapidly and wiped them out, shooting the fallen riders as they endeavoured to crawl away. After a lull more cavalry attacked from the right. One of our tanks appeared from nowhere and, assisted by our machine guns, soon turned them.

As dusk approached we sent out a patrol. They never returned, and a second patrol, consisting of a drunken major and myself, was sent out. We wandered about aimlessly when a hut window, about 600 yards in front, lit up. The major ordered me to put that light out. In the dark I pointed my rifle in the direction of the light and fired. The light went out, and I surmised that some German, having lighted his cigarette, had blown out the match. On our return the major swanked about me as being the 'best shot in the British Army.'

We were then ordered to withdraw to the new line some 12 kilometres back, where the enemy advance was finally stopped. We moved up behind Ypres, where it was my privilege to instruct the first American runners in the line, although they first objected to being taught by 'a boy.'

On leaving the line we were sleeping in a hut when I suddenly felt horribly afraid and told the others, who laughed at me. I got up and dressed, and had just lain down when a shell hit the hut. We lit candles and found, in the next partition, two medical orderlies, one almost blown to pieces and his friend wounded. In the room at the other side the colonel's servant was dead, and in the next hut some were killed and many wounded. As we carried one man up, I saw the wounded orderly dying bravely. Smoking a cigarette, he told the medical officer to dress those who would live. He died in the ambulance shortly afterwards. There was a gaping hole in my steel helmet, a piece of shrapnel in my towel, and the hut was riddled, but I was untouched.

Soon after this our big push that was to end the War started. We kept the enemy on the move and talked excitedly when the first rumours of the Armistice came through. On the morning of

November 11th I was with a section in the front, and had orders to harass the Hun until 11 a.m. when hostilities would cease. At eleven o'clock we halted at an estaminet and amazed the landlady by demanding beer and shouting 'Le guerre finis.'

Following the Germans next day to make sure that they were retiring, we met frightened figures in strange clothing – men of the Allied Armies, fearing and starving, staggering towards freedom. Some died by the roadside, dead on the day of their delivery from a living death, turned out by an enemy without any provision for their safe return.

Corporal Robert William Iley enlisted in 21st (Service) Battalion King's Royal Rifle Corps (Yeoman Rifles), November 20th, 1915. Transferred, to 41st Battalion Machine Gun Corps about March 19th, 1918. Wounded, September 20th, 1917. Awarded Military Medal, June 1917. Mentioned in Sir Douglas Haig's Despatches, April 9th, 1917. Demobilized, January 1919.

IN A HIGHLAND REGIMENT

1917–18

H. E. May, M.M.

The individual who finally sank his identity under number S/41250 of the Gordon Highlanders could not by any stretch of imagination have been called brave. Nevertheless he joined the khaki throng. And he did so voluntarily, though conscription was in force. He had received a protection certificate under the Military Service Acts unsought, being in a protected occupation. He was, in fact, a London policeman.

Then a journey north to Scotland by night, with the whole of the Highlands a vast sea of white.

At the Regimental Depot the conscripts – and the old swaddies used the term quite often – were required to wait outside the dining-hall until the Depot Staff, time-serving soldiers, and men returned unfit from the B.E.F. were seated. Then the orderly sergeant gave 'Go' and the conscripts were at liberty to enter and take seats below the salt.

There was the good corporal who trained them. He had Gaelic and would cast a disapproving eye over his squad. 'Holy – !' And an acid stream, descriptive of their shortcomings, would flow. One of the missing words was perhaps the most obscene that can be uttered.

Musketry training and draft leave and that glorious journey to France for the great adventure – full of hope, expectation, and wonder. And so by the Bull Ring of Etaples of happy memory(!); by the rose-covered chateau at the Divisional Reinforcement Camp, with its placid stream running through the grounds and dragon-flies darting to and fro in the sunlight. And the rumble of the guns heard for the first time.

Trenches in a quiet sector on the Somme, 'Drumming up' in a mess tin, using for fuel wood cut finer than matches in order not to cause smoke. Gargantuan feeds of bully beef and pork and beans, fried up in a biscuit-tin lid, with a candle and a piece of sand-bag for fire!

A movement north to take part in a big battle.

Ypres, city of the lowlands. What memories does the name conjure up! The Salient! Dyed with the blood of men who faced the hell that existed there right through the War. A dark night, with the pale moon beaming fitfully between the flying scud of the clouds. Under the shadow of what had been a convent and the walls of the stately Cloth Hall! All quiet. One could nearly feel the presence of the 'Old Contemptibles' of 1914; could almost see their ghosts as they, perhaps, smiled approval on their successors.

A day by Hell Fire Corner, plastered the while with shrapnel, H.E., and incendiary shells. No sleep. Thunder of guns continuously until parade. Onward by Wilde Wood. The sky was cloudy and obscured the moon. A phantom host flitting through the black night. And so across the Ypres battlefield with its dead, its debris, and its horrible stench. Past some old gun-pits. The moon gleamed fitfully for a few moments and there was a vision indescribable in its naked horror. Pieces of metal that once were cannon; and, if good Krupp steel had been so shattered, what of the humans who served the steel? Heads, legs, arms, trunks, pieces of rotting flesh, skulls that grinned hideously, bones cleaned by exposure, lay about in hopeless riot. And so to No Man's Land.

Two hours' sleep, then the thunders of an intensive artillery barrage. 5.50 a.m. – over! Men falling. Ahead a burn shown on the map as being 30 inches or 3 feet wide, but found to be a morass 50 feet wide. Wading through mud waist deep, with kilts floating on the surface like water-lilies. Midway over, when the searchlights from the pillboxes swept the countryside and the vicious spit of the machine guns was heard. Many fell, killed outright or to suffer the horrible torture of suffocation beneath the mud. You cannot help them; you must push on. A stretch of firm ground and signs of daylight coming up. You see a line of stumpy tree-trunks that, dimly, you realize is the objective. You creep up. A wild melee; stabbing with a bayonet. A gushing of blood from many wounds (oh! the nauseating smell of freshly spilled human blood in quantity), and then a cry of 'Kamerad!' and a whine for mercy. Unheeded, for all the enemy died.

Stuck in the mud for four days. Shelled and sniped from the front; sniped and bombed from the air. Casualties every hour. Ten counter-attacks for the lost ground before nightfall on the first day. And all broken up and withered away by our artillery and rifle-fire.

No sleep. Then on the fourth night came relief. Staggering out to a rest billet and dropping exhausted. A feed of bacon, bread and butter, and tea. Real hot tea, scalding; plenty of it, and you rejoice – until you remember you're eating dead men's rations beside your own, for without the dead men there would be no plenty.

Holding on at Joy Ride and Crucifix Street. Built up of German dead. Skulls peering hideously; mute decaying arms and legs jutting out at every step you took along the trench. Then badgered about practising attacks in diamond formation, in depth, on woods and in open country which were destined to be delayed for many months

In again at the fag-end and to help consolidate such gains as remained after Cambrai. Bovis Trench. Doubtless in appearance something akin to what we shall find Hades when, in due season, such as meet their just deserts reach there. An absolute shambles. The ground twisted and torn; shell and trench-mortar holes everywhere. Trench walls crumbling; on all sides evidence of decay, but fairly dry. Then on the first. night snow, which changed, through sleet, to hard rain, and morning light found 18 inches of the finest mud one could wish to see. Black, oozing, liquid, penetrating. It stayed and clung in deep and abiding affection, soaking through boots and rubber capes. Counter-attacks by Jerry for the lost ground; raids and counter-raids; general conditions so appalling and losses so heavy that the Brass Hats took compassion and gave relief after four days.

Relief on Christmas Eve after a spell of eighteen days, on eleven of which battle hardly ceased by day or night, though officially activity was defined as 'engagements of no importance.'

Into the line on January 26th, 1918, and 'right sector,' 'support trenches' and 'left sector' in turn, changing at six-, three- and six-day intervals. On the night of March 17th a maelstrom of hell in the shape of British artillery in action from Ypres to Cambrai. Outside news none. Wild rumours of heavy enemy successes in the south, of which confirmation was forthcoming in the way of German Verey lights appearing much farther behind our backs on each succeeding night. The front line untenable. Shelled from the front and from a point seven miles in rear. An evacuation to cut the angle out. Then, as the enemy attack came north, desperate attempts by him to take our ground. Harassing attacks day and night. Then, on the evening of the 27th, a curious lull – an absolute and awe-inspiring silence.

Three a.m., 28th. Boom! Bang! Biff! Crash! A confused jangling; a succession of heavy explosions rent the air; shrapnel whined and flew in all directions. A holocaust of shell-fire. Shell after shell poured about the position; high explosives tore the earth up; gas shells polluted the atmosphere, and shrapnel hurtled from the sky above. Hours of it and with the first faint light of dawn, deploying from the village and the height behind, came the enemy. A huge grey mass. The British infantry held their fire. The enemy bombardment ceased and their infantry drew nearer. Artillery there was none; not so much as a solitary 18-pounder covered the British front. All had been withdrawn. The enemy came nearer; close up to the wire. Cutters were handled and made ready; then the Lewis guns belched forth and the riflemen opened rapid fire. Huge gaps in the enemy ranks and all confusion. They broke and fled; were re-formed, came again, were beaten back and again were driven forward, this time with sticks and at the point of the revolver. Seven attacks and not one gained an inch of ground.

9 a.m. A fresh bombardment and the enemy rested awhile. Picture a valley, low hills on either side, and along it a light railway. Down the track went a constant stream of battered humanity. Men minus an arm; those with huge dark stains on their uniform to show where they had been hit – Highlander

and Sassenach. Here a man badly burned by a petrol bomb; there a poor devil with his leg gone at the knee, who dragged a weary way backward, using his rifle as a crutch. On the faces of all a look of hopeless horror as they fled from the terror behind them. One must see something like that to realize the insane folly of war.

Midday. There had been a slight lull in the shelling; then it suddenly increased. A veritable tornado. Shells fell unceasingly; they ripped the earth tip. Hundreds of tons were blown into the air at once. Shrapnel everywhere; the earth shook with seismic quaverings. Then, racing madly across the intervening space came the remnants of a brigade; the front line had gone. There were two gaps in the wire. The colonel sprang for one, two H.Q. company sergeants for the other. Some coaxing, a turning about; spreading out to open order, they went back through that barrage of death. The shelling went on with unabated violence; men were swept to Eternity at every yard. But the line went on without wavering, without faltering, without a look behind. So steady, it might have been a drill movement on parade, Through that awful hail of steel and lead they passed and at 1 p.m. had regained the shambles of the Third Defence System. And the words of a famous Frenchman uttered at Balaclava might equally apply to the charge led by the old 75th Regiment of Foot.

No rest. Isolated attacks by the Hun and bombing parties; the spraying death of the machine guns on every hand. At 4 p.m, the enemy again lashed down his devastating barrage that blighted everything within its radius of action. That ended any hope of holding the advanced trenches and a withdrawal to the Green Line took place – the line the enemy would cross only when none remained alive to stay him. Another night and day; minor attacks and bombing-raids all the time and then relief...relief after sixty-two days in trenches without having been withdrawn. What relief to get one's clothes off after wearing them continuously for a month! What comfort to cast boots aside after nineteen days' wear! What savage delight to scratch and drag the damned lice from shirt seams and the more exposed portions of one's anatomy? *Lousy* doesn't properly express it.

Twelve days out. A promise of rest and a quiet sector. A long line of M.T. A hurried dash across country. Civilians streaming back – old men, old women, young women, and children. Some had carts loaded with their worldly goods; others pushed perambulators or small trucks loaded with their more treasured goods. Others – the greater number – carried what they had snatched in a handkerchief, and wandered wearily backwards. An attitude of helplessness and resignation that perhaps brightened a little when they saw the Tartan and the Soldats Eccosse.

The M.T. column halted behind a crest. Packs were piled. A Staff car flying up at 50 m.p.h., a hasty consultation, a rapid distribution of maps, a quick move to diamond formation, and the battalion moved forward. A 6-inch battery, drawn by motor lorries, pulled up and at once opened fire, without pits or masks.

A runner came up to report German cavalry on the right. Through a village and ahead a strange sight met the eye. A riot of green of every tint. The spring grass of verdant hue; budding trees clustered here and there; red-roofed houses peeping amid the green. Orchards of apple, cherry, and almond blossoms were dotted about. A riot of colour – green; red, white, and pink. Toward the horizon the bright flashes of the big guns, the whole lit gloriously in the dying splendour of the sun. Yet more than that was seen. There were the remnants of the 51st Division, slaughtered for the *n*th time, fighting desperately in an endeavour to stay the onslaught of the enemy. Now scarce a brigade. But they fought on in isolated groups. Sections scattered over the countryside and fought till they died or were overwhelmed by vastly superior force. The Gordons moved rapidly forward, crossed the La Bassée Canal, and plunged on to conflict. Surged forward and came up; plunged madly on the field-grey that swept up to break and swamp the heroic Highlanders. A short, grim struggle; bayonets flashed in the dying rays of the sun.

The field-grey wave rolled sullenly back from whence it had come. And then came the darkness. A line was dug. In a near-by farmhouse were cows, calves, horses, chickens, rabbits, pigs, and the varied stock one finds about a farm. In a cellar were hundreds of bottles of red and white wine, port, and champagne, to say nothing of a dozen barrels of beer. The troops lived very well in the ensuing days when not engaged with the enemy, on consolidation, or wiring. Out for a day, then into the other sector doing labourer's work. A sergeant took a party out one night to fire farmhouses in No Man's Land. They were nests of machine guns and the party's arms were tins of petrol. Under a rising moon petrol was lavishly poured away. Some under a table. Some on the cloth and a sofa, walls quickly splashed. A flight of stairs in a corner quickly doused when a door at the top opened and a stream of light shone down and there was the noise of much guttural speech. The sergeant had a sheet of newspaper folded lengthwise. A match, a touch, and instantly a flame shot upward. A rapid touch to table and sofa and the sergeant dashed through the door with his kilt apron alight at the rear. They set light to each of four houses; fell foul of a German patrol, and surprised them by fighting with their fists, which seemed so to alarm them that they broke and fled... The incendiary party returned without loss.

They stayed on the sector for a while. The enemy used much gas. At this time they were using a very pernicious gas, which caused one to weep and sneeze and which infected you with dysentery at the same time. Unpleasant!

A working party was required one night to dig a cable trench. It is impossible to do navvies' work in a box respirator and the party mainly worked without. A deluge of gas shells. Eyes swollen and red; throats parched; flesh inflamed and almost raw where the mustard variety of gas had burned it – a serious disadvantage to a kilt. In the morning the gas lay across the valley, thick and nauseous as the miasma vapour of an African forest. Large green banks of chlorine gas threw back iridescent colours to the sun, while rising from it came a fetid, urinous stench that came near choking one.

In the garden at the billet lying about the grass were close on a hundred men, denuded of their clothing, who lay about and writhed in veriest agony. The worst gas cases. With the passing of a few hours huge blisters were raised by the mustard gas. One man had a blister that reached from his neck to the bottom of his spine and extended the whole width of his back. In their agony they were retching horribly; straining till they sank exhausted, and then suddenly vomiting a long, green, streamer-like substance. And they were nearly all blind.

Christ! This happened on the morning of May 25th, 1911, in the village of Chocques, after nearly two thousand years of Christianity.

Would you believe it?

Sergeant H. E. May joined the Cameron Highlanders in January 1917, and was sent to France in May 1917, and transferred to the Gordon Highlanders, with whom he served continuously until the close of the War, when the battalion marched to Germany. Held the substantive rank of Sergeant, and in 1918 acted as C.S.M. or C.Q.M.S. on occasion. Was awarded the Military Medal in October 1918 for operations in the early part of that month.

OPENING OF GERMAN OFFENSIVE

March 1918

Alfred Grosch

Turmoil and confusion are everywhere. Troops, baggage, and all the litter of war, lumbers up every available space. R.T. Officers are here, there, and everywhere. They sort us out, guide, and lead us to our trains. We file in.

Where are we going? No one knows. Where's the 8th? Where's the 7th? Where's the 6th? Where is any regiment?

We move. It is night, we travel all night, and are joining or rejoining, new troops or casualties returning to cur units.

Sergeant S. is with me. He already has the D.C.M. This is his third lot. He does not relish it, none of us do. This will probably finish him; he realizes it. We all do. That is, the men. But what of the others? Boys, boys, boys – always boys. They have no right here. They are brave enough now, but, in a few hours, shells, gas; machine gun, and rifle will play hell with them. Daylight comes. Nesle slips by, and Ham, and right on to rail-head we go. There the track ends, and we detrain.

Officers claim us, and the troops break up, going each to their corps reinforcements. Here we spend a day or two. There are parades, and instruction. We drill the boys; they hate it – so do we.

Then they give me a map, point out my direction, put me in charge of a party, and off we go. We belong to the 8th Londons.

Autreville is our headquarters, and I have to shepherd these lads safely to their destination, which, according to my map, is about seven miles away.

The going is heavy. Loaded like pack-mules, some of the lads soon crack up, so I rest them a bit, and take the opportunity to make adjustments to the equipment of one or two, in order that a better fit will make it easier for them. We go on; aircraft, flying high, are being shelled; it gives the boys their first experience of shell-fire. They do not mind, it is so far away. We watch the puffs and listen for the 'Krupp! Krupp!' A transport wagon overtakes us, it belongs to the 8th, our unit. I hail the driver. He says that we have three miles to go yet, and suggests relieving some of the boys of their equipment.

I agree. I know that it is wrong to do so, but I chance it. You have to chance everything in this war; and if you get caught, well, it does not matter much. He loads the equipment into his wagon, and goes on. The lads keep their rifles, and the going is easier for some. We reach Autreville.

Of course, we have our rations – at least, we did. A bag of tea, one of sugar, and milk in tins. No, they're gone? Dumped somewhere, no one knows. I don't mind very much. The quartermaster fumes and curses, but I know perfectly well that he will have to provide more. The boys, however, are appalled. They think that they will have to go short, Why does the Army stick to this idiotic system of loading men, already overloaded, with rations that can, and often have to be, provided at the next depot?

We lounge here for a day, and then I take my party up the line. As I have only three miles to go this time, they give me a guide. He leads. I am instructed to take the rear, and keep an eye on stragglers. He sends me no word back. We pass a guard 'turned out'; we don't salute, because I do not see them until we have almost passed them. Further on we pass a general with his aide, both on foot. We do not salute; we take no notice. He looks surprised, but passes on without a word. Wise old man! Some of our old Blighty dug-outs would have doubled us up and down for ten minutes.

At last we reach the battalion. Captain P., the adjutant, takes the list. 'Any old friends here?' he cries; then 'Yes,' and he reads aloud my name. I step forward. 'I am new to you, sir. I belong to the other battalion. My cousin was here with you, but he is now home, wounded.' We are divided up, and go to various companies. I go to 'B' Company. The first man I meet is Alf K., V.C. 'Oh!' he cries. 'Here's a bit of luck; we've got a sergeant.' That means that he, and his N.C.O.s, will be a little less overworked. Our platoon commander is Lieutenant P., a

Canadian, a real dare-devil, afraid of nothing. For the moment we are in caves at Barisis-au-Bois. Wonderful place, these caves, they afford a complete shelter for two battalions, one French and one English.

This is the extreme right of the British line; we join up here with the French. At night in the front-line trench we have a post which consists of one French and one English sentry. This post is in my care. I find it very difficult to keep the boys awake; as soon as I turn my back they are asleep.

My officer is away on leave; his place is taken by Lieutenant S., whom I do not like, and consider a bit of a fool. I see him in the dark just removing a rifle from beside a sleeping boy. He is handing it back to his runner, and has not seen me as he is half-turned away. I decide to give him a fright; so as he turns again, he finds the point of my bayonet an inch from his throat. He hears my fierce whisper of 'Who are you?' and replies hurriedly, 'Rum!' the password for the night. I tell him, that he is lucky, as I thought of thrusting first and enquiring afterwards. I tell him that I view the disarming of one of my sentries very seriously. For the sake of the boy we patch it up, and say nothing about it.

Things are very quiet, and Alf K. goes back home for a commission. I take over the platoon. We are continually changing officers, and the greater part of the time are without one, which is as well, for some of them are perfect fools. Barisis is a quaint old place. Our front-line trench winds in and out of the main street, through back gardens, out into the fields, and right up to Grottoir Hill, where it curves round the base. But this is the French line, and we do not enter it.

Opposite my dug-out are the remains of a convent and chapel. There is a well in the convent and we can get fresh water from it. Attached to the convent is a little cemetery, where sleep the departed sisters of happier days. Wild cats and rats abound. Far out in No Man's Land is the village cemetery 'Where the rude forefathers of the hamlet sleep.' We think Jerry is there, and bombard it mercilessly. He thinks we are there, and returns the compliment. Stones, crosses, and other sacred emblems fly, in all directions. No one is hurt. We have only one casualty, poor Dan G. I stop a moment and speak with him, then go on, I hear a crash, run back, and find him dead. My life is spared by thirty seconds.

We know at what time the German sentries are relieved on the guns during the night. For they fire off all four guns in the battery, and reload. They are then quiet for another hour. The machine guns on all sides kick up an infernal din all night long.

Trench mortars come fussing over, but no one is hit; our nerves get rather frayed. The weather is dry, but horribly cold. It freezes all night, every night.

We have finished; to-night we are to be relieved, and everyone is pleased. My corporal is sick, but he remains on duty. He takes his overcoat out of his pack, and dons it; his pack will be lighter, and easier to carry; but he gets hold of someone else's pack, and so moves off with two overcoats instead of one. Poor Joe, we very nearly carry him out.

We rest. That is – we drill, dig, and make up roads. An unpopular sergeant-major is leaving us for good. The boys line the road, and give him a send off that makes him come off the top of the bus, and hide himself inside. The usual bombers come over at night, splash us with dirt and little else. Our Company Commander comes back from a course of something or other, and with him come rumours of big attacks by Jerry. We parade for pay, but it is cancelled and we don't get it, but instead, get into 'full marching order,' draw rations and ammunition. Then we stand by. N.C.O.s are called together. The news is: 'The attack has opened; situation obscure.' We know exactly what that means.

At six o'clock a fleet of motor lorries arrives, and all embark. Bugle-major K. wishes me 'Good-bye and good luck.' Off we go, further in to the west, St. Quentin way.

Many of the boys realize the significance of events. They are silent. Twenty-four hours hence many will be silent for ever. We pass through Chauny, which I recognize in the twilight, and later, at a cross roads, get out. Here is a concentration of troops, who are slowly moving off in various directions.

Jerry has been successful. He has smashed the 153rd

Brigade, and nearly got their brigadier. Where he is or what he is doing no one knows. To my company is given the job of finding out. I am to take my platoon, search for a bridge, find out if it is held. If it is, I must take it, and hold it, preferably with bayonet. I arrange accordingly. We dump our packs, and with them my supply of tobacco, which is most unfortunate for me.

We move on, march, deploy, circle, get lost, dig in, get moved on, dig in again, are moved on yet again, and at dawn are still digging in, far from where we should be.

We get into our correct position about seven in the morning. No question now about the bridge: there it is, not a soul on it. Some R.E.s attempt to blow it up, but do not succeed. More digging. The morning is misty; all is quiet; some sleep, some dig, some make tea, and some eat.

Presently two Fusiliers come over the bridge; they have a Jerry prisoner. They tell us that the three of them slept in 153rd Brigade Headquarters. This is supposed to be in German hands, but actually he is 200 yards from it. These lads are lucky. They take their prisoner with them.

I have no officer in my platoon; the other platoons have one each, but two of them are no better off than we are, for early on their officers go off to the rear, and are not seen again.

How they explain themselves at Headquarters I do not know. They get through all right; but their platoons are captured and wiped out. At noon the attack opens up on us. Casualties are heavy. In going for a German bomber, I myself am hit and put out for a time. I come to, but cannot keep quiet. I go along, and examine my platoon; it is nearly *non est*.

Lieutenant W. calls for volunteers to go to Headquarters for help. I set off, and take a boy with me who is badly hit in the head.

The area we cross is swept by rifle and machine-gun fire; we crawl and escape it. The boy is in pain and crying. Presently he jumps up. 'Here they come!' he cries. I pull him down. 'Who?' I ask. 'Jerry,' he says. I look cautiously up. There he is right enough, the first wave almost on top of us.

'Leave it to me, boy; we're done; we're prisoners now. Do

whatever I tell you.' I wait a second, then 'Up!' I say, 'and take your helmet off.' We do so. The German in front of me says, 'Ach!' raises his rifle and takes aim. I mutter to myself, 'I hope to God he won't pull that trigger.' For ten seconds we remain so, then he lowers his rifle, and says what I take to be 'Wounded?' I nod, and say, 'Yes, yes.' He beckons, and we approach. We still have our equipment on, and the Germans utter shouts, pointing to it. 'Slip it off!' I cry to the boy, doing so myself.

The German has spared us. Would we have spared him under the circumstances? God knows! Perhaps not.

We go back, through our own barrage, to the rear of the German line, passing through successive waves of troops going forward.

Only one thought now: to get out of this hell, and as far back as possible. But the Germans in charge of us do not know the country. More prisoners join us, little groups of dead are here and there where they have fallen, English and German together. It is very hard, many are only boys.

One of our officers from 'A' company is lying on a stretcher badly wounded in the stomach. He is delirious with pain. It hurts to see him writhe, and hear him call his N.C.O.s one by one. I know each one he mentions, and wonder whether they are living or dead.

We carry this, officer about for some hours, until we reach a German casualty clearing station, where we leave him. He has grown much quieter, and I think his end is near. But oh, for a sleep; my head is fit to burst.

Relentlessly onward we go. Back, back, right clear of the battlefield, moving all night.

Morning comes, we reach a camp where the remnants of my company are already assembled, having travelled by a quicker route. I greet them, and am glad to meet the survivors. But I go off to sleep, and am oblivious to everything. I get just an hour. We are off again, no stopping here. What a crowd: hundreds, perhaps thousands, French and English – a long column stretches down the road before and behind us. We are escorted by Uhlans, not bad fellows. They rest us frequently, and after each rest I am shaken vigorously before I come round. They send a horseman in advance, we go through a village, the inhabitants line the road with pails of water, we drink as we pass. The women wring their hands at the sight of us, and when they can pass us a piece of bread quickly, so that our guards cannot see the action. We go to Guise; the castle on the hill is visible some way off.

We enter the town, which, though in German occupation, is still full of French inhabitants. They rush into the ranks, push tobacco, bread, and food into our hands. One woman braves the guards, and rushes to me with a can of hot coffee, then she is gone. The men throw their caps to those who are without. Tears are in all eyes.

We stay here the night. We who are wounded are taken to a dressing station, they give us bread and jam to eat, with weak coffee to drink. The place is full of German wounded. Some are terrible; a man is near me with half his jaw blown off; they are trying to feed him with a little teapot. The sight is ghastly. Poor fellow. He is only one. The whole place is overflowing. They come in one long stream all night and all day. The push is costing them dear.

We must go away next day; there is no room for us, others are on the way. Down to the railway we go. A huge train is waiting. From many trucks come cries of men in mortal agony. What a load; whither are we going? Sixty of us, all wounded, all packed in one truck. We pass Le Cateau. At Diedenhofen, a German says, 'Here you get hot eat.' We do, and it is good.

The Jerries scrounge an issue of cigars and cigarettes for us. We are at Trier West, and change from trucks to carriages. On we go into Germany. Adventure is at an end; henceforth we are prisoners.

Private Alfred Grosch joined Post Office Rifles (8th London) October 13th, 1915. Wounded (acting Sergeant) and captured at La Fère, March 22nd, 1918. Nine months in various camps in Germany. Reached home on New Year's Day, 1919. Discharged, February 28th, 1919.

RETREAT

R. G. Bultitude

In the early hours of the morning of March 22nd, 1918, our own front-line troops retired through us. At the time we were occupying a shallow trench forming the support line before Marcoing, in the Cambrai salient, and a little later we also withdrew.

Our first halt was on the slope of a hill. We could not see the attackers, but their artillery plastered the hillside with shrapnel, and we were not sorry to get orders to move again. During the halt one of our officers handed me a bottle of whisky to 'look after' for him. I did not see him again, but the whisky came in useful.

My company was leading, and we were under fairly heavy shell-fire for some time. As we passed through one village, evidently some sort of headquarters, the mixed assortment of clerks, storekeepers, and other oddments were making a hurried exit. A hundred yards or so ahead of us, a two-horsed wagon, containing stores and half a dozen men, had just started off when a shell burst, apparently immediately over it. We made a detour round the mangled remains of horses and men.

Although our latest spell in the trenches had only been the normal one of eight days, we had been relieved, had marched back to the reserve line, a distance of about eight miles, had immediately been exposed to a protracted shelling, with gas, and then, without food or rest, had returned to the line.

During the spell of trench life, too, there had been considerable activity; it had been difficult to get rations up when we were in the front line, and there had been no rest during our four days in support. The infantry-man is a soldier by day and a navvy by night. Sleep is a luxury in which he is allowed to indulge only on rare occasions, and then for very brief periods.

We did not start on our long trek any too fresh. We marched all day, with very few and very short halts. A little after dark we came to some cross-roads, went straight across them, and very shortly after, walked plump into the arms of the enemy!

For several hours we had been marching at ease in apparent security, and were therefore taken completely by surprise on the first challenge in a foreign tongue.

We scattered in open order on to the fields on either side of the road, and lay flat awaiting developments. A sergeant shouted out that he knew the place as the site of an Indian Labour Corps encampment.

An officer and one or two men went forward, calling out that we were English, and were promptly shot.

The fight that followed remains in my recollection as a confused medley of bursting bombs, rifle and machine-gun fire.

I found a shallow hole in the ground, and from its shelter fired point-blank at forms just seen in the darkness under the unmistakable squarish German helmets, until my ammunition gave out.

A form appeared, and Johnson's voice said, 'I've got one in the thigh, old man.' I felt the wet blood on his trouser-leg, but by the time I had fumbled for and found my first-aid outfit he had wandered off again. I heard afterwards that he acted as orderly in a German War Hospital.

Among the confusion of shouts, groans, curses, and the detonation of bursting bombs, I thought I recognized a voice calling for help as that of a company stretcher bearer and one of my pals. He was known as 'Blanco,' from which anyone acquainted with Army humour will at once realize that he had coal-black hair and a swarthy complexion.

I crawled towards the voice, and found its owner in a shell hole with five wounded whom he had collected by the exercise of I don't know what powers of sight and physical exertion. He bandaged their wounds in the darkness with my unskilful assistance.

Loud commands in German, and a sudden intensification of firing apparently from all sides told us that we were almost if not quite surrounded. The only chance seemed to be the road; obviously if the enemy were behind us there we were completely ringed round; if not, there might be an avenue of escape by the way we had come.

By the time we had got our wounded companions on to the road (I have no idea how), the enemy were pretty fully occupied in guarding and disposing of their captives. Luck favoured us, and we got clear. A few others, possibly a dozen, also escaped, as we found out eventually.

We had, of course, no idea as to the whereabouts of the remainder of our battalion, and when we reached the crossroads any direction seemed as likely as another to lead us into trouble again.

Providence, sheer chance, or a sense of direction led us to turn left.

During the rest of that night, and, I think, the whole of the next day we struggled along. By good fortune we all escaped being hit by splinters from a huge ammunition dump which had been fired by our engineers, and from which a shower of red-hot metal rained down over a large area of the road and its surroundings.

The noise of the explosions completely shattered the nerves of the most seriously hurt of our comrades, and it was almost impossible to control him. We got him past the blazing dump somehow, and I then remembered the officer's whisky. We all had a swig, and we poured a very generous quantity of the neat spirit down the delirious man's throat. We had practically to carry him, after that, but he became quite quiet. He died an hour or two later, and we were able to leave him by the roadside.

The other four needed more and more support as time went on, and our progress became a crawl.

I retained a few small personal belongings, my haversack and rifle, but had to discard the rest of my equipment.

At last in the distance we saw a group of huts, but now also we came under sporadic machine-gun fire. It was not very heavy in our direction, and we got safely into one of the buildings. In a field a little further on British troops were digging themselves in, but the space between them and ourselves was swept by bullets and it would have been suicidal to attempt to reach them.

One of our charges had been hit in the head; his mind now was wandering, and he was babbling and muttering. The other three were in some sort of shape to help themselves, and we decided that when darkness came on 'Blanco' should try to get them across to 'the line,' and then if possible send someone to help me in getting the fourth over.

The first part of the programme was more successful than we had hoped, 'Blanco' and his charges went off on hands and knees, hand and knees, or hands and knee, according to where they had been winged, stumbled on to a sort of dugout, which they found occupied by our own American medical officer and a number of other casualties, and heard that the diggers-in comprised the other three companies of our own battalion!

I, of course, had no knowledge of what had happened to my companions at the time, and it soon became apparent that there was very little hope of any help reaching me, for the firing again became very heavy, and the hut itself was constantly being hit.

The effects of the whisky had long since worn off. I had had no other food or drink for considerably more than twenty-four hours, during most of which time I had been on the move and heavily encumbered. I could hardly remember when I had last slept. My companion became violent, and I had to sit on him to prevent him rushing out of the hut, which contained other occupants in the shape of two dead men. My vigil seemed interminable.

Towards morning I had practically given up any hope of leaving the hut alive, because it was obvious that sooner or later the enemy infantry would advance, and we were pretty certain to be 'mopped up.' I fished a piece of paper out of my pack and wrote a short farewell letter to my wife, in the hope that some decent German, finding it on my body, might manage to get it sent on.

Daylight came at last, and with it a slight lull in the firing. My comrade had sunk into a condition of lethargy, and I determined to risk the journey. We reached the M.O.'s dug-out; I think I carried my companion part of the way and dragged him the remainder. I never knew his name, and have heard nothing of him since – but I hope he got home safely. The M.O. was killed the same day whilst evacuating the wounded.

I joined the rest of the battalion. My first action upon reaching the half-dug trench was to tear up the letter I had written an hour or two earlier and thankfully scatter the pieces to the winds.

For the next week or so (one quite lost count of time) the retreat resolved itself into a test of endurance. The battalion managed to keep more or less together, but there was no pretence at any sort of order. Some had to drop out, either through exhaustion or wounds, sometimes stragglers from other regiments joined us or were overtaken. A few were killed by the enemy's ubiquitous machine guns. The latter were always more or less at our heels (and as often on our flanks), but, after all, bullets drill a fairly clean hole, and one does not mind them – much. The thought of great gaping wounds caused by jagged bits of shell, to say nothing of the shattering of nerves by concussion, is a different thing. The absence of shell-fire was our one cause for self-congratulation.

In some ways the attackers probably had a worse time than we. To a certain extent we could and did choose our own places and times for halting and showing fight. Our artillery, too, frequently continued to fire over our heads almost until we reached the guns.

The enemy troops, however, probably did get some orations. Our food was such as we could 'scrounge' from' deserted canteens and Y.M.C.A. huts, when anything had been left by those who had preceded us: perhaps a few biscuits, a packet of chocolate, or, as happened on one occasion, a tin of pineapple chunks. We were badly troubled by thirst; there seemed to be no water anywhere except that collected in shell holes, stagnant and impregnated with gas. Eventually we were driven to crawling about in the early mornings and licking the dew off the grass.

But the almost insupportable hardship was the lack of sleep. The longest uninterrupted spell I remember was one of about a couple of hours, wedged with three fellow slumberers between the outstretched fore and hind legs of a dead horse (for shelter from a biting wind), its belly for a pillow and the cobblestones of a village street for a bed. For the rest, we dozed as we walked, or fell asleep, willy-nilly, whilst making some sort of cover, only to be prodded into wakefulness almost immediately in order either to move off again, or to be ready to repel an attack.

There was no lack of ammunition, for cartridge-belts, haversacks, and other equipment, even rifles and smashed Lewis guns, were lying about in the wake of the retreating troops, whose physical exhaustion was such that an extra pound or two in weight might mean the difference between capture and liberty.

Sometimes we were in open country, sometimes we took to the roads, but night and day we tramped on. I found somewhere a rake-handle, and but for this third leg probably could not have stayed the course. I walked the soles off the two pairs of socks I was wearing, and raised blisters on my feet which gave me hell until they burst.

We passed over the old Somme battlefield, a desolate stretch of overgrown and fallen-in trenches, with rusty barbed wire, old tins, and other 'junk' scattered about.

We crossed the river – the Aisne, I suppose – near Albert, and halted on a grassy plateau on the far side of the town.

One of the historians of the War says: 'At eleven on that date [March 27th] an inspiriting order was sent along the line that the retreat was over, and that the Army must fight out the issue where it stood. It is the decisive call which the British soldier loves, and never fails to obey.'

Our old colonel didn't put it quite as nicely as that, but he was a sportsman, we liked him, and we appreciated his way of delivering the message. Strictly expurgated, it was, as near as I can remember, as follows:

'Now, you men, that's Albert, and this is as far as we go.

When the Boche tries to come through the town, as he will, we attack. There's to be no more retreat, and no surrendering. What the hell are you going to sleep for?'

He walked in front of our ragged line as we advanced to the attack, and gave the signals by a wave of his cane. We had no cover, and advanced in open order under a terrific machine-gun and rifle-fire – a few paces forward, then flat on the ground, then on for a few yards again.

I had a foolish notion that if I had an umbrella I should feel safer.

I have not yet read an account of troops attacking whilst asleep, but this was true of many of our men. The man on my left was fast asleep immediately on throwing himself prone, and on each upward wave of the colonel's cane I had to prod him awake with the butt of my rifle.

My 'tin hat' was hit twice. A bullet pierced the exact centre of the top of the helmet of the man on my right as he walked forward with head down. He spun round as he fell, and with a stream of blood spurting out of the circular hole in the top of his head, scrambled back on hands and knees for perhaps 10 yards, and rolled over.

A short, white-haired lad rushed screaming right along our line, with an eye shot away.

As we threw ourselves over the edge of the plateau to the ploughed land below, another near neighbour was hit in a most painful part of the body, and lay in the ditch at the foot of the slope, screaming.

Very few of us reached what shelter the ditch afforded, and it was impossible to advance further. Our casualties already were very heavy. Eventually, with four others I reached a shell hole which provided some sort of reasonable cover, and from there, and a few other similar posts of vantage, those of us who were left managed to check any further advance of the enemy. One of us had a penny stick of chocolate, which he divided into five pieces, and which formed our sole nourishment for many hours.

If Alf's magic button had suddenly come into my possession, I should have thus addressed the attendant genie:

'Send up immediately large reinforcements of fresh troops – not ragged scarecrows like ourselves; mind, but real live soldiers, and *let them be Colonials*.'

No magic button was needed. Up they came, rank – after rank, clean, shaved, in spick and span uniforms, properly armed. The awed exclamation of one of my shell-hole companions seemed to sum up our feelings to a nicety.

'New Zealanders! Well, Gawd help Jerry!'

Private R. G. Bultitude joined the 1st Battalion Artists Rifles in 1917, and served on the Western Front until May 1918, when he was severely wounded whilst occupying an outpost in Aveluy Wood. The stretcher bearer referred to in the narrative as 'Blanco' came over, in broad daylight, bandaged his wounds, and carried him to safety in circumstances involving the risk of almost certain death.

'STAND-TO' ON GIVENCHY ROAD

Thomas A. Owen

It was near the end of the great German bid for victory in April 1918. We left Beuvry and passed the hamlet of Le Fresnoy and crossed the bridge over the La Bassée Canal into the village of Gorre. There we struck a route past the famous Brewery to make for the open fields and the front-line trenches. We knew our destination was 'somewhere between Festubert and Givenchy' – a new sector to us – and, as we marched, we sang softly a popular ditty of those days. It went to the tune of a sentimental song then going strong in Blighty, about a Tulip and a Red, Red Rose. Our own exclusive lyric had pointed reference to certain gentlemen at home and ended in averring that:

You stole our wenches
While we were in the trenches
Facing the angry foe;
You were a-slacking
While we were attacking
The Huns on Givenchy Road.

Now, in reality, we were to know what it was like on Givenchy Road, and it was said that there was plenty of 'dirt' up in 'the doings.'

The 'Pork and Beans' had broken in disorder on the left, and it was rumoured that the Germans had captured the Portuguese commissariat and were even raiding and reconnoitring in Portuguese uniforms. The 55th Division had made a stand and held up a veritable horde of the enemy with great slaughter. Now, utterly weary, they were to be relieved, and we of the 1st Division were to hold the renewed attack of the enemy.

A part of my own company relieved a detachment of the Liverpool Scottish, and we occupied a section of the trenches almost square-shaped in form, with three sides facing a miniature salient of German troops, who surrounded us more or less in the form of a horseshoe. Our post was evidently a key position in the line. Dead men lay about here and there; the communication trench to Headquarters – a small pillbox in the centre of the square had partly collapsed at the sides and was sickeningly yielding underfoot with the bodies of buried men. Here and there a leg or an arm protruded from the trench side. The wire was cut in places and the gaps in the trenches, caused by trench mortar attacks, were staringly open and dangerous.

We arrived in the dark of the evening, before the moon had risen. Silently we filed into the trench at a corner of the square. A line of bare trees, tall and ghostly, marked another boundary of the line. The Scotties trailed out, with whispered greetings, and we settled down to the eternal vigil. The silence was of the dead. Not a gun fired. Not even a Verey light flared. The bloated trench rats squeaked now and again and only intensified the silence.

There was nothing to do but overhaul equipment: place Mills bombs at strategic points, with slack pins ready for throwing; play cards; smoke interminable cigarettes. During the night we examined the wire and sent reconnoitring patrols into No Man's Land. They met nothing, heard nothing, saw no one, and came back scared and craving rum. Above all we must not remain still to brood on things. For two days the silence continued, unnatural and nerve-racking. Old soldiers talked with bated breath of the horrors that were surely coming. On the evening of the third day, as we shook our limbs and set guards and patrols moving, a whispered word went round that at 'Stand to' at dusk the Germans might attack in force. We lined up along the trench, and gulped our rum ration and literally ached for something to happen. But the sun went down and the gloom came on, and not a sound broke the solitude. Well, it would be at 'Stand to' at about six o'clock in the morning – a bloodchilling time.

Morning 'Stand to' came in due course, and once more the rum went round and the whispered word of warning. A watery sun peeped through the mist and still no enemy appeared. No lark rose to greet the dawn. Not a gun hurled its load of venom.

I sat down with my section of eight men and I looked at our ration of bread, bacon, and cheese. It was small enough, and God knew if we should ever get another. 'Shall we cook the whole issue?' I asked, and a nodding chorus signified assent. We lit the 'Tommy' cooker, and made a good job of the cooking, and ate a great bellyfull and smoked a Woodbine at the end.

Suddenly a gun barked and a heavy explosion shook the trenches. The frantic rats squeaked and scuttled past us: men shuddered, and clattered their arms and sprang to attention. The barrage had started. I heaved a sigh and was almost glad the suspense was over. The barrage was pitched about 40 yards short of our line of trench. Evidently it would creep to us after first smashing the wire.

I placed five men on the fire-step and fixed one man with a Lewis gun and two men to fill containers for it. We waited with livid faces. The barrage crept nearer. Now it was 30 yards, now 20 yards. We were in a hell of din and slaughter. The trench was crumbling slowly to pieces. One of my men suddenly sank to his knees. A piece of a shell had torn at his middle and he sat down quietly to die a slow death. I shook with stark fear, but I held to my rifle and kept my place on the crumbling fire-step.

The barrage lifted again and moved nearer.

The man with the wound in his side moaned at intervals, and fixed his field bandage and held his hands to it as if to hold the very life in him. His groans, coming during the briefest lulls in the shelling, were unnerving us all. We crouched at the bottom of the trench, abject and trembling. I passed the rum bottle round and took a long swig myself.

Rum numbs you at times like these. It gives you Dutch courage and a lurching contempt for danger. You die more or less decently; neither whining nor squealing – which is as it should be. A moment later the machine gun to the right of us went up in the air and its team of men went up with it: a direct hit. The shells were dropping practically on the very brink of the trench.

Now the worst had come. We were face down in the slime, with boot and finger and knee clutching and scraping for the veriest inch of cover; hiding our eyes, as we did once from childish terrors; now whimpering, now cursing, with bowels turned to water and every facility at agonized tension.

...Who shall say where Providence came in?

Death grinned at us and yet not a shell hit full on our dozen yards of entrenchment. Still leaping forward, the barrage blundered over us and beyond us. It left us stunned and deaf and prostrate. The dying man mercifully breathed his last in the midst of it. Still we cowered in the mud and the slime. At nine o'clock in the morning the barrage started. It ceased as suddenly as it had begun, at exactly 11.30 a.m., It might have been a year of time.

The deadly stillness came on again but I ran among the others kicking right and left in a frenzy because I knew the attack was coming. The man would follow the machine. Looking over the top I saw the long grey lines sweeping along four hundred yards away. They were marching slowly, shoulder to shoulder, heavily weighted with picks, ammunition, and rations.

We scrambled to the fire-step. We fired madly and recklessly. The Lewis gun rattled and the two magazine fillers worked with feverish haste. It should have been horrid slaughter at the distance, for the Germans seemed to huddle together like sheep as they lurched over No Man's Land. But there were thousands of them and our aim was hurried and bad. We fired in abandonment rather than by design.

Still the grey hordes advanced.

A hoarse voice shouted at the back of us. It was Sergeant Winnford: God knows how he got through to us; and he yelled 'Retreat back to support line: you, corporal, see them all out.' He made for a gap in the trench. The survivors followed him. As he reached the open a stray shot, or splinter, splattered his brains out and he fell without a sound.

Stupefied, the others crept through and got clear, and raced across the open land with the enemy in full cry behind. Barker was the last to crawl out. I howled at him to hurry, but he was tall and lanky and dead beat. I raced at his side. 'Slip off your pack,' I shouted, as I got out of my own trappings. He did so, but he was ashen and panting.

I felt a smart above my elbow and found there was blood trickling from the tips of my fingers. 'Barker, Barker!' I screamed. 'Hurry up, chum, for God's sake!' I might have saved my breath. As I turned my head to him, and as he made a supreme effort to hasten, I saw the bullet hit the back of his tin helmet and spurt out at the front. He curled over in a heap. He was past aid.

I ran a dozen steps further. Something hit my other elbow, searing hot and smashing through, and I spun round like a top and lay once more in the slime.

I thought my arm had gone. If it was death I was numb, careless and content. I sank into a dull stupor and the hordes of grey uniforms trampled over me, round me and by me, and forgot me in their own terror. '

They swept on and on to meet another wall of steel and flame. How many of them would see another dawn?

Presently I came fully to myself and found that my arm was still there but was bleeding profusely. Laboriously, I got my field dressing somewhere near where the blood was flowing, and I got to my knees, then to my feet in a half-blind endeavour to get somewhere, to someone… I staggered to meet the second wave of the advancing Germans. Would they shoot me again as they passed me? An officer, with revolver in hand, waved me through the ranks.

They parted to make a road for me. At every other step I fell with weakness and the spikes of the ground wire stabbed into my hands, my limbs, my very face, as I fell. I remember weeping like a child because I could not help falling and suffering this torture.

I cannot say how far I walked. I passed a first-aid post in an old trench, but they waved me off despairingly. They had too many to see to. Stretcher bearers passed me, carrying a pole, with a blanket slung to it, and inside an agonized bundle of broken humanity – blood trickling and dripping from the pendulous blanket.

Eventually I simply fell into another portion of trench and there a sad-eyed, black-bearded man whispered 'Armes kind' – meaning little child – and stripped off my tunic, leather jerkin, and cardigan, and took his own field dressing and patched up the mess of my arm. A prisoner indeed; receiving succour from a man whose countrymen I had blazed at in hate but a while ago, and from whom I had suffered this shot in my elbow.

Truly the quality of mercy is not strained. I had none of his tongue, nor he of mine, but he gave me a drink of warm coffee from a flask, and his hands were as tender as a woman's as he bandaged me. If ever I had felt hate for the German I was cured of it now. I had had my job to do and he his. The responsibility was not ours and our fate was none of our choosing. I to-day; perhaps he to-morrow. But I could not stay here.

The English barrage had now started; tearing and rip-snorting along all the roads and communications. It was intended to hold up the reinforcements for the German attack.

For me there was the sickening necessity of walking through the menace of our own barrage; to risk death from our own shells; to get to some place of refuge.

Three others joined me. They also had staggered from the shambles of No Man's Land, and we bled from various wounds all along that pitiless road to the rear.

How we escaped the shelling I know not. German transport wagons lumbered past us at intervals, the drivers whipping the horses to a mad gallop. Here and there dead or dying horses lay among the splintered ruins of shafts and wheels. The very road was greasy with blood. Yet even as the horses fell the poor brutes were dragged to the side of the road and the matter-of-fact Germans whipped out knives and cut long strips of flesh from the steaming flanks. Heaps of intestines lay in the ditches.

At last a German unter-offizier dashed out from behind a ruined house and took charge of our little band. He took us a further short walk till we came to a large church with the Red Cross flag flying from the tower. We were placed in a queue of men all waiting for attention to wounds. Gradually we got inside the church. May I never again see such a sight.

All along the nave improvised stretchers lay side by side and reached to the step leading to choir and chancel.

Up there a dozen surgeons in ghastly stained white overalls performed operation after operation. Amputation after amputation.

The smell of chloroform and ether pervaded everything. The horrible rasping sound of the silver saws grated on the ear.

Attendants carried limbs away in tall baskets. Men died before aid could get to them. Each had inexorably to wait his turn and the surgeons, with white and drawn faces, sweated and toiled silently: no time for consultations.

I was attended to in my turn, and left that charnel house for the near-by prisoners' cage, where I was questioned and had my papers examined and my letters from home confiscated.

It was now nightfall. I was in a small town – La Bassée, maybe, though I had no means of knowing.

Twenty-four hours previously I had 'stood to' on the fire-step and awaited the coming of the attack. Now it was all over. There is enduring stuff in youth, and I was young and craved for life with every fibre of my being. I was not done for yet. So I staggered among the ranks of a draft of prisoners to be entrained for the rear hospitals. We marched in columns of four to the station, and we held one another up and marched as if in a dream. They placed us in open trucks; Black Watch, South Wales Borderers, and others, and we clanked through a pitch-black night of hail, rain, and storm, through Lille and on to Tournai. I was half delirious by then: the numbness had given place to agony, and with all of us the bitter night did its worst to finish off the work that even the shells had failed to do.

So we ended up away in high Germany, and the Army Lists posted me as 'missing.'

Lance-Corporal Thomas A, Owen. Attested November 1916: called up February 1917. Service in France and Belgium, chiefly on sections of the Ypres Salient, 1st Battalion South Wales Borderers, 1st Division. Wounded and taken prisoner near Festubert, April 18th, 1918. Thence to Schleswig. In hospital for

6 months, then discharged for labour at Munster Prisoner of War Camp, till Armistice. Repatriated December 2nd, 1918.

WHEN TANK FOUGHT TANK

F. Mitchell, M.C.

On April 23rd, 1918, three tanks covered with their green camouflage nets were lying hidden in the gas-drenched wood of Bois-l'Abbe, near Villers-Bretonneux, awaiting the impending German attack. The crews had worn masks for the greater part of the day and their eyes were sore, their throats dry.

Darkness came, but with it two enemy planes flying low, over the tree tops. They dropped Verey lights that fell right in our midst, showing up the bulky outlines of the tanks in vivid relief.

We were discovered!

An hour later, when clouds hid the moon, three huge, toad-like forms, grunting and snorting, crept out of the wood to a spot some hundred yards to the rear.

Just before dawn on April 24th a tremendous bombardment deluged the wood. I was aroused in the dark by someone shaking me violently. 'Gas, sir, gas!' I struggled up, half awake, inhaled a foul odour and quickly slipped on my mask. My eyes were running, I could not see, my breath came with difficulty. I could hear the trees crashing to the ground near me.

For a moment I was stricken with panic, then, suddenly, a thought sped through my confused mind, 'If you are going to die, why not die decently?' I listened to that inner voice and pulled myself together, only to discover that I had omitted to attach my nose clip!

Holding hands with my section commander and the orderly who had aroused us, we groped our way to the open. It was pitch dark, save where, away on the edge of the wood, the rising sun showed blood red.

As we stumbled forward, tree trunks, unseen in that infernal gloom, separated our joined hands and we were tripped up by bushes and brambles. Suddenly a hoarse cry came from the orderly, 'My mouthpiece is broken, sir!' 'Run like hell for the open!' shouted the section commander. There was a gasp, and then we heard him crashing away through the undergrowth like a hunted beast.

Soon I found my tank covered with its tarpaulin. The small oblong doors were open, but the interior was empty. On the ground, in the wrappings of the tarpaulin, however, I felt something warm and fleshy. It was one of the crew lying full length, wearing his mask, but dazed by gas.

Behind the trenches a battery of artillery was blazing away, the gunners in their gas masks feverishly loading and unloading like creatures of a nightmare. Meanwhile, as the shelling grew in intensity, a few wounded men and some stragglers came into sight. Their report was depressing, Villers-Bretonneux had been captured and with it many of our own men. The Boche had almost broken through.

By this time two of my crew had developed nasty gas symptoms, spitting, coughing, and getting purple in the face. They were led away to the rear, one sprawling limply in a wheelbarrow found in the wood. We waited till an infantry brigadier appeared on the scene with two orderlies. He was unaware of the exact position ahead and, accompanied by our section captain and the runners, he went forward to investigate. In ten minutes one of the runners came back, limping badly, hit in the leg. In another ten minutes the second returned, his left arm torn by shrapnel, then, twenty minutes after that, walking, unhurt and serene, through the barrage came the brigadier and our captain. The news was grave. We had suffered heavy losses and lost ground, but some infantry were still holding out in the switch-line between Cachy and Villers-Bretonneux. If this line were overwhelmed the Boche would obtain possession of the high ground dominating Amiens and would, perhaps, force us to evacuate that city and drive a wedge between the French and British armies.

A serious consultation was held and the order came, 'Proceed to the Cachy switch-line and hold it at all costs.'

We put on our masks once more and plunged, like divers, into the gas-laden wood. As we strove to crank up, one of the three men, turning the huge handle, collapsed. We put him against a tree, gave him some tablets of ammonia to sniff, and then, as he did not seem to be coming round, we left him, for time was pressing. Out of a crew of seven, four men, with red-rimmed, bulging eyes, only remained.

The three tanks, one male, armed with two six-pounder guns and machine guns, and two females, armed with machine guns only, crawled out of the wood and set off over the open ground towards Cachy.

Ahead, the, German barrage stood like a wall of fire in our path. There was no break in it anywhere. It seemed impossible that we could pass through that deadly area unhit. I decided to attempt a zigzag course, as somehow it seemed safer.

Luck was with us; going at top speed, we went safely through, the danger zone and soon reached the Cachy lines, but there was no sign of our infantry.

Suddenly, out of the ground 10 yards away, an infantryman rose, waving his rifle furiously. We stopped. He ran forward and shouted through the flap, 'Look out! Jerry tanks about!' and then as swiftly disappeared into the trench again.

I informed the crew, and a great thrill ran through us all. Opening the loophole, I looked out. There, some 300 yards away, a round, squat-looking monster was advancing. Behind it came waves of infantry and further away to left and right crawled two more of these armed tortoises.

So we had met our rivals at last! For the first time in history tank was encountering tank!

The 6-pounder gunners crouching on the floor, their backs against the engine cover, loaded their guns expectantly.

We still kept on a zigzag course, threading the gaps between the lines of hastily dug trenches, and coming near the small protecting belt of wire, we turned left and the right gunner, peering through his narrow slit, made a sighting shot. The shell burst some distance beyond the leading enemy tank. No reply came. A second shot boomed out, landing just to the right, but again no reply.

Suddenly, against our steel wall, a hurricane of hail pattered, and the interior was filled with myriads of sparks and flying splinters. Something rattled against the steel helmet of the driver sitting next to me and my face was stung with minute fragments of steel. The crew flung themselves flat on the floor. The driver ducked his head and drove straight on.

Above the roar of our engine could be heard the staccato rat-tat-tat-tat of machine guns and another furious jet of bullets sprayed our steel side, the splinters clanging viciously against the engine cover.

The Jerry tank had treated us to a broadside of armour-piercing bullets!

Taking advantage of a dip in the ground, we got beyond range and then turning, we manoeuvred to get the left gunner on to the moving target. Owing to our gas casualties the gunner was working single-handed and his right eye being too swollen with gas he aimed with the left. In addition, as the ground was heavily scarred with shell holes we kept going up and down like a ship in a heavy sea, making accurate shooting difficult.

His first shot fell some 30 yards in front and the next went beyond.

Nearing the village of Cachy, I saw to my astonishment that the two female tanks were slowly limping away to the rear. They had both been hit by shells almost immediately on their arrival and had great holes in their sides. As their Lewis guns were useless against the heavy armour-plate of the enemy and their gaping sides no longer afforded them any defence against machine-gun bullets, they had nothing to do but withdraw from action.

We still were lucky enough to dodge the enemy shelling, although, the twisting and turning once or twice almost brought us on top of our own trenches.

Whilst we were ranging on the leading German tank our own infantry were standing in their trenches watching the duel with tense interest, like spectators in the pit of a theatre.

Looking down on one occasion I saw to my horror that we were going straight down into a trench full of men who, huddled together, were yelling at the tops of their voices to attract our attention. A quick signal to the gears-man seated in the rear of the tank and we turned swiftly, avoiding catastrophe by a second.

Another raking broadside of armour-piercing bullets gave us our first casualty, a bullet passing through the fleshy part of both legs of the Lewis gunner at the rear after piercing the side of the tank!

We had no time to put on more than a temporary dressing and he lay on the floor, bleeding and groaning, whilst the 6-pounder boomed over his head and the empty shell cases clattered all round him.

The roar of our engine, the nerve-racking rat-tat-tat of our machine guns blazing at the Boche infantry, and the thunderous boom of the 6-pounders, all bottled up in that narrow space, filled our ears with tumult. Added to this we were half-stifled by the fumes of petrol and cordite.

Again we turned and proceeded at a slower pace; the left gunner, registering carefully, hit the ground right in front of the Jerry tank. I took a risk and stopped the tank for a moment.

The pause was justified; a carefully aimed shot hit the turret of the German tank, bringing it to a standstill. Another roar and yet another white puff at the front of the tank denoted a second hit! Peering with swollen eyes through his narrow slit the elated gunner shouted words of triumph that were drowned by the roaring of the engine.

Then once more with great deliberation he aimed and hit for the third time. Through a loophole I saw the tank heel over to one side and then a door opened and out ran the crew. We had knocked the monster out!

Quickly I signed to the machine-gunner, and he poured volley after volley into the retreating figures.

My nearest enemy being now out of action, I turned to look at the other two, who were coming forward slowly. As the German infantry were still advancing, the 6-pounder gunner sent round after round of case shot in their direction which, scattering like the charge of a shot gun, spread havoc in their ranks.

Now, I thought, we shall not last very long. The two great

tanks were creeping forward relentlessly; if they both concentrated their fire on us at once we would be finished. We sprinkled the neighbourhood of one of them with a few sighting shells, when to my intense joy and amazement, I saw it go slowly backwards. Its companion did likewise and in a few minutes they both had disappeared from sight, leaving our tank the sole possessor of the field.

This situation, however gratifying, soon displayed numerous disadvantages. We were now the only thing above ground and naturally the German artillery made savage efforts to wipe us off the map.

Up and down we went, followed by a trail of bursting shells. I was afraid that at any minute a shell would penetrate the roof and set the petrol alight, making the tank a roaring furnace before we could escape.

Then I saw an aeroplane flying overhead not more than a hundred feet up. A great black cross was on each underwing and as it crossed over us I could see clearly the figures of the pilot and observer, when something round and black dropped from it. I watched it for a fraction of a second, horrified! The front of the tank suddenly bounded up into the air and the tank seemed to stand on end. Everything shook, rattled, and jarred. We fell back to earth with a crash and then continued on our journey unhurt, Our steel walls had held nobly, but how much more would they endure?

A few minutes later, as we were turning, the driver failed to notice that we were on the edge of a steep shell hole, and down we went with a crash, so suddenly that one of the gunners, taken unawares, fell forward on top of me. The driver, in order to right the tank, jerked open the throttle to its fullest extent. We snorted up the opposite lip of the crater at full speed, but when just about to clamber over the edge the engine stopped. Our nose was pointing heavenwards, a lovely stationary target for the Boche artillery!

A deadly silence ensued...

After the intolerable racket of the past few hours it seemed to us uncanny. Now we could hear the whining of shells, and the vicious crump as they exploded near at hand. Fear entered our hearts; we were inclined at such a steep angle that we found it impossible to crank up the engine again. Every second we expected to get a shell through the top. Almost lying on their sides, the crew strained and heaved at the starting handle, but to no effect.

Our nerves were on edge; there was but one thing left, to put the tank in reverse gear, release the rear brake, and let it run backwards down the shell hole under its own weight.

Back we slid and happily the engine began to splutter, then, carefully nursing the throttle, the driver changed gear and we climbed out unhurt.

What sweet music was the roar of the engine in our ears now!

But the day was not yet over. As I peeped through my flap I noticed that the Boche infantry were forming up some distance away preparing for an attack. Then my heart bounded with joy, for away on the right I saw seven small whippets, the newest and fastest type of tank, racing into action.

They came on at ten to fifteen miles an hour, heading straight for the German infantry. I could see the latter scattering in all directions. The whippets plunged into the midst of them, ran over them, spitting fire into their retreating ranks.

Their work was soon over. They had nipped an attack in the bud, but only three, their tracks dripping with blood, came back out of the seven; the other four were left burning out there in front. Their crews could not hope to be made prisoners after such slaughter.

Then, near Villers-Bretonneux, about 1,000 yards away, appeared a fourth German tank. The left gunner opened fire immediately and a minute later the reply came swift and sharp, three shells hitting the ground alongside of us. Pursuing the same tactics, we increased our speed and then turned. We heard a tremendous crack and the tank continued to turn round in a circle. 'What the hell are you doing?' I roared at the driver in exasperation. He looked at me in bewilderment and made another effort, but still we turned round and round.

Peeping out, I saw one caterpillar track doubled high in the air! We had been hit by the Boche artillery at last, two of the track plates being blown clear away! I decided to quit. The engine stopped. Defiantly we blazed away our last few rounds at the slopes near Villers-Bretonneux and then crept gingerly out of the tank, the wounded man riding on the back of a comrade. We made for the nearest trench, when 'rat-tat-tat-tat' and the air became alive with bullets.

We flopped quickly to the ground, waiting breathlessly whilst the bullets threw up the dirt a few feet away. Then the shooting ceased and we got up again and ran swiftly forward. By a miracle nothing touched us, and we reached the parapet of a trench. Our faces were black with grime and smoke and our eyes bloodshot. The astonished infantrymen gazed at us open-mouthed, as if we were apparitions from a ghostly land. 'Take your bayonets out of the way,' we yelled, and tumbled down into the trench.

F. Mitchell enlisted September 1914. July 1915 to February 1917 A.O.C. attached 21st Division in France; March 1917 to end of War Lieut. in Tank Corps; 1st Battalion. March Retreat 1918, Villers-Bretonneux, April 1918, attack of August 8th (Battle of Amiens). M.C. gained for fighting enemy tanks at Villers-Bretonneux.

BRAVERY IN THE FIELD?

Alexander Paterson

In the summer of 1918, when I was twenty-one years old, I rightly considered myself a war veteran. I had seen one after another of my friends 'go West' at the Somme in 1916, both in the heat of July and August at High Wood and Delville Wood, and in the terrible slough of despond around the Butte de Warlencourt in November. I had lived for weeks on bully beef and biscuits as one of the victorious army which 'chased' the Germans at Arras in April and May 1917, till it was brought to a halt by the Hindenburg Line. For months during the winter of 1917–18 I had never been further away from the line than in 'rest' billets at Ypres. By some lucky chance our battalion missed the disastrous March 21st, 1918, when the enemy broke through in the south. Nevertheless, I had taken part in almost hand-to-hand fighting in Flanders for a whole week during the month of April.

With such a campaign behind me I was a careful and experienced soldier with an expert knowledge of all the strange sounds and smells of warfare, ignorance of which may mean death to the man who is not quick to apprehend their meaning. My hearing was attuned to every kind of explosion from the hacking cough of bombs to the metallic clanging of 5.9 shells bursting in re-echoing valleys. My nostrils were quick to detect a whiff of gas or to diagnose the menace of a corpse disinterred at an interval of months.

The strain of the summer of 1918, with its big outbreak of influenza, tended to a mood of utter war-weariness. I had entered the Army grudgingly, but in obedience to irresistible social pressure. I had hated strife, yet lacked the courage to be a pacifist, Military service seemed not so much an adventure as a disagreeable, inescapable task. I coveted neither rank nor glory, and my twenty-first birthday found me in the ranks of a Scottish regiment performing the duties of that military maid-of-all-work, acting lance-corporal (unpaid).

My mood during 1918 changed from a stoicism which looked on and, with difficulty, conquered fear, to one of blank despair which tried to mask itself in a spirit of care-free military enterprise. I was in a frenzy for something to happen – wounds, death, anything! There were various contributory circumstances. I had received a letter from home, stating that my father expected to be conscripted. I had seen a father and son in France together. The son now lay trussed in his groundsheet at Passchendaele and the sight of the father was not easily forgotten. Perhaps, also, the fact that I had suffered the ignominy of 7 days No. 1 Field Punishment for a purely imaginary military 'crime' helped my disgust. Whatever the cause, I found myself volunteering for every job that came my way, and running unnecessary risks in a thoroughly unsoldierlike manner.

In September 1918 our battalion was occupying a frontline position which had just been vacated by the Germans. At this stage of the War Jerry was fighting a magnificent rearguard action. The day before leaving this position he had repulsed our attack, inflicting heavy losses. Next morning he was nowhere to be seen. Cautiously we crept over the parapet in an uncanny silence, advancing in little groups. Just in front lay a Highlander with face upturned, red bubbles at mouth and nostrils. Further on a young subaltern, a few weeks from home, had fallen, striking an attitude with walking stick outstretched. Their faces were still quite recognizable, the weather being cool. A couple of hundred yards from our starting-point lay the main body of our comrades who had fallen the previous day. Their bodies were strewn in every direction. Dozens were heaped around a pitiful little 2-foot trench which they had dug. Many of them were without boots, for the Germans in retiring had taken sufficient time to satisfy their crying need for good footwear.

Our objective, a ridge about a mile off, was reached without opposition. We dug in on the crest of a hill overlooking a deep valley. Along the bottom of the valley ran a canal.

Soon after dusk our patrols penetrated to the canal bank, where they were peppered by rifles and machine guns. Even to the brass-hats at Corps Headquarters in some distant chateau, it was obvious that the passage of the canal would be a difficult operation. A hurried decision was taken that before attempting any general advance we must ascertain the disposition of the enemy. For this purpose it was proposed to send a patrol consisting of an officer, a sniper, and a signaller to reconnoitre in daylight next day. Without much difficulty I secured the post as signaller. I was glad to find the officer was a cool youngster of about my own years. I had known him whilst he was in the ranks. He gave me a hearty welcome when I reported at the commanding officer's dug-out for instructions. The careful instructions of the colonel suggested our task to be one of some importance and some danger. On leaving we received stiff tots of whisky. Here was confirmation of my suspicion. All doubt was expelled when the sergeant-major handed me a water-bottle with rum as part of the equipment of the expedition.

My duty as signaller was to lead a signal wire all the way travelled by the patrol, so that we would be in continuous communication with our unit. I was carrying three drums of wire, a telephone, a rifle, and infantry kit.

Climbing out of our front-line trench in the dark between four and five o'clock in the morning, we proceeded gently downhill to the towpath of the canal, where the previous patrols had been fired on. Nothing disturbed the stillness of the early morning as we walked warily forward. The first signal station was soon established in a gun-pit in a small hillock overlooking the canal. Our plan was to spend the day there scouring the further bank with the telescope to locate enemy positions. By wartime standards, we had comfortable quarters, and considered ourselves, entitled to celebrate our safe arrival by broaching the rum. I was physically weak after the exertions of the previous day or two. Perhaps the rum was particularly potent. Anyhow I awoke in broad daylight with a raging thirst, a confused head, and a Webley revolver staring me in the face. Stone, the subaltern, threatened with curses that he would shoot me if I didn't keep awake, I sat up and tried to appear interested. He and I were good friends. I suggested breakfast and instantly my somnolence was forgiven. In my haversack I had a selection of eatables from a parcel just received from home. Out came a piece of cake, a black pudding, a tin of *café-au-lait*, and a 'Tommy' Cooker. It was the work of a minute to commandeer the water in the sniper's bottle, and a brew of coffee was soon prepared. A short time later slices of black pudding were sizzling in the mess-tin lid. Small tots of rum completed the banquet. Once more we could resume interest in the War.

Through the telescope Smithy the sniper scanned the towpath of the canal while Stone gave me in an undertone some of the more scandalous episodes of a recent leave. He was interrupted by Smithy, who put a finger to his lips and motioned Stone towards the telescope.

There was little need of the telescope, for about 100 yards from us on our side of the canal was a small emplacement with two machine guns. A German sentry sat behind the guns keeping a lazy look-out. Two other Germans were a few yards from him, with tunics off and shirts open, washing on the canal bank. Evidently our presence was unsuspected. Beside the emplacement, a small plank bridge had been thrown across the canal.

Stone and I exchanged understanding glances. Slowly he led the way on all fours through the narrow sap leading from our gun-pit to the open. I divested myself of the telephone headpiece, which I handed to Smithy, who nodded comprehendingly. Grabbing my rifle I followed Stone, lying flat when clear of the sap. The ground outside was uneven and there were low shrubs affording some concealment but we crept forward on our stomachs till half the distance was traversed. 'I say, Jimmy' – it was a furtive whisper – 'what next?' There was no answer for a moment whilst he examined his revolver. In dumb show he looked at my rifle to see if the safety catch was up. 'Come a little closer,' he whispered, 'and we'll try to capture them. Brigade wants prisoners for information. You cover the two on the bank while I rush the sentry.' Cautiously we tried to carry this out and just when I had judged it was nearly time to put the plan to the test there was an excited shout from one of the bathers, who was pulling on his tunic and had looked in our direction. Both of them rushed towards the sentry. Quick as a flash Stone and I ran forward. But the Germans were quicker. Over the plank bridge they scuttled, throwing themselves flat on the ground on the other side. A bullet whistled past us as we jumped into the little emplacement containing their abandoned machine guns. I fired a round or two of my rifle into the opposite bank but there was no answering fire. They lay low and probably crawled away to safety. The ground on the other side was undulating and offered good cover. Stone had taken down their guns and turned them the other way round. For an hour we awaited events, but all was still and peaceful except for a breeze rippling the canal.

A short distance to our right were the remains of a stone bridge which had been mined. A good road led to it on each side. During the hour which had elapsed we had watched the road on the German side without seeing any signs of life. Stone was getting restless as we were out to spot Germans and as yet knew nothing about the troops across the way. He sent me back to bring our friend the sniper to our new post and to extend the telephone. This was easily done and Stone was soon reporting progress to the colonel at the other end of the wire.

I could see that my own daft mood had its counterpart in Stone's. It was, therefore, no surprise to me when he invited me to 'walk the plank' and reconnoitre the other side. Judging our three Boches to be a forgotten outpost, we made boldly on foot for the road. I had still remaining one drum of telephone wire which was connected to our line in the emplacement. The telephone was slung on my shoulder. On we walked, looking to right and left, but seeing nothing, Half-way up the hill we were brought to a halt, as the drum of wire was exhausted. It was reassuring nevertheless to connect the telephone and find we were still in contact with our battalion. In the ditch ran a number of German field cables. I grabbed one, nipped it with pliers and bared the end with my knife. In a minute it was joined to the end of our own cable. This German wire, I thought, must lead somewhere. Taking it as guide I walked up the road, followed by Stone, who nodded understandingly. About 200 yards ahead, the ditch was bridged over and at this point the cable was led upwards to a pole. The pole stood on the lip of a large chalk quarry which sank from the roadway. We lay beside the pole peering into the deep hollow.

There was no movement in the quarry, which appeared to have been recently abandoned. German clothing and equipment littered the place as if hurriedly discarded. Facing us in the side of the quarry were five doorways, leading to what we thought was a big dug-out. Souvenirs running in our minds, we entered the quarry carefully, avoiding noise. We approached the nearest dug-out shaft and furtively peered in the entrance. I gasped. The shaft was deep and probably not quite completed, as there were no steps, only boards reaching from the ground level downwards, with one or two wooden treads. Leaning against the wall inside the doorway was a German sentry fully equipped. Half-way down another German was seated with his back to the door, crouched on one of the treads. The sentry gave a queer cry and made to seize his rifle which was propped against the wall opposite him. As he did so he lost his footing and stumbled headlong down the shaft on top of his comrade. Both slithered to the bottom. Instantly a chorus of voices from below was heard in protest.

The situation called for only one remedy – flight. The dug-out had five doors and might be swarming with men. We were without even one Mills bomb. In a twinkling we were speeding down the road, but before we had gone any distance rifle bullets were whistling around us. We jumped in the ditch and crawled laboriously back to the canal bank, where we rejoined our sniper and once more connected the telephone.

The moment the instrument was affixed a loud buzz indicated that someone was calling us. The colonel had come to a company station in the front line accompanied by the brigadier, who wished to speak to Mr. Stone. I retained the headpiece telephone whilst handing him the speaking set. The brigadier was a professional soldier of the most efficient type, and I wondered how heroics of this kind would appeal to him. He listened in silence whilst Stone reported the position in the quarry. Stone went so far as to ask for a platoon to be sent out with bombs to capture the dug-outs. 'Stone,' said the brigadier, 'we've had quite enough damned silliness for one day. Lie low where you are and I'll phone Corps to strafe the quarry whilst you make your way back here over the open.' Stone acquiesced meekly.

It was now afternoon and Stone considered he deserved another drink. I handed him the rum bottle, and he drained it at a gulp. Shortly afterwards he was asleep.

Telephonic communication must have, been in good working order that day. In a very short time the message to the Corps had its effect. Shells of every calibre were whistling over our heads, bursting in and above the quarry. This was the moment arranged for our retreat. I phoned to the signaller, back in the front line, that I was disconnecting. Turning to Stone, I gave him a shake. He was like a log. I shouted and punched, but all to no avail. He would not move. I thought of threatening him with his own Webley. We were compelled to await his awakening. This came with the darkness, and we walked carefully over to our front line praying that the sentries would not mistake us for Germans. We were challenged, gave the reply, and were once more back in a forward trench, although not with our own battalion, which had been relieved at dusk.

I have told this incident in as simple a way as I can; I feel I owe that to my conscience, because there is a romantic version of it in the London *Gazette* which does not say one word about rum or revolvers.

Private Alexander Paterson enlisted at Glasgow on October 21st, 1915, at the age of eighteen. Trained at Glasgow, Ripon, and Richmond (Yorks). Went to France, July 1916, and remained with the Glasgow Highlanders in the 100th Infantry Brigade, 33rd Division, until within four weeks of Armistice. Fought on Somme from July 1916 till March 1917. At Arras, April to June 1917, in

Ypres Salient, September 1917 till April 1918. Saw severe fighting during retreat in Flanders, April 12th to 17th, 1918. Took part in final offensive operations till wounded near Le Cateau on October 13th, 1918. Was also wounded (slightly) at Delville Wood, on August 22nd, 1916, and gassed (slightly) in October 1917. Received Military Medal in respect of episode dealt with in narrative.

NOYON

March 23rd, 1918

Dr. F. O. Taylor

The most unhappy hours which I can remember during my
service in France and Belgium were spent in and near Noyon,
on the third day and night of the great German attack on the V
Army. I shall not describe the first two days of our retreat. They
are very blurred in my mind now, but I still dream of what
happened to two of our field ambulances, to one of which I was
attached, which had been withdrawn from active work after
these first two days and nights.

Blistered heels seem a small thing to grouse about, but they
are enough to cause acute misery, and I had unfortunately
contracted, as the Americans say, 'a good case of them.' Owing
to the fact that at the beginning of our hasty retreat I had been
wearing an old-fashioned pair of field-boots, ideal for riding,
but the worst of walking footwear, my ankles above the heels
were unbearably painful, and when our ambulance was
directed to proceed to Noyon and await orders there, I got
permission from my colonel to precede them in a motor
ambulance which was going on with baggage. Arriving at
Noyon, I soon heard that the German Army was advancing
rapidly from La Fère, and that Noyon shortly would be
evacuated. I managed to find the French barracks, where I was
to await the arrival of my unit, and found myself in a large open
space, which was guarded by a long castellated gateway, just
inside of which there was a small macadamized drill-ground
sloping up to a pretty grassy field with small trees at the side.
For about 50 yards up from the gate and on the right were some
small tarred-felt huts, and down near the gate a small lane
turned sharply to the right, leading to some buildings.

It was a perfect afternoon, the sun was as warm as on a
summer day, and, having had practically no sleep for more than
two days and nights, I sat down to rest just inside the gate on a

bank at the side of the lane. Though I began to read a book, I dropped sound asleep with my head between my knees, and the next thing I knew was our Padre waking me up with the words, 'They're in.'

If that unsympathetic soul had not disturbed my slumbers, I do not think that I should have ever awakened again, at least, not in this world! I must have been very sound asleep, for four motor-ambulances had parked in the lane right in front of me without disturbing me at all.

'Oh! Right-oh!' I yawned, and staggered to my feet. 'I'll walk up and see them.' Then I strolled up the barrack yard, casually looking up at a British aeroplane, which was flying very low and coming towards us. I stopped about 50 yards from the gate to talk to a group of our men, noticed the colonel talking to two or three other officers in the centre of the macadamized space, and was admiring the pretty aeroplane – the first British plane we had seen for days – glittering in the sun, the red-white-and-blue rings clearly visible, when there came an indescribable explosion. It was the most terrific, though not the loudest, perhaps, that I have ever heard, followed immediately by dull thuds and the sickening sight of men falling, groaning, spouting blood – whole limbs severed, horses frantically breaking loose... But in the moment of frightful surprise I could only grasp the fact that two more explosions followed, luckily outside the gate, and believing that a Boche long-range gun had found us, I waited a few seconds flat on the ground for more – but no more came.

Beside me was one of the youngest men in the ambulances; the calf of one of his legs was torn right out, and the wound was spouting blood. I dragged him into the nearest hut and compressed his femoral artery, managing to stop the bleeding. The hut seemed full of frightfully wounded men; I could do nothing but hang on to my poor little private's artery. What terrible faces they all had, pale as ashes! 'Water,' they groaned. 'Oh, sir, can you do nothing for me?' It was frightful. I saw two men die in front of my eyes, and no one came to help; my thumbs were nearly breaking, when to my horror, a badly wounded horse came galloping straight at the door of the hut, reared up, and appeared to want to come in! It would have trampled us badly. I was half-turned from the door, and was just able to keep it shut by holding my foot against it, my right leg braced against the weight of the poor horse, which was frantically beating the door with its fore-feet! All the time I hung on to that femoral artery! Just when I felt that I could keep my leg up no longer, the horse fell dead, and I was released from my uncomfortable position by the arrival of a sergeant, who first had to open the backs of two wagons to get enough dressings, as we were all 'packed up,' and then was able to give me some assistance with first aid to the wounded in our immediate vicinity.

All this must have taken place in a matter of a few minutes, for when I was able to get out of this ghastly hut (by the way, why did we all crowd into it?) things outside were still appallingly confused. I gathered from quick questioning that the aeroplane must have been one captured by the Germans, and that a bomb had been dropped, the hole which it had made being just inside the barrack gate. The terrible nature of the damage to everything in the neighbourhood of the explosion was due to the impact of flying fragments of road-metal. The vagaries of explosives were illustrated in this case by the fact that our colonel was standing within a few yards of the spot where the bomb went off, and though a French interpreter just beside him was stone dead, he was not touched or affected in any way by the concussion.

Piteous sight after sight met my eyes as I got more into the centre of the holocaust; more than fifty non-combatants were dead, dying, or wounded. One face haunts me to this day: a fine young American medical officer lay in the hut at the foot of the row, his expression the most horrible and soul-searing I ever saw. He was half-sitting up, waiting for his turn for attention, both legs bending, not at the natural place at the knees, but half-way up the thighs, and he was praying for morphia to ease his agony. All the wounded seemed to suffer more than any I had seen before, owing probably to the awful bruising and smashing power of these lumps of road-metal. Just where I had been sleeping a few minutes before, the greatest damage was apparent. The two foremost ambulances were completely wrecked, two men had been hideously mangled on the front seat of one of them, and along the bank one could see the ground furrowed by the flying stones, many pieces of which were almost as big as one's clenched fist.

I found the strain of helplessly watching so much suffering while waiting for dressings and drugs to be unpacked so insupportable that I asked the colonel if I could go down to a casualty clearing station for liquid morphia and perhaps some help. My memory here is somewhat blurred, but somehow I got hold of a car and managed to find the clearing station or stationary hospital – I cannot remember which it was – with great difficulty, as the place seemed deserted. I found a nursing sister – her face of sorrow is another painful memory. I blurted out to her, 'We've had an awful catastrophe with a bomb – thirty or forty men crying for morphia. Can you give me some?' Her sad face hardly changed its expression. Then she made me understand why. 'Come this way,' she said, and led me to the largest marquee. I stepped inside and recoiled, aghast... Row upon row upon row of silent forms on stretchers – nothing else.

'There are several hundred stretcher cases here who still have their first field dressings on.' The sister sighed. 'And we are leaving very soon!' She had reached the limit of unavailing regret, and I felt quite ashamed of mentioning such a trifling matter as thirty or forty wounded!

When I returned to the blood-stained barrack yard, order of a kind had been restored, but another row of forms, alas, still for ever, lay side by side in the evening sunshine. The less seriously wounded were being got away somewhere in our available transport, baggage was being cleared from wagons to make room for them, and the obviously dying were in the biggest hut. We survivors could barely raise our voices to speak. I was detailed to take a certain number of men to dig a grave near the abandoned hospital.

A beautiful chestnut mare stood patiently tethered to a tree, bleeding slowly to death from a small wound in the belly, through which a flying fragment had passed; the blood dripped steadily on, and one could not think of the poor animal's final and tedious death; as I had at one time been a combatant officer I was beseeched to put an end to its misery with a rifle which was produced from somewhere. All that I can say about this is – that I did it...but it is another haunting memory.

Then followed the burial of twenty-nine officers and men. The grave took several hours to dig. The service and filling in of the grave took a couple of hours more, and then, in darkness, began the crowning agony of that awful day. Twelve miles to march with exhausted men to a destination which never seemed to come nearer; every halt a torture – thinking of starting again; whipping in stragglers whom one pitied from the bottom of one's heart, while cursing them for their bad discipline; trying to be cheerful, when we were all in the darkest depths. What a night! It ended by our arrival at a place called Lassigny, which had once been a village, and where the main body of our ambulance had crept into a muddy field and erected tents. I at last could lie on my face on the ground and moan to myself, 'My heels!... Oh! my heels!' until someone – perhaps my servant, perhaps my friend Captain Barton – came to help me off with my boots...

Dr. F. O. Taylor served in France in the R.F.A. and the R.A.M.C.

A CASUALTY CLEARING STATION

Dr. John A. Hayward

In April 1918 I volunteered to go to France in response to the urgent call for more surgeons. For twenty years I had been in general practice in a suburb, and did a fair amount of surgery among patients and at the local hospitals. I had also had some war experience as one of the surgeons at the British Red Cross Hospital, Netley, in the first six months of the War, but I had no experience of cases fresh from the battlefield, and the surgical technique which had recently been adopted in dealing with them.

I had been longing throughout the War to get to the Front, and I set out full of enthusiasm and with no little pride and satisfaction to my family and myself.

It was a great disappointment, after a wait of four days in Boulogne, to find that I was posted to a large Base hospital at Trouville. Here I remained till the beginning of July, not at all happy, and hampered at every turn by red tape, rules, and regulations. The hospital was full of the wastage of war – men sent down from the Front, suffering from the ordinary diseases of civil life, which should have precluded their enlistment. The Front knocked them out almost at once, and they came to be patched up, to convalesce, and return. The mess was full of rather war-weary men, who had endured much, and were glad of an easy berth. I had plenty of operating on ordinary civil-life disabilities, and, when not engaged in filling up 'forms,' enjoyed myself in field expeditions to collect butterflies and flowers, but the distant sound of guns was often disturbing. Through the influence of a kind consulting surgeon at G.H.Q., and to my great delight, I was appointed early in July as a surgeon to a casualty clearing station at Crouay, near Amiens.

A greater contrast to a Base hospital could hardly be imagined. All military discipline, red tape, and formality were reduced to a minimum. Within the camp, officers donned flannels or shorts, and the mess, a dozen altogether, formed a family party; there were a small number of highly trained sisters, and forty or fifty orderlies.

The institution of these small mobile hospitals near the fighting line had revolutionized the surgery of the War, and was the means of saving thousands of lives. It was found that the fatal sepsis and gas gangrene of wounds could be avoided if effective operation was performed within thirty-six hours of their infliction, and all dead and injured tissue removed, in spite of the extensive mutilation incurred. The essential parts of a C.C.S. were:

(1) A large reception marquee. (2) A resuscitation tent, where severely shocked or apparently dying cases were warmed up in heated beds, or transfused before operation. (3) A pre-operation tent, where stretcher cases were prepared for operation. (4) A large operating tent with complete equipment for six tables. (5) An evacuation tent, where the cases were sent after operation, to await the hospital train for the Base. (6) A ward tent for cases requiring watching for twenty-four hours, or too bad for evacuation.

I had two days to settle down, and get some idea of my new surroundings, and everyone was immensely kind, but I realized how entirely inexperienced I was in the work which would be required of me; my colleagues were all young men with two or three years' War service.

Vast reserves of men and transport had silently for two nights been moving up the road to Amiens to support the Australian attack at Villers-Bretonneux. On my third day I was orderly officer, and after my day's work had to be on duty all night as reception officer. On that evening the attack began, with a continuous roar of heavy guns, while the horizon was brilliantly lit with the flashes of exploding dumps, Verey lights, and star shells. The camp was quietly resting, and I was left with a few orderlies in the dimly lit reception tent. About 1 a.m. the ambulances began to arrive.

It is impossible to convey an adequate picture of the scene. Into the tent are borne on stretchers, or come wearily stumbling, figures in khaki, wrapped in blankets or coats, bandaged or splinted. All of them stiff with mud, or caked with blood and dust, and salt sweat, and with labels of their injuries attached. They come in such numbers that the tent is soon filled, and what can be done? I can't cope with them all! Many are white and cold, and lie still and make no response, and those who do are laconic, or point to their label. I have had no instructions how to dispose of such numbers, or the method of procedure, but realize that they must be examined briefly and sorted, and sent to one or other of our hospital tents. But my non-com. orderly was at my side with whispered suggestions, and soon we had the stretchers on one side and the standing cases on the other, and, leaving the slighter cases to be dressed, I gradually sorted out the bad ones for the 'resuss,' 'pre-op,' or 'evacuation' tents. I had never seen such frightful wounds, and could not conceive how we three surgeons could deal with them on the ensuing day. It was 7 a.m. before I had cleared the tent, and I felt tired out after nearly twenty-four hours' work, but at 10 a.m., I should have to begin to operate for another twelve hours and on cases like these!

It was extraordinary that in this charnel tent of pain and misery there was silence, and no outward expression of moans or groans or complaints. The badly shocked had passed beyond it; others appeared numbed, or too tired to complain, or so exhausted that they slept as they stood. Even the badly wounded often asked for a smoke. Here were lying uncomplaining men with shattered heads or ghastly disfiguration of their faces, others with shell and bullet wounds of the chest, spitting blood and gasping for breath; and, worst of all, those quiet, afraid-to-be-touched cases with the innocent tiny little mark where the bullet had entered the abdomen, but already with the thready pulse, drawn corners of the mouth, anxious look, and rigid muscles which betoken hopeless disaster within. And here were 'multiple wounded,' their bodies riddled with large or small shell fragments, terrible compound fractures in Thomas's splints, and the stumps of torn-off limbs.

Well, I got a bath and some breakfast, and at ten o'clock began the operating: three of us at first, and later on in the day we were reinforced in response to S.O.S. calls by four visiting teams from distant C.C.C.s each consisting of surgeon, anaesthetist, sister, and trained orderly.

As the day wore on I felt nearer and nearer to collapse. The appalling wounds, my ignorance of the new methods of dealing with them, the utter fatigue of standing at the table, and the growing feeling that my assistants must be noticing my incompetency began to take away all self-confidence. I began to think of the bad luck of the wretched victims who came under my knife. How confidently they went under the ether, relying on my skill: how their lives and the happiness of their homes depended on me; how much better for them had fate brought them to the next table. Every feeling and introspection that should never cross a surgeon's mind began to possess me and shake my nerve, and it was only concentration on the actual technique of the operation that kept me going. The hours dragged on. Would the 'Resuss' and 'Pre-op' wards never be emptied.

'Resuss!' 'Pre-op!' – abbreviated words always to be fixed in memory with the haunting faces of their inmates. 'Resuss' was a dreadful place. Here were sent the shocked and collapsed and dying cases, not able to stand as yet an operation, but which might be possible after the warming-up under cradles in heated beds or transfusion of blood. The effect of transfusion was in some cases miraculous. I have seen men already like corpses, blanched and collapsed, pulseless and with just perceptible breathing, within two hours of transfusion sitting up in bed smoking, and exchanging jokes before they went to the operating table.

The orderly in the 'Resuss' was a wonderful lad. A boy of twenty, he had served without relief for months in this tent, attending to the worst cases and the dying. He had all the patience, tenderness, and devotion of a woman, the gentle hands and skill of a nurse, and an enduring fortitude. He was recommended for the D.S.M., but his best reward must be the memory of many a farewell message home, many a silent grasp of hand, and the last look of grateful eyes.

That dreadful day of my first experience of a C.C.C. rush ended at 7 p.m., after thirty-six hours of continuous work, and somehow I had got through. I was completely exhausted with anxiety and fatigue, and felt I could never go on with it, and was not up to the task: but to give in was even more terrible. I could hardly articulate at dinner, but my condition escaped notice, and I crept to my tent to fall dead asleep before I could make a decision.

I woke refreshed on a glorious July day: we were encamped on cultivated down-land untouched by war, and the air was alive with the song of larks and the fields gay with poppies and marigolds and down flowers. The camp and country a picture of peaceful calm and beauty, if only one could forget the scene inside the tents. Fortunately, there were only a few cases left by the night shift, and in the afternoon I was able to leave the operating tent and get out among the birds and butterflies and flowers. It was this walk, I think, which saved the situation for me. I got time, alone, to pull myself together, and though many times afterwards even worse rushes occurred and more terrible scenes were enacted, I never became overwhelmed with the same panic of my first experience.

That evening we took in nearly 200 Australians who had been caught by gas shells without their masks on. Entirely whitened with dust, every man was temporarily blinded and in agony with the difficulty of breathing from the mucous fluid in the lungs. It was a weird sight to see them led away through the camp in the moonlight, in long single files, holding on to each other and guided by an orderly as leader.

As the days wore on, I began to feel my self-confidence returning, and that I should be able to face another ordeal with more equanimity. The friendliness and camaraderie of our little mess was an immense help: I was popular and enjoyed it like a schoolboy. I think they looked on me as an 'old sport,' and I had to live up to it.

It was not long before I was again put to the test. Our C.C.S. was ordered to take up quarters with two others in a huge deserted asylum close to Amiens, in expectation of the grand attack of the IV Army around Villers-Bretonneux, and for lack of transport we had not been able to complete our preparations before the attack began on the day after our arrival; nor had visiting teams, coming to our aid, yet arrived. On that evening our barrage opened – a continuous roar of heavy guns which shook the ground, and trembled the walls of our building, and the sky and fields were lit up with the flashes and explosions of dumps and star shells. In the early hours of the morning came the ambulances in a continuous stream. Quickly we took in our quota of 200 cases, and the 'take-in' was 'shunted' to the adjoining C.C.S. located in the same building, and within two hours to our third sister station. And then our turn began again, long before we had made any impression on the first lot.

The stretchers filled the numberless rooms, and then flowed out into the corridors, which became blocked except for a narrow passage. Every unit, except those engaged with the nine operating surgeons, was occupied in sorting, dressing, and doing what was possible for the masses of wounded, but the numbers were too great and many had to lie for hours without help, or die unattended. A quick surgeon might get through from fifteen to twenty cases in a spell of twelve hours. I certainly could not do more than ten or twelve.

Among so many cases it was a sickening thing to have to make a choice for operation. We were dealing with a mass, not individuals, and if selection had to be made, it must be made in favour of those who by operation had a chance of being made fit again to return to the Front sooner or later, to keep up our man power and afford fresh fodder for the guns.

In such circumstances, nothing seemed to matter. It had to be got through somehow. Action, doing one's best, rightly or wrongly, mistakes or no mistakes, precluded all thought of self, and drove out fear and anxiety, and so I gained confidence as I tackled whatever came, along on the table, or went down the 'pre-op' rooms and chose out my cases – learning much from what I saw others were doing.

All that night and the following day, when the visiting teams began to arrive, we worked; night shifts took our places, and on the following morning, I went round the vast building to see what was happening. The wounded, including many Germans, had now overflowed from the rooms and corridors and were lying on stretchers in the open squares of the asylum. Through the night, with dimmed lanterns, doctors and orderlies went down the rows doing what they could, but we were snowed under – and we could neither operate on nor evacuate cases fast enough to make much impression on the heaps. Many of the Germans evidently dreaded they would meet with but rough treatment, and, unable to make themselves understood, clasped our hands and with imploring looks and despairing gestures tried to convey their meaning. Except for precedence in operation it is perhaps needless to say they were treated with the same care as our own men.

Entering an outbuilding, I found it strewn with rows of corpses – a human *battue* – and in another, a piled-up heap of arms and legs, freshly amputated. I write of these horrors, not for the sake of sensation, but to bring home the realities of war as I saw it, and the work and scenes in the three C.C.S.s behind the fighting. It took nearly a week before we had cleared up and evacuated the cases, and everyone was exhausted. It was clear that insufficient time had been given to the medical side to organize for the number of casualties that might be expected in a battle of this magnitude, and the exigencies of the fighting must have the first call on transport. It was probably unavoidable, but, the pity of it; and, after all, as old Caspar said, 'It was a famous victory.'

A lull the fighting for a few days on our immediate front now ensued, and we had some rest, and I even went butterfly hunting, and on another day went up to the Front, and saw our guns firing, and heard the German shells coming over and bursting. I remember, too, one night we had to spend operating on a number of men, brought in dressed up for theatricals, some of them as girls in ballet costume. A German aeroplane had dropped a bomb through the tent on to the stage, and the tent had collapsed on top of the crowded audience and the dead and wounded.

It was these violent contrasts that, to me, make up the vivid memories of my days in France. Outside, the sun and the larks, the birds, butterflies, and flowers; inside the tents, Nature violated, outraged – and alternating with the dread and anxiety and physical and mental exhaustion was the happy mess and bridge, picnics, and concerts. It seemed hardly real at the time. It is fast becoming a dream, and, though I had many other experiences, as our C.C.S. followed the advance, at Albert and Brie and Peronne, Roiselle, and Bellenglise, none remain in my memory like those of my first 'blooding' at Cronay and Amiens, where I came so near to collapse and disaster.

John A. Hayward, M.D., F.R.C.S. 1914–1915, Assistant Surgeon (rank, Captain) British Red Cross Hospital, Netley. 1915–1917, Medical Officer, Queen Alexandra Hospital, Roehampton. April to November 1918, Temporary Captain R.A.M.C., B.E.F.

RATIONS

C. Goddard-Chead

It was our third day 'in.' The front line was no longer well-made trenches – or trenches at all, in fact – but merely small 'posts' a few yards distant from each other, each holding about half a dozen men.

These 'posts' were actually strips of trench with a rather high parapet – open at the rear; made up with very little sand-bagging, protected in front with the usual rows of barbed-wire. The defences here had been made hurriedly: this, the region of the Lys Canal, had been the latest scene of German thrust. Thus we were on ground that had but lately been in civilian occupation, and still retained much of its peaceful country atmosphere, even trees were still standing.

I found myself in charge of a 'post,' some distance to the right of where the main road ran from St. Floris, Immediately behind our position was some rough ground, showing where, at later seasons, a little stream evidently ran, but which was now apparently only a ditch. All movement on this sector was impossible by day. 'Jerry' held slightly higher ground, but even he seemed content to rest after daybreak, for with the exception of his artillery at intermittent intervals and a very occasional burst of some machine gun, daylight to dusk was a period of peacefulness.

Just now we were very glad that the weather was in our favour. Some of us at least (though the battalion was mostly young kiddies, newly out from home) knew what it meant to carry on war in pouring rain and always mud – interminable mud.

Now after some weeks of hot, dry weather it was dust we were struggling with – at all costs, to keep it out of the rifle, even if it was impossible to keep it out of one's mouth. Dust and grit had replaced slush! There always seemed to be one amongst us, at all times and all places even, who could give expression to our troubles, whatever they might be, and at the

Front they were certainly pretty numerous. Surely we must have thrived on troubles! Such a fellow at this time was Bert. Bert had come to us from the Liverpool Scottish, I think it was. Anyway, he was anything but a dour Scot, and always reminded one of East London. Language was always unparliamentary with us. 'Gor' blimey' was Bert's preliminary, and its force had to be heard to be realized. That expressive opening always seemed to call for some attention.

'Gor' blimey,' he would say. 'Wonder what the 'ell they'd say to this lot at home. Blast, it's dust all the bloody time. If you get a bit of 'rooti' to eat, it's all dust while you eat it. When the stew comes up, it's got a layer of blasted dust on it thicker than drippin'!' Another voice broke in: 'Yes, and how many times have we chivvied the ol' wife about a speck of something in the Sunday dinner.' 'Here, who's that talking about Sunday dinners?'

'Gor' blimey! put a sock in it,' was Bert's reply of course.

What happened in this post on our third morning in was the prelude to the experience I shall relate here. We had seen dawn gradually break through – and yet no sign of the ration-men, who must be up before daybreak, in order to reach us safely. Someone said, 'That's b – it now! They'll never get across that road once it gets light.' Feeling that to be true, all eyes watch alternately the streaks of daylight above, and behind us the faint line of that strip of road that connects us with the supports. Uncovered road (and the only place with a movable 'spider' in the barbed wire that permits getting through) every inch of it 'marked' by a German gun, which opens at the slightest movement after daybreak. It is a bad spot, evidently covered by some 'observation post' on Jerry's side. 'Here they come, look!' hushed voices – words almost unsaid. Inwardly one cheers up. Thank goodness the rations are coming up! Heads first appear indistinctly, then slightly clearer outlines: one carrying something that makes him appear dwarf-like in that half-light; the other, more upright, has something beside him. They seem to hesitate; they must be through the wire; they separate. Then the first one moves forward quicker, followed on his right by the dixie carrier. 'Gor' blimey! They'll never get up here. Them bloody Jerries have got eyes like – 'awks on that roadway.' Bert is always a fatalist, but we realize the truth in his expression. 'Wonder what it is this morning?' someone asks. 'Stew – 'corse it is. We had 'char' last time up' – the words are said briefly by men inwardly cold and hungry, yet tense with quiet excitement for the safety of the men carrying those rations, as well as concern for the anticipated meal.

'Those blarsted cooks again, you can bet – keeping the carriers too late, or they'd have been here by now,' and Bert spat vigorously. Evidently his mind was working savagely about cooks and field-kitchens. 'Blimey! They're moving, anyway. Jerry ain't spotted them yet.' Only one man ventured that remark; fear kept others silent – double fear – for pals and for rations, and yet we must stand here helpless and watch. Why were they so late – we wondered!

Only for a second did it seem that Jerry hadn't seen them. 'Zim-Boom,' and a shell has burst only a few yards from the two figures, now being watched – watched more keenly than ever two runners on a sports-ground, or even two horses on a course. Two men burdened with our rations, yet even for sake of their own lives racing with time and death to reach the nearest post! They are our pals, too, and those damned cooks must have made them late getting away. Curse these wallahs behind the line; we forget that they are necessary to feed us; only now they are thought of as the cause of the danger in which our mates and our grub seemed doomed! We stand and watch – helpless to render any aid to those figures struggling over that ground about twenty yards away. And they cannot race for it – a dixie full of stew is, I suppose, the most awkward thing imaginable – certainly impossible to run with. They are quite clear now. Surely it's got broad daylight in the last few seconds; yet, really its only half-light, but enough for some Jerry's glasses to spot a movement on that road. Someone overstrung with the tense excitement of all of us who watch shouts, almost yells: 'Run, Jock, run for Christ's sake!' just as one supposes he had yelled to some player on a football ground: 'Go on, shoot! Shoot! Now!' Then 'Oh-h-h!' in a cry of dismay from the crowd that the ball had gone wide perhaps – that is the sound now from us, as a second shell, ranged with greater precision, bursts almost in front of those two!

The platoon officer's shouted order to us to 'Keep down there!' was half lost at that moment. The explosion cleared. There was only one man now, dragging a sack, he could be seen to rise from the ground. The other is gone, but that looks like a dixie there in the road – on its side! And how cold it is at dawn too! – we shiver and almost turn away in silence. There goes all hopes of 'something hot,' anyway, and we don't speak about the carrier – yet. The voice of Bert, that had merely swore about cooks and those behind the line, broke the silence again and cursed now. 'Bloody – cooks and all the – rest, what do they care? Wait till I – well, get out of this.' It's a decent mouthful, but we know Bert's sentiments are right, and if we don't all use those words we agree, and under those conditions out there we all become 'Berts' now and then. It did ease things a bit to have a good 'blind' about somebody.

'Look! That's 'Chunky'!' and we turn to see someone climb out from the post on our left and race madly towards the man with the sack coming on, but slowly. Another shell bursts, full in the road again, but just a little too far back. Involuntarily some of us have ducked – it became sheer habit out there. When we look up again, 'Chunky' has reached the other and together they are covering the last few yards like mad, carrying the sack between them. Yes, they're there. We only see two bodies disappear unto the nearest post, and someone voices 'Good old Chunky.'

We learnt afterwards why the ration carriers were late starting back out there. One of them has doubtless 'Gone West,' the other slightly wounded in the leg. It is lighter now. There's something lying doubled up in the road, and the stew dixie is quite clear – mocking us as it lays empty on its side. The ration sack 'caught' a lump of shrapnel, and two loaves are now lying out there somewhere too – so near – yet not one of us dare risk life to get them until dark! For twelve hours at least, more probably eighteen, we must 'carry on' with what has reached us, bully, some cheese (mostly broken), jam, biscuits, and a loaf between six of us. Nothing hot! – nothing to drink at all, and yet they tell us how they had to wait in Blighty for hours, perhaps, to get their rations of butter or meat! And the bread was half-black they say! So we must carry on another day, and only hope that the carriers are sent off early enough to reach us safely next time.

The day developed hot, terribly hot, with the sun blazing down on that unsheltered trench-post, in which some of us tried to snatch some sleep in various curled-up positions. Finding rest in that heat impossible – it burnt our face and eyes, it seemed, while we slept – we dug forward: lay there digging out holes with entrenching tools – holes that would go in under the parapet sufficiently big enough to get one's head into at least. Anything for shelter. Somewhere about midday we decided to eat what we had if only to alleviate our misery for half an hour. Two pals and myself opened up a tin of bully between us. One only wanted a little, he said. 'Awful bloody stuff anyway to eat without bread or drink' was his opinion. Bottles were empty and bread had been eaten for 'breakfast.' Iron ration biscuits were turned out, and so we managed a 'meal,' only to feel more parched than we had done before...

At last it came to my turn to keep a look-out. This meant standing up in one place, watching through the periscope, and readiness to sound the gas alarm if necessary. I didn't spend all my hour looking Jerry's way, however. I had a good view of the country behind me, and I looked round in all directions at intervals. 'Where the hell could one get some water?' was all that seemed to matter. What about that ditch I had nearly broke my leg in last night, when we were moving about. I could see the irregular ground. The nearest point was about 15 or 20 yards away. Wonder if it was quite dry. I remembered when I had half fallen one foot had squelched in wet mud. Apparently it was a decent stream in the wet season; it shouldn't be quite dry yet. That ditch was all I could think of till the next one took over the look-out.

'D'ye hear, Wally. I wonder if there's any water left in that ditch over there.' He stirred uneasily. 'I shouldn't think so after this heat. Besides it would be pretty blasted dirty, anyway. What good's that?' 'Come and lie down,' said Reggie, moving sideways a little. I persisted, however, 'Well, we could boil it. You've got a 'Tommy' cooker, Reg.' 'And I hope you'll remember Reg has got some sense too,' that worthy exclaimed slowly. 'That ditch is filthy, man. Don't you know what some of them used it for at night.' 'Oh, Gord! there goes windy Reggie again,' broke in Bert. Reggie's voice always seemed to move Bert. 'We're at the bloody War now, not in your – fancy restaurants.' But I cut him short. Wally appeared to be interested, anyway, and we appeared to be the only two who could seriously consider any hope of water from that ditch. But how to reach it? Could we get out there over the exposed ground? These pros and cons continued, and so did our parched throats. Enough is it to say, that thirst overcame fear or caution or even orders to 'keep down all day.' One of us took two mess-tins, and crawled out and worked towards that ditch on belly and face almost, got there, and started back, which was slower work. How long it took we never knew, but it seemed hours before we were in possession of one can nearly full, and the other about half-full of liquid thick with green scum, just exactly what one finds in any stagnant pool or ditch in the country.

We surveyed that capture, for which life had been risked, and perhaps we made little comment beyond one who said, 'And now what the devil will we do with that?' To me occurred the notion that if we strained it and then boiled it it might not be so bad. We could then make some tea. Several of us had tea and sugar ready for any chance of a 'drum up.' I was doubted and besides we hadn't got 'any damn thing to strain it with!' I produced a khaki handkerchief that had washed a bit thin by now, and was not too dirty. I had probably rinsed it out about a week ago, though, of, course, it had doubtless wiped other things than my nose since then – principally my rifle! I cannot give the debate that took place between us over this except the general opinion: it couldn't be any worse! Would it strain through that rag? It remains with me as an outstanding experience, because I was the one to think of this particular 'outfit,' that somehow we did with great care and expenditure of time strain off the thickest of that green scum growth! My handkerchief was used. Then the 'Tommy' cooker was fitted up in one of the holes we had scooped out earlier in the day, the 'water' was boiled and the tea brewed. That drink of tea was shared out between four of us and I remember we continually assured each other that 'anyway the boiling would have killed the germs!' It was drunk, by Reggie and Bert alike, in comparative silence. And we thought of homes that afternoon (I wrote to my wife on the pages of a little notebook), and the grumbles some of us had made in old days in those homes over little things at meal-times! I remarked that the 'tea' we drank could do us no more harm than a 'packet from Jerry' would probably.

That night Wally was killed outright. The following night, going out of the line, I was severely wounded, and never went back again.

C. Goddard-Chead volunteered August 1914. Actual service did not commence until fourteen months later, because he was three times rejected – unfit. Served over three and a half years with Argyll and Sutherland Highlanders, at home, in Prance and Near East (Turkey). Twice wounded, slight shell-shock, once blown up in France. Returned to Blighty, May 1918 – wounded in thigh by bomb dropped by night bomber just behind lines.

A PADRE'S STORY

Anon.

The war treated me kindly. I was wounded, gassed, and had shell-shock, but they were all relatively slight. I received decorations which thousands earned quite as genuinely without recognition. As a combatant private and a brigade chaplain, I was in almost every part of the line on the Western Front. I came through with a great pride in men and a bitter hatred of war.

Memories besiege my mind. I can only select. I remember vividly certain bonny lads of twelve or thirteen haunting our billets behind the line, touting for buyers of their sisters' bodies at 50 centimes. I remember also a mother offering her daughter of sixteen in a whisper as she handed out eggs and chips.

During one spell in the line a bantam battalion was on our right. They were sturdy fighters. One day a party of Prussians raided them and a huge German ran off with a bantam under his arm.

Our platoon sergeant during one period was an old Regular. He could carry drink well from long practice. Once when we were out of the line someone made a bet of 20 francs that he could not get drunk on French beer. He tried hard all one night. They carried him to his billet at closing time. He was very ill, but as sober as a judge.

There was no romance in the War for private soldiers. There were great days when there were comfortable latrines available and when the bread ration was four to a loaf. Such days were infrequent. Life was unutterably boring. I was a company runner, but most men had an almost unchangeable routine. We knew nothing about the meaning of our masterly inactivity. We received shells but saw no Germans save on occasional raids. We felt that the War would outlast us all. Most men longed for a Blighty.

When I became a chaplain I saw more actual fighting. I think of Arras. I was with the first brigade that lived in the catacombs under the town. They were very deep below the ground and were lighted by electricity. They were huge, irregular caves out of which the stone of which the cathedral was built had been hewn. They were connected by passages with each other and with the sewers under Arras. They were very silent, for men went out to work or fight and came back to sleep. We rested there before the Easter Battle of Arras, 1917.

In front of Arras I saw my first German booby traps. They had withdrawn quietly from their line, destroying most of their dug-outs as they went. Our troops thrust out patrols to discover their new line. I visited a new company headquarters. In the corner of the dug-out there was a heap of dirt out of which a beautifully carved crucifix projected. I reached down to examine it. 'Good God! Don't touch it!' the company commander yelled. The bottom of it was attached to a bomb. Battalion headquarters was in a huge German dug-out which had four entrances. Three had been destroyed and the fourth partially destroyed. In the main room there was a huge fire-place with a wide chimney. In the chimney the brigade bombing officer found a large bomb and in other parts of the dug-out eight other bombs. A fire would have exploded the lot. In my unit there was a superstition that it was dangerous to carry French cartridges. I was going round with the C.O. during the later stages of the Easter show when we passed a dead soldier of our battalion. The C.O. examined his pockets and, curiously enough, found a clip of French cartridges.

We spent eight months in and out, of shell-hole positions in front of Ypres. Often we came out less than half as strong as we went in. It was an animal and often beastly life. The wonder was that there was as much morality behind the lines after such an existence. In this area I had my first experience of sportsmanship among Germans. The Menin road between Hooge Tunnel and Clapham Junction (a captured pillbox) was a raised road. Any working party setting foot on it was strafed by machine-gunners, who had it under direct observation. As a result, troops journeyed under the shelter of the right bank of the road. In one show for a number of hours I made journeys with wounded men down the road itself. Machine guns never opened on us. Round the entrance to the tunnel, however, we lost over seventy stretcher bearers by shell-fire.

One of the men we carried out was Private C. of a Cornish regiment. He was only twenty. Later I saw him at the advanced dressing station. He had one leg blown off, the other badly injured, and other wounds in the body and face. The doctor said he could not live, but he did. I was with him as they dressed his wounds. Only seldom did he groan. Each time he looked up and said, 'S-sorry, padre.' He had a stutter. When they had almost finished he gave a twisted smile and said, 'P-padre, the c-c-canary that k-kicked me had g-got hob nails in its b-boots.' I saw him later in England. I wish I could see him again.

Early in 1918 we took over from the French down south. It was a very quiet part of the line. Here the brigade was reorganized on a three-battalion basis. Each battalion was 800 strong. A Scottish unit came into my brigade and I lived with them. The officers and men were a great lot! After a time the second in command, Major F., took charge. What a man he was! He stood over 6 feet. The men worshipped him. He was in charge of the first daylight raid. On that occasion he arranged a sweepstake for the men on the number of prisoners that would be captured. Soon after joining our brigade, he had an attack of jaundice. It was a good Blighty, but he would not go down. Each night he had a 'bivvy' put up on the top of headquarters dug-out and there he slept. One day in the communication trenches he met a new youngster carrying a dixie and stopped him. 'Well, my lad, are you a Boche-eater?' The lad, quite puzzled, said 'No' sir.' 'What the devil are you then?' ' Please, sir, I'm mess orderly.'

We were to conduct a raid in front of Moy. 'Mad Macduff,' as the men lovingly called him, prepared the party. There were two belts of wire, according to information received. A Bangalore torpedo was to be inserted quietly under the first. The two men were to run back. It would blow a gap. They were to rush through and insert the second. torpedo which in turn would be exploded. Then, according to programme, the party would rush through, snatch a prisoner and return. The whole thing was rehearsed again and again behind the lines. On the night of the raid the party paraded, well camouflaged with grass-covered coats. There were to be two officers on the raid, one of whom was an Engineers officer. Actually, there were five who took some part in the raid. 'Macduff' went with them. The raid involved a journey of 1,000 yards along a bit of a valley to a place where the German line was a fair distance away. The night was quiet. The party went forward and lay down. 'Macduff' went ahead further to examine the wire. He found a gap in the rear belt. He returned. He stood upright and passed along the line telling the good news. He spoke in an ordinary conversational tone, which seemed strangely loud. A machine gun opened and the bullets seemed to be right at the party. Every head save 'Macduff's' was buried. He never even ducked. Instead, in level tones he said, 'Away and have a course, Boche. You can't shoot for toffee. We'll show you how to shoot.' Shortly after, the signal was given, our barrage opened on the German line, the gap was made in the wire and through the men went. At the head of them was 'Macduff.' There was a German machine gun right opposite the gap, but the gunner was too stupefied to open fire. The major got him. He was first in the trench. He was the only casualty. It was soon over. The prisoner was a poor frightened youngster. As soon as the party knew 'Macduff' was injured they wanted to kill the prisoner. I stopped one of them with difficulty. We were soon journeying along the safer valley. The stretcher bearers rested a while. I offered to relieve one, but no one would give way. The wound was an abdominal wound and the end was obviously near. He smiled at me and said, 'Did they get the Boche?' 'Yes.' 'Good! Good!' he whispered. He was carried into an improvised aid post in front of the line. He lived but a few minutes. He whispered once, 'The Boche!' and it was all over.

I shall never forget that night. I went round the posts. Men called out, 'Padre, 'Macduff's' no deid! He's no deid!' More than one wept. We buried him at Montescourt. The raiding party made a coffin out of biscuit-box wood and lined it with tin-foil.

Contact with Major F. is one of my most poignant memories. 'We knew each other but a brief time, but we were friends. He was kind, generous, and a true gentleman. I am proud to have known him.

The weeks passed – quiet, nerve-racking weeks. Again and again we manned battle positions. Again and again there were false alarms. Our transport lines were at Remigny. There were football matches on March 20th. In the mess that night there was once again certainty that *It* would happen at dawn. The company commander in my mess was losing his nerve. That night he was dreadful. Again and again he said he knew he would get killed next day. He drank neat whisky to steady himself. Presently we were alone. The others could not stand it any longer. 'I can't help it, padre, I'm a damned coward. I know I am, but I shall get killed to-morrow.' He was not drunk, but his nerve was going. More than once during that evening he had said, 'The men are fine, but I'm a white-livered cur.' At last I persuaded him to go to bed. Next day early on he was hit in the leg. He carried on, rallying his men and retaking captured machine guns until he was killed.'

That night was quieter even than usual. Just as dawn was breaking I went to a cooker for some tea. As soon as I returned to my hut the barrage opened. It was incredible. My hut was near the cross-roads at the top of the main street of the village. I bolted for the nearest dugout. The men were getting their blankets rolled in bundles of ten. Four men had to fall in and take them to B.H.Q., past those cross-roads. We never knew whether they arrived. The men went out with blanched faces to find their battle positions. One of them had mislaid his tin-hat. I gave him mine. I was without until nightfall. I went to other dug-outs.

In one, just as they were filing out a boy went mad and shrieked, He was quickly quietened. My nerves were dreadfully shaken. For half an hour I skulked in the deep dug-out which the signallers occupied. They had had no contact with anywhere after the first few minutes. I would like to have stayed there, but my faithful batman said headquarters would wonder why I had not appeared. He knew I was funking, and that was how he helped me.

It was now about 10 a.m., Headquarters was opposite the aid post. There was no aid post left. In the dug-out the C.O. was just arranging to fall back to try and find contact with Division. I remained behind with my batman and a man detailed to watch the precious blankets. I thought we could direct stragglers. There were no stragglers. The Germans were obviously moving their guns forward. After about a quarter of an hour the blanket guard ran in shouting, 'Good God! padre, the Boche are coming down the hill.' We bolted out the back. Our headquarters was less than a hundred yards from the top of the street. We pelted on. We passed no infantry, but just before we reached the canal at Jussy we passed a battery of 18-pounders plugging away steadily. By nightfall Jussy was our headquarters. The sky seemed full of Fokkers. During the first two days I didn't see a single British plane. For days after, the Germans were overwhelmingly more numerous.

At one time the Germans were one side of a railway embankment and our men the other. They had bombs. Ours had scarcely any ammunition. On the fifth day my brigade consisted of twelve officers and not more than 260 men out of three battalions.

Of course, some may have got with other units, but the casualties were terrific and none had joined us from the battalion that was in the line when the show opened. For some days it was a case of running back to dig fresh positions, making a brief stand, then back again. Demoralization seemed complete. The men were hungry, tired, and hopeless.

At last, after several days, we were in front of Noyon. One of our R.A.M.C. units was marching into the barracks when a plane swooped down and bombed them. There were over a score of casualties. Ten days or so later we were talking about this in mess. There was a young lieutenant there who had been with the Air Force for instruction. He turned white as death. The plane that bombed our men was a British plane and he had been in it. They believed the troops were Germans.

After what seemed an eternity, we were crowded into lorries and rushed away from the line. The French had come forward to relieve us, and we thought we were going to safety. We were soon disillusioned. We were being rushed up to the front of Amiens. Our whole division was little more than the strength of a battalion. We were rushed as a composite battalion straight into the line. Our uniforms were all sorts. Our R.A.M.C. remnants were not with us. We had no stretchers. We were in despair. We were dug-in on the banks caused by plateaux which rose in terraces. Quite suddenly a tremendous bombardment started. It lasted two hours. Then equally suddenly it ceased and no attack came. I walked along the banks that were occupied. In one 'cubby' sat a soldier without a head. In another a sergeant lay asleep from exhaustion. He had slept through the barrage. Soon a lot were asleep. That night we were finally relieved by the Aussies. They came up fresh and singing. We had thought the War was over and we were licked, but as we went back we saw, to our amazement, a newly erected prisoners' barbed-wire cage. By the next night it was filled with Germans.

Three months in hospital and in England followed. Then once more in the line until a week before the end. I am glad to cut this part of the story short. The moral of new drafts of officers and men was often very bad. There were incidents one would like to forget. I remember a show at the end of October. We were believed to have an easy task, but camouflaged machine guns made the event a tragic fiasco. There was an aid post on a sunken road which was safe until you turned the bend that led into the village we were to capture. Then it was under direct observation and almost point-blank range from machine guns in and round the village church tower. I had taken a casualty back as dawn was breaking. My nerve had gone. Instead of returning to my work, I cowered in the side of the road trembling like a leaf. When walking wounded came I walked as though I was going forwards and then when they had passed I hid again. This went on for half an hour. Then it was getting light. I took hold of myself, and, keeping to the side of the road, walked right down to the outskirts of the village. Not until I saw a German did I realize that they were still in occupation, Fortunately, he had not seen me. The rest of the day was spent carrying wounded. Once, perforce, we had to come up that sunken road. The machine guns kept quiet till we rounded the bend in the road.

I took six frightened boys back to their company. They were hiding and might have been shot for cowardice. I used a number of Germans as stretcher bearers. We dressed one boy's wound as he lay in the sunken road. A German lay flat on the far side. I lay on the near side. He died when we dragged him to a sheltered spot. The German was a man of about fifty! He wept like a child. I asked him why in French. He said he had had four sons killed, and that boy was like his youngest. I sent him back to safety, I could write much more. I hate war. I fight now to end it.

The writer of this narrative served in the Scottish Battalion in 1916 as a Private. In 1917 he became a Brigade Chaplain, and was awarded the M.C. and Bar.

MESSINES

October 1918

A. B. Kenway

It was a cold wet day towards the end of September 1918, and we had pulled our guns out from our position on Pilkem Ridge from which we had been firing on Passchendaele. We were resting in an old school at Hazebroucke while our O.C. had been finding a new 'possy' for our guns.

I had been with this particular battery about five months, having come out from Prees Heath as a reinforcement the previous April. 'Jerry' had presented me with a cushy 'Blighty' at Ypres in November 1917, and coming back to the same part of the line after five months in England did not make me feel very comfortable. In fact I was 'windy,' more so than at any time during my first spell of fifteen months in France. Day after day we had had casualties: a few killed, some wounded, others gassed. When was I going to get mine? I wondered how it would come.

Would half my body be pitched up into the branches of a tree as had been the case with one poor gunner on the canal bank? I hoped not, please God, not that! Nor like that boy who got it in the stomach at Reninghelst, who, when we let down his trousers, found his intestines bursting through the two holes the shell fragments had made. I prayed that I should not be mutilated. If I had to go 'West,' let it be a quick death – a hole in the head perhaps; that wouldn't be so bad. But let my body be in one, and not scattered, when they came to bury me.

There was one man in this battery who gave me comfort. His name was Bob Lawrence. He was a bombardier and the No. 1 of our gun. He and another gunner, Frank Thomas, were my particular chums. The others of our gun detachment who formed our clique were Jimmy Fooks, the oldest man in our section, whose time was nearly up: he was looking forward to going home soon for a month's leave; Harris, a fair-haired youth, who had just come back from leave and had left a young bride behind; and Kempton, who was due for leave and expecting to go any day.

Bombardier Bob Lawrence was a butcher in civil life. He was very easy-going and good-tempered, and never appeared to have the wind up. He was slow in his movements – a plodder. Nothing upset him: shells didn't worry him – at least he didn't show it if they did. He floundered about in the mud as if he enjoyed it, but the lice played hell with him. He would spend an hour cleaning up his shirt, killing the vermin until his thumb nails were covered with their blood. As soon as he put his shirt on, he would start itching again and scratch himself raw. He was quite bald, without eyebrows, or eyelashes; his body was as hairless as a baby's. He used to wear a wig of a dirty ginger colour which was beginning to show signs of wear, so that at the artificial parting you could see the soiled leather or rubber that formed its foundation.

At this time Bob had been in France three years, and I thought he was safe for 'duration.' He had never been hit, and I thought he never would be. If I was one of a working party sent to prepare a forward position or build an observation post, I was nervy and 'windy' if Bob was not of the party. I would start off with my limbs trembling and my heart in my mouth, and, until we were well on our way back to billets, I would be nothing but a bundle of nerves. Indeed, it was only by exercising all my will power that I was able to hide my feelings and control my actions. If Bob was with us, how different I felt! 'It's all right; nothing to worry about,' and off I would go contented and almost care-free.

We had made a fire in an old oil drum which was planted in the middle of the class-room of the school that was our temporary home at Hazebroucke. The room was full of smoke, and this made our eyes water and rendered the atmosphere so thick that one could cut it. About thirty men were lying about, some reading, some writing letters, others having a 'crumb up,' as we called the process of picking lice from our shirts. Steel helmets, gas respirators, and the remainder of our equipment were hanging from nails in the walls, and sand-bags filled with spare clothing and private property acted as pillows.

Harris had been giving us an account of his leave, telling us what it was like sleeping between sheets again and taking his meals off a clean tablecloth. He told us, too, how a flapper had presented him with a white feather one day when he was out in 'civvies' with his wife. Then we started talking of our chances of coming through the War. We had all seen over twelve months' fighting, and had overlived our allotted span of life as R.G.A. gunners. Bob, with his three years of active service, had become quite a fatalist. 'It's no use worrying, Ken,' he said, turning to me. 'If a shell has got your name written on it, it will get you; it will turn round corners to get you.' Then he started singing in his flat, cracked voice, 'What's the use of worrying, it never was worth while,' until someone suggested a game of nap.

Bob couldn't resist a game of nap. He would go 'nap ' with the most impossible of hands, and I am afraid he was 'rooked' shamefully. He would lose all his pay the very day that he received it, but he never went short of anything as long as one or the other of us had it. Parcels from home, cigarettes, tobacco, toothpaste, shaving soap, and writing paper were property common to our little clique. If you wanted something that one of the others had, you just helped yourself in front of his eyes. If he wasn't about, you helped yourself just the same, and told him, if you thought of it, when he returned.

You would curse and swear at each other to the best of your ability, but never with any bad feeling. If your chum came back to billets too drunk to stand, you would just put him to bed, tuck his blankets around him, and put an empty biscuit or fruit tin near his head in case he should need it. Then you would turn in beside him, and cuddle up to him for warmth, and share his lice with him. In the morning you would fetch his breakfast of bread and bacon and canteen of tea to him in bed, as he would probably awake with a thick head.

Bob always slept with a Balaclava helmet on his head. In fact his head was always covered, and I believe he was rather conscious of his wig. When I think of it, it amazes me that we didn't pull his leg about his wig, but we never did. It wasn't that his stripe protected him, as we chaffed him as much as we did each other. We often told him to 'go to hell' or to take a 'running jump at himself.' He would then threaten to run us in for 'insubordination'; that was his favourite saying, but never once did he report any man.

Though he was an N.C.O., he always did his share, and often more than his share, of all the hard and disagreeable tasks that fell to our lot, such as humping 6-inch shells and boxes of cartridges weighing over 1 cwt. If the caterpillars had to be fixed to the wheels of the gun on a dark, shell-swept road covered with thick slimy mud, Bob would do his whack, getting his hands all bashed and cut, and his fingers pinched between the blocks. On duty at the battery, though there was no need to for him to do a turn on guard, he always would, so that each man's turn might be a little less. He wouldn't even choose his turn, but always took his chance out of the hat as we gunners did. Perhaps we would have to do a harassing fire during the night at the rate of ten rounds per hour on roads behind the enemy's line. Then Bob would split his detachment into two, working the gun with four men and himself, while the other four got what sleep they could in the dug-out. When the night was half through he would send his four men in and call the other four out, but he would stick to the gun throughout the night, with no rest at all.

On October 2nd about twenty of us were sent forward over Messines Ridge to prepare positions for two guns that were coming up during the night. A lorry took us as far as safety would allow; then we made our way on foot along a road up the Ridge. The Germans had this road under observation, so we went along in parties of three and four, 50 yards or so separating each party. A day or so previously this road had been held by the enemy and now the bodies of Germans and horses lay about, the stench from which was fearful. Some were headless, some limbless, while others looked just asleep. A German gun team had been caught by one of our shells as it was getting away. Two of the horses lay dead in the traces, two gunners in grey lay in the road, while a third was doubled across the muzzle of the gun, all dead. One of the wheels was smashed, and under the gun was a hole in the road where the shell had burst.

In charge of our party was Sergeant Ellis, D.C.M., and we passed the spot on the left-hand side of the road where he had gained his medal by getting three of our guns away and blowing up the fourth as the Germans came over the Ridge when they attacked in the previous March. The remains of the blown-up gun were still there.

Running along the right-hand side of the road was a bank about 2 feet high, from which the ground sloped away to flat country below. Bob Lawrence, Frank Thomas, and myself were trudging along together in tin-hats, gas masks at the 'alert,' and loaded up with picks, shovels, petrol tins of drinking water, and rations. Suddenly there was a 'Phee-ew, crash! Phee-ew, crash! Phee-ew crash!' and three 4.2s burst about 20 yards to the left of us. We dashed to the side of the road and cowered beneath the 2-foot bank while Hell opened its gates and poured a storm of fire, gas, and flying jagged pieces of steel on the road: 77-mm. shells coming with a 'whizz-bang!' 4.2s coming with a sighing moan and a crash, and big 5.9's with their 'Phee-ew-ew!' rising to a crescendo and culminating in a roar like that of an express rushing through a station. On top of the bank were the bodies of two Jerries, and these gave us a little more protection, for we could hear the 'Phut! Phut!' as flying pieces of red-hot steel found a billet in them. We endured this torment for about ten minutes or a quarter of an hour, though it seemed ages. During this time Bob didn't turn a hair, though he didn't speak a word. Neither did I. All my energy was directed towards making myself as inconspicuous as possible!

The shelling stopped at last, and continued 200 yards further along the road. The only remark Bob made was, 'Bit hot while it lasted, Ken, blast 'em.' Then we made off as fast as we could down a side road to the left into a bit of a hollow. Here was a pillbox of concrete, together with a big signpost bearing the word 'Last-Kraftwagen,' and it was near here, on the side of a narrow road, underneath a few scarred trees that we had to prepare our gun positions. We called this position 'Last strafed wagon' because of the signpost. Away to our left front, about two or three kilos. away, rose the spire of a church which we were told was Wervicq and held by the enemy. We were ordered to lie low and do nothing till dusk, as we were visible to any observation that might be carried out from that spire.

About 100 yards or so to the rear of our gun position was a little shelter of rotting sand-bags filled with earth, and this we made our cook-house. Here we gathered and hid ourselves till dusk, when we made some tea, after which we started work on our gun-pits. We levelled the ground and made a platform of railway sleepers. The other section did the same a little distance down the road.

Just after midnight we heard the rumble and clatter of lorries and guns, coming down the road, and in a couple of hours we had both guns in position and camouflaged, and the shells, cartridges, and fuse boxes, etc., all stored around the guns. The major; who had come up with the guns, told us we should be relieved at ten o'clock in the morning. Then he went away, leaving another officer in charge.

As there was no shelter against shell fire, Sergeant Ellis ordered us to dig a fire-trench to the rear of our gun, big enough to accommodate ten or a dozen men. This we proceeded to do and by daylight had dug a trench about 4 yards long by 1 yard wide and about 5 feet deep, our intention being to cover it over later and make it into a dug-out.

About eight o'clock in the morning we went across to the cook-house for breakfast, which consisted of tea, bully beef, and biscuits. There was a heavy ground mist, so we could move about without fear of being observed from Wervicq. After breakfast we went back to our trench to await our relief. Sergeant Ellis went into the gun-pit under the tarpaulin to get a little sleep while the rest of us squatted in our trench talking. Ten o'clock came and the mist was rising, but no relief! 10.30 and no relief. Eleven o'clock and we were getting very impatient and angry, but still no sign of the relieving party. We were tired out. It had rained during the night, we were wet and cold and covered in mud; our eyes smarted and our feet felt like clay. We were grimy and lousy, and our cigarettes were all gone; we had descended to the depths of misery. We were afraid to walk about in case we were spotted from the spire at Wervicq. Presently Frank Thomas said to me, 'What about going across to the cook-house, Ken, to see if there is any tea?'

'Too much fag,' I replied. A quarter of an hour later something came over me, and I turned to Thomas and said, 'Come on, Frank, let us go now. Come on, Bob,' but Bob wouldn't come, so we promised to bring him some tea back if there was any. So Thomas and myself scrambled out of the trench and, keeping the scarred trees between us and the church spire, we made our way to the cook-house, only to find biscuits, but no tea. We munched a few biscuits and begged a cigarette from our temporary cook, and warmed ourselves by the dying embers of his fire. We had been there about ten minutes when Thomas suggested that we should go back to the trench, but I was in no hurry. If the relief came up we wouldn't have so far to go from where we were. Just then we heard someone shouting 'Is that – th Battery?' and, looking around, we saw it was one of our officers who had brought the relief along. He sent Thomas and myself to tell Sergeant Ellis that the relief had arrived.

We were half-way back to the trench when suddenly there were four or five explosions, following quickly one on another. We flung ourselves flat on our faces and heard the 'Whirrphut! Phut! Phut!' as fragments of steel flew around. I was scared stiff, and a cold sweat came over me. Bob wasn't there to give me the comfort of his presence. We lay there a few minutes waiting; then there was another salvo of shells and, peeping up, I saw a cloud of black smoke and a fountain of earth rise in the air over the trench where Bob and the others were. We waited a little while, but, as nothing else came over, we made a dash towards the trench.

God! what a sight met our eyes! A shell had landed right among the boys. It was a slaughterhouse – just a mass of mangled flesh and blood. Bob's head was hanging off; you could only recognize it by his poor, worn-out; dirty little wig. Jimmy Fooks was squatting on his haunches, not a mark on him, quite dead, killed by the concussion. You couldn't tell which was Harris and which was Kempton – what was left of them was in pieces. I was numbed. I felt as if a great weight was pressing on my head. I was choking. In a dream I heard the sergeant's voice, 'For God's sake get away. Get to hell out of it before they start again.' He had been asleep in the gun-pit and was untouched.

Somehow I got back to the lorry which was waiting to take us back. Then I broke down and between my sobs I cursed the Germans. Though I had always felt I could not kill a man, at that moment I could have killed with my bare hands the Boche gunner who had fired that shell.

We knew the enemy was beaten; we knew it couldn't last much longer, and at this time, after three years in France and the end so near, Bob must be killed! Harris, who had left a young bride in England – killed! Jimmy Fooks, whose time was nearly up – killed! And Kempton, who was due for leave – killed also! Why hadn't they come across to the cook-house with Thomas and me? Why hadn't the relief come up to time? If either of these things had happened Bob would still be alive. And then I remembered his fatalism. 'It's no use worrying, Ken. If a shell has got your name on it it will get you; it will turn round corners to get you,' and it had done that to Bob and the others; it had found its way into that trench and got them.

They left them where they fell and covered them over. The trench which they dug to give them shelter in life proved to be their grave, and sheltered their bodies in death.

Gunner A. B. Kenway joined Glamorgan R.G.A. (Territorial) November 1915. Age twenty. 2/3rd Coy. Went to France, September 1916, with 172nd Siege Battery. First time in action at Vimy Ridge, then at Hébuterne from October to December 1916. Battle of Arras (April 1917.) Third Battle of Ypres (July 1917). Battery position: on Canal bank. Later, position near the China Wall, not far from Hell Fire Corner, to the right of the Menin road. Was burned there, but stayed a few days with battery, but, as it was ordered to Italy, had to go into hospital. Sent to Mile End Military Hospital, London November 1917. April 1918, back in France as reinforcement, posted to 155th Siege Battery, which was in action near Reninghelst, in the Ypres area; later at Borre, near Hazebroucke. From there to Pilkem Ridge; later to Gapaarde near Messines (scene of narrative). Then to Dottignies, a hamlet near Tourcoing, until the Armistice. Demobilized January 26th, 1919. Resumed civil occupation February 2nd, 1919, as a ledger clerk.

A BOY AT GALLIPOLI

Fred T. Wilson

When the Territorials in 1914 were asked to volunteer for active service, I went with the others. I left England in September 1914, when I was seventeen years old.

We embarked at Southampton in the S.S. *Corsican*, and reached Alexandria seventeen days later.

In Alexandria and Cairo eight months went by and my experiences were varied. War seemed very distant, the Egyptians themselves appeared to be quite unmoved by our presence or the reason of our coming. I am afraid we didn't get their true opinions.

It seemed to me in those days that the main idea in the Army was to get you as fed-up as possible, so that you welcomed any change. They caught us in this mood when orders came to embark for Gallipoli; so lustily we sang all the way from Cairo to Alexandria, sitting in cattle trucks, regulating the beat of the song to the clip of the wheels.

At Alexandria, after hours of delay, we embarked on a captured German liner, the *Derflinger*. Iron plates above, iron plates below, and riveted iron plates each side, bordered our bedroom.

Closed and covered portholes kept out light and air, the darkness being partially relieved by a few electric globes in cages. In this half-light confusion attended the hanging of our hammocks as we tripped and fell over bits of unfamiliar ship's tackle. All this appeared more ridiculous when we slept on deck owing to the heat down below. We slept as we were. Nobody thought of undressing.

For three days and three nights four men lived where one would have been cramped in that iron-cased floating stinkhole, eating badly-cooked food and drinking warm water. By the night of the third day, as we neared Gallipoli, we were in the mood for anything. We'd fight anybody for anything; we didn't care what.

Looking towards the land, we could see flashes here and there and hear intermittent firing, punctuated occasionally by the boom of heavy guns. Rumours were numerous, but the only one that proved true was that we disembarked that night. With all lights out, we crept slowly in towards the land, alongside the *River Clyde*, and were taken ashore in flat-bottomed barges. Everything was quiet, as though the guns were silenced to give us welcome. It was raining. Raining as it can only in the East. The barges grounded and we got no wetter by wading ashore. Everything was in a wonderful state of chaos. Nobody met us. Friend or foe could have done what we did. It was May 1915, and the Gallipoli campaign was new. Soaked kits are heavier than dry ones, and we were glad to lie down on the top of a cliff, in the pouring rain and mud, and sleep.

The sun shone in the morning and we looked round. We were all eager for information, and this was given to us readily by a few wounded Lancashire Fusiliers from the front line.

Cape Helles, where we had landed, was the general stepping-off place, and a mile of land had been taken. The loss of life had been out of all proportion to this gain, due to the prepared positions of the Turks right down to the water edge, which enabled them to mow down our men with ridiculous ease. Very bitter were our informants as they related the hurried preparations for battle, the taking of practically impregnable positions, and the terrific hardships endured under constant bombardment.

That morning we were treated to a new sight: a Turkish prisoner, bandaged about the head, lying on the ground, his face, hands, and arms painted green, and wearing a green uniform. He had been shot down from a gun-nest in a tree, and, before he had been located, his accurate sniping had accounted for a considerable number of officers. Now he was slowly dying. His eyes searched our faces, and no doubt read pity there – the pity that goes out to a dog with a broken leg. We had not yet acquired the callousness of war veterans.

Enemy aircraft kept us on the move all that morning. They seemed to have command of the skies. No airmen of ours challenged their activities. A few anti-aircraft guns tried to bring them down, but did no apparent damage.

More troops arrived during the day and it was interesting to watch them land under heavy shell-fire that sank a few barges and scattered us on land as they fell short of the water. The daily bathing parade in the sea continued, however, and the shelling did not seem to upset the troops swimming about near the beach.

That afternoon we paraded ready for a move up towards the front line. A shell blew away a few of our men in the rear company, then, regardless of procedure, we turned right and 'Follow me!' was sufficient for the moment. The leading officer was an old hand. He knew the way or we might have marched straight into the enemy. A series of gullies, about 50 feet deep, one joining with another, ran in all directions, and up and down these we twisted and turned for about three hours, stopping occasionally for rest. At dusk we were told to stand easy until further orders were received. We were then on a lip on one side of a gully about 500 yards from the front line. As night advanced the flies left us. Then the shelling became more intense and rifles and machine guns helped to swell the noise. After an hour this subsided and the gully became full of other sounds. The small stream that ran in the bed, full of slime and blood-coloured in patches, was full of frogs. Hundreds of them, all croaking together. Very weird and uncanny this was in the darkness and unnatural silence. We trod on them as we moved off, but the croaking continued.

We now heard officially that we were to relieve the New Zealanders in the front-line trench, and, led by the same officer, we pushed off in a long single file.

The communication trenches from the front line went back about 10 yards, then a dash over open country before one reached the shelter of a gully. Leaving the gully we had now to cross this open space before we could drop into the communication trenches. Only about 200 yards. Not far, we thought, but a long way when under fire. Here we got our first small taste of war. The enemy guessed a relief was taking place, for their machine guns found us, and as the whine of bullets became more marked, we were ordered to lie down. I lost my first friend at that moment, and it was hard to realize he would never again share with me the things we both enjoyed. As I flopped down, my equipment falling on top of me, I felt the handle of a spade on the ground. Instinctively I covered my head with the spade end and burying my ear in the mud, felt very well protected. I saw the man in front of me lying still with head well down; and waited with him for the next move. It came in the shape of a sergeant, who, crawling up to both of us, wanted to know why the hell we didn't follow the others – we were keeping back all the men behind. I realized then my mistake in waiting for the man in front, and, crawling over him, I caught up with the others, who had waited after the break had been noticed. One by one we dropped into the communication trench with a splash. Last night's rain still lingered, finding no outlet. No comfort or safety was to be found in the trenches in those early days. Sand-bags had not arrived. Dug-up dirt thrown out served as a shield from bullets, a shield that fell in when rain came, and a roughly cut step in the side of the trench served for a seat. We slept on the floor of the trench or propped up along the side.

In the blackness of the night we stumbled and splashed along the trench. All we could do was to obey orders and if we received none, we thought we were doing right. We didn't know where we were or what might happen next. There was an awful din and the order for absolute silence had to be shouted from man to man. A stream of men going in the opposite direction ploughed their way through the mud past us – the New Zealanders going out. It was a tight squeeze and many a curse followed us as we tripped over one another or bumped them into the sides of the trench.

The guns were silent again now, and upon arriving at our appointed stations word came down the line to fire 'fifteen rounds rapid' at the enemy trench. With fingers cold, wet, and fumbling we loaded, fired as quickly as we could and got a volley in reply. This was our first shooting at the enemy even if we could see nothing, and proved so exciting that our discomfort was forgotten. The New Zealanders had, now gone and we Territorials held the line, or rather our part of it, for the first time. A great honour, and we meant, if possible, to do all we could to uphold that honour.

By dawn, having 'stood to' all the night, we were tired and hungry, and thought nothing much of the honour thrust upon us, but as the day became brighter we found interest enough in having a peep over the thrown-up dirt at the part of the landscape occupied by the Turk, and at the chaotic condition of No Man's Land. Barbed wire there certainly was, but it hung in shreds from wooden posts, and nearer to us a small trickle of water flowed alongside the trench, coming through the trench side a little lower down. In this, opposite to where I stood, lay a couple of dead Turks. There was no need to tell us not to drink this water, but we had to later, after it had been boiled.

That day our time was taken up chiefly with making more comfortable the trench that served as a home, and in the days that followed there was no great excitement. Only a few big shells and sniping.

Then a fifteen-hour bombardment by our guns commenced. The noise we now heard was terrific. A continual roar; thousands of big shells hurtling through the air at the same time. If more noise had been added it would have passed unnoticed, so great was the din, but the Turks did reply, as our casualties that night were very heavy. I was losing most of my friends. We were in the support trench at the time and received an order to carry ammunition for the gunners from the dumps. Dozens of us carried heavy shells through mud that was impassable for mules. Instead of the fifteen hours, the bombardment lasted only seven hours. Ammunition had run out. There was only sufficient left for desultory shelling by our guns for one more day. The ammunition boats had not arrived according to schedule, and the bombardment took place, as we afterwards learned, to impress upon the enemy how well supplied we were with shells. A peculiar thing is war. The Turks could, this night, have driven us into the sea.

A week later we advanced about 50 yards, half way into No Man's Land, under a full moon. Our hectic digging with entrenching tools into rock-like earth as we lay flat on the ground was a sporting chance given to the Turk to try a little sniping. Our barrage did not cover us well enough and a large proportion of our men were killed. By dawn we were out of sight if we knelt down and we did a lot of kneeling that day. We had no time that day to complete communication trenches back to the old line, so when the counter-attack came, no way of retreat was possible except over the intervening open high ground. Our guns got the range soon after the Turks attacked, but that didn't stop them, and, after a short hand-to-hand struggle, we had to give way. It was a sorry retreat and our casualties, if not heavy, were ugly. I was surprised at what man is capable of enduring in a semi-conscious state; how he can stagger to safety, leaving parts of himself behind. When we got back our machine guns opened fire and we laughed like maniacs as the Turkish advance crumpled and fell. That attack had failed.

So it went on, day after day, week after week; a bit forward here, a bit back there; very little ground gained and very little lost, but death always. Disease helped to swell the death roll, but still the senseless game went on. New blood came from England but was soon spilt, and old blood faced days with hope of quick release. We became infected with the spirit of hopelessness. Such was the state of things when I was forced to crawl 100 yards to the nearest dressing station to have a shrapnel wound plugged. Two days later I found myself on a hospital ship. I saw no more fighting.

Private Fred T. Wilson enlisted 1/6th Battalion Manchester Regt. (Territorial Force), January 26th, 1914. Demobilized, March 31st, 1920. Active service, 4^1/$_2$ years. Foreign service, Egypt and Gallipoli.

THE FLOOD AT SUVLA BAY

F. W. D. Bendall

If you broke a wash-basin in half, the line of the break would give you a good idea of the trench lines at Suvla. High, almost mountain-high, to the north, they ran down the stony slopes, where nothing grew but prickly Turkish holm-oak in dense, scrubby patches, down to the cultivated fiat land at the bottom of the basin. Over grassy hillocks they ran, and away southwards to the Anzac position, which we saw dimly, but did not know, and up the distant cliffs to the precarious foot-hold we had on the summit there. From 70 to 400 yards apart they ran, our trench and the Turkish line.

Standing in the middle of the basin, we saw a curved line of hills some miles away. To the left these hills went on behind us to the northern end of the blue bay, where the battleships rode snugly at anchor inside protecting nets. The ground here was like a rough farm at home. There were hedges and ditches, trees, some poor olive-groves, and here and there a vineyard.

All the ravines and water-courses on the distant hills led the winter rainfall into the middle of the basin, and in August we found in the clayey soil hoof-marks and foot-marks inches deep, made in the previous winter, when the farms were a puddle, and the farmers were at peace, and now baked and set till the rains should come again.

Our division held the middle of the basin. My battalion was on the left flank of the divisional sector, and my left-hand company was on rising ground, where the slope of the northern hills began. The battalion trenches were shaped like a bent bow with an arrow on it. The front trench was the string, about three-quarters of a mile long. From each end a communication trench led back. These curved towards each other and met some 300 yards behind the firing-line. They formed the bow. The arrow was a third trench, which was really a field ditch dug out and widened, and which ran from the middle of the front line to the junction of the two communication trenches.

Battalion headquarters were just off this straight trench on the south side. A trench with a fire-step led to them, and from this ran several narrow slits in the ground 2 feet wide and 6 feet deep. Each of these opened out into a small room, about 6 feet by 7, in which an officer or some men lived. One room was a good deal larger than the others. This was the mess-room. These rooms were covered with corrugated iron and a few inches of earth, and in them lived four or five officers and about twenty men, runners, signallers, and the like.

It was a Friday in the last week of November 1915. I had been out for some hours with the Brigadier and the other C.O.s, walking over the line of the trench which was being dug close to the beach to cover the evacuation, which we knew was coming. Heavy rain had fallen all day, and I was very wet. When I got back to my little room in the earth I changed, putting on dry 'slacks' and shoes, a British warm overcoat, and a Balaclava helmet, for it was cold. The time was now about six o'clock, and it was quite dark.

So I walked down my private slit and turned into the mess-room, where we had a lamp. Here the second-in-command, the M.O., and the adjutant were sitting on seats made of filled sandbags, at a rough table made of rum cases. The Adjutant told me nothing had happened, and we all cursed the weather, for the floor was muddy and the roof was dripping. There was an hour before dinner, and we began to discuss the evacuation, some details of which I had learnt during the afternoon.

As we sat talking there were noises of splashing in the slit outside, and the figure of an orderly was dimly seen, saluting with difficulty in the restricted space.

'Front line all correct, sir,' he said.

'Very good,' said the adjutant, and looked at me.

'All right, Jones, no messages,' I said, and the splashing sound faded away up the slit. This was the usual procedure during the hours of darkness. Each company reported to battalion headquarters every hour, and we reported to the brigade.

The rain sounded more heavily than ever, and there were by now some 3 inches of water on the floor. To keep our feet dry we took the top row of sand-bags from the seats, and used them as foot-stools. Hopes of a meal seemed rather dim. The cook-house was not likely to be drier than the mess-room, and it would be no joke carrying things along the slit. Even as the M.O. gave voice to this thought there was more splashing, and the adjutant's servant appeared, a waterproof sheet over his head.

'Sorry dinner will be a bit late, sir,' he said. 'Cook's doing 'is best, but it's raining something awful, and keeps a-puttin' the Primus out.' 'All right, Smith,' said the M.O., who was Mess President on the grounds that he had less to do than anyone else. 'Tell him not to worry. We'd sooner have it late and dry,' and Smith paddled away.

Another unpleasant quarter of an hour went by, and the water on the floor rose slowly but steadily. Then, almost suddenly, the heavy drumming noise became less heavy, died down to a mere patter, and ceased. The M.O., who had on gum-boots, splashed outside and sniffed. 'It's stopped, sir,' he said; 'I can see a star or two.'

'Thank Heaven!' I replied. 'If that's so I'll just wade round to my dug-out and see how much of my kit is dry. I'm afraid I didn't cover up my valise.'

It was very unpleasant in the slit. 'The water was over my shoes, and it was pitch dark. Gradually I began to see a little, and by the time I reached my dug-out had picked out several stars to the north.

My dug-out was furnished simply. There was a stretcher resting on filled sand-bags, and a packing-case in the corner. My valise went on the stretcher, and my kit on or under this. I lit a candle and began to pile things on the valise. The cover was turned over, after all, so my flea bag was dry. As I fished about underneath for gum-boots I heard a strange sound. I could have sworn it was the sea, washing on the beach! But the sea and the beach were four miles away. I stood in the doorway and listened. And as I listened in the flickering light there was a curious slapping noise in the slit outside, and a great snake of water came round the curve – breast high – and washed me backwards into the dug-out. I was off my feet for a moment, and then, sodden and gasping, I was in the doorway again. Another moment and I was in the open air, and the horror of drowning under the dug-out roof was gone. What was left was bad enough! The water was at my throat, waves of it licked my face. I reached both hands to the top of the walls, but I could get no hold there. My fingers tore through the mud. Slowly I forced my way along the slit. If I could get to the main headquarters trench I should be better off, for this, like all trenches that faced east, had a fire-step, a broad ledge some 2 feet higher than the trench bottom. I do not know how long it was before I turned the last corner. But suddenly I felt that the slit was wider. I turned round and with great difficulty got one foot up. Thank God! there was the ledge. A great heave and I was on it – another heave and scramble and I was on the top – panting and dripping but out of the water, out of the greasy prison-walls of that horrible slit.

I stood there in the dark for a minute to get my breath. Then I called out, 'Hullo, headquarters party, is anyone here?' Answering voices came from a few yards away, and, moving towards them, I found the M.O. and five or six men standing by the hedge which ran along the centre communication trench. They were all sodden and shivering, and the M.O. and one of the men were clearly in a bad way – the others were supporting them. The ground was covered by the water – my feet told me that – and I realized that there was a flood from the hills, and that the water must have come through the Turkish lines. They were worse off than we were! But our lot was bad enough.

I could see the hedge clearly now, and the break in it where the trench I had just left opened into the centre trench. Taking two of the men with me, I walked carefully to the break, and turned along the headquarters trench, which, of course, I could not see for the flood water, calling out as I went. Answers came from more than one point, and I heard the adjutant and the second-in-command. Moving on, I found they were on the top, each with two or three men, but separated from me and from each other by the small trenches that led to the dug-outs. Gradually, going carefully hand in hand, and feeling with one foot ahead so that we might not step into a hidden trench, we came opposite them, and as one man had a stick which would reach across the slit, we were able to help them over in turn, and in the end we collected most of the party, though some were missing. We moved cautiously back to the hedge, and in it or near it we spent the night. Most of us stood on the lower branches to keep out of the water. It was bitterly cold.

My memories of that night are growing a little dim. One memory is of shouting from the darkness beyond the hedge. This came from the Captain of 'C' Company – which was in the support line. He told me many of his men were drowned, and nearly all collapsed from cold, and he asked me what to do. I told him to keep his men together and moving about while it was dark, but at the first sign of light to lie down behind the parados of the trench. His voice had a desperate sort of ring in it, which told me more than his words did. Other shouts were heard at intervals, and to those who came close enough the same orders were given. During the night several of the men near me collapsed, and the M.O. seemed to be dying of cold.

With the first streaks of light came a young officer from 'A' Company, which was on the right flank – and the lowest ground. He had managed to jump out of the trench when the flood came pouring over the parapet, and was dry, fit, and strong. He had got a plank from somewhere and crossed the intervening trenches by means of it. And he came splashing along in the grey dawn with the plank on his shoulder. He had a dismal tale to tell of his own company. Many were drowned, others missing, He had left a few men behind the parados.

I told off the strongest of our party to salve two spades as soon as the water sank a little, and to dig a hole for the others to sit in – a shelter of some kind.

I decided to try to get up the front trench with the young subaltern and his plank. All the trenches were abrim and the water swirling along strongly. The torrent had eaten away the sides and each trench looked like a small river in spate.

We went up the hedge side. This gave us some cover from view, and also led straight to the front line. We crossed several trenches and ditches with some difficulty, and reached the front line in the middle of the sector.

No Man's Land was a lake. No attack would come over that for some time. North and south the front trench was full of sullen brown water, and behind it was no sign of life. Only here, where the hedge joined the front trench, were there any men. Fifteen of them were there, with the company sergeant-major of 'A,' a very stout fellow, who had saved several from drowning, and was cheering them up as best he could. They were all blue with cold, shivering and wild-eyed.

'B' Company lines ran on to higher ground, so we turned north to find them. For some way the trench was full, and the muddy water hid its dark secrets. At the extreme end of our line the slope of the ground told, and here, behind an old stone wall, we found some twenty men and three officers. They had got their machine gun in action, and I told the company commander that he must watch the whole front carefully, and be prepared to cover most of it. On our way back to Headquarters we saw a number of bodies of men who had obviously died of cold and exhaustion.

The men were digging when I got back. Eight of them were taking turns with two spades, and they had dug down about 4 feet in a square of 9 feet.

In this hole we existed for another forty-eight hours. In the afternoon two runners got up from the Brigade. Our orders were to hang on for the present, and I learnt that the whole front was disorganized, ration parties drowned, trenches impassable, and floods everywhere in the basin.

No rations came up in all that time. We found one tin of gooseberry jam and a rum jar half full of rum and muddy water. These were shared out among the party. We had nothing dry of any kind, no matches, tobacco, paper, clothes. That evening it began to freeze and the night was bitter. The M.O. died in his sleep, and two other men also.

Next day there was not more than 2 or 3 feet of water in the trenches, and we had about forty rifles in action as well as the machine gun, but all the men were exhausted. One Turk sniped at us from a tree, and hit several men before we got him. It was quite impossible to get the wounded men away. Five other Turks struggled across No Man's Land (it took them an hour) and gave themselves up. Poor devils – they were half-dead already.

On the second day the brigadier waded up. He stood thigh deep in the trench to hear my gloomy report and went back with hardly a word. He had seen all that was necessary – and there was nothing to say. Moving about carefully on the top we found a number of bodies. None was wounded, all had died of cold and exposure. Two brothers of 'C' Company had died together. The arm of one was round the other's neck, the fingers held a piece of biscuit to the frozen mouth.

It seemed a strange and inexplicable thing that these men who had come there to fight, and had fought bravely, had been killed by the elements.

The trenches were a foul sight. Everything was covered by a slimy scum of mud. The front trench in the southern half was unspeakably horrible; this was where the flood had been deepest and strongest.

On the third day we were withdrawn. Forty-five of us all told crawled back to a ravine near brigade headquarters – many on hands and knees. Forty-five out of 500. The adjutant was killed on the way by shrapnel from a solitary shell.

In the ravine we camped under tarpaulins, and slept round a fire. They sent us up brandy and tinned chicken from the medical stores, and dry boots and clothes. On each of the succeeding days we stumbled up to the trenches to collect identity discs and to bury our dead.

Lieut.-Colonel F. W. D. Bendall was before the War captain, unattached list, Territorial Army. 1914, promoted Lieut.-Colonel to raise and command 2/3rd Battalion The London Regt. (Territorial Army). 1915, Malta; The Sudan; Gallipoli, Suvla Bay. 1916–1917, France, commanding 8th and 7th Battalions Middlesex Regt. Wounded August 1917, Battle of Passchendaele Ridge. 1918, Home service. Despatches (2) and C.M.G.

THE EVACUATION OF SUVLA BAY

W. H. Lench

After six months' training in Scotland I was as fit as drill, fresh air, and mutton stew could make me. I could route march all day with full pack; I could make four bulls at 500 yards; and I could run as far as any man in the battalion. I was an efficient robot-soldier the morning I went on board the *Olympic* bound for Gallipoli. On the trip out from Liverpool to Mudros I was inoculated five times. My body was sore, my head ached, and my tongue stuck to the roof of my mouth. Before I landed I was a physical wreck.

The peninsula loomed up black and foreboding. The lighter that took my company from the troop-ship grounded on the beach and the men jumped ashore. The guns were booming along the whole Suvla Bay front; Verey lights sizzled in the sky and the orders were passed from one to the other in whispers. The men formed up near a shelter and moved off and then halted.

Gallipoli, and I was sick before I started.

'Sergeant, you will go to the front line immediately,' the landing officer told me.

'Follow me,' a guide said; and I followed him with my men across the beach and up through a gulley into the darkness. When I reached the top of a hill a bullet whizzed over my head. I ducked and the guide laughed at me. I felt the top of my helmet. The whole place smelt of sage and decaying flesh – a rich combination. So this was war! I stumbled on and on through the darkness with my fears. The machine guns rattled away on my left. The smell of death was everywhere.

I jumped into a trench. I followed the guide through the darkness. The guide was blotted out two paces in front of me. I would have lost him but for the click, click of his entrenching tool. I arrived with my draft at regimental headquarters without a casualty. The adjutant came out of his dug-out. His clothes were covered with mud, his face had three-weeks' growth, and his left hand was bandaged. He had been struck with a bullet only a few minutes before.

'Nice clean lot of men you have,' he said. 'You are badly needed.'

We were. Ten hours before a storm had swept the Peninsula of Gallipoli, and the ruin of it! Desolation everywhere. Thank God it was dark! It was better to have the first experience of trench life before the dawn. I stumbled over men lying on the ground, moaning, crying in their agony; their legs frozen to their hips. There was an utter utterness about it. There was no one to attend to them; no one to carry them back to the beach. Everyone was demoralized; everyone was sick, waiting, waiting for the stretcher bearers who never came.

I had only a hundred men, and the adjutant divided them equally between the four companies. I was detailed to 'C' Company. I was shown the communication trench. 'You will find your company officer in a dug-out up there,' the adjutant said. I found the captain and reported to him. 'Twenty-five men,' he said. 'What a landfall.' It was just before the dawn.

'We stand-to at dawn,' the captain said to me. 'Post some sentries; we haven't had any since the storm.'

I posted the sentries and walked up and down the trench. I linked up with the companies on my flanks. There was little rifle fire, but it had its terrors. Everywhere I moved I stumbled over dead bodies; they floated towards us on the receding flood. The dead bodies were washed over the parapet, and the rains had opened the shallow graves. The first hours in the trenches were horrible.

I worked for twenty-four hours. The next night I took out a patrol across the mud of No Man's Land. I fell into the abandoned trenches; I crawled through the water with two men after me. I got within 20 yards of the Turks' wire on my first patrol. I saw them digging in the darkness, improving their trenches and putting up new wire. They were as demoralized as we were.

The next morning the sun came up in a blaze of orange. It became very hot before eight o'clock and it was middle

November. The company spent many days digging trenches to let the water run off from the front line. And there were orders for deep dug-outs as the winter loomed ahead.

There was not much sudden death, but there was slow death everywhere. The body was slowly dying from the inside. We talked to each other; we laughed occasionally, but always the thought of death in our minds – our insides were dying slowly.

The water was death; the bully beef was death; everything was death. I was afraid to eat a thing. It terrified me; it made me feel dead. A man would pass me holding his stomach, groaning in agony, and a few minutes later I would take him off the latrine, dead. The men contracted dysentery and fever every day. The bullets did not take a big toll. It was the death of germs.

I worked with my men all day and all night. I was lucky to snatch a few hours' rest in the middle of the day. The company had now thirty men to hold 200 yards of front. The sentries were posted at incredible distances apart. And for ever the patrols and the fatigues and digging day and night – digging, digging, infernal, intensive digging.

The company had been in the line twenty-five days; it was a record. There was no talk about going out for a rest; there was nowhere to go, only down to the beach, and the beach was shelled incessantly. It was safer in the line.

The food consisted of tea and biscuits. No meat. There was plenty of jam, but if a man was 'fed-up' with war all he had to do if he wanted a nice bed on a hospital ship was to eat a tin of jam. Many a tired man looked longingly at the flaming red cross on the side of the hospital ship at night and opened a tin of apricots. They carried him away the next day or the day after.

There were rumours every day – cook-house rumours, latrine rumours, and trench rumours. They were always different. The regiment was doing this to-day and that to-morrow. No soldier will deny the psychological blessing of them. They were the hope of tired men, of fed-up men, and sick men. They were lovely rumours, always original and timely. Nothing came of them. Dig and dig; patrol and patrol; raid and raid. Above all, over all, hopeful, glorious rumours! The company is going out of the line to-morrow for a month. The company has been ordered to Mesopotamia. The company is going to Egypt for the winter. There were rumours all day and all night.

One morning the captain called me. 'Our trenches must be deepened 3 feet,' he told me. Why, God only knew. They were quite deep enough if a man went about at the stoop. Three feet deeper, and only twenty-five men left in the company to do the work.

'Three days to do it, sergeant; and see it is done; don't care how.' It was done.

A few days later there was an incredible rumour. The General Staff would pass along our trench at noon. The men had to scrape off the mud with jack knives; they were given a pint of water to shave and, God above, their buttons had to be polished. The joke of the deepening of the front line trench was now obvious. The war must be made safe for the generals.

At noon the order was passed along to 'Stand at attention.'

We did, and Lord Kitchener passed and his general's cap was just six inches below the parapet. There were a number of Staff officers following him, and as they passed around the traverse of the trench their footsteps seemed to echo: 'It's hopeless! It's hopeless!'

The next morning the company officer called me into his dug-out. He was a hard drinker and a brave officer.

'There are rumours of an evacuation, sergeant,' he said. 'Kitchener does not like the look of it for the winter; but there is nothing official. Perhaps we shall have good news to-night.'

I smiled as I went back to my trench. When did the British Army ever retire? It was impossible. Here for ever. Flies in a spider web – million to one against ever getting out. Evacuation, no! I was sorry for those sick men who would believe the story. There would be more raised hopes, more denials, and more silly talk.

However, the impossible did happen. It was to be in ten days, the captain told me. Ten days, and the regiment would go to

Egypt, the captain said – perhaps Cairo, certainly Alexandria. It was not a bad War after all!

The remaining days were full of feverish activity. Small mines were sunk; bully beef tins were filled with explosives and scores of rifles with time fuses were stuck about the trenches. I worked like a galley slave all day and all night. The British Army was going to leave the ghastly place and outwit the Allahs on the opposite hill. Yes, the British Army would sneak away in the night under the cover of darkness, what a story to tell my grandchildren! 'Once upon a time, my young hearers, I fought in the rear-guard action when my regiment ran away from Johnny Turk at Gallipoli.'

The days passed with the usual routine work. There were only fifteen men now to carry on, and there were still three days before the evacuation. Three days! Would I get away safely? The web was drawing closer around me, around the company, around every man left at Suvla Bay. What if the Turks suspected?

The preparations were completed. I was detailed to fight the rear-guard action with five other men. I should do something to win the War. There was a conference in the company officer's dug-out to talk over the latest plans. In twenty-four hours, with a bit of luck, I should be sailing down the coast in a destroyer.

I went back to the trench and made up a bed on the fire-step. I lay down and pulled a blanket over my shoulders and closed my eyes. A pain shot through my belly, a terrible biting pain. My whole body ached and ached; but tomorrow it would be good-bye to Gallipoli for ever. I slept, a sleep of pain, incessant pain.

'Stand to! Stand to!'

Someone poked me in the ribs with a rifle butt. I sat up and rubbed my eyes. I tightened my belt and felt for my rifle. I stood on the fire-step and peered through the dim light out over No Man's Land.

I felt a throb in my head; a rush of blood through my body. Darkness...black...black...darkness.

I was warm and snug. I woke up and looked around me. Where was I? In hospital – a whitewashed room with many beds.

I did not ask any questions; I was still and quiet. I wished I would feel so warm and peaceful throughout eternity. A young nurse came to my bed: 'Sister! Sister! No. 10 has come round!' She smiled at me, a lovely smile.

'Nurse, where am I?'

'Malta,' she answered, and she mentioned the place as if it were only a few hundred yards off W. Beach, Suvla Bay.

'Malta!' I mused. 'Not Egypt... What happened?... The evacuation?...'

I slept again. When I awoke I took more interest in the ward and the beds around me. A patient in the next bed was reading a London newspaper. I saw the headline: 'Suvla Bay Successfully Evacuated.'

Sergeant W. H. Lench enlisted early in January 1915, at St. John's, Newfoundland, and arrived in England in April the same year. Joined the 1st Newfoundland Regt. at Edinburgh, and finished training at Stobs Camp, afterwards going to Gallipoli, where his regiment was attached to the 29th English Division, the only colonial unit that fought at Suvla Bay. At Gallipoli until the day before the evacuation, was in hospital in Malta, and sent back to England for convalescence in April 1916. After months in London hospital became staff instructor at the regimental depot at Ayr, Scotland, until March 1917, when he went to France, and was gassed near Monchy Le Preux in June 1917. Invalided home to St. John's in July 1918, discharged unfit for further service.

THE END OF BULGARIA

N. C. Powell

After nine months in France, I joined the East Lancs. at Gugunci, travelling overland from Cherbourg to Taranto, thence by steamer to Itear, and finally by motor and rail across wild Greece to Salonica. On disembarking at Dudulah, an enemy aeroplane greeted us with its heavy drone, but proceeded on its way to bomb an ammunition dump some distance away. After going through the usual routine (bound by broad red tape), at Summer Hill Camp, I was, along with sixty or seventy others, duly despatched to my unit. I was thankful to find the unit at rest, occupying dug-outs in the base of a large hill.

As it was early March, the weather was cold but fine. Occasionally the cold was accentuated by the laziest wind I have ever known – 'the Vardar Wind.' Our 'rest' was short-lived: orders to return to the line awakened us to our senses, kits were soon packed, and we moved off in good time to reach our objective about dusk. In Pearce's Ravine we were joined by a squad of Greek muleteers who carried our rations and rum. 'A' Company, led by a dour Scotsman, then branched off and took a direct route over the top. On we ploughed our way in silence, meanwhile breaking up into platoons with 50 yards or so between, until the line was in sight. I was marvelling on our good fortune so far, when the serenity of my thoughts was rudely shattered. There was a terrific series of explosions. I had barely time to throw myself flat, and take cover behind my steel helmet. I felt the ground tremble beneath my body. Pandemonium reigned. The company was scattered as if by magic, and the cries of men and mules rent the air. After what seemed to be an eternity, we pulled ourselves together and reached our sector. Instead of going to posts as arranged, we were picked out haphazard. Specialization qualifications did not count; signallers, Lewis-gunners, bombers, and riflemen were jumbled together, sorted out in threes and fours, and sent to various posts.

Along with two others, I was found a post in No. 3 bay, and, feeling much like a jelly, I took first turn on the fire-step. My rifle I placed on the parapet, and I peered out into beyond for the next two hours. My turn over, I paced the bay in an effort to speed up my circulation, but with little success. Few words passed between us until midnight, when a corporal ordered us to relieve an outpost in Jumeaux Ravine. We slouched off and wended our way down a sap until we reached our destination and relieved our comrades, who made all haste back.

Our physical position was uncomfortable, having to stand on sloping ground: all on sentry together, one facing half-right, ready to call for artillery assistance by means of a Verey light pistol, the other facing his front, rifle in position with one 'up the spout,' whilst the third turned half-left, holding two icy-cold Mills bombs that were to be thrown to cover our retreat in case of attack. Our cover consisted of sand-bags piled breast high in two rows. Long before time for returning the cold had numbed our bodies, our tongues were silent, and, had the enemy chosen that particular time to pay us a visit, our resistance would have been feeble indeed.

The hours dragged wearily on, and as dawn pierced the blackness of night we turned about and scrambled back to our trenches. We all 'stood to,' and I peered beyond the parapet, waiting expectantly for the full light of day, which revealed the magnificent Belachitza Mountains, standing grim and gaunt frowning upon us from afar. Lake Dorian rested at their feet in quiet repose, a haven of rest for thousands of wild birds that met in wailing congregation each mom. Directly in front of us stood Petit Couronne, backed up by its parent, Grand Couronne. Both had been bombarded incessantly, and they seemed to tower over us hurling their defiance in our teeth. Away on our left the 'Pips' arrayed themselves, five in number, all in line, each succeeding one taller than the other. They glared at us with their bulk and seemed to say: 'Five sentinels are we. Pass us if you can.' I was awakened from my reverie by the terse order 'Stand down!' A rum issue followed; we didn't get drunk off it either: and breakfast consisted of tea with no quality excepting a high temperature, bacon which had been fried to the crispness of a frosty morn, and bread. After devouring our portions, we recovered our composure to some degree. 'Tis a wonder to me we ever recovered anything after the happenings of the previous night. Not being required for further exertions, we found sleeping places, mostly small dug-outs capable of holding three or four at once, and 'got down to it.'

I was awakened by a sergeant ordering me to fall in at 6.30 for burial fatigue. My whole being revolted against the necessary reminder of last night's jolting; I never could face the gruesome task of giving the last rites to fallen comrades. I ascertained the casualties from unofficial sources: these being nineteen killed and wounded, along with four mules; among the dead were one sergeant and two other ranks who came out with me. Poor devils! They never had a chance to fight, being put out before seeing the front line or the enemy.

I duly fell in and was one of the party detailed off to dig pits to bury the carcasses of the four mules. We laboured through the night. A drizzle set in to our discomfort, and our greatcoats felt like lead casing. Interruptions were many; a machine gun kept us bobbing up and down at irregular intervals. We left off at dawn, but the results of our work would have made a decent navvy laugh. Four nights it took us to complete our job, including the dragging of the carcasses a distance of 80 yards; and how they stunk as their bellies burst when we rolled them into the pits! If it took us four nights to excavate those pits, we filled them up in less hours, relieved to get away and return to normal trench duties.

Winter gave way to summer, and the weeks lengthened into months. We held the front line, reserve, and finally a short spell of rest. We returned to the fray looking the worse for our exposure to the merciless rays of the sun, with faces and knees resembling the colour of mahogany. Horse Shoe Hill proved to be our residence, and from there a good view was to be obtained from Doldzeli in the west, stretching along the front beyond Dorian and along the Belachitza Range. How different they looked after casting their winter mantle, donning a covering of magical light; beauty of an untamed variety was there, even to my hard-baked eyes.

The 'pips' stood up in front of us, not unlike a huge railway embankment reaching to the clouds. Many hours have I spent in roaming the lower and nearer ones, in the darkness of night or by the light of the moon. Owing to a large decrease in strength. caused by the playful antics of Johnny Bulgar, who treated us to many displays of accurate shooting with trench mortars, cramps, grenades, machine guns, and a few personal visits, these, coupled with malaria, played havoc amongst us – despite all precautions, including nets for bivouacs and faces. I was posted as linesman to 'A' Company and I thought myself in for an easy stretch, but I was soon to have my illusion dispelled. For a few days everything went smoothly, until one day, after a 'strafe' on our right, the line of communication was down. Waiting until early dusk I ventured out without rifle, but kept my helmet and gas-mask. Running over the wire with one hand, it led me a dance, down ravines and up again, over and round much scrub until I found a dug-out at the other end. After introducing myself and the nature of my visit, I turned about, baffled, but determined to, trace the wire more carefully. In ceasing once or twice to regain my breath I could not help but admire the beauty of the scene. The silvery moon, spreading out her beams of light to play in phantasy among the hills and ravines, held me momentarily enraptured.

My breath regained, I eventually discovered the cause of my wanderings. Having found both ends of the wire, I sat down close to some bushes and a path. So engrossed was I that the challenge, 'Who goes there?' startled me out of my wits. I managed to mumble back, 'East Lancs.' These spirits proved to be a party of pioneers led by an officer who were out on wiring duty. They passed by. I completed my job and took a circuitous route back to our lines. I was pleased with myself on returning, every line being in order, and I snatched a short sleep before I took myself off to the cook-house for an early drink. On popping my head through doorway a corporal bawled at me. 'Who was out on the b – lines last night?' 'Me,' I replied. 'Why?' He answered, 'You lucky b – . The colonel received a complaint concerning a shady looking suspect on the wires. He immediately collared me and two men and sent us out to shoot at sight, but nothing could we see of him.' I then informed him of the route I had taken in returning. A jolly good job for me that I had entered into the spirit of the night that whispered of peace and tranquillity. The incident passed over, and I made my way back to the dug-out with a firm resolve that never again would I attempt alone the dangerous duty of repairing broken lines (and I never did).

Some time later, just as we were about to be relieved, the line running out to Pip 41 was down, so it had of necessity to be repaired before handing over. We were short-handed and no one could – or would – go with me. I waited, during which time our relief came up. Upon explaining the situation, one of them volunteered to accompany me. Off we went, like two hares, intending to be as sharp as possible; we found the break and, kneeling down, started to work, when a hail of bullets whizzed past. We threw ourselves flat. After a few minutes' wait, we crawled about to find the ends we had let go. It was an eerie experience, and fraught with danger, for each time we arose bullets zipped past us uncomfortably close. We hugged the ground in our efforts for safety, and stayed there until our task was completed. Beads of sweat stood out on my forehead as we crawled to a knoll about 100 yards away. There we paused to recover our equilibrium and made a dash for our line. It was no joke being out in front of our lines open to attack by raiding parties of Bulgars, who knew every inch of the ground.

We arrived back at our starting-point panting like a couple of old cab-horses and looking like ghosts. I wasted no time in clearing off, after thanking my comrade for his valuable assistance. Arriving at our camp rather early I was able to pick a comfortable place to sleep, and did so like a dead man. The following day we were sorted out and put in order, just like a lot of papers put into their respective files. Some were sent to a special rest camp at Gramatna for a fortnight, whilst I was despatched along with two other signallers for a course of heliography at the brigade headquarters. To me this was a stroke of luck: it meant a good time, good grub, and no fatigues. It was a great time I had for a month, but little did I know what lay beyond it all. The ways of the General Staff seemed at all times peculiar to the average Tommy, but no doubt they had method in their madness. During our last days there many rumours gained currency. 'We are going to attack' was the gist of them; but where and when was matter for speculation. I felt in a state of perturbation, knowing that the moment was at hand when the giant bulwarks that had looked down upon our forces for three summers and two winters had to be taken. It was the inevitable, and the prospect could hardly be faced with a smile.

In the meantime our brigade was attacked by a severe epidemic of flu and malaria that swept men off their feet, so that, instead of being shock troops, they had to be withdrawn. I was returned to my unit and soon after my arrival I was laid low, for I too had succumbed to the prevailing malady. The M.O. sent me to the field ambulance. I lay helpless for days, my body trembling like a leaf and wanting nothing, not even food or drink. I lost all desire to live, but my time was not finished. I slowly recovered, and within a fortnight I was pushed out to rejoin the battalion and take part in the pursuit of the enemy.

The Serbs (gallant fighters) had smashed their way through the Bulgar line, causing them to retire, and we held the mountains that once were theirs. From stretcher to sleeping out under the open skies, on the move all the time, was drastic in the extreme. I felt a sense of novelty in the pleasure of seeing the other side of Macedonia right up to Bulgaria.

After the surrender of Bulgaria we returned to the scene of our former struggles and I stole away one day to visit the Devil's Eye on the summit of Grand Couronne. It was an impregnable O.P. with a mighty view stretching down to the Gulf; even the shipping could be plainly seen, along with every position in front of it. We eventually turned our backs upon our newly won territory and marched day after day, weary and weak, towards Stavros. I stuck it until Janesh was reached. My feet had swollen and my toes were like stumps of raw meat. I reported sick the following morning and was left behind to be sent down to hospital suffering from septic poisoning. In a way I felt glad, but the knowledge that my comrades were equally sick and weary of it all pained me not a little. Hospital was reached; I was popped into a bath and a bed, and indulged in a comfortable sleep, to be awakened by a sprightly nurse requesting me to suck a thermometer. Recovery was slow, the Armistice was Signed, and when the sister announced the fact not a cheer or murmur came from anyone in response. I was too full for words and so were the other inmates. The only thing left was to wait for the ship, home, and loved ones.

Private N. C. Powell, joined the 3/5th East Lancs Regt. on April 27th, 1915, at the age of seventeen years. Drafted to the 7th Battalion of the same regiment in France when he reached the age of 19. Served on the Somme and Flanders until the Messines Ridge Attack on June 7th, 1917. Wounded whilst advancing with the first wave over the German third line. Invalided home, June 13th, 1917 until Christmas Eve the same year. Arrived Salonika, January 1918. Served with the 9th East Lancs. Regt. on Doiran sectors until February 1919. Demobilized the following month on St. Patrick's Day.

A SAPPER IN PALESTINE

H. P. Bonser

THE first few months of training were curiously unreal. I seemed to be watching someone who wore my face and features doing a hundred things fairly easily that I hadn't imagined I could do at all. He even, I believe, achieved a little swagger on occasions.

I went through my training camps, 'passed out' in musketry by the aid of a sergeant firing half my course for me, missed a Mesopotamian draft through a cook getting drunk, and found myself in Alexandria in the autumn of 1916.

On the voyage out one of the fellows struck a match after dusk. He was promptly shoved into clink, a comfortable cabin, on the well deck. As it was inconvenient to take him his meals, he joined the rest of us during the day, returning to prison in the evening. He had a mat to lie down on, and was the only one of us who had room to stretch himself at night. On making port one of the ship's officers came along and told him he was several kinds of idiot and dismissed him.

After a spell in the Signal School at Cleopatra Camp, I was drafted to the 74th Divisional Signal Company which was then being formed. My first experience of war was at the Second Battle of Gaza, when we were in reserve.

It was a nightmare of interminable marching, thirst, and tiredness. On the third day of this commotion I was on a cable wagon which was picking up a line in order to lay it again wherever needed. The horses were restive, and while I was undoing a tangle they jerked on and I was thrown with my foot in the winding gear. The wheel driver brought his horses back on their haunches when I yelled, and I found myself scrambling round on the sand 'on three legs,' trying to shake the pain from my foot.

By eight o'clock next morning preparations were being made to retire. I asked the sergeant-major to let me ride on a G.S. wagon, and he told me they'd no room for casualties, and I must look after myself. We could not see much because of the hills, but the sound of rifle-fire was getting nearer and nearer. I felt very unhappy.

A sergeant familiarly known as Charlie, and of whom the only other thing I remember is that he swore fluently and frequently, came to my rescue. I hung on to his stirrup leather and hopped while he rounded up a passing sandcart ambulance and put me inside.

The sandcart got into an area where one of our batteries was being shelled and bombed at the same time. The Egyptian drivers dismounted and crawled underneath the cart. The mules stood quite still. I was so done up that the only sensation I remember is one of violent anger because the noise kept me from going to sleep.

I went down the line on a camel ambulance – two men to a camel in little swing seats. We met a squadron of Australian Horse coming up, and a Taube flew slowly just over our heads machine-gunning them.

The casualty clearing station was so full that the lighter cases were given the staff tents. We lay on the ground, and three times a day an orderly came round with two buckets. There was tea or cocoa in one bucket and stew or porridge in the other; we dipped in whatever receptacle we had.

There was a fellow in the tent with a dislocated shoulder, and the similarity of our damage drew us together. I used to hop along clinging to his sound shoulder, and in return fasten and unfasten his buttons. Six weeks later I was discharged from convalescent depot with 'Temporary Base Duty,' and as a result found myself posted to a section stationed in Abbassia Barracks, Cairo.

In my new unit, U.U. Cable Section, I found a couple of enquiringly minded fellows, and we spent many evenings exploring native Cairo. We met with far more courtesy than hostility.

One evening we found ourselves in a kind of courtyard where men were sitting smoking, and where children were playing. In a corner were three or four not-too-fat cats. Dusty –

so called because his name was Miller – bought a piastre worth of meat at a little shop and we cut this up with jack-knives and fed the cats. This caused quite a stir. The men made friendly noises, and a number of them offered us sweetmeats. Afterwards in that quarter we were always greeted as 'The *askaris* who fed *pussini.*'

There were quarters in Cairo and in Alexandria that one doesn't talk much about in decent society. Places where girls sat on chairs outside a door, waiting for hire. I think most of our chaps went to look at them for curiosity. One of their tricks was to snatch a soldier's hat and run into their room with it, in the hope that he would follow.

I knew one man who used to go to see one of these girls every week; if he hadn't a shilling he would take a vest or shirt, and she would hold it in pawn until he was in funds.

One evening in barracks I was working out, on a big sheet of paper, a kind of charm or soothsayer I had come across in Lane's book on Egypt. It consisted of circles of letters so contrived that if you selected a letter at random and picked out every fifth from that starting point you got a sentence which was supposed to be an answer to your enquiry.

There were two fellows with us who had arranged to meet two French girls from one of the shops that evening. There was nothing wrong in the proposed meeting, just a squeeze and a kiss, perhaps, but the lads were not quite easy. One had left a bride at home, and the other carried a photograph; at any rate they asked me to consult my soothsayer.

While all the room stood round watching, the answer spelt itself out: 'Whoever does this thing will be doing great wrong.' I felt sorry for those French girls.

September of this year found us on the borders of Palestine. The chief hardship was lack of water – a good wash was a luxury.

Our final preparations for the advance (1917) took place in a sandstorm. For three days we were working with goggles over our eyes and handkerchiefs round mouth and nostrils. The job was recovering and loading cable ready for the dash up. It was impossible to see a man 20 yards away; there was sand all over our perspiring bodies, sand on every mouthful of food we ate, and a sip of tepid water left sand on our lips. Half the fellows were suffering from dysentery pains and passing blood.

The storm ceased, and we had a clear and beautiful night. We washed, and we stretched ourselves under the stars utterly content with just the absence of physical discomfort. I have had the same feeling in miniature when a tooth has stopped aching. The noise of the bombardment added a pleasurable touch of excitement. We felt things were afoot.

Morning saw us setting off in earnest. Curiously enough, it was the drivers who suffered most from the sand, and it was a job getting men well enough to sit the horses. My pal and I found ourselves riding in an eight-horse cable team. It was an exciting ride. Straight down the side of a wady and top speed at the opposite bank before the momentum was spent.

About midday we clattered through Gaza, an untidy dilapidated Gaza from which most men had fled. Here and there a dark face peeped stealthily from a doorway, but, apart from the troops hurrying through, it was a place of desolation. Yet I felt an indescribable sense of elation riding through this town heaped with the debris of war; an elation akin to those lines of Macaulay's about the thick, black cloud of smoke going up from a conquered town; an elation that seemed to have no basis in reason.

North of Gaza we off-saddled for a meal. We found a patch of grass on which both men and beast rolled for pure enjoyment. While we were eating a man and woman came trudging along the way. They were of village Bedawi type and looked hard pressed. They sat down as though waiting for any leavings. The woman had a baby.

My pal and I had a half tin of condensed milk, and we slipped over casually, and soon had the baby sucking it off biscuit. The man grinned and nodded when we gave him the rest of the tin, but the woman looked at us without saying a word. Although she was Mohammedan, she made no attempt to draw her veil. She just looked at us. I don't think we fitted in with her notion of invading soldiers.

We trekked northwards, rigging up signal offices wherever we stopped, until we settled down in the Wady Surar as a transmitting office to the divisions.

It was a mud and misery winter. Supply lorries were stuck fast in the mud, and supplies often scarce. Our Christmas Day ration was two biscuits, a tin of bully to four, and a tin of jam to seventeen men. We were sleeping in wet clothes, and even sleep was scarce, as pressure of work in the signal office necessitated us working all through every alternate night. I had the additional misery of neuralgia.

Three telegrams I handled that winter stick in my memory. One from General Allenby to the 60th Divisional General when Jerusalem was taken. It read 'Congratulations. Psalm 122, V. 2.'

I looked it up. 'Our feet shall stand within thy gates, O Jerusalem.' I thought it rather decent of Allenby.

The other two struck me by their contrast to one another. One wet and shivery night I handled a telegram from a G.H.Q. general asking for his hot-water bottle to be collected from Fast's Hotel, Jerusalem, and forwarded by despatch rider, as the nights were chilly. The next telegram was from 163rd Brigade reporting how many men had died of exposure during the last twenty-four hours.

My only other encounter with General Allenby – perhaps 'other' is hardly the word – was at Haifa nearly a year later.

One hot morning, with a bandolier slipped over my shirt, and a coil of wire hung round the handle of my wire cutters, so that any enquiring red-tab might assume I was out mending a line, I set off on a fruit scrounge.

A coil of wire and a blue armband were very useful passports in those days.

Plodding homeward with the spoil, I became aware of a mounted party approaching, and quickly detected the particular polish and aurora of staff officers.

There was nowhere to dodge, so I squared my shoulders and tried to forget the pomegranates bulging my shirt. Suddenly I realized that the leading horseman was the G.O.C. himself.

He was spruce and polished; his equipment glittered, and his buttons shone.

I was tunicless, covered with dust, and couldn't even have pretended to a lance-corporal that I'd seen any polish that morning, but I gave the regulation salute.

The Staff eyed me a trifle disdainfully, I thought, but General Allenby returned my salute with the precision of a full parade.

There was no perfunctory lifting of the forefinger. The gesture was full and complete. It could not have been more so had he been taking the salute at the march past of a whole army. I thought that, too, rather decent of Allenby.

With spring we moved on to Birsalem, and how we revelled in the orange groves. I got the idea of sending some home to my youngster, posting them in old petrol tins. The fellows laughed at me, but several of them followed my example later on.

G.H.Q. came to Birsalem, and we shifted onward, setting up a signal office by the side of the Turkish Railway near Wilhelma.

It was fairly quiet, but a Turkish battery at Kalkilieh used to shell fairly frequently. I remember being in the signal office one day when they kept our range for exactly an hour. They carried away every telegraph line we had, and as there was no proper dug-out the continuous whine and shatter were disconcerting. An Edinburgh fellow suddenly burst out 'Oh Christ! When the hell will they hit us?' I felt like that too.

We drove up north again with the September advance. There was wreckage everywhere, and the veterinary sections were kept busy looking after abandoned animals. Among some we passed one day was a young bullock that looked as though it had been a regimental mascot. We were real hungry for fresh meat, and the forty-four of us ate three-quarters of that bullock for supper and breakfast. It was a case of take the good things when you can.

By Christmas we were in Sidon maintaining lines of communication.

It is because of two children that I remember Sidon most. A Hugh Mactaggart and I struck up an acquaintance with some

American Syrian Mission folk. Hugh and I used to go along once a week and romp with their kids. It was the first association with civilized life we'd had for three years.

One evening Mrs. Byerley suggested we should all go out on the flat roof. The way led through her bedroom, and its delicacy and whiteness filtered round me and lifted me into a sweeter world.

Hitherto the only women we had spoken to were those who wanted to save our souls and those who did their best to make us lose them. Here was a woman who, by this action, put us on the same plane as herself. I wonder if she realized how dear a thing she did.

Hugh and I had many a day's ramble in the bills around Sidon, often striking villages where British troops hadn't been seen before.

At one such they prepared a wonderful feast at which Hugh and I were guests of honour. The 'grandma' of another had been in domestic service in New York, and greeted us in strident American. After entertaining us to figs preserved in aniseed, she produced two attractive Syrian girls.

'These are my nieces,' she explained. 'They are good gals.'

'You're married,' she added, to me. Then turning to Hugh, she shot out:

'You're not. I want my nieces to marry Englishmen. Which one will you have?'

These were Christian, villages, and I think the hand of the Turk had been heavy.

There came orders to proceed to Beirut. Hugh and I, doing rations and orderly room work, got a comfortable room as combined office and quarters. We'd hardly settled in when a knock came at the door and two young women who spoke pleasant English made the proposition that they share room and rations with us.

We declined and they apologized. Afterwards they often called to see if there was any mending they could do for us. 'Won't Mamma be pleased!' was their usual exclamation if we gave them a tin of bully or jam for darning our socks.

They never referred to their original proposal again, though once, when I asked the elder girl why they chose that livelihood, she answered, 'It was this or starve, Mr. Harri.'

A chaste friendliness with a prostitute seems a contradiction, yet I felt a tribute in their tears when we came away. We were out of touch with our ordinary conventions, and I think fellows hammered out standards for themselves. For instance, among the drivers of our company was a Sheffield lad, a rough handful. I was in where he slept one day over something or other, and on the wall was a long string threaded with packing needles. I think there were eighty-seven of them, all sizes.

The Syrian prefers a packing needle to a whip when he's on a donkey. It's less trouble and more effective. This lad didn't agree with the practice, and used to take the needle away from anyone he saw using one.

On one occasion he stopped a portly Maronite priest, who got quite angry and held the needle clenched in his fist with one end dug into the pummel of the saddle, and the other end under his thumb. This lad brought his first whack on the priest's thumb; there was a yell of pain and the priest tumbled backwards off the donkey. Our young driver walked off with the needle.

But this is getting beyond the War, although it was the more interesting time to me because I was more drawn to the idea of learning about people than of killing them. The only thing I killed all the war was a marauding dog, and I feel sorry about that still.

Sapper H. P. Bonser, Royal Engineers (Signals), February 1916 to July 1919. Foreign service units: 74th Divisional Signal Company, Egypt, Southern Palestine; Detached Duty, Fayoum Area; U.U. Cable Section, Royal Engineers, Egypt, Palestine, Syria.

TELL-EL-SHERIA

William G. Johnson

When the 321 V.C.s sat down to dine with the Prince of Wales on November 9th, 1929, one man present, Lieut.-Colonel Arthur Drummond Borton, V.C., D.S.O., might possibly have experienced just one tinge of regret. For had the great function taken place two days earlier it would have coincided with the twelfth anniversary of his winning the coveted honour.

I know just a little about the winning of that V.C., and the man who won it, but I doubt whether the colonel would recall the fellow he swore at during that most critical moment of his career.

It happened in Palestine on November 7th, 1917. The day is Wednesday. We are hard on the heels of the Turk. Gaza has fallen, we have taken Beersheba, and are now on the way to Sheria. There are wells at Sheria, and we are very thirsty!

From dawn all Tuesday we have ploughed through sand and sun, no food to speak of – a nibble of bully and biscuit; and, though warned at the start to hang on to our water, there isn't a man with a fly's bath in his bottle when we come to a halt in the evening. The grit on my teeth! The mud on my tongue! Lord! I can taste it now! Trekking the best part of a month, we are tired, ragged, verminous, and itchy with septic sores. Now we have halted and know we are close to the Turk. Petulantly through the twilight half-spent bullets whine out their last breath overhead. Nobody cares; we are too fagged out to heed them. Dropping our packs, we unload the mules and feed the poor brutes a mouthful of corn.

We stretch our backs on the warm sand. Our aching backs! Oh, for a little green apple to quench this blistering thirst! Our spirits are low with fatigue and thirst and dirt. This hopeless, unending misery, this madness, this ultimate futility! Would I could sleep for ever. Would I could wake in the morning and know all this for a nightmare. Ah me, have we not dreamed thus a thousand times through twenty unthinkable months!

I sleep. The four hours seem but a minute before I am awakened with the toe of a corporal's boot.

'Get dressed!' I rise and shiver, hating that corporal. I dress as a dog might shake himself. It is dark, but away to the left the sky glows red. I hear faint crackling sounds. The air is full of whistling lead.

'What's up?'

'Moving off.'

I groan and drag my stiff legs over to my mule and tug and punch him into his harness. Taking his cue from me, he shows his teeth in a succession of mighty yawns.

Shadowy forms are everywhere moving to and fro in the darkness; tired and expressionless faces show palely out of the gloom, and pass.

'Stack packs!'

Ah, we're in for it now. Grimly I smile as I hump my clobber to the pile and pitch it with the rest. I meet Silburn on the way

'Another stunt, Sunbeam?'

'Dunno, Gunga. Looks like it.'

'What's that light over there?'

'Johnny getting breezy. Blowing up his ammunition dumps.'

'Best thing he can do with 'em,' I grumble. 'Why not let him get on with it!'

'Fall in for rum!'

'That's about corpsed it!' mutters Tich Webster, divining that not for nothing is he to get a noggin of rum in the Plain of Sharon.

But the rum's good – dashed good it is! It stings our leathery tongues and stops our shivering. It calms my damnable nerves. I join a little group; Baker is there, the Welsh miner, our last remaining tenor, the red-headed, unquenchable 'Scrounger.'

'What's doing, Scrounger?'

'Oh, nothing much. Clearing snipers. 'Colonel can't sleep.'

I smile sceptically. 'Who told you that?'

'Harold,' says Baker.

'I thought as much.'

'A knowing bird, that mule of yours, Scrounger?' sneers Holland.

'He is,' replies Baker. 'Fed on bully and four-by-two, is Harold. In return for which he tells me things.'

'He's a b-blatant liar,' growls Durrant. 'That's w-what he is. It's b-bullets 'e wants, not b-bully!'

Then Durrant is ashamed of himself. 'Sorry, Baker. M-my n-nerves,' he says, and turns away.

'I suppose you didn't ask him if we're getting any water to-night?' enquires Evans.

'I did,' answers Scrounger. 'And he kicked me in the – !'

I go. Yes, as always, the officers will know all there is to be known when we start. We shall know nothing. We batten on rumours. Rumours! And are led like lambs to the slaughter. My blood boils. Are we such cowards we may not be told?

'Fall in! No noise! No talking!'

We line up. Bombs and additional bandoliers of ammunition are served out. Ten rounds are loaded into the rifle magazines. Things look bad. Contrary to orders, I slip a cartridge 'up the spout,' adjusting the safety-catch.

Now we are shuffling out over the plain. Someone coughs; entrenching tools, haversacks, empty water-bottles clatter and rattle; here and there an iron-shod heel strikes a flint, igniting a shower of sparks; a man stumbles and that man surely curses.

Rob and I march side by side. We talk little. A Yorkshireman is Rob. His calmness reassures me. His sturdy bulk is a tower of strength to me. *Vive le* rum!

We trudge on in silence. I think of those at home – all warm and clean in bed. Perhaps they turn restlessly now and then and think of me. May they sleep deep and long to-night. *We* have work to do. Keep your eyes skinned, lad. Steady and cool! Don't fumble. Strike – swift as the lightning! I feel braced up and fit. God bless the distillers of rum!

I glance at Rob. His face in the dark is bloodless and dirty; there are streaks of grime on the cheeks where sweat has dried in the night; and a four-day growth of beard gives him a strangely spiritual expression. I think: This might be the face of Christ! A distant look in his eyes, has Rob. *I* know. He's away and playing on his old violin. 'How feeling, Rob?' But Rob makes no reply.

Then the silvery voice of Baker, just behind me, breaks the silence, singing:

How lovely are the Messengers

That preach us the gospel of Peace!...

'Put a sock in it, Baker!' says a sergeant, irritably.

The roar of the burning dumps grows louder; and flames, leaping into view, send out cascades of sparks; we hear the crack of rifles; bullets whistle shriller, filling the night with little spiteful devils. We stop to unload the mules. I strap on my chest and back two wallets of spare Lewis gun magazines. The weight of them! We are leaving the mules behind. I am the mule – a proper soldier now!

And now, suddenly, we enter a world writhing in its last agony... Deafening crashes, flames and smoke, unearthly boomings and rumblings! Above this din comes the splutter of machine guns; and, from a towering structure to the left, massive fragments of masonry are being pitchforked into the night! It is grand! The Turk is blowing up the world!

'Shiverin' saints!' comes a voice.

'Strike me pink!' says another; and I catch a glimpse of an illuminated face uplifted for a moment in the glare.

Now we are off at the double. We zigzag about; then, swinging to the right, plunge over the edge of a deep but narrow wady, and fall into dust and darkness. We regain our feet, bewildered, shaken. Officers dart hither and thither, shouting orders. 'Steady now, boys! Steady! Lock-up, lock-up! Keep together!... For God's sake, don't bunch up!'

Then out of the gloom and the confused medley of men emerges the colonel. I see him in the light of the conflagration. Like the rest, he has a steel helmet on his head; but he wears no tunic, his shirt-sleeves are rolled up past his elbows. How clean and neat and fresh he looks! His hair, sleek and parted, shines in the glare.

He is lean and tall; his face is red. He carries his head as though his neck was stiff. His gait seems a shade unsteady. He waves a cane in his hand, and, in the crook of his other arm, he hugs a football! Borton is laughing!

'Twenty-second Queen's!' he bellows. 'It's your turn now to cover yourselves with glory! Follow me!'

'Stone me paralytic!' gasps Tich.

He leads us along the *wady*, every gun in creation going mad at us. In that dusty inferno we are merely shadows. We come to an opening in the wady. Borton gets across, but not so others following; they seem to stagger and wilt and crumple up and fade away into the gloom. A murderous fire from concealed machine guns sprays death along that alley...

'Stand fast!' cries the colonel. 'Now quickly...in twos and threes!'

Rob and I plunge into the abyss. I hear a cry and Rob sinks into the dust. A momentary halt. I see heaving breasts all round me, and drawn, white faces. I hear curses unmentionable. I curse unmentionably too. But there's one man as cool as a water-melon – a man with a stiff neck, and a football under his arm.

'Fix bayonets!' yells the colonel. And the shining things leap from the scabbards and flash in the light as they click on the standards. They seem alive and joyous; they turn us into fiends, thirsty for slaughter. We scramble out of the *wady*.

'Charge!' And away goes the colonel, flourishing his ludicrous cane!

The hail of lead! We greet it with a blood-curdling shout, ripping our throats; and, as surely as I have eyes, there's Borton driving ahead, taking the hill at a bound, and kicking the football!

Breathless, we gain the, top. The Turks have bolted. Torn tents flap in the wind; pots and pans are about our feet. Away now from the flaming dumps we pick our way at a walk, peering into the dark, bayonets ready to stab. Then I go sprawling over a vessel of porridge standing among the remains of a weed fire. I rip out an oath as an ember burns me. Scrambling up, a sticky mess, I flounder over something that is warm and groans as I clutch it. Again I stagger forward, and a strand of barbed wire catches me in the leg. I tear myself out of its grip. Near me, Scrounger Baker trips over a tent rope, and, attempting to rise, is shot. A raking fire sweeps the darkness, but still we advance. The ground is rough and treacherous. Men are falling. Where's the colonel? Has he also stopped one? I hear his voice! God save Borton! We know him. The mad major of Gallipoli! He'll fetch us through, this man with a broken neck!

Suddenly the darkness lifts, paling to grey, and a ridge looms out ahead. 'Down! Down! Down!' and flat as a sack I go. Men are moving on the skyline. What use to take aim! I blaze away madly, striving to silence those swine on the ridge. I sweat. I gibber with glee when a form flings up its arms, dances a second between earth and sky, and vanishes. A little ahead of me, on rising ground, lie two pals working a Lewis gun; its bark, its spiteful rat-tat-tat, is music to me.

Spells of the tensest concentration are followed by moments of terrible fatigue. My strength ebbs away; I feel unutterably weak; I could sleep. There succeed intervals when my senses seem to stalk abroad, icily alert and alive; periods when my mind is a whirling wheel, my brain a furnace white-hot, my pulse a sledge-hammer. When my nerves seem about to snap there come instants of exquisite calm. Death! What does it matter? I am alone. Surrounded by friend and foe, I am alone in the world! But the will to live wells up – the desire to live is a torment, a torture, a devilish, damnable agony!

A man near by groans and rolls over. A yard or so away an officer lies quiet as though sleeping. I see a friend writhe and twist. I hear a man scream. A sergeant, rising from the ground, staggers forward, shot in the back! I hear sobbing. No stretcher bearers here. Vaguely, as in a dream, I am conscious of flashes and rumblings overhead and regular crashes and slams to our rear. Where's *our* artillery? Where are the guns? Bring up the guns? O God!

The barrel of my rifle blisters my fingers; then the bolt sticks fast, fouled with grit. I tear and swear at it, and my hand goes stiff with cramp. The reeking breech sickens me.

Now I become aware that the gun ahead is silent, and

motionless the men beside it: one on his back with his eyes open, his hand outstretched as though beckoning; the other, his head on his arm. I look at the thing in a daze. It is getting lighter. A clammy sweat breaks out on me. I am a Lewis gunner! Turning my head, I gaze at the ridge. My hand shakes as I grip my rifle and take aim; but the bolt is jammed, the trigger limp. I lie there panting... 'You're a coward – a dirty, crawling coward! That one gun...that one gun might stop those...curs!'

A stone, struck by a bullet, jumps from the ground and hits me on the knuckle. It stings me to terrible anger. Next to me, Tom Rolls gives a yell as blood spurts from his wrist and splashes me in the face. I spring to my feet and race to the gun, heaving aside a corpse to get to it. I lie down to the gun, between the two dead men, and...I feel fine!

But the magazine will not rotate. I strain and strain at it. The cocking-handle is stuck fast. I squeeze the trigger. I change the magazine. I talk to it, swear at it, do impossible things to it. Then, glancing down the barrel casing to the sights, I see that the muzzle is frayed and torn and broken, and the gas-regulator blown clean away. The gun is as dead as the men beside it.

At this moment the colonel appears. His face is black and sweaty; his shirt is torn to ribbons. 'Don't lie here!' he roars. 'Come on!... With me!'

We scramble to our feet and follow him down a long, rocky slope in the half-light, but heavy fire breaks out anew. We cannot stand it, and are forced into the dust again. Ripping out the bolt of my rifle, I lick it clean, spitting out the grit. It is hot and scorches my tongue. Now a worse enemy attacks. Shells scream about us, exploding overhead, on the ground, everywhere; they tear up the dust; they cover us with stones; the air is a hell of whizzing shrapnel. I see Harman with his back ripped open. We bite into the earth. Our mouths are full of muck. Not so Borton. He's on his feet (has he yet been off his feet?); he crouches, his neck thrust outward. His grey-blue eyes are searching, searching...

'Ah, good!' he cries, and, tossing away his cane, pulls out his revolver. 'Now I have them! Follow me!'

I go staggering after him down the slope. Had every man been shot he would have gone alone. Dimly ahead I see a hedge of stunted cactus swathed in smoke from which come flashes – white, knife-like flashes. Then I see figures moving, and, pausing, fire from my hip.

'Don't stand there like a palsied idiot!' shouts the colonel. 'Come on!'

I go on. Something warm is coursing down my face and trickles into my eyes, half-blinding me. I stumble on – my head is bursting...

'Camarade! Camarade!' Men in grey-coloured uniforms and 'pork-pie' caps are coming forward, their arms above their heads.

'Austrians!' The colonel's voice is hoarse and husky. He rams his revolver into a man's ear.

Beyond – across the open – men run for their lives; and I, breathless, land up against the smoking nozzle of an artillery field gun, the point of my bayonet stuck into the tunic-button of a burly Austrian bombardier; while the colonel, with a man or two, strives desperately – but without success – to get another gunner to turn his gun and fire on his fleeing comrades.

Daybreak! I stand panting before my prisoner; a breath from whose smoke-blackened mouth could bowl me over. He towers above me, smiling. I am trembling.

'Mercy, Johnny,' says he quietly, dropping a sooty hand and holding it out to me. 'You brave feller. You haf face all bloody! Have mercy!'

He smiles. He looks a decent sort. His glasses and ginger hair remind me of Baker. Scrounger Baker! Rob! It is touch and go with the Austrian. Blood for blood! He smiles. *Camarade!* I cannot kill him...

Next to me on my right, little Sid Avery has a similar problem confronting him, and quickly he solves it, as well as mine:

'Cigarettes...or yer life!' puffs Sid.

Private William G. Johnson joined London Rifle Brigade, November 1915. Age twenty-three. Volunteered for transfer to 60th (London) Division for active service. Sent to 2nd Battalion 22nd London Regt. ('Queen's') June 1916. July 1916, France. Five months in trenches. January 1917, Salonika. Three months in mountains on Doiran front, and three months on Vardar Front. Took part in operations against Bulgars. July 1917, Palestine. Took part in operations against Turks, resulting in capture of Gaza and Beersheeba, the wells at Tell-el-Sheria, Nebi Samwil, etc. At the capture of Jerusalem, December 9th, 1917. Also in engagements around Jericho, crossing of the Jordan, and the attacks across the Jordan Valley and Moab Mountains on Es Salt and Amman in the Hedjaz country in an attempt to link up with Lawrence of Arabia. Took part in forced marches across Palestine to sea above Jaffa, which ended in final rout of Turks on September 19th, 1918, at Tul Keram, towards Damascus.

THE CORRIDOR

T. Clayton

The camp at Sheikh Saad in March 1916 was bearable. The soil had not been powdered by the feet of the multitudes who later passed through it. The desert beyond was clothed with a rich verdure, which in the early morning was drenched with dew. The Tigris flowed past in flood, for the snow was melting on the distant mountain peaks. We strengthened its bonds as we had improved the roads on Lemnos previously.

We learned something of the position before Kut-el-Amara, where Townshend was beleaguered, though not much, conjecture and rumour filling the gap. We learned of the Turkish position at Um-el-Hannah – the gateway of the corridor to Kut.

One night we set out for an unknown destination. The day had been hot, but just before dusk there came a thunderstorm, and the rain was torrential. Very soon we realized that the going was unusual. On the granite-like subsoil was a thin layer of mud, and our feet would not stick in it. Soon men and mules were floundering in a sea of slime. Darkness closed in on a scene unparalleled, and the flickering lightning added to its weirdness. Towards the Euphrates the horizon glowed like the front of Mars. Through the long night we struggled and scrambled over the nullahs, blaspheming and cursing; until the sun rose, disclosing a mob of exasperated and exhausted men, reeling through the morass towards the camp at Orah.

Later in the day we crossed the Tigris, and evening saw us drawing near to the ominous mounds of earth at Um-el-Hannah. For the first time we heard the scream of shrapnel in that country, and to many of us it was our baptism of fire.

The trivial details of our life in the trenches are now almost lost to the memory, but the night of April 4th looms conspicuously. There was a dug-out open to the sky. In the centre the dying embers of a fire glowed feebly. The night was bitterly cold, and we huddled near it for warmth, for we were clad in drill and without greatcoats. Through the opening to the dug-out could be seen others of our company sitting on the fire-step of the trench. Their faces were grimly apprehensive, for the Turks were peppering the sandbags with machine-gun and rifle-fire. The sand was trickling down from the parapet, and over the dug-out poured a continual stream of whistling bullets.

There was a man of my own town near by, young Brandreth, and we discussed the morn and its chances. There was also a man with unusually bright and piercing eyes and gypsy-like countenance. He sat apart and was very quiet. I was smoking a cigarette. The tense atmosphere must have got on his nerves, for he turned towards me and said, 'Can you spare a cigarette, corporal?' 'Yes,' I replied. 'Here you are, Jaspar. I'm nearly stumped, but you can have one.' Our talk ceased and drowsiness overcame us. I must have slept. I was awakened by a hand gripping my shoulder and the voice of the platoon commander saying, 'Here, corporal, a couple of hard-boiled eggs for breakfast; put them in your haversack.' Hard-boiled eggs. How funny! I held out my hands, and felt the contact of cold metal and the familiar knobs of the hand-grenade. I came back to reality with a start. 'And waken us,' he continued, 'at three o'clock, please.' The night grew colder, and we watched the glittering galaxy of stars move overhead, and waited for the hour.

At dawn the company, filed into another trench, and we cut notches for our feet, for it had no fire-step. Our guns were bombarding the front heavily. In the opening of a fire-trench near-by a white-faced, scared-looking boy leaned against the parados with blood streaming down his face. He had done his bit; ours was to come.

The height of the trench was well above my head, and the soil loose, but the friendly hand of a more nimble comrade helped me to a view of the war in microcosm, for the front here was narrow, not above 2,000 yards at a guess, with the Tigris on the left and the marsh on the right.

Right in front was a mound, and the shells were bursting about it, and the clouds of dun and white smoke were interspersed with vivid flashes, like a volcano in eruption, both beautiful and terrible. On the mound was a man gesticulating wildly, signalling the gunners to cease fire. The Turks had fled and our men were in the shambles intended for them.

Leaping the criss-cross of trenches we soon found ourselves on undisturbed soil, on which were strewn the bodies of our own people. They lay very quiet and very still, and took no notice of our passing.

On we went, now the vanguard of the little army which broke the barrier at Um-el-Hannah. We formed column of route and pursued the vanishing Turk down the long corridor to Kut-el-Amara. Falahiyah was now the objective. Shell-fire and the crack of rifles compelled us to open out, one of our company dropped. Very soon the gleaming earthworks were visible. We advanced over the level field by sectional rushes. Brandreth and I had a canvas water bucket containing bombs. Its presence was abominable. We speculated fearfully on the result that might follow a broken pin. On one occasion we rested rather longer than usual. Jaspar was second on my right. A boy lay between us. Without raising his head, he turned his face towards me, and observed that Jaspar was asleep. 'Asleep?' I replied incredulously. 'For God's sake waken him!' The boy stretched his arm to waken him, but turned again quickly. 'Corporal,' he said falteringly, 'Jaspar's dead; his neck's bleeding.'

Soon we were well within range of the Turkish guns, and the whole battalion in alignment. The order came to make cover with our entrenching tools, a grievous task lying prone under a broiling sun. Mason, a wiry little fellow from a cotton town, was on my left, with Brandreth between. Mason, when his task was accomplished, settled down to rest and observation. Over-curious, he raised a shoulder above the level of his little parapet, a rifle crashed, and with a groan he subsided. Brandreth had the task of giving first aid. It was accomplished without further mishap. Mason was very restless and breathing heavily. He turned, exposing himself once more, another crack and another groan, and he lay very quiet. On my right was a tall strong youth who used his cutting tool to great advantage. An excellent parapet was the result and an oblong cavity sufficiently long and deep to shelter his whole body. As the sun rose to its zenith we became hot and weary. The tall youth lay on his back and fell asleep. It must have been his habit when sleeping to draw his knees up. I had to caution him about it. Unobserved by us, he must have slept again. A crack from a rifle and the tall youth collapsed with a bullet through both knees. So the long weary day passed, until dusk came and the order to evacuate the wounded. Later we followed, crossing the new trench dug under our protection, leaving Falahiyah and the Turks to other and fresher troops.

We returned to Um-el-Hannah, and going there we were once more caught in a deluge of rain. How the wounded fared is unthinkable. Eventually we reached the place of bivouac, and stood about drenched and cold waiting for the dawn. Great was our relief when the camp fires gleamed in the early morning mists, and loud were the acclamations and shouts of joy when o'er the eastern hills the sun arose and ushered in bright day.

April 5th and 9th, 1916, stood out in our battalion annals. So I can safely say that the eve of the 9th saw us tramping down the corridor once more. This time to Sanna-i-yat, Falahiyah in the meantime having fallen into our hands. Once again the night was overcast. So thick was the gloom that the nearest objects were hidden from us. The path was fairly good and well-trodden. At one point we seemed to run close to the Tigris bond, and it was here that we passed a stack of discarded rifles with bayonets attached. The platoon commander slipped from the ranks and took one from the stack. A stern reminder of coming events.

What other troops were making for the rendezvous and what already there I could not say. Of Sanna-i-yat defences we knew nothing. Eventually we found ourselves drawn up in line. In front was impenetrable darkness; no stir, no rap-tap-tap from a machine gun; no crack from a sniper's rifle.

We were told to lie down. Of the distance between us and the Turkish trench we had no knowledge. The herbage was wet with dew, and while I lay there shivering I thought of

Magersfontein, for I was as old as Brandreth, who lay by my side, when news of the Black Week came through from South Africa. And now we were up against troops adept in the use of small arms and trench defence, many of them veterans of the Balkan wars.

At last the agony of suspense was over. A rippling movement from the left and we were standing, a similar movement and we were moving forward. The silence was now broken by the swishing of many feet through the herbage, by the rustle of clothes, and the clicking of bayonet scabbards. We were uncomfortably crowded. Brandreth and I had decided to remain together if possible. The order came to incline to the left. The men on our right were soon in difficulties. Possibly some trench or nullah interfered with their formation. There was a tendency to run, and then to buckle. Shortly we had a phalanx instead of a line.

I was separated by the crush from Brandreth, and very soon lost view of the platoon commander. At all costs, I must regain touch, I thought, and was still worrying about my predicament when a flare curved over, showing up our front in a great white light. Then out of the dark came a hurricane of screaming lead and shot, so staggering that the men reeled under it in confusion. There was a rush forward on my left, instinctively I followed, and found myself against a bank or nullah, behind which I took cover along with the others.

I quickly realized that this was wrong, so turned from the nullah and ran forward. I found myself going over a white patch of ground, bare of grass, and already littered with the accoutrement of the wounded. I was alone. The machine-gun and rifle-fire seemed to gather intensity. My sole thought on that short run was where the impact of the bullet would be. The irresistible impulse for self-preservation came uppermost again, and I flung myself on the ground, this time my cover being a discarded valise. I was now conscious of the dawn, and, peering forward, saw a trench. My first thought was, I am there!

This did not seem to worry me much, not near so much as the infernal screaming overhead; but when I became accustomed to the gloom I noticed that the faces in the trench were turned from me. Then came a hoarse voice calling, 'Come on, mate!' The firing was now less intense, I rushed forward and saw at once that the attack had failed. The Turks remained secure behind their wire.

All was quiet in front. The dim outline of the Turkish trench showed no breach. The scattered forms of the wounded and dead lay round about. On the left a few Turks came through the wire and began to bludgeon the wounded with the butt-ends of their rifles. They were soon driven back.

Nothing further could be done. So when the morn advanced we sought our depleted and scattered units – feeling subdued and shaken in spirit. The platoon had suffered severely. The commander was killed, also the sergeant and many others. Brandreth I never saw nor heard of again.

Soldiers have a nice sense of delicacy. They did not pry too closely into each other's movements on that fatal morning. They realize that success in war, as in other affairs of life, depend largely on circumstance. Neither did they blame their harassed leaders, though there was bitter comment because they felt they had not been given a fair chance.

Corporal T. Clayton enlisted January 1915, in the Cheshire Regt. Embarked for Gallipoli in November 1915. Arrived in Mudros harbour, but sent to Alexandria. Back at Lemnos at Christmas, stayed until the 8th Cheshires arrived from Cape Hellas, and joined them. Sent to Port Said in January 1916, and from thence to Mesopotamia. Took part in the Townshend relief operations on both banks of the Tigris, in the spring and early summer of 1916, and in the offensive against Kut 1916–1917. Took part in operations on the Shatt-el-Adhaim in April 1917, and in subsequent minor operations. In the Abu-Hajar pass until the end of the War.

THOSE DESERT DAYS

Robert Harding

It is dawn and we are marching towards the sunrise. Khaki-clad British soldiers with bare, brown knees and wide-brimmed topees swing cheerfully along, marching to they know not where, for at nightfall we shall bivouac somewhere in the Arabian Desert.

Behind us plod the camels, carrying the kits and the very few necessities of desert warfare. They are controlled by coloured-turbaned Indian drabis, who know these ships of the desert as a captain knows his ship.

And then come the Gurkha boys, with a merry stride. Every one of these stocky little fellows wears a beaming face – all ready and willing to march until their limbs sink beneath them. Some are leading the chafing mules, which clink noisily in the harness, and pull along the iron wagons which carry the precious water-tanks.

At the rear slow-moving oxen draw the small, dome-shaped wagons with the Red Cross painted on the sides.

We are approaching the last outpost of the Basra Cantonment. The next camp is 140 miles away. Where, only the scouts know. It does not matter where; the order is to march hard and fight hard.

We march on. Loneliness closes around, creeping, sinister, and comfortless, till all that is real loses its reality in a monotonous circle of horizon and hard, cracked sand.

'Keep step, mate!' says one to another faltering in front. It is easier going in step.

'I'm dying for a drink,' says another. But the allowance is a pint a day, to be drunk when ordered.

We trudge on, and men bow beneath the weight of ammunition, equipment, and rifle. The brazen sun burns; clothes become wet with sweat; topees heavy and big.

At hourly halts we sink to the ground, and rise again with stiff joints and aching shoulders. At given times we drink, and march again, until the sun sinks low and tinges the desert red.

A halt is made. The camels are unloaded and fed, the water-tanks stacked together, and those detailed dig a trench round the camp.

Field kitchens are soon brewing tea, and a frugal meal of bully beef, hard biscuits, and milkless tea is taken by famished men. At last blankets are unpacked from the camel lines, and those fortunate ones who are not on guard sink like logs and remain so until Reveille.

The camp awakes by a shrill voice calling: 'Camels! Fetch the camels!' Fellows stir in their blankets, as stiff and weary as though they had just laid themselves down. It is a little before dawn. The moon has sunk low.

There is a roaring, and the camels, as irritable and as tired as all, loom in the morning mist. Blankets are rolled and packed on the camels' backs: bitter, black tea and some more biscuits are swallowed for breakfast; and then we move on again as the sun lifts its dreaded golden light over the horizon.

A corporal plays a tune on his mouth organ to keep spirits up. Plucky devil! He is as tired as the rest of us, and yet he forces out that little extra bit, and is admired for it.

A man collapses in a heap, sweat pouring out of his pores. But someone bathes his face with a moist handkerchief and passes on. The ambulance is behind!

Suddenly there is a halt. What's that? Bones? Yes, a camel's. But the others, white and glistening...and the skull and ivory teeth? A Gurkha's, we are told; and our plight, too, if we fall and faint by the way.

A sergeant gives a ghastly shriek, and begins to charge his magazine desperately with live rounds. He is grabbed by an officer and held to the ground, shrieking the while: 'See them? Look! Thousands of them – all charging upon us!' He struggles frantically, roaring like a mad bull, until the sound makes the marrow creep, Then he falls back unconscious...and the column passes on, leaving him behind till the ambulance comes.

Evening again: camp is made and trenches dug. But the order is 'Stand to.' Hostile Arabs are near; and through the night every eye is skinned to pierce the darkness for the glint of a curved knife or rifle.

Dawn comes. Men's eyes are heavy, and limbs weary and limp. But still we plod on. Nerves are keyed high: a small, prickly bush to be avoided or a clump of hard earth irritates. A soldier looks at his comrade and sees fixed, glazed eyes and cracked lips. His own tongue is swollen, furry, and leathery.

Corporal Ben tries at his mouth organ again, but fails at the first notes, for his lips are blistered and cracked.

The only thought is for water. A sparkling waterfall to lie and drown under, drinking, drinking; the tap at home; the green, green water in stagnant pools – all would taste delicious.

We come to a stagnant oasis, fast drying and black with dead insects and flies. And deaf to the warning shouts of the medical officer and others, many sink upon their knees and drink.

At midday there is an unexpected halt, and the scouts ride into the horizon and are lost to sight. We rest our lean, unshaven heads on haversacks and sleep fitfully. There is no sound save the jingling of the mules in the harness. Even the camels rest.

The column stirs again, though no one knows the reason why. Camp lines are marked out, deeper trenches dug, every man stands at the parapets, officers consult together.

A mug of warm tea, beef, and biscuits brighten spirits a little; but the word is passed to keep a sharp look-out, for Arabs are near.

A large-limbed man falls to the floor of the trench, groaning in agony and bent double, his knees pressing against his chest.

The medical officer is summoned, and comes with two orderlies with a stretcher. He knows the curse that has stricken the regiment: he had warned us that in that green pool, passed a few hours before, there lurked the germs of cholera.

Men fall quickly after that, at the very thought of having swallowed the stuff. Corporal Ben and myself are left in the trench where there had stood a dozen men. Corporal Ben who still smiles with lips that quiver, and whose bloodshot eyes are heavy with sleep.

Evening comes; and the moon shines and the stars. And around we lonely two at the parapet looms the desert, ghostly, still, and sinister.

We do not speak, or know how our comrades fare near by. We gaze into the night, tired soldiers and weary – too tired to care for life.

Dawn stirs the darkness. The early mists cling to the ground.

They are there! right in front of us! – a good 600 Arab horsemen. But the sight does not rouse the sluggish pulses of the soldiers.

Volleys are fired – rapid, continuous volleys which make gaps in the Arab lines, but the fighting blood of our men is cold.

The Arabs charge; are beaten back like a wave against a rock; and then there is a silence.

An orderly arrives, grey with sand and sickness: 'Beat a rearguard action quickly, and join the Gurkha boys!'

And Corporal Ben smiles. 'Retreat before *them*?' he says slowly, wearily raising his heavy lids... '*We British retreat!*'

He jumps to the top of the parapet and, kneeling, charges his magazine full ten rounds. He fires off five of them. Then a bullet enters his brain. He rolls over with a sigh.

Private Robert Harding served in the ranks of the 1/4th Battalion Dorset Regt., Territorials, from September 1914 till early 1916; from 1916–1918 was attached as Staff clerk to Headquarters, 15th (Indian) Division.

THE DEVIL – MY FRIEND

Charles Trehane

The first time we tried to saddle him he sent two men to hospital.

It wasn't viciousness: he was young; he had never been backed before; he didn't understand. He only knew an unmolested life on a South African farm, and the sudden change upset him. The herding down to the coast and the long stifling sea voyage up to German East must have been unpleasantly strange.

He landed at a malarial little port called Kilwa Kissiwani, and, the day after, was handed over with a batch of remounts to an Indian cavalry regiment. He came to my squadron, and I picked him out as a charger because his head and ears, fine muzzle, and wide nostrils showed breeding.

My orderly christened him *Shaitan* (the Devil), mainly, I think, because the first thing the horse did was to bite him in the seat of the breeches.

He certainly was a devil at the beginning. His was the nervous kind of temperament one should have coaxed. But we hadn't time for that; we had to be ruthless. We had to throw him. All horses hate that, and he soon gave in. In three days he was ridable, and when, on the fourth, we started off, I took him as my charger.

The country was unlike anything I had seen before. In places we came across open grassland, but most of it was dense. Oppressive. It shut one in. One longed to push it all away and hold up one's head and breathe. All around huge trees towered up out of the ground, bent and twisted into grotesque shapes as they fought each other for the space to live. Here and there thin, knarled branches hung down like the withered tentacles of some great forest octopus groping in the earth. Up above the canopy of leaves and intertwining branches almost blotted out the sky.

One learnt, for the first time in one's life, to value water. Through those long weary days of striving Shaitan and I got to know each other, though he often did try to give me a nip in the seat of the breeches when I mounted. And he had a great heart. He never slacked. He never spared himself. He was always willing. When everyone else was worn out and weary, he'd hold up his eager head and stride along as if he never knew fatigue.

But the strain told. It was a very different Devil that stood beside me somewhere south of the Rufiji four months later.

We had had a hard day. A night without water or fodder, a long march round behind the German position to cut off the retreat, and some fighting. Late in the afternoon we were waiting to rejoin the column.

It was a remnant of the squadron that rested, the men silent, dirty, and dejected, the horses with drooping heads. Tunics were torn. Many men looked ill, with sunken eyes and thin, pinched faces. The horses were like skeletons.

Rawlins, the adjutant, had gone to find out where we were to camp, and we were waiting for him to come back. I felt dreadfully weary and sat down on the ground. Jackson came and sat beside me.

'Bedford is pretty bad,' he said.

'Really? I thought he was only hit on the arm?'

'Yes, but it's a ghastly hole. Must have been a soft-nosed bullet.'

'Elephant, perhaps.'

'Quite likely… The sods!…'

'Poor devil.'

For a while we sat silent. Behind us a man started spewing. I looked round. He was leaning up against a tree holding his stomach and being violently sick. The malaria there must have been a particularly virulent type; it seemed to knock the men out altogether.

Jackson lay back and shut his eyes. After a while Rawlins returned and told us we were to camp inside the old German perimeter.

We marched in. The ground was undulating, and intersected here and there by deep trenches. A strong boma of twisted branches enclosed the whole position. Most of the other units of the column were already in camp and several fires had been lighted, at which men were cooking. We led up the main centre road and turned off on to the site that we were to occupy.

As the men were putting up the long line from tree to tree to which head ropes are fastened, the C.O. came over and spoke to me, and Rawlins joined us.

'I've just seen Colonel Stone, sir. He says we can't water to-night.'

'Can't water! But that's preposterous!'

'I know, sir, I told him. I – '

'But – Good Lord! Doesn't he realize we were out on the flank last night? He must be mad. I'll go and see him myself.'

He hurried off towards the Column Headquarters tent.

Rawlins shook his head.

'It won't do any good,' he said glumly, 'But 'C' Squadron has had practically no water for thirty-six hours,' I protested.

' I know. But I don't think we shall get any. It isn't that Stone doesn't realize. He was quite upset about it. But apparently there are 3,000 porters who haven't had water yet.'

The C.O. came back. If we must have water we could clear the water-hole, but we should probably have to use bayonets.

'Which sounds ridiculous, doesn't it?' he said. 'You'd better go and see what is happening there, Rawlins.'

I went along with Rawlins, We found out from a gunner that the water-hole was behind a low ridge, which he pointed out at the far corner of the camp.

As we approached we heard an incessant babel, quite distinct above the hum of the camp noises. It grew louder as we got nearer. We found ourselves in a jostling mob of porters. The crowd of them on the road was so dense that it was impossible to force one's way along. We climbed up on to the low ridge and looked over.

The ground in front of us was alive – a great crawling mass of black heads and khaki bodies, pushing and struggling, like maggots crowding about a rotting carcass.

No water-hole was visible, only a sea of moving bodies. In the dusk it looked like a huge heaving blanket and one could hardly realize it was composed of human beings – porters mad with thirst.

In the middle of the mass an arm would stretch up, the hand holding a *chaghul*. Immediately a dozen arms would snatch at it, pulling and jerking until the water spilt down on upturned faces with mouths gaping open to catch the splashes.

Those in the centre must have been standing in water up to their thighs, while those at the edge stood in mud, but their bodies were packed so tightly together they could hardly bend down.

I saw a man struggling to get out. In one hand he held his dripping water bottle pressed to his body, with his other hand he shoved and pushed the bodies near him. He heaved and writhed, but he hardly moved a yard. Then his arm got wedged, and another man grabbed the bottle and drank. The first man tried to wrench it back, beating the other's face, but he went on drinking even though his nose was torn.

As we watched, I believe a man was trampled into the mud. His body was down amongst a mass of legs. I couldn't see properly what happened, but it looked as if they just stamped on him. It was impossible to do anything.

We came away. It was not an edifying sight.

To water the horses that evening was obviously out of the question, so when I went along to *Shaitan* I took my water bottle.

He looked round when he heard me coming and gave a low whinney, as he always did, pushing his soft velvety muzzle into my hand when I went up to pat him.

I pulled his ear. Usually he pretended he didn't like it and gave a playful nip at my leg, but to-night he was too utterly weary to play. He just rubbed his nose against me.

I took up my water bottle and, while my orderly held up *Shaitan*'s head, I pulled out his lip and poured a little water into his mouth. Poor old thing, he got so excited. I could feel him trembling. I'm not sure it was a kindness really; I could only spare such a very little and he was so frantically thirsty. And the smell of it made the horses near him restless. But they quietened down after a bit, and then I gave him his dope – a sprinkle of white powder on a handful of grain. Arsenic. We dosed all the horses with it every night because we were in a tsetse belt, and it was supposed to be a prophylactic for 'horse sickness.'

But I doubt if it really did much good. They looked dreadful, poor brutes; their withers and hip bones stuck right out, and the flesh had fallen away from their backs, leaving backbones standing up like ridges. Of course the fatigue, the lack of fodder, and the long spells without water had a lot to do with it, but it was the 'sickness' that made them seem to fade away.

I went back and sat down on my valise. Brent was opening a tin of melon jam by the light of our hurricane lamp, turned very low because we had no spare oil.

I got my tin of bully beef and started to eat, scooping it out with a pocket knife. I expect it tasted rather tinny, it usually did, and possibly it was a bit mouldy, but one didn't notice that in the dark.

We were very low in food just then: bully beef, jam, and ration biscuits – the latter so hard that one had to saw off pieces with a knife because one couldn't bite them. And we were nearly always hungry – so hungry that if anybody took a little more than his share of jam it made the rest of us angry.

I can see that scene now: around us the dim forms of the horses, the trees, the camp fires flickering out of the darkness. Jackson stretched on his back with his eyes shut; Brent beside him munching. On the ground the lamp, burning in that absolutely still air without a flicker, showed dimly their sweat-stiff shirts, their cropped heads, their scrubby beards, and the hollows on their dirty faces. It made them look like Russian prisoners.

As we ate, a noise in the bushes behind made me look round. Two figures were moving slowly through the undergrowth beyond our light.

'*Kaun hai* (Who's there)?' I called out.

'*Do admi aur ek mard.*'

Two men and one corpse. I don't know who they were, I suppose they were trying to find some spot where, undisturbed, they could perform the last rites for a brother killed in the attack. Nobody seemed to heed them. We went on eating.

When we had finished we put up our mosquito nets. Jackson had thrown his away, but Brent and I still had ours. They were small – just big enough to lie under – and dyed a dark brown. We tied the four top corners to sticks stuck in the earth. Brent's was quite good, but mine was torn and full of holes. It didn't keep out the mosquitoes, but I imagined it kept out the horrid things that slid to and fro in the undergrowth – snakes, scorpions, centipedes, and huge warrior ants. In the dark one never knew that they were not creeping about over one's body. They did sometimes. Once in the middle of the night something slimy crawled over my throat.

Jackson had a high temperature that evening. He took fifteen grains of quinine, and Brent gave him some aspirin, but it didn't seem to ease him much, because I heard his teeth chattering as we lay there in the dark. I got up and collected a couple of horse blankets and wrapped them round him.

He looked worse next morning.

I told him he'd better report sick, but he tried to make out it was nothing.

'Only one of my goes of fever, old thing. I'll be all right in a couple of days.'

But I fetched Doc. And Doc shook his head. He sent Jackson down the line straight away by the empty ration convoy that left before we marched.

Poor Jackson. He was the kind who never gives in, but the beastly country got him down in the end. He seemed awfully weak when we said good-bye. I felt it was unlikely that I would see him again.

I wasn't feeling too great myself. As I was thinking about opening my bully beef, I felt a pain in my stomach; a sharp gnawing pain. I knew what that meant. I'd had dysentery twice already. I decided to give meat a miss for a day or two.

'It's an ill wind – ' Brent philosophically remarked when I gave him my ration.

Shaitan got water all right, though it was very muddy. But he had a fairly easy day in front of him, as we only had to march fifteen miles to join another column.

The Intelligence Officer attached to my squadron came along as we were forming up – a lean, dark-skinned fellow called Van Ponk, a Dutchman, with a scar across his left cheek which was the result of a bullet wound he received fighting against us in the Boer War.

He had collected a couple of local bush inhabitants to act as our guides, and I found them waiting at the corner of the camp as we moved out. They were a comic couple; a thin wiry old man with curly iron-grey hair and a young boy. The boy was naked except for a strip of the fibrous bark of a tree wrapped round his middle, but the old man was more dressy. He had a two-piece suit made out of a couple of grain sacks. He'd cut holes for his legs in one, which was pulled up and fastened round his waist with a thong, and the other had holes cut for head and arms, and was worn like a shirt. It might have been quite an effective shirt, but, unfortunately, he had only been able to get hold of a very small sack, so it looked like a very coarse little brown vest that had shrunk in the wash. Rawlins grinned at me as we started off.

'If in doubt,' he' said, 'rely on the fellow in the plus fives.'

At first the air was fresh, almost cold, but as the sun got up it became hot, and one's skin dried up as if there was no moisture in one's body at all. Those hot, dry marches always made me long for wet pavements. I used to picture Piccadilly in the evening when it was drizzling, with all the lights reflected in the wet.

The bush we went through varied: sometimes it was more or less open, like a thickly tree'd park; sometimes the undergrowth was so thick the Hankers could not keep in touch; sometimes the path led through a dense forest of bamboos. Never could one see more than 100 yards ahead.

It was like playing a fierce, relentless game of hide-and-seek in a strange garden in the dark. And though one might march from dawn to dusk without meeting any enemy at all, without even hearing a shot fired, one was utterly worn out with the mental strain of it at the end. One's mind could never relax.

After we had been marching for four hours or so, we got on to a road down which a squadron had raided a few weeks previously. One couldn't help knowing it. The dead-horse smell was nauseating. It made Brent sick. Several were lying quite near the road, their legs sticking straight up in the air, their bodies swollen like balloons. The stench was quite awful. Thank goodness it only lasted for about a mile!

Shaitan began to get very sluggish. I had to keep urging him on, a thing I had never had to do before. I guessed he must be feeling pretty rotten, because, though for the last three weeks I'd missed the eager springing step of old, he had never slacked. Worn out as I knew he must have been at times, that great spirit of his would never let him rest.

To-day I hated riding him. It was cruel having to urge when I could feel the effort it was to him to keep going, and I knew how bravely he was trying.

Twice he stumbled badly, and at the second time I called up my orderly and told him to bring me one of the spare horses at the next halt.

'Old *Shaitan*'s tired out,' I said. 'We'll give him a rest.'

But the rest came sooner.

A few minutes before we were due to halt he suddenly stopped, turned off the path, walked a few paces, and stood still. And then he sank. I only just had time to slip off before he collapsed. We got his girth undone and pulled the saddle away and slipped the bit out of his mouth. And he lay there on his side, a poor worn shadow of what he used to be.

I rubbed the velvet muzzle gently with my knuckles, I pulled an ear that was cold and damp with sweat…and said good-bye to him.

There was nothing else for it.

I brushed aside a wisp of forelock and put my revolver to his temple – and shot him.

Captain C. H. Trehane entered the Army from Sandhurst in 1912. Attached 2nd King's Regt. and 8th Hussars, and joined 25th Cavalry (Frontier Force), I.A., in 1913. 1914–1915, operations at Miramshah, North-West Frontier; 1917, German East Africa; 1918, Mesopotamia and Persia (attached 5th Cavalry). Eventually invalided from the service.

'THE CIRCUS'

F. Suckling

By the side of a cottage in an insignificant French village one morning in the spring of 1918, a group of khaki-clad figures stood gazing intently at a sheet of foolscap bearing a few typewritten names. By the cap and cut of the jacket, these lads, none of them more than nineteen years and all just from England, could be seen to belong to the Flying Corps, and they were eagerly scanning the newest list of postings. One of them, by hurrying out from his billet immediately after breakfast, had been the first there, and although he had been at the Pilots' Pool only two days, it was with intense satisfaction that he read:

To X Squadron: Lieutenant S.
                   Lieutenant K.

'X seems to be having a thin time; that's ten new pilots in a week,' a voice remarked.

'Heaven help those two poor devils. They've got the 'Circus' on their front.'

For a moment Lieutenant S. felt a tinge of dread; he had heard much of the 'Circus' of forty picked fighters, led by the redoubtable Richthofen, and here was he – a mere child in matters of aerial warfare – to be pitted against the best pilots of the German Flying Corps.

About eleven o'clock that evening a tender came for the two 'unfortunates,' and after a chilling ride which brought them ever nearer to the sound of big guns and a sky perpetually bright with their flashes, S. arrived at his squadron in the blackness of night that preceded dawn. War seemed far away when a few hours later, looking out from the tent flap, he found himself in a little wood where a bright sun made the dew on the green leaf-buds glisten and revealed patches of violets among the moss. The sight of these flowers brought to his mind a vivid picture of Sussex woods and an English girl. It was her favourite flower!

At the end of a fortnight he was told to be ready to be one of three for a two hours' 'show' over the lines. As he gazed up at the blue sky, broken from time to time by drifting clouds, which the enemy well knew how to use as a hiding place, the young officer pondered over his first outing. There was his 'bus,' a scout which needed delicate handling, and instruments which required occasional watching. He must keep a wary eye all round and at the same time look out for landmarks; he must also keep his place in formation, and an eye on the leader's plane for the 'waggle' which should tell of hostile aircraft.

Once up aloft, all apprehension left him and the clear spring air acted as a tonic. The sense of adventure became uppermost. In a close triangle the machines climbed to gain height before crossing into enemy territory, and after an hour's flying the planes of the front machine rocked.

Enemy! Another waggle, more violent! He looked in front…behind…above…and then over the side he saw them. A few hundred feet below cloud vapours were drifting across the sky and as the machines circled above a gap in the golden mist he could see an old R.E. 8 lumbering along with three 'tripes' buzzing round like hornets. Only the 'Circus' flew triplanes, and here were three of them, their variegated colours turned into gold by the brilliance of the sun, playing about with one of the slowest machines then on the Front. Why didn't his leader dive into them and give him a chance of using his guns on a live target, instead of letting the unequal battle go on?

Suddenly across the sun shot some black specks, and a flight of Camels streamed down on to the scene below. There was a mix-up of red and blue circles and black crosses, and one machine went down in flames, but the three machines above flew straight on, and finished their patrol.

When they came down S. asked the leader why he had not taken them into it, for they had been in a good position and the numbers were even.

'Say, youngster, do you realize who they were? If we had

mixed it, you would have been dead meat before now. They are not new hands! And I had seen our chaps – even if you hadn't!'

A few weeks afterwards he met the 'Circus' again, not three of them, but the whole bunch.

For several days things had been quiet on the Front, and the absence of hostile planes, which was attributed to a threatened offensive against the French south of Moreuil, had engendered a greater boldness in our young flying lads. Miles beyond the trenches they would fly, a few feet from the ground, bombing dumps and 'shooting up' anything moving. There was no opposition whatever until a certain Sunday in mid-June when, at a height of 15,000 feet, three of them had ventured about eight miles into the enemy's territory. The clear sky, the absence of noise beyond the hum of the engine, the apparent peace all round, made it seem really a day of rest. Once during the patrol S. had noticed about a mile away and 1,000 feet below a large flight of machines. Since his arrival at the squadron he had learned how to identify all types of machines in the air, and now, with the momentary thought 'Bristol Fighters,' he dismissed them from his mind.

For a few minutes only!

Suddenly, without any preliminary waggle, the leader climbed sharply to the right. S., flying on the right corner of the triangle, climbed at an even steeper angle to keep formation, and what happened then was recorded as a series of blurred impressions. As he turned, the air was filled with tracer bullets and before he was on an even keel his partner on the left burst into flames, fell, and went out. He had heard such happenings reported by others, but the quickness of it appalled him. There was by now no sign of his leader, and coming straight at him was the 'Circus!' His mind, in a flash, remarked the bizarre appearance of these triplanes with the sun behind them; they resembled so many sets of empty bookshelves as they flew at him, the first a blood-red one. Only Richthofen flew a blood-red machine!

The air seemed alive with white-hot bullets passing over his head, beneath his wheels, and even between his planes.

Instinctively he pressed his gun controls, there was no time to use telescopic sights. He blazed away in a vain effort to stop these flaming specks which were streaming past like fiery hail, and forgot that he had been told to fire always in short bursts. His guns stopped – jammed; the 'Circus' all round and he helpless at a height where the thin air made his controls slow to act. There was one thing he could do, dive – and the 'tripes' could not dive steeply for long without a plane lifting off!

Pulling the joy-stick over to the right, he kicked the rudder bar hard with his right foot. Up and over came the nose of the little Camel, then down, down, engine full on. The pointer on his air-speed moved rapidly round 150, 170, 200, and still he kept his nose down. Even as he had begun his dive he had seen four enemy machines dive out of the crowd and give chase. Could he go more steeply? He had heard of his own type of bus sometimes not coming out of a vertical dive. By this time the rush of cold air would have cooled his guns, and he could scrap again, but one against four of Germany's best! A backward glance revealed the enemy beginning to flatten out and lose distance, so he himself flattened out. By the time he was out of the dive and had turned his machine back, only two of his attackers were at all near. He climbed after them, but instead of turning to fight they simply flew eastward. His own bus, built more for rapid manoeuvring than for great speed, was gradually outdistanced and all he could do was to fire a burst in farewell.

On his return home he found his flight leader awaiting him, unhurt.

'Gee, that was a warm two minutes,' the captain said.

'There were well over thirty of the blighters.'

Two minutes! To S. it had seemed a lifetime!

July came in and was very hot, and in that part of the Front, both on the ground and in the blue, there was great activity. No longer did our young pilots seek adventure in threes or sixes, a 'squadron show' was now the rule.

Every evening at 7 the whole of the eighteen machines went up together, and as soon as they were high enough and formation was made, the three triangles, each of six machines, flew east in quest of trouble with the red sun behind them. Nor did it take much looking for. Invariably about the hour of 8, the 'Circus' was there, always waiting at the same spot, and a perfect formation dive soon developed into a 'dog-fight.' It was then a case of every man for himself, singling out an enemy 'bus,' and sticking to it until one or the other went down or ammunition gave out.

In the twilight of the evening our machines returned singly or in pairs; names were checked and the pilots gathered together by a hangar, looking out for those not yet in. Soon all but one were back, and as long as light permitted them to discern anything moving in the sky, so long they stood there, cap, goggles, and gloves in hand, just as they had climbed out of the cockpit. But something strange was happening, and as the days wore on a gloom settled upon the squadron. Every night with unfailing regularity one of the lads did not return, and this went on for the greater part of a fortnight. On no occasion had a Camel been seen to go down in flames or out of control. In the excitement of a 'dog-fight' this was to be expected, but there seemed something uncanny in the monotonous regularity with which just one failed to return. A less buoyant air was to be noticed among the pilots on the 'drome and in the mess, and unconsciously everyone knew the unspoken question uppermost in every mind, 'Whose turn to-night?' Something had to be done and quickly.

One evening during the middle of that month, the men in the trenches must have looked up when they heard the roar of more than fifty English scouts crossing over like three great arrowheads.

The boys in those machines that evening were feeling 'bucked,' for that self-same morning another squadron had met a section of the 'Circus' and satisfactorily disposed of ten of them. With this knowledge and no time to think of the nightly missing pilot, they sailed across to their evening tryst.

Of the scrap that followed, one of the largest ever seen over the lines, one vivid picture remains to S.

He is on the tail of a small, fast German scout, barely 100 feet away and, even while keeping an eye on it until he cannot fail to hit it, he is able to glimpse in the sky all round him countless specks of different sizes, wheeling, 'split hairing,' half-rolling, diving, at times spitting flame. To his right and just above him there are five balls of fire falling earthwards, a moment ago swiftly moving machines guided by living minds. As he watches, flames lick out of the side of a bus not far away; in a fraction of time it is consumed with fire and hurtles down, leaving streaks of flame behind. No shrieks are heard, the comfortable hum of the engine removes any sign that a boy has gone to his death.

His own quarry is doing its level best to escape, but, although actually faster, it is inferior at stunting, and the crowd of eighty odd specks makes straight flying impossible. Suddenly; during a short dive, the German pilot's neck fills the ring in his sight. S. presses his gun controls. There is a short burst, a wisp of grey smoke, but before he can see the result the nose of his machine rises quickly and turns to the right. Why he never knew; he hears the rattle of machine guns, and, looking to his left, sees within a few feet a black bus with tiny white crosses on the upper plane streak past in a headlong dive. The pilot's head is turned towards him, so near that he would recognize him again. In a flash he pushes the joy-stick forward to the left, rudders in the same direction and dives after this new adversary. Comes another burst of bullets, more prolonged, and an S.E.5, in a vertical dive, shoots between them and separates them.

How he went into the fight, what else happened in it and the flight home, have gone from memory.

Back at the hangars, pilots related individual experiences, and there was great satisfaction when it was clear that the Camels alone, apart from the other two squadrons, had accounted for eleven of the 'Circus.' But no one had downed a red machine. That honour fell to Brown of 209 on the following Sunday morning. On the evening of the same day S. saw the dead body of the famous German pilot. As a doctor cut open the leather flying suit, Richthofen's underclothing was revealed – of the same blood-red colour as his triplane.

F. Suckling joined Army, April 1917, at eighteen years of age. Served in infantry training battalion for three months. Became an officer cadet in Royal Flying Corps. Received Commission in October 1917, and 'wings' as flying officer in March 1918. Went to France in April 1918, and served with 65 Squadron until October of the same year. From April to August 1918, engaged on the Somme front, chiefly against hostile fighting machines. Did first 'show' before nineteen years of age. August to October 1918, on the northern section of the front, chief duty being the escorting of bombing machines to Bruges and other Belgian towns. Returned to England for brief period of Home service, during which time the Armistice was signed.

THE CASUALTY

Rev. John H. W. Haswell

It happened over Ypres.

I was a member of a Royal Air Force unit, nineteen years of age.

The infantryman was one in a tiny circle of pals, each circle but one wavelet in a huge-sea. His was a hard life – mud and blood and losing chums, and ever conscious of being but a cog in a mighty and soulless machine.

We, on the other hand, were neither wavelets nor cogs. We were *it*. Our squadron was, like a battleship, a unit in itself, and every individual was important.

We were a small family of officers living in decent huts, partaking of decent meals, sleeping in, clean pyjamas, and generally living in comfort for eighteen hours of the twenty-four. In the remaining six we might plunge into the welter of war in which the infantryman lived, but we did our particular job in a clean atmosphere in a clean way, and when we killed or were killed it was done in that same inevitable and highly respectable manner.

The infantryman looked up from his rathole and said, with his hair on end, that he wouldn't have our risky job for anything, while we looked down on his muddy wastes and said, 'Poor devils!' (or words to that effect), and flew home to a hot dinner served on a clean tablecloth while he cut his fingers opening bully-beef tins.

The family were, of course, occasionally bereaved, and we talked rather awkwardly at dinner and avoided each other's eyes, and were relieved when, at the end of the meal, the O.C. briefly called us to silent remembrance, But coffee, smokes, and piano quickly saved us from overmuch thought. When these bereavements became frequent, we had to receive others into the family, and every few days there would arrive a number of strangers looking very self-conscious and humble, as well they might before us hardened warriors of two or three months' experience! Only a few hours after their arrival each one was instructed to report to a senior pilot, and the process of initiation began. 'The observers had revision of the mysteries of maps, machine guns, cameras, and many other strange things with which these poor benighted ones deal, while the pilots, to whose skill (or lack of it) the former entrust their lives, were told to memorize the map of the sector until they knew it better than anything else on earth, and then were taken to 'have a look at the War.'

I was a senior pilot of about ten weeks' standing, and to me there was detailed a new pilot, a youngster of about twenty-one (two years older than I!) and, after a serious conversation on what London looked like when he left and what 'shows' were running at the time, we agreed to go and have a peep at the front line.

My machine stood waiting; we put a couple of bombs in "for luck,' and in a few minutes were heading eastward towards that horror of mud and waterlogged trenches. We soon caught sight of the flooded area which had been the Yser Canal, and then of that dark blotch called Ypres and, being now about 10,000 feet up, I beckoned my 'pupil' to lean over from his seat behind me, and, shutting off the engine and falling into a glide, I pointed out to him the various beauty spots of the district, Ypres, Poperinghe, the Menin Road, etc., yelling the names at the top of my voice, lest the fierce wind should snatch them out of hearing. He nodded, glancing at his map, and I saw with joy that he was keen.

For some little time we flew up and down the line (but keeping on our own side of it!), waved our hands to some kite-balloon folk who occupied lofty positions in a row behind Ypres, while at the same time I took the opportunity to indicate the cables mooring the balloons, for it is not wise to collide with them. Then came the second stage of the initiation – to go over the line and receive a baptism of fire from 'Archie,' the enemy anti-aircraft batteries.

There is an art in this game. On a cloudy day one can hop in and out of the clouds, greatly to the annoyance of some Archie commander who, just when he has got range and direction and is about to let fly, finds that his bird has disappeared into a cloud. He fills that cloud with H. E., but his quarry emerges from another near by with a gesture of derision which the gunners below may imagine, though cannot see.

On a sunny day, Archie is up early, for he knows that aircraft will be silhouetted against a blue sky. Then the experienced pilot hops in and out of the sun, there being no clouds, while the Archie commander rubs his smarting eyes and uses strong words.

To-day favoured the latter game, which we played with zest for some little time. Then, having carefully spotted the A. A. position, we got it carefully on our bomb sights, and sent our greetings in the form of the two bombs we had brought.

I was about to swing round and head for home and tea, when I espied a spot on the horizon towards the south-east. It might be an enemy raider coming to pounce on our helpless balloons, or it might be one of our own. Anyway, we would see, and, pointing out my intention to my companion, we speeded off in pursuit. We were in luck! From far off the shape of the aircraft showed its alien origin, and we began to prepare for chasing him home again.

First I pressed the trigger of my forward gun, which loyally answered with a rapid 'Ta-ta-ta-ta,' a noise which, my companion told me afterwards, nearly made him jump overboard with fright. I had forgotten him and he had forgotten my front gun! Then quickly I beckoned him, quietened down the engine and shouted a series of instructions, and, as the engine roared out again, I heard a few rounds fired from his rear gun and knew that all was well.

The next minute we had come to grips with the enemy, a wicked looking single-seater, much lighter and faster than us, and with every advantage except that his one gun fired only forwards, while, in addition to my similar gun, my companion had one on a swivel mounting which revolved easily and allowed him to fire in almost every direction.

Our plan of campaign, therefore, was that I should

manoeuvre the machine so as to keep the enemy in a position where he would be a good target for the rear gunner, who could give all his attention to firing.

We circled round each other looking for an opening. Then I suddenly reversed my direction, bringing the other alongside us, and within easy range where he would be simply raked from stem to stern, while his fixed forward gun pointed harmlessly away from us. I waited to hear my companion's gun as he took advantage of the position, but not a sound came, and the next fraction of a second I was swinging round for dear life with the 'Zip-zip!' of bullets round my ears. The second's delay had given the other the chance he wanted, for he was now under our tail out of reach of both of our guns and it was some seconds more before I could shake him off.

However, I got him once more in a good position, waited for the sound of gun-fire, but again silence, and again I dived desperately out of a stream of bullets.

'Fire, you fool!' I yelled, though not a word could reach him, and I dare not turn round, while all the time the darting little wasp, who seemed aware of my plight, came buzzing behind and resisted all my efforts to avoid him.

There was only one thing left to do. I must try to fight him off with my forward gun, and I turned to do so, when, wonder of wonders, I saw him fall into a steep dive and make for home, having seen a triangle of our machines appearing out of the blue.

And now for an explanation from this idiot behind! I spun round angrily, but words were impossible. He was sitting there strapped as usual to his seat, but with his face a mass of blood, while his gun hung uselessly from its mounting!

After a rapid spin to earth and a landing at the first favourable spot, he told me what had occurred.

We had not been hit by Archie's shrapnel. I had seen him quite fit after that. The disaster had befallen him before we engaged in the air duel.

It was that silence after the first gun-test which should have told its tale. He had decided to test the gun-mounting also, but, being accustomed to the poorly kept machines at home, had expected to find it equally difficult to move. He had not thought that here on active service, where the space between life and death is measured in hundredth parts of a second, each mounting is kept thoroughly oiled, and will spin round at a touch. Consequently he had seized the mounting, pulled it round quickly, and the heavy gun, resenting such rough treatment, had revolved on its easy bearings, and had smitten him violently over the head, knocking him out completely.

Well might I have waited for the sound of his gun. *He had not even been aware of the fight!*

Rev. J. H. Haswell enlisted as a private in the Royal Welch Fusiliers in 1916, became corporal, and in 1917 commissioned in Royal Flying Corps as second lieutenant. Promoted lieutenant in May 1918, and proceeded to France. Served there until 1919 (May) with the Royal Air Force. Became missionary in West Africa (Primitive Methodist).

AUGUST TO NOVEMBER 1918

H. F. Taylor

August 8th, 1918. Who of those who were on the Somme will forget that day when we started to push the enemy back along the long, straight road which leads from Amiens to Peronne?

I had just joined my squadron as spare pilot. It happened that an observer had been wounded the previous day, and my flight commander asked if I would act as an observer for a time. Of course I said 'Yes.' What else could I say?

Thus it was that on August 8th I had my first experience of a bombing expedition over the lines. The objective was an ammunition dump somewhere along that same long, straight road. Fourteen machines flew in V-shaped formation, so close that an observer on one side could make faces at his friend flying on the other.

For an hour we circled on our own side of the lines, gaining height. Referring to my map, I found I could look down on the Forest of Crecy, where centuries ago another army of ours had fought, but with what different weapons!

Now we were heading east, sweeping along at ninety miles an hour, three miles up. At such an altitude, details below cannot easily be picked out, and because of my lack of experience we were over the target and dropping bombs before I realized we had crossed the lines. At a signal from my pilot, I pulled the two wires and released the bombs from their rack below the fuselage. Then I leaned over the side to watch them fall.

Have you ever looked down from a high building and felt as though you must throw yourself down? As I watched those two bombs falling, second after second, getting smaller and smaller until they became invisible, I felt an almost irresistible impulse to slip over the low wall of three-ply wood that was the side of the cockpit, and follow them. I had to turn away.

So far, we had had the sky to ourselves, but as we turned for home I became aware of a number of black specks on our left, rapidly growing into a flight of enemy scouts. They did not dive on us, but hung behind, peppering away at the end machines of the V formation.

Everyone of us opened up with his two Lewis guns, and I had my first sight of a machine sent down in flames. Who hit him it was impossible to say, since he was the foremost in the attack, and the target of at least six guns. He suddenly dived. Petrol vapour streamed out like smoke behind him, then burst into flames. I watched as he rushed downwards, to fall to pieces 1,000 feet below.

His companions disappeared, and we were left to go home in peace. In the distance I noticed a number of machines carrying out most wonderful evolutions. There must have been twenty, twisting and turning like worms writhing in a fisherman's bait tin.

At the lines we dived and broke formation. My pilot flew low, perhaps 100 feet up, and we looked on the ground that had been fought over that morning. The earth was tom up. Here a tree stump, there a heap of ruins, a wrecked gun, a dead horse, a deserted tank half buried in the mud. It is impossible to describe how desolate the scene appeared. Soon we were back at the aerodrome, taking off our flying suits.

'Poor old Baker's done,' said my pilot. 'Didn't you' see him go down?' I had not noticed any of our men drop out, but it was true. Only thirteen buses landed. I was no longer a spare pilot.

'Those fellows were having a good time stunting, just before we got to the line, weren't they?' I asked.

'Stunting?' said Johnson grimly. 'That was a dog fight. Our bombers and Jerry's scouts. That's what would happen to us if we didn't keep formation.'

'Why didn't we go and give them a hand?'

'Nothing to do with us. Our business is to drop bombs and get home as quickly as possible.'

One soon gets to know people in an Air Force squadron. There was Mills, who always stayed in bed until the last possible moment, and at the cry 'Raid on!' would hastily don his flying kit over his pyjamas and climb into the machine.

There was Macdonald, who, unknown to the C.O., was so short-sighted as to be unable to judge his height, and had to give the controls to his observer when about to land. Biddard, who rouged his cheeks and reddened his lips; and Machin, whose father was a boot manufacturer, and kept his son supplied with an extraordinary collection of footwear.

I was soon to see changes. One by one as the days went by, familiar faces disappeared, and new ones came.

Mills went off one day alone, on a photographic expedition, returned with a dud engine, and was well cursed by the C.O. for not getting the job done. He went off again, and never came back. Whether he was killed or spent the rest of the war roaming a prison camp in pyjamas, I never knew. It was not the C.O.'s fault. He was being hurried by the wing commander, who in turn, no doubt, was responsible for the photos to someone higher up. One machine and its occupant was a small price to pay for them.

Macdonald was lucky. He went home after six months' flying with 'nerves.' Biddard came down one day in a raid on Namur, and was taken prisoner, unhurt, but no doubt sadly missing his rouge and lipstick, which he had left behind. That evening in the mess, raid orders were posted up just like the football teams we used to put up at school only a few months before. Machines, with pilot and observer, were set out each in its position in the formation. Being a new pilot, I was given a comparatively safe position near the front.

At dawn next morning we were awakened by the cry 'Raid on!' and hurried out for a quick breakfast of boiled eggs. The engines were being run up by mechanics, and we were soon in. A heavy mist hung over the ground. One by one the engines were opened out, the machine moved forward, gained speed, and at last rose up.

Soon we were in formation, circling to gain height. Below us stretched a sea of cotton wool, the earth being obscured by ground fog. Ahead, we steered into the rising sun, straight for the lines. I had no difficulty in keeping in formation; we had practised that when in the training squadron.

Nothing happened as we crossed the lines and neared our objective. Then suddenly, a dirty yellow cloud unrolled itself about 20 yards on my right, and a hoarse 'Woof' followed. It was 'Archie,' an anti-aircraft battery.

Another and another followed, and we were soon flying through slowly dispersing clouds of smoke. It seemed impossible to avoid being hit, and before I realized it, I had soared 200 feet above the rest. I was no better off. As I turned to avoid one burst, I would see another appear in front of me.

The range had been changed, and while the formation sailed peacefully below I was catching the lot. However, we left it behind, and I resumed my place. On several subsequent occasions, I have seen young pilots do the same thing, to fall easy prey to Fokkers lurking above waiting for 'Archie ' to disrupt the formation.

Over the target we dropped our cargo, then as we turned, we met the enemy scouts as before. Why they did not dive on us from the front and split us up I do not know, but their policy was always to hang on behind. Our observers opened fire. Streams of tracer bullets shot out from each gun, and our machines began to sway from side to side, and up and down, yet still keeping in the V shape, which it would have been fatal to lose.

For fifteen minutes it went on. Above the roar of the engine could be heard the sharp rattle of machine guns. Little rags of fabric would spring up in the wings as bullets tore them, and all the time the pilot must keep his hand on the throttle and his eyes on the machine ahead, swinging and dipping until collision, seemed imminent, yet always keeping a little above and to one side, so that the guns in front might protect his blind spot under the tail.

We reached the lines, and our attackers vanished. We could fly steadily now, and I had time to look behind. My observer was leaning on the side, white-faced, and gazing longingly at the ground below. I realized he had been wounded, and the awful thought flashed through my head that he might fall across the controls, setting the machine into a dive from which I might be unable to pull out.

Hastily I motioned to him to sit down, and dived steeply for home.

Every minute I expected to feel his weight on the elevator wires, and I was never more thankful than when my wheels touched the aerodrome. My engine stopped as I landed, and I stood up and waved. The ambulance, always ready, dashed across, and my observer was carefully lifted out. I never saw him again: wounded men were always hurried away, lest the sight of them should affect the nerves of the rest.

I looked at my bus. The planes were torn, and the ailerons sagged loosely.

It was half an hour before the next man came in, then one by one the stragglers arrived. Three messages came later, reporting forced landings up and down the country, but four of our machines were never heard of again. That was my first air raid as a pilot.

Of course it wasn't always like that. We made two and sometimes three raids a day. Sometimes we had trouble with aircraft or 'Archie' or both; often we had none. Twice we took over new aerodromes, following our slowly advancing infantry. New faces appeared and old friends dropped out, and in three months I found myself senior pilot of my flight.

It was late in the afternoon of a day in October. We had done our two raids, and imagined our work was over for the day, when a message came from the wing commander, asking for volunteers to bomb Peronne, the possession of which our troops were stoutly contesting.

Everybody volunteered; we couldn't refuse. We were assured that it was an easy job, that there would be no 'Archie' left in the town, and that we should be back before dark. There was no time to gain height and we must do our job at 2,000 feet, a most unusual thing for us, with our engines specially designed for use at high altitudes.

We approached the lines as dusk was falling. All around us guns flashed incessantly. It seemed that the air must be full of projectiles. I have no idea how high a shell travels, but I went in fear of being knocked to pieces any minute.

Then 'Archie' started. At such a range he could be very effective, and we had experienced nothing like it before. Still we kept steadily on, to meet a new horror as we approached the town.

Long strings of balls of fire began to float up. Sometimes slowly, then accelerating, one could not judge their speed. Sooner or later one must become entangled and fall to a hideous death.

Now we were over the town. I signalled to my partner to drop his bombs. As he did so, the engine began to splutter, and the nose dropped. I looked at the revolution indicator: the engine had fallen off to half its speed. Hastily I swung round, so hastily, indeed, that for some seconds my compass card continued to swing and I could not be sure in which direction we were flying. Our only hope now was to clear the lines. We could no longer fly horizontally, the only thing was to glide at as small an angle as possible and trust to luck.

Now we were alone 'Archie' recommenced, and so near were his shots that in the disturbed air we were tossed like a leaf in the wind. Tracer bullets pelted from below as we crossed the lines only a few hundred feet up.

We kept up as long as possible, but a very convenient field not badly scarred by shell holes enabled us to make a safe landing. Even then we were not really sure we were among friends until a khaki uniform appeared. My observer was so overjoyed that he wrung the hand of this bewildered artilleryman, then complained of a wound in the head. Gingerly we untied his helmet. Not a scratch! It was a case of shell shock. 'Archie' had been a bit too close. '

I spent the night with a battery of howitzers near by, and after phoning up my squadron got my engine repaired, it was a minor mishap, and I flew back next day.

As I say, these particular flights were exceptional. The one I remember best was the last one I ever did. It was uneventful, but I was panic-stricken the whole time. I was to go on leave next day, and I could not drive away the fear of catching a stray bullet on this raid, after having done over 100 without a scratch. However, I did come back safely, and next morning, as I waited for the car to take me on leave the C.O. popped his head out of his hut and said, 'The war's over!'

It was November 11th.

Harold F. Taylor was commissioned in the R.F.C. in January 1918 at the age of eighteen, and after the usual training was sent in July 1918 to 205 Squadron, operating on the Somme. He flew the DH4 and the DH9 daylight bombing machines, carrying out reconnaissance, photography, and bombing, sometimes doing two and three raids a day, and visiting St. Quentin, Busigny, Namur, and Dinanl among other towns. Richthofen's famous 'Circus' was still lively. Though three observers were wounded when flying with him, Lieutenant Taylor came out unscratched to the end of the War. Moving up after the Armistice, his squadron was engaged: on the earliest air mail, carrying mails from Cologne to the French coast. He was demobilized in April 1919.

AUGUST 1914

Esmée Sartorius

Like so many others when war was declared, I applied at once to the St. John Ambulance, to which I belonged, to know if there was any possibility of their making use of me, my only recommendation being three months' training in the London Hospital.

I was told that only trained nurses were wanted, and so gave up hope, but three days later the British Red Cross got an appeal for forty nurses to be sent out to Belgium; five St. John Ambulance nurses (V.A.D.s later on) were being sent, and I was asked if I would go. I naturally accepted with alacrity, and August 14th found us in Brussels. Most of us were taken to the Hotel Metropole, where we were to await orders. As there was a big battle expected any day, we should all be badly wanted.

Next day some of the nurses were sent to hospitals outside Brussels, and others, including M., my cousin (who was a fully trained nurse), and myself, were given posts in the Royal Palace, which posts, however, we never filled, as the next thing we heard was that the Germans were outside the gate of Brussels, and all the allied wounded were to be evacuated to Antwerp.

We were then given the option of returning to England at once; some returned, but we, M. and I amongst others, elected to remain, as we were told we were wanted outside Brussels.

At 3 p.m. next day the Germans marched in; it was a soul-stirring sight, seeing these impassive and tired-looking troops marching in to what seemed like a deserted town, every door and window shuttered and barred, and not a civilian to be seen, or a sound to be heard, save the steady tramping of the German troops, regiment after regiment, guns, cavalry, Uhlans with their fluttering pennons on their lances. One felt that thousands of Belgians were waiting and watching behind their shuttered doors and windows, with bated breath and terrible anxiety lest anyone or anything should cause a disturbance, and so bring down the punishment of the enemy. However, nothing happened, owing to the notices which had been posted up everywhere, and the wonderful influence of Burgomaster Max, who had implored everyone to be careful and to give no cause or excuse for trouble.

Brussels being an unfortified town, he had begged the people to help in a peaceful occupation. His words had the right effect and, after a time, doors and windows were opened, and cafes put their chairs and tables outside again, and the town gradually resumed its everyday life, but with a strong undercurrent of fear and consternation at the terrible feeling that the enemy was really in occupation, and Brussels under German rule.

Panics were easily started these days, and one sometimes met a crowd tearing down a street terror-stricken, crying that the French were outside the gates and a battle beginning, and one had to turn and run with the crowd till the panic was over.

We heard there were a number of wounded lying not far outside Brussels, and M. and I tried to get a car to take us out there to pick them up, but the Germans would not allow a car outside the gates just then, so we took a tram as far as we could, then walked, but could find no trace of them.

On our return from a trip out beyond the gates we heard we had been applied for, M. and I, to go to Charleroi to join a matron and two nurses who had gone there a few days before. We were given ten minutes to get ready, and were very glad to leave the hotel (which by this time was full of German officers), and to feel we were at last wanted. As there had been no fighting in Brussels, there was very little need for nurses.

We were raced off in a car by the Belgian Red Cross, and were dumped down late in the evening at one of the hospitals in Charleroi; but could find no trace of our compatriots, though we searched all the hospitals, nor could we get any news of them. The town was still burning, and most of the houses were shelled, and had gaping windows and large shell holes, and the streets were littered with broken glass and bits of furniture; but every house flew a white flag of some sort, which had been no help to them, as the Germans said they had been fired on.

It was now getting very late, and we were told nothing could be done till the morning, so we gratefully accepted the offer of one bed from a kindly Belgian. We spent a sleepless night. The guns sounded so close and shook the house, and it was with great relief we saw the day break, and we started once more on our search, this time with more success, as we heard they were at a hospital at Marcinelle, five miles out of Charleroi.

We trudged there, leaving our luggage to follow, and found the matron and nurses in a semi-equipped hospital, desperately busy, and worn out with all the wounded who had been brought in a few days before from the battlefields nearby. The German wounded, slight cases and dying, had all been evacuated the day before we arrived, and we took this as a good sign that the Allies were near, especially as we heard the guns so close, but this was not the case, as the fighting was in reality getting further away.

We had plenty of work, though no fresh wounded. The hospital was originally intended for a civil hospital, but before it was finished the War broke out, and it had to be hastily equipped as a front line hospital, and in consequence was very badly supplied, and though we found beautiful electric appliances none of them were in working order, and all water had to be heated on a small stove, and many beds were without mattresses.

Our matron very soon left us to look up some other nurses in Brussels. She took the offer of a seat in a car going there, and that was the last we saw of her. M. had been left in charge.

The wounded were all French, and we found them extremely nice to look after. They were most grateful for all we did, and were much amused at the amount of cleaning and washing required by the English nurses, those of them that were well enough.

We had many exciting incidents and thrilling moments, especially when the German guards came round, as we never knew what they might be coming for. It was sometimes a search for a deserter, or to see that none of our patients were escaping. We never knew that it might not be to march us off, as rumour had it that we should be sent to Germany.

Life was one continual series of shocks; strange noises made us think we were being shelled; the electric light going out one night made us vividly imagine we were going to be blown up. Many of these scares ended in laughter, the Frenchmen ragging us for our *crises de nerfs*, but they did not quite like it themselves, lying helpless in bed.

We had a very busy time, but our patients were being gradually taken to concentration hospitals in Charleroi or to Germany as soon as they were fit to move, and we realized that our work before long would come to an end, and we began to wonder what was to become of us.

We had had no news for a long time, all means of communication having been stopped. We had no idea what had happened anywhere, or what the English nurses in and around Brussels were doing, so thought we must try and get news somehow from Brussels. We found a Belgian who had means of going there, and we asked him to put our case before the American Minister, who, we knew, had been asked to look after British interests. We wanted some money advanced on our cheques, as we had practically nothing left, and for help to return to Brussels or England.

The only answer we got to our appeal from the U.S.A. Legation was that we were on no account to go to Brussels; that they could give us no money, and that we were to ask the German Commandant in Charleroi to give us a pass to England or Maastricht via Germany.

This answer completely nonplussed us, as we did not want to advertise the fact that we were four English nurses alone in a hospital inside the German lines, especially as we had heard a rumour that some of the nurses who had been in and around Brussels, and who were supposed to have been sent to England by the Germans, were last heard of in Russia.

All these reports made us very unwilling to apply to the German Commandant for passes; so we decided to wait till our last wounded had been taken, hoping something might turn up.

Food was getting beautifully less and less, meat very occasional, and we lived for the most part on beans and potatoes and soup made of the same, flavoured with many fryings in the frying-pan. This, by the way, got me into severe trouble with the old cook, Mme. Gustave, because when I, on night duty, had to warm up our scanty meal, washed and scoured the frying-pan, I was told next day that I had completely ruined the soup and beans for ever, as we now would never get enough meat or onions to bring back the flavour of so many fryings. I never heard the end of that flavouring. The bread was black and sometimes so hard we couldn't eat it, and other times so doughy that when thrown at the wall it stuck. We very, very rarely, as a great treat, had a mouthful of white bread given us by some kindly Belgians.

By now our last man had been taken from us, and we felt that something must be done at once, so, much against our feelings, we bearded the German Commandant, who kept us waiting for a very long time, and we heard the orderly we had spoken to first, and who spoke English very well, telling the Commandant that we wanted passes to England via Germany or Maastricht. This he flatly refused, saying we must remain in Charleroi; nothing would move him, and so we returned crestfallen to Marcinelle.

Having now no work to do, we spent our days making definite plans to escape. Our only anxiety was to get away quickly before the Germans could get any inklings of our efforts. We had been cheerfully assured by the Belgians that, if they did get wind of them, we should undoubtedly be shot. This we were more than ready to believe, and many a time had visions of being lined up against the wall.

We managed at last to get a small sum of money lent us by our Belgian friends, and after many hours of talking we finally came to the conclusion that our best plan would be to accept the offer of a Belgian mine-owner, who offered us the use of his coal miners' ambulance to take us part of the way. We were advised to leave in the dead of night, and we arranged to dine with our friends the following night, telling the concierge at the hospital, whom we did not trust, that we should be spending the night with them. This we did, taking only a string bag with toothbrushes, etc., and dressed in mufti, with our Red Cross brassards sewn in the bottom of our skirts.

After a marvellous dinner to speed us on our way, the ambulance picked us up at 2 a.m. Two Belgian women accompanied us, as it was thought safer to go, in a party. We had many nerve-racking moments when we met sentries and guards, especially crossing the bridge out of Charleroi, the driver explaining that we were a miners' ambulance; after a few words he passed us on. In the early morning we arrived at Fleurus, where we took the tram to Namur, and where we arrived in a snowstorm, and then on to Liége, partly trams, partly trudging. These last two towns, as well as villages along the route, were in ruins.

We had palpitating moments when the sentries on the trains asked for our papers; all we had were 'laisser-passer' as far as Liége, which our friends had somehow managed, to wangle out of the Germans; stating we were Belgians going to see sick relations. These we showed, but fortunately we struck men who could not read French, but we murmured something which seemed to satisfy them. Before starting on our journey we had agreed that M. and I would do the talking, as the other two nurses did not speak French, and we naturally did not want it known we were English.

We spent the night at Liege, a room having been found for us, starting off the next morning early, feeling we had the most difficult part of the journey before us with the frontier to pass. We were thrust into a market cart going to Maastricht with vegetables. All this had been arranged for us by our Marcinelle friends, who had found out that Liége market-women carried on a trade taking refugees over the border.

Just before arriving at the frontier the owner of the cart said she could only risk three across, so that the other three must manage as best they could. A Belgian, one nurse and myself got out, and the cart drove on with the others. We walked a bit, then started to cross a field, and had just crawled under some barbed wire, and were beginning to feel we had escaped, as we thought it was the frontier, when, to our horror a loud voice called on us to halt, and we looked round and found a sentry covering us with his rifle. So we turned back, as we knew that if any of us tried to run for it one of us would, at least, be shot. The sentry then asked for our papers. This was a blow, as they only allowed us to Liége, and here we were well on the way to Maastricht. However, the man seemed only to worry about the German stamp, and, seeing that, told us we must go back to the road and in through the proper *douane*. This we knew we could never do. There wasn't a hope of our being allowed through, but we walked in that direction, and further on tried again to cross, where we came on another sentry. This time we did not try to pass him, but came back again to the road, making up our minds as we walked on to bluff the next one if we met with one.

We did meet with one and he was busy with a young Belgian who wanted to cross, so we hurriedly pushed our German stamp out for him to see and pressed some money into his hand and walked away as unconcernedly as we could, and again crawled under the barbed wire, expecting any moment that we might be shot at. However, this time we were safely across, but to our horror another sentry appeared, only he turned out to be a Dutchman who laughed at our scared faces.

By this time we were almost without feeling one way or another: the strain since leaving Marcinelle had been so great, as we were always terrified that our escape had been discovered and that we might be arrested at any moment.

We stumbled on to the market place at Maastricht, where we found the others, who had got safely over.

We had no sooner found rooms in a hotel when a message was brought us from a man who wished to see us, and it turned out that he was an Englishman over there on military business, and wanted some very important papers taken to a certain Government office in London. We were not too keen about it, but eventually agreed to take them.

The next day we took train to Flushing, and after some difficulty, owing to our having no papers on us; and only our Red Cross brassards stamped with the German stamps in Brussels, we got passages across to Folkestone, where the authorities found it difficult to believe our story, and where we were detained till they had made enquiries at the British Red Cross headquarters in London.

So this was the last of our troubles, and we were thankful to be back once more in England.

Our reward came in the shape of the Mons Star.

Miss Esmée Sartorius, after returning from Belgium, continued nursing for the Red Cross in England until 1918, when she was sent to a British Red Cross Hospital for Italians on Lake Garda.

THE GREAT RETREAT IN SERBIA IN 1915

M. I. Tatham

The field hospital had been busy for eight months trying to stem the awful tide of death which was sweeping over the country, and, together with other volunteer units, had pretty well succeeded. The typhus, sinister legacy of the Austrians when they evacuated Belgrade at Christmas 1914, had been carried to the farthest corner of Serbia by soldiers going home on leave – to the little farms and cottages where, under Turkish domination for hundreds of years, the ideas of hygiene and sanitation were practically undeveloped. With the result that nearly a third of the total population succumbed.

By October 1915 the typhus had been fought and beaten, and then the human enemy overwhelmed the country. The Bulgarians declared war early in October. Simultaneously, the Austrians attacked on the north, and the field hospital had to retreat with the Army. We were in the town of Kraguyevatz, arsenal of Serbia, which had suffered the bombardment of Austrian aeroplanes for weeks before the evacuation, and was left an open city. Having sent off every man who had sound feet, and left those who were unable to move in charge of American doctors (who were then neutrals) the trek southwards began. It was southwards at first, for we had been told that, if we could reach Monastir, there was the possibility of transport to Salonika. The single railway line from Belgrade to Salonika had been cut the first day after the declaration of war by the Bulgarians; and there was the life-line, as it were, severed, for on that railway line all the stores, men, and ammunition were transported.

We started off with bullock-wagons with as much of the hospital equipment as we could carry, and for three weeks we trekked south – a long, slow procession of springless carts, each drawn by oxen, moving deliberately at the rate of two miles an hour-day or night was all one. Several times the unit halted, hoping that the retreat was stayed, for all the telephone wires were down, and no one knew exactly what was happening. There we would rig up a dressing station, and dress the wounds of the men as they marched by, and there we were invariably sent to join the retreating mass again, as the sound of the guns drew nearer and the towns behind were occupied by the enemy. The stream of the refugees grew daily greater – mothers, children, bedding, pots and pans, food and fodder, all packed into the jolting wagons; wounded soldiers, exhausted, starving, hopeless men, and (after the first few days) leaden skies and pitiless rain, and the awful, clinging, squelching mud.

The roads were obliterated by the passage of big guns – those guns served by that wonderful 'Last Hope' of the Serbians, the old men, the Cheechas, the 'uncles,' who held the enemy for the priceless few days or even hours, and so saved the youth of the country. For every Serbian boy – every man-child over twelve – had to retreat. The Serbians had at last realized that the enemy were out to finish her as a nation, and the only way to save herself was to run away. And at first all those battalions of boys, gay with the coloured blankets they carried coiled across their backs, camping round the great camp-fires at night, were happy – until the days grew into weeks, and the rain fell and fell and there was no bread anywhere. But the rain, which churned up the mud, and soaked the ill-clad people, was called by the Serbians 'the little friend of Serbia,' for it held up the Austrian advance, and consequently saved practically the whole of Serbia's remaining Army.

We camped one night in an old monastery, deep in the heart, of the mountains, the residence of the Metropolitan, dating back to the thirteenth century. Here it was decided we might stop for a time, and the monks gave us their new school-house for a dressing station. We had high hopes of being able to remain the winter, so entirely ignorant were we all of the real conditions, and we actually did remain for a fortnight, amongst the most beautiful hills, clothed in their gorgeous autumn colours, for the country thereabouts was one glowing wonder of beech-woods. Until again came the order to evacuate, and in haste, for we were not on the beaten track, and were in danger of being cut off.

We had orders to go to a town called Rashka, and we trudged there in a jam of ox-wagons and soldiers, big guns and refugees, in the most appalling mud and pelting rain and quite unquenchable good spirits. Until we were nearly there, when one of our number was shot through the lungs – an accidental shot, fired by an irate farmer after some flying refugees who were stealing his horses. The injured girl was taken to a Serbian dressing station about eight miles back along the road, with two doctors and a nurse; after which the rest of us tramped unhappily on, knowing that they would inevitably be taken prisoners, which they were two days later. They were well treated, however, by the Austrians, and when the girl who had been shot was sufficiently recovered to undertake the journey, they were all passed through Vienna and Switzerland, and so home to England. But that is another story.

Meanwhile, the rest of us arrived, soaked to the skin, at Rashka, and were cheered by hot soup and cocoa, in the awful little hovel in which the earlier arrivals were housed. We slept that night under a roof, but infinitely preferred our previous nights under the stars, for about twenty of us were crammed into an indescribably filthy room, over a stable full of Army horses, and next to a larger room in which they were making shells! In those days there was no time for factories. Things were made anywhere. Most of the Army had no uniforms. The country had not recovered from the Balkan Wars of 1912 and 1913, and there was no help outside the country when all Europe was engaged in her own bitter struggle.

Then, two days before we would have reached Monastir, the Bulgarians took it. We had no choice now but to cross the mountains – the mountains of Albania and Montenegro, which we had been told were impassable for women in the winter. The three weeks' trek south had made us three weeks later in the beginning of the attempt, and the very first night we got to the narrow ways, the snow came. The roads were now too narrow for wagons, even though at the beginning they had been sawn laboriously in half, so that two wheels might pass where four would not, and the only means of transport were pack-mules or donkeys. These carried what food we had, and the blankets without which we would have perished. For many died on those pitiless mountains, and the snow fell and covered up their misery for ever.

Yet, with all hope gone, their country left behind, their women left behind (for when we reached the mountains the only women were the Red Cross units), starving, beaten, miserable, how wonderful were those soldiers! Peasants, driven from the soil which bred them, these men had no high education to tell them how to hold themselves in this disaster. But every Serbian is a poet: how else had they kept their souls free under 500 years of the Turkish yoke? And ever down those years, entirely through their songs and stories, and through their religion (for, to give the Turks their due, they did not interfere with that), they had kept alive and burning bright the flame of the belief that one day their country would be free. And in the year 1912 it came true, for the small Balkan states banded together and pushed the Turks out of their country – back to Constantinople. But for a pitiful short time, for in 1914 came Armageddon.

These retreating men, even if they won through wounds and starvation and exposure and hardship unspeakable, had only hope of exile. For us who were with them, the end of our journey was home. So it was easier to bear things cheerily, though hearts could hold no more of pity. Simple as children, with the unquestioning gratitude of such, no one ever saw them other than forbearing with each other, when men fell dead of starvation while waiting for the ration of bread and were laid by the roadside and left for the snow to shroud; no one ever saw them other than courteous to women. And when one remembers how the conditions of retreat can turn men into animals, when things are down to the bed-rock of primitive passions and desire for life, then it is a proud thing to remember also the high courage with which this people bore their disaster.

To add to the horrors of the retreat, there fell upon the mountains in that December one of the worst snowstorms for decades, and then was the pathway indeed bordered by death. We were crossing the higher passes, and only a 2-foot track wound upwards. On the right were snow-covered cliffs, on the left a sheer drop to the river 1,000 feet below. Two mules could not pass each other on that path, deep in snow or slippery with ice, and when a pack mule fell and died (brave little faithful beasts of burden) there they froze and the trail passed over them. The worst night of the storm we sheltered in an Albanian hut. The fire smouldered in the middle of the mud floor, the smoke escaping through a hole in the roof – and round the fire squatted the family – unto the third and fourth generation! Around them again, the refugees, soldiers, and nurses, and the livestock of the little farm. (My neighbour on one side was a warm and comfortable calf!) Everything that could be sheltered was sheltered; those that had no shelter remained out on the mountain and died. In the morning, the pack-mules, which were under the lee of the hut, were frozen stiff; and again the blankets and gear were reduced. At the last, when the mountains were crossed, and the weary, muddy miles to the sea lay before us, nothing remained to most of us but what we carried ourselves. But we had our lives, and many had left theirs on those cruel heights. But for those exiles, literally bereft of everything that made life worth living – family, home, country – what use, after all, seemed even that?

Those last days, towards the sea and the ultimate hope of rest, were even more dreadful than the rest. For now it was not the snow which covered death and corruption, but mud. It seemed as though there never had been and never again could be anything else than rain, rain, rain. And in all the world there is surely nothing more depressing than rain which falls soddenly on mud, and mud which receives all sullenly the rain.

Then, as the uttermost depths seemed reached, the skies of

the nearly-last night cleared. It was late, nearly midnight, but the little fishing village on the Adriatic coast had somehow to be reached by morning – for a ship was to be there to take us off. (It was torpedoed, and we sat on the shore, as it happened, for three more days.) And suddenly, out of the welter of misery, the road burst out on to the sea – lying dark and shining under stars; and perhaps the most vivid memory of all those weeks of adventure is the sight of her – sudden, beautiful, clean. 'Who hath desired the sea, the immense and contemptuous surges'; after all, what was starvation and death?

The Italian ship which was to meet us at San Giovanni di Medua was, as I said, torpedoed, along with every food-ship which was being sent by the Italian Government to meet the refugees. The little harbour was full of the sprouting masts and funnels of unhappy ships which had been sunk, a pitiful sight at the ebb of the tide. And the surrounding hills were quivering at night with the little fires of innumerable soldiers, who had survived starvation on the mountains only to meet it again on the shore. While overhead the Austrian aeroplanes circled, and dropped their bombs.

Then, after three days, a ship got through. Little as she was, she was able to take off all the Red Cross units. The soldiers had to set off again on that everlasting trek, down to Alassio and the further ports. No man of military age was allowed on board, but many refugees who were quite hopelessly smashed, and women of the coast as well, filled the little ship literally to overflowing. There was not room for all to lie down. Twice she was attacked, and tacking, swerving, zigzagging across the Adriatic, we came at last at dawn to Brindisi. And as the light grew, to port and starboard of the little ship, loomed in the mist first one and then another protecting form. And hearts at last believed in safety, for they were British gunboats. We landed at Brindisi, and had our first real meal for over two months.

Miss M. I. Tatham served (1915) with Stobart Field Hospital (Serbian Relief Unit), Kraguyevatz, Serbia. 1916–1917, Corsica, S.R.F. Unit. 1918, Scottish Women's Hospital, Royaumont and Villers-Côterets, France, until the Armistice.

THE STORY OF A W.A.A.C.

A. B. Baker

This is a girl's contribution. It has few thrills.

First, as to why I went: at home, my father was too old to go. Also, he had the farm. My sister and I have no brother. Many relatives lived near us. All had men-folk who could go to fight – and did. Uncles, cousins, and cousins' sweethearts were all in the trenches or in training for the trenches. Three or four times a week an aunt or a cousin would bring in her letter from the Front, and read it proudly. They were anxious of course. One cousin was killed. One uncle was wounded. But they were proud, above all. They said that Father and Mother were lucky, to have no one about whom they need be anxious. Yet even my young sister could see that they pitied us, too.

I do not know what Mother felt. I quickly discovered that Father did not count himself lucky. Their pity hurt his pride. With him, it was not only pride. The farm had been the family's for two hundred years. The country meant more to Father than flags waved and glib patriotic cant uttered. The old sorrow that he had no sons had become, I guessed, a new bitterness.

To be brief, there you have the reason why I joined the W.A.A.C.s. I joined first and told my home-folks afterwards. (I had to call myself twenty-one. They would allow no girl under twenty-one to go to France. I meant to go to France. But I was not nineteen.) Mother was upset. Father said little. Yet I knew that he was glad.

I was sent to camp near Oswestry. My humdrum training days are of no interest to Everyman. Here are two impressions which remain. How good it was to wear (unofficial) riding breeches! How queer in the small villages of the Glynceiriog Valley to feel myself the foreigner that I was! I had not left Britain: yet I was a stranger in a strange land, with strange speech in my ears.

We went to France, via Folkestone. Our billet was a big hotel by the sea. I liked its luxury. It had not occurred to me before that riches have their good side. I seemed to grow taller in those lofty rooms. The many bright lights and the soft, thick carpets made me feel quietly content. I think that I must have had the feeling which our cat has when it purrs on the rug before the fire at home.

Our draft was posted. The end of Folkestone was excitement and inoculation and leave.

That last English leave of mine was rather wonderful. Mother cried. Daddy took me down to the pig-sties and talked. He told me that he was proud of me. He knew, he said, that I should be good. He wanted me to be kind as well as good. The Tommies were heroes, but they were men, too. I had only to respect myself, and they would respect me, also.

I did not understand all this at the time. I did later.

Daddy scratched Dolly the sow's back while he talked. The old sow grunted. Months afterwards, those grunts came back to me. A Tommy who wasn't a hero, and not much of a man, tried to make love to me. He was the exception to Daddy's rule: I had respected myself, and this man wanted not to respect me. I got away from him, and ran. He ran after me. I could run better than he. Soon, he was grunting much like the old sow. No other Tommy behaved like this one. They did as Daddy said they would do.

The Channel brought my first real war thrill. Like the other girls, I was, I think, both sad and exalted at the thought of England behind, and of France in front. The zigzag course we kept was because of German submarines: with these our destroyer escorts were there to deal. Foolishly, I wished that the submarines might be there with which to be dealt. I had my wish. A torpedo missed us by a few feet. In a flash, I discovered that I did not want to die. Especially, I did not want to die in that horrible green water that was under and on every side of us.

The excitement died away. Our course grew less erratic. Our escorts became sedate once more. I had never heard bells more cheerful than those which rang below-deck as we entered harbour at last!

I had got to France, but I had not got to the War. I was never very near the line. The devilish guns rumbled day and night. By day, the click-clacking of my typewriter keys drowned the rumbling of the guns. In that, I see now, lay a parable. I saw only unheroic monotony, then. By night, the rumbling grew louder and seemed nearer. Wakeful, I would make impossible plans to get hold of a Tommy's uniform, in it to break camp and to make my way to the line.

There I was to be a second Lady of the Lamp, or something equally ridiculous. It was all very schoolgirlish and absurd, I have no doubt. But, then, I was absurd, and I had been a schoolgirl not so very long before.

I did not get to the War. But twice the War got to me. On each occasion it was at Étaples in 1918. Let me tell of one of the two.

The bridge at Étaples meant much to the Allies: in consequence, the enemy made incessant attacks upon it from the air. Near it, in the sunlight of a spring day, I saw half a company of men blown to pieces by bombs. Some of the latter fell into the adjoining cemetery. Coffins and dead men were blown from their graves. Into those graves limbs of living men and fragments of shattered dead men were flung.

Our N.C.O. shouted: 'Quick, girls, quick! The dugouts.' In the shelter and comparative safety of one of them, I found myself laughing hysterically, and crying: 'The quick and the dead; the quick and the dead.'

I remember that I was very sick, I said my prayers; I thought of Mother. I wished that I were home.

A few days later I had a letter from our curate. In it he talked about war as noble discipline. He said it purged men of selfishness, and by its pity and terror brought men nearer to God. I felt sick for a second time. He put with his letter a printed Prayer for Victory, and told me to say it every night. I remembered that my prayer in the dug-out had been just this, said over and over again: 'O God, stop this war; stop it, and let me go home.' At home the curate had been rather a hero of mine. He wasn't my hero any more.

Soon after this my chum and I thought that we would go to the cinema. In the town we came upon a queue of Tommies.

One of them was shouting out: 'This way for the one-an'-thruppennies.' We tacked ourselves to the end of the queue. The Tommies tittered. For some reason we seemed to amuse them very much. Then one rather nice boy came to us, and said: 'Missies, this performance is for men only.' He blushed as he said it. We did not understand, but we went away.

Afterwards, when we did understand, I wondered what the curate would have said about that queue.

In the 'office' I had, as part of my work, to translate into English letters written in French. (It was my knowledge of colloquial French, rather than my white lies as to my age, which had got me to France.) A number of these were from the parents of French girls who were with child. At first, this seemed very terrible to me. It shocked me most that my superiors should be shocked so little. 'Another Mamzelle like it,' one would say. 'Damned little fool!' a second would answer. That was all. They looked upon it as natural and normal, a necessary nuisance of war. They called it a 'beastly bother' when I was about. They used stronger terms when they thought I was out of hearing. Never once did I hear an expression of pity or sorrow or indignation.

Sometimes, one of these girls would come to the office, alone or with her parents. One was Hélène. She came alone, at midday, when I was in sole charge. She was frantic. She said that her father would kill her: she said that she would kill herself. She implored me to help her find the man. She would kill him when she had found him, if he would not marry her. Suddenly her rage left her. She sobbed like a child. She refused to tell me anything but her Christian name, and went away. For weeks the sound of her sobbing haunted me. I never knew what became of her.

There was, too, the old grandmother of another girl. Her back was bent, but not her spirit. She cursed me; she cursed the Colonel; she cursed the British Army; she cursed England and all the English. She went away, cursing. I sat shivering and ashamed.

In the beginning I condemned these girls and their men in

my heart. Later, I learned not to judge. I myself became very friendly with a young sergeant named John. He had been in France for over three years and had been several times wounded. Gas and shrapnel had left him fit only for a job at the Base. When the big German advance began in March, 1918, however, he was put on draft for the trenches. He had to report at ten o'clock. At seven o'clock he asked me to go for a walk with him, as I had done several times before. We went into the woods. The stars were clear. The night was very beautiful. There were rustlings at our feet, and twitterings over our heads. The guns rumbled in the north, and the ground shook slightly beneath us as he talked of his Surrey home and the woods near it, which he loved. He said that he was afraid – more afraid than he had ever been in his life. He was sure that this time he was going to 'collect something worse than a packet.' He wanted to know what I believed about death. I forget what I told him. He made me promise to write to his mother if anything happened to him. When I promised he said that I was a 'dear kid.' I was very near to crying. He asked me if he could kiss me. I said, 'Yes.' He kissed me many times, and held me very tight. He held me so tight that he hurt me and frightened me. His whole body was shaking. I felt for him as I had never felt for any man before. I know now that it wasn't love. It was just the need to comfort him a little. I am an emotional girl. I might have forgotten what Daddy had told me by the pigsties, if John had not been so decent. Before he need have done, he took me back into the town, saying: 'This won't do. You shouldn't get so sorry for a chap. It's risky for you. You're only a kid.'

It was not till later that I realized how decent John had been. Yet Daddy, I know, would have called him 'common' and 'not my sort.' He was killed before March was out.

It was in April that my own great grief came to me. A telegram was sent, telling me that my Mother was very ill. They gave me leave, and I went home. When I got there, Mother had been dead six hours. Influenza had killed her in three days, as it had killed many thousands more. The sun shone when they buried her. The cherry trees were white. 'It is God's will; His will be done; for He is good,' the Vicar said. I thought of the men blown into pieces at Étaples, and of the corpses blown from their graves. I thought of John, dead near Arras, and of Mother dead in our quiet churchyard. I thought of Daddy, who had cried because Mother was dead, and of Hélène, who had cried because her unborn child was alive. It set me wondering whether the Vicar knew any more of God than the Curate did of war.

My leave ended, and I went back to France. One of the first letters I received was from a boy friend of mine. He was a Quaker, and he had written his letter from prison. He had been put in prison because he had shown in times of war that he had meant what he had said in times of peace. Till then I had abominated his opinions. At least, I thought I had. Yet – his letter was a queerly happy letter. He said that, thinking of France and the Tommies there, he had been miserable until they had put him in prison. He said that he wasn't miserable any more. He was sure that he was doing his bit for England.

I read that letter, written on blue prison paper, many times. I had begun to doubt whether there was any God, or, if there was a God, whether He was good. In some way and for some reason that letter made me doubt my doubts. I wondered what Sergeant John would have thought of it.

The spring and the summer went on. The Germans began to go back. The Allies began to go forward and to take prisoners. Part of my work had to do with prisoners quartered in a camp near to our own. Those Germans were friendly men. They were clever with their hands, and would give me little carvings which they had made. One of them had a look of Father about him. He talked a little like Father, too. He said that he was sure that I was as good as I was kind. (A few packets of cigarettes quickly made one a paragon of kindness in the eyes of prisoners of war.) I found it strange that he should seem so genuinely concerned for me.

These German prisoners would sing in the evenings. They would often sing hymns. Many of these hymns were the old, familiar hymns which, or the tunes of which, I had sung in church at home. They had rich voices. They put much feeling into their singing.

It must have been at about this time that I found I could say my prayers again. Or, rather, not my prayers, but this one prayer: 'O God, stop this war; stop it and set all us poor prisoners free.' That seemed to cover the Tommies and me, the German prisoners and my friend in prison in England.

The day of Armistice came, and the War stopped. I remember that I drank four glasses of champagne, and afterwards had a very bad headache. Later I felt ashamed.

Demobbed, I went home. There they wanted to treat me as a sort of heroine. Their talk hurt me, even Daddy's. They praised me for all the wrong things. When I tried to tell them what the War had taught me; they were hurt in their turn. When I went to visit my friend, not yet released from prison, they were angry. When he and I – but that is another story.

The War Office sent me two medals after many months.

Mrs. A. B. Baker joined the W.A.A.C. in mid-1917; trained at Kimmel Park, Oswestry, etc.; went to France late 1917, Étaples, Rouen, Dieppe; demobilized 1919.

WAR AT SEA

J. Willey

When war threatened in 1914 I was stationed in the East Indies on board H.M.S. *Fox*. She was an old cruiser and due for the scrap-heap. We were to return to England in August, 1914, but on July 27th, being on that date in Muscat taking in coal, orders were received that caused us to leave that afternoon for an unknown destination.

We began to prepare for war immediately we got our orders for sea. We were taking in coal on one side of the ship, and changing our colour from white to grey on the other. Once we were at sea, we took down all awnings and rolled them up, placing them – along with our bedding – around the most vulnerable parts of the ship. Splinter nets were rigged over each battery of guns, and rails cleared away, and rigging 'snaked' down. We kept station at our guns, torpedo tubes and searchlights at night. We had almost settled down to war routine before war began – at least we thought we had.

With the exception of preparation for war, our trip was uneventful, and Wednesday, August 5th, we entered Colombo. At 11 a.m., our skipper came off from shore and the crew were informed that War was declared.

We now put all our boats ashore, excepting two cutters, and, to reduce our silhouette, our ventilating cowls were taken down and dumped. Stores were taken in, and off to sea we went. Our job was hunting down German merchant-men, putting a prize crew on board and sending them back to Colombo for internment.

At this time I had just turned twenty-one and felt jubilant at the outbreak of war. It was to last about six months, and such was our confidence, we thought it was to be more or less a picnic. Besides, we might possibly get a medal. The men either due, or approaching their time, for pension were not by any means pleased. They had cause for displeasure. War doesn't choose her victims, and some of these chaps went under during the conflict, and instead of a middle age of comparative ease, it meant hardship, suffering, and death.

Our first real thrill came on the night of August 11th. War had been declared with Austria, and during the night we had stopped a big Austrian liner for inquiries. We were at action stations – I was at a searchlight – and prepared for any emergency. Our position at first was exactly abreast of the Austrian, and about 300 yards distant. Whilst signals were exchanged we had drifted to a position at right angles to the liner and lay across her path. Suddenly we noticed her lights getting nearer and nearer still.

At my position on the after shelter deck I could observe everything. It soon dawned on me that the liner was going to ram us. I wondered why the order was not given to open fire. Our engines began to throb. I could feel the ship vibrating, and slowly we went astern. But only just in time, for as the liner passed us one could have tossed a biscuit on board. It turned out that we could not seize her. She had twenty-four hours to get clear after the declaration of war, but for a moment or two I thought my time had come.

War was now beginning to be irksome, and the novelty wearing off. Hatches were battened down most of the time – it was the monsoon season – but water found its way, just the same, into our quarters. The air was foul, and hardly breathable. On deck we did only necessary work by day. At night we closed up at action stations and slept in turns at the rear of the guns.

In September, we escorted three troopships to Mombasa – the first troops to land in East Africa. Passing down the harbour at Kilindine on our way back to Bombay, we saw the *Pelorus* lying calmly at anchor, ignorant of her fate. She swung with the tide as we passed and narrowly escaped hitting us.

Our next job was to help to escort the Indian Expeditionary Force across the Indian Ocean. There were about fifty merchant ships in the convoy, and six or seven warships as an escort. They were a fine sight, and our hardest job now was 'gingering' up stragglers.

Three days out from Bombay we were ordered back to East Africa. The *Königsberg* was getting active and had sunk the *Pelorus* at Zanzibar with heavy loss of life. We began to feel the monsoon now, and I should think a quarter of the crew were down with fever.

Once on the African coast, we began a hunt for the *Königsberg*. We were informed on one occasion that we should probably meet her the following day. This was somewhere north of Madagascar. I'm pleased to say we did not meet her. Our guns were obsolete, and she was faster and could easily out-range us. Some of us were even disappointed over this, but a watery grave at the very least would have been our fate, without a shadow of doubt. The *Königsberg*, when the chase got too hot for her – there were five warships on the coast looking for her hiding place – finally retired up the Refugi River.

About this time fighting was going on thirty miles distant from Mombasa. Our assistance was required for the transport of wounded, and a difficult job it was. They had first to be carried through the bush to our cutters, and then several miles out to sea, where, on arriving at the ship, they were hoisted inboard. We landed them at Mombasa.

The lack of nourishment began to make itself felt, and a number of us were sent to hospital at Mombasa suffering from beriberi. After three years' scouring the Red Sea, Persian Gulf, and the Indian Ocean, this was a heaven of delight for me. Good food, and plenty of it, and the kindnesses of the nurses I will never forget. All good things come to an end, and after a spell at Nairobi I left for England.

My next ship was a destroyer – H.M.S. *Melpomene*, and based at Harwich.

Our job was patrolling, submarine-chasing, escorting ships to and from Holland, acting as a screen in co-operation with the ships further north: 1915 for us was dull and monotonous. The only time we fired a gun was to sink a mine.

On Easter Monday, 1916, we, and three more destroyers from Harwich, were protecting a monitor on the Belgian coast, off Zeebrugge. A large number of trawler mine-sweepers, and small motor submarine-chasers were in the vicinity as well. It was my afternoon watch on the paravanes (an anti-submarine device), and my mate and I were walking up and down – probably talking of our next leave – when the alarm bells sounded, and the crew ran to action stations. We quickly rendered our paravanes safe, and ran to our torpedo-tubes, already trained upon the beam. We wondered at first what the 'spasm' was. A tall column of water just astern of us, soon enlightened us. We were under fire! This would be about three o'clock in the afternoon, and the sea as calm as the table I write on. The sun was bright and the weather warm. In short, it was an ideal spring day.

Zeebrugge lay several miles off, but was clearly visible; the first sausage balloon that I saw used in the War hovered above the town and 'ranged' us. Three black streaks – which we knew to be German destroyers – steamed a steady course up and down outside the town. They were the decoys. We were to provide the sport, although at the time this did not occur to us.

Owing to the restricted area – due to the minefields thereabouts – the only tactics we could adopt were to put our helm hard over and steam in a circle. There were the four of us – the monitor was lying-off, practically motionless, firing very slowly – going around hell-for-leather, about a ship's length separating us, and firing away steady at the three Germans.

The chaps at the guns were busy, and not having too bad a time. Anyway they had no time to philosophize on the matter. I was sitting astride a torpedo-tube, awaiting any orders that might come through. In the meantime, I watched the fight. The other chaps near me did not seem the least excited, but a feeling, a gentle elated sort of feeling pervaded us.

The shells were falling around us pretty thickly, and throwing up great dark columns of water. We had the fire of the Zeebrugge forts and the three destroyers concentrated on us. It occurred to me that their marksmanship was rather bad, or else a destroyer was a very difficult thing to hit. Our three 4-in. guns were going at it steadily, I cannot say if we registered any hits. There were no visible effects, anyway.

After about half-an-hour of this sort of thing, as, in our turn, we came broadside on to the Germans – the ship having a list of about 25 degrees through the helm being nearly hard over – something was evidently wrong below. We heard nothing on deck, although we were immediately above the engine-room. The first sign was that of a stoker coming up from the engine-room hatchway in very quick time. He shouted to us that we had been torpedoed. I jumped down from the tube I was sitting on, and looked through the engine-room fanlight. The sea was pouring in through a great hole in the side. Here I had better explain that a destroyer is only a very frail shell, split by bulkheads into watertight compartments. The engine-room is the largest by far of these compartments.

The order was given to 'out collision mat' to attempt to stem the flow of water. We had ceased fire in the meantime. The Germans, for some unknown reason, had done the same. By the time the mat was in position the engine-room was flooded completely, and we were only a foot out of water at the stern.

The *Medina* and the *Milne* now came to our assistance – one on either side of us – and after we were secured with wires, they began to tow us out of danger. The *Medina* also was running out of ammunition, and we passed her some of ours.

The three ships, lying together as they were, must have presented a splendid target to the enemy. They took advantage of it and opened fire again. We were stem on to them and could only use our after-guns – that is, the one gun on each ship. The Medina decided to get away from us and, without waiting to cast off the wires, she went full steam ahead – carrying away the ropes.

The *Medina* and the *Medusa* carried on the previous manoeuvre of steaming around in a circle and drew the fire away from us and the *Milne*. Tied together as we were we still fired our after-guns, the remainder of our crew were employed shoring bulk-heads and watching the fight.

Between 5 and 6 that evening we got away, and met a flotilla of boats coming up from Dover. We reached Dunkirk next morning and were docked right away. A hole about 4 feet long and 18 inches wide had been torn in our port side. The shell had caught us as we listed over in our turning. The curious thing is that the shell did not explode, and probably is still in possession of our captain.

It took a week at Dunkirk to patch us up, but what a week it was! Every morning, just after daylight, we got an air-raid. A merchant ship in the next dock to us showed some of the results of these raids. A bomb had dropped into one of her holds and knocked the bottom out of her.

When we were fit for sea a tugboat towed us to Portsmouth to be overhauled. We were there when Jutland was fought and our division of destroyers took part in it. The boat that replaced us – the *Termagant*, I think it was, was sunk. This, I suppose, is the luck of war, but it's not much use to the poor fellows who get it in the neck.

Later on, in the year 1916, about August or September, we were ordered to sea suddenly. We had an idea something was in the wind, rumour was always rampant, and 'spasms' more than frequent, so that we were more or less sceptical in our outlook. I had the middle watch below and was trying to get what rest I could, stretched on a wooden locker – in full kit of course.

The alarm bells sounded about 1.30 a.m., and I hurried aft to the tubes. They were trained on the beam, and I placed myself astride one as usual. We were somewhere off the Dutch coast, and a lightship flashed her warning light at intervals. The night was fine, but about as dark as it's possible to be. These, briefly, were the conditions. We were steaming full speed and had hardly got to action stations before fire was opened. We dared not switch on our searchlights; the Germans were in the same predicament. Our only guide for point of aim was an occasional flame from one of their funnels or the blast from their guns.

If there are human beings who exist that want to see hell realistically staged in this world I can recommend an action on a destroyer on such a night as this. The guns crews were again lucky in being occupied with their tasks.

The noise of battle that one hears and reads about was absent. The guns, of course, kicked up a row, and there was the throb of the engines and the swish of the water, and an occasional sea spent itself along the deck. These noises we were more or less used to, and regarded as normal, so when I say the silence seemed uncanny, I will not be misunderstood.

The deck of a destroyer is open – no shelter exists. Every time the guns fired it seemed to me like sheet lightning gone mad. The glare was blinding. All this time the lightship lay between us and the Germans, and continued doing her work as if nothing were happening. We found afterwards it was the Maas Lightship. During the action my mind kept turning to the plight of the Dutchmen on board that lightship. I wondered what they thought of the business that night.

Whilst the fight was still in progress we got news that we had been hit forward, and several wounded. Shortly afterwards we lost sight of the Germans and they disappeared into the night. After the 'cease-fire' had been given we found a shell had gone through our wireless office and charthouse, and three men badly hit about. I said men. One was a boy of seventeen who had a big piece of steel in the middle of his back. He died next morning, poor kid. One of the other cases was a bit hard too. Goldspink, a torpedoman, had joined us the previous week, and, for night action-stations, was posted at the bridge searchlight. Because he had nothing to do up there, he went down to the forecastle gun and helped to pass up ammunition. He got hit on the head and thigh, and was carried out of the ship in a stretcher a week after he joined us, almost to the minute.

The events of this night, although we were the only ship hit – stand out in my memory. I cannot easily explain why, but it appeared to me at the time as peculiarly awe-inspiring and terror-striking. I do not admit fear; we got inured to that sort of feeling – at least, I did, and my outlook was decidedly fatalistic.

To illustrate how easily ships were sunk, I'll give the following instance. We were a large convoy bound for Holland. It was August 15th, 1918, and our pay-day – that's why I remember the day so accurately. The whole flotilla was out escorting them. The weather was fine and the sea like a millpond. About 11.30 a.m. I thought to go in for my dinner, as I was due on watch at noon. I casually looked across to the destroyers on the other side of the merchantmen and saw a cloud of water ascend in the air near a destroyer; shortly afterwards, only a few minutes, her bow went up in the air, and she slid, stern first, under the water. Before she sank the Scots had gone alongside and taken off survivors. Suddenly she began to settle down, and in about ten minutes she had gone. The two ships were hit and sunk in a quarter of an hour. The *Ullswater* was the name of the first one hit.

The marvel of it was that no one seemed disturbed or upset. We were two ships short, that's all. The remainder of us carried on, the merchantmen on a steady course, and us with our zigzagging. Although I witnessed in broad daylight the sinking of these ships, at a distance of not more than two miles away, I did not know then, nor do I know now, what it was that sunk them, whether mine or torpedo. Such is modern war at sea.

J. Willey's war service was prefaced by 2¹/₂ years in the Persian Gulf under semi-active service conditions in H.M.S. Fox. *During the first few months of war this ship patrolled trade routes, captured merchant vessels, convoyed troops to British East Africa, and the Indian Expeditionary Force half-way across the Indian Ocean. After a period on East Coast of Africa was sent to hospital (Mombasa), with beriberi. Invalided to England about the beginning of February 1915. After a period at the Torpedo School, Devonport, sent to H.M.S.* Melpomene, *and stationed at Harwich, under Commodore Tyrwhitt. Remained in the* Melpomene *until January 1917. Then served until the end of the War in H.M.S.* Satyr, *patrolling, mine-sinking, etc.*

ZEEBRUGGE

W. Wainwright

The early days of February 1918 found me a minute cog in the machinery of the greatest Armada known, the Grand Fleet – a seaman on board the Superb, stationed in the melancholy regions of Scapa Flow.

One evening, in the midst of our usual festivities, namely, looking mournful at each other, Nemesis in the shape of a large overfed 'crusher' (ship's police) overtook me, and I was informed that a large piece of 'Gold Braid' living an exclusive life at the far end of the ship had become interested in me, and would I favour him with an interview?

I followed the pompous 'body-snatcher,' along brightly lit passages, feeling dismayed, but on reaching the Commander's cabin all fears were dispelled, as I was cordially invited to enter and found myself in a circle consisting of the Commander, Secretary, Master-at-Arms, and five able seamen, all wearing a vacant expression.

With my arrival a full quota appeared to be made up, as the Commander, rising to his feet and producing a paper, informed us that the Commander-in-Chief had sent him a signal for six seamen, for special service.

He went on to say that, not knowing himself what the stunt was, he could not give the least idea, except that it was dangerous work, and nine out of ten chances that we should 'snuff it,' and we should be under twenty-three, single, physically fit, and able to use a revolver and oar.

From these conditions it appeared to us as though the result of the War rested on us, and, needless to recount; oil was poured on troubled waters with phrases of honour, and glory. After letting his words sink in he gazed at the condemned 'six' and stated that if any did not want to volunteer nothing would be said, and the man could just carry on.

However, no one moved, and no doubt, thinking I looked the silliest pigeon there, the Commander asked if I would go.

Having served a miserable six months in that, ship, and my third year in that dismal theatre of war, I informed him promptly that I would be glad of it. To get away from his tender care had been a cherished ambition of mine. Needless to say, the remaining five jumped at the idea, and we were beamed on with pride, solemnly shaken by the hand, and called heroes, and bidden to depart to our habitation and say nothing, but by that time all the ship was seething with excitement as to what was going to happen, and we found ourselves the centre of an admiring crowd all agog with excitement.

I never knew I was so popular; even old sailors of twenty-one and abouts who had hitherto passed me by with disdain (I was only nineteen), gave me fatherly advice. I retired happy.

The glamour had not worn off the next morning, and vainly I tried to concentrate on the day's work, that bugbear of civilization known as 'Saturday's routine,' a mix-up of salt water, sand, and scrubbers, and I was wandering round in a state of oblivion when an autocratic personage in the shape of the Captain's Messenger came with the startling news that the 'old man' had expressed a desire to see us immediately. My scrubber was dropped and I was on my way to his cabin before he had finished his message.

Here, again; we were royally received with more handshakes and words of praise, and our tender young ears must have burnt, but by far the best news was that we would work no more in that ship, but confine our energy to physical training and revolver exercise.

Monday morning saw us step off in a fine style, in athletical garb, led by a high-stepping physical training instructor and watched by an admiring, envious and cynical crowd, and we were kept at it all the afternoon, our only respite being the ju-jitsu lesson, and later we landed for revolver practice, wandering round on a deserted island and practising drawing and shooting. I think it was a good job at first that the island was deserted.

As the days went on we grew into whalebone and whipcord, thanks to the slave-driver who had us in his care, and we understood the whys and wherefores of revolvers and the art of firing, the days passing all too quickly.

Again it was a Friday and we were beginning to think the affair was a fiasco, when the bombshell burst, and our instructions were to the effect that we were to leave the ship at 5 a.m. the following day and report on board H.M.S. *Hindustan* at Chatham the following Friday, thus giving us a few days' leave to say farewell to all relatives and any other affair before being killed.

That journey south appeared the longest I had ever done. In fact, it took thirty-six hours before I arrived at the home station, but all was forgotten in the reunions, which might have been for me, as they were for many, the last.

But, like all good things, they soon came to an end and I took my leave of all with an uneasy feeling, wondering if I should ever come back. But at nineteen cares are light, and I slept soundly in the train that was taking me to this new adventure.

Holborn Station presented a curious spectacle the following morning; groups of seamen could be seen talking with suppressed excitement and looking questioningly at any seaman wearing the ribbon of some ship in the Grand Fleet.

The Chatham train drew all these adventurers into its compartments, and here the question, 'Are you in this stunt and what is it going to be?' was freely debated, but no one could throw any light on the subject, and whoever had organized the whole business had preserved its secrecy in no uncertain fashion.

A couple of hours later brought us to Chatham, and, knowing the dinner that would await us, we decided to join the ship with a good meal stowed away, so dined in town before attempting the miserable walk to the dockyard. Our knowledge stood us in good stead, as, once aboard the *Hindustan*, the usual emergency dinner was served, bully beef, bread and pickles, but, for once, 'sailors didn't care,' and the natural excitement and high spirits took the edge off everybody's appetite.

The remainder of the afternoon was spent in recovering our belongings, which had been dispatched from Thurso the week previous; and getting to know the lay of the ship and making acquaintances. In the evening a strong contingent made their way to the barrack canteen in such a jovial mood that the clash that came with the men of the barracks later was inevitable (it's a curious trait with a seaman, but he'd fight his own brother just for the sake of being antagonistic if the brother belonged to a different depot or fleet), and it was only after the guard had been turned out and the dockyard police reinforced that peace was obtained.

During the next few days we were formed into companies, platoons, and sections, introduced to our leaders and put through our paces on St. Mary's Island both day and night, and then handed over to the instructors of the 5th and 6th Middlesex Regt. to be polished off and to be instructed in the fine arts of land warfare.

The weeks that passed then were one mass of bayonet drill, pointing and parrying, blob sticks, bombs, trench mortars, gas, night attacks, final assaults, and musketry, and we were gradually becoming excellent soldiers.

A slight change in the run of things found our section transferred into a 3-inch Stokes trench-mortar battery, and we were armed with a combination of nautical weapons, the pistol and cutlass (the latter article is only useful for deck cricket, when three of them make good wickets), and our training regarding the wielding of this barbarous weapon began again.

The whole of this period spent in training was glorious, the new surroundings and atmosphere, the unfamiliar work and the keenness to become proficient at it, and the high spirits between officers and men combined to make the work a most pleasing task, and, although our leave was stopped, we found ways and means of having a run ashore, a proceeding which was given the blind eye by our officers. The worst punishment a man could be threatened with was expulsion from the party. 'The Mecca' of our pilgrimage was gradually growing nearer, but we were still in the dark regarding the actual intention of all this strenuous training.

Our training was now nearing completion, and our massed attacks were taking on a sameness which pointed at some concerted item we were rehearsing for, and many inventions were tried, with a view to saving as many lives as possible, and we had practically reached the acme of perfection and were in danger of going stale.

One morning, about this period, our usual route was changed, and we found ourselves inside the Royal Marine Barracks, and, after being thumped, patted and pushed round by a rotund sergeant-major, we emerged into fresh air, in a dazed state, and a suit of khaki.

There was another trial and tribulation put upon us, the difference between our nautical garb and this warrior's suit being as wide as the Poles, and the weather being warm for the time of the year, there was a distinct, subdued and muffled up feeling amongst our detachment, but in a day or so all strangeness wore away, and the mess-deck mirrors did a roaring trade. It had now reached the beginning of April and we had finally finished our training with the Army, when we got the order to get 'under way' and proceed to a certain rendezvous, and accordingly the same evening found us in a desolate waste of water known as the Swim just off Sheerness.

A couple more days aboard the *Hindustan* and orders were issued that we should embark in that curious stranger that had just arrived, an obsolete cruiser with a strange Noah's Ark look about her, the *Vindictive*, and we were conveyed to her by the Liverpool ferry-boats *Iris* and *Daffodil*. Our going aboard of her synchronized with the arrival of three detachments of Marines, and the living accommodation was taxed to its utmost.

The ship itself was an exceedingly unique specimen of warship, there being no comparison to her former days when she had been a pride to all who sailed in her. She had been stripped bare of everything bar the essential parts, her mainmast having gone and her foremast cut short above the fighting top. Along her portside ran an immense wooden chafing band reinforced with huge hazelwood fenders and on the port quarter a part of the main-mast had been cemented to the deck to enable her to lay alongside any wall without swinging out, head on stem.

Covering her port battery ran a false deck lined with sandbags, and towering above this deck was an array of improvised gangways, sixteen in all, flanked by two huge metal huts housing the foremost and aftermost flame throwers. At the break of the fo'c'sle and the quarter-deck were two grapnels fitted to wire pennants and leading respectively to the foremost and after-capstans. Here fore and after guns had been replaced by 7.5' howitzers and midships abaft the after funnel was an 11-inch howitzer, the port battery had been replaced with 2-pound pom-poms, with the exception of the foremost and after 6-mch gun, whilst two pom-poms adorned the fighting-top.

There is no denying it she was ugly, as she lay there, a veritable floating fortress, a death-trap fitted with all the ingenious contrivances of war that human brain could think of, but we took unholy pride and a fiendish delight in her, and if it were possible for men to love a ship, we loved her.

Now came the awakening: the platoons were gathered together under their commanders, who, fortified with models and aerial photos, explained to us our objective – we were to block the entrance of the Bruges canal at Zeebrugge and Ostend and our objective was to land and obtain possession of the Mole, to enable the blockships (*Iphegenia*, *Intrepid*, and *Thetis*) to get into position for sinking, and to cause a diversion to facilitate that project.

The magnitude of the scheme overwhelmed us, the sheer audacity of tackling a place like Zeebrugge under the muzzles of the world-famed Blankenberghe Battery, where a change in the wind or tide at the critical moment would undoubtedly result in the total loss of the expedition. Viewing the whole outlook in cold daylight the large element of luck that must accompany us for the scheme to be successful was evident, also the knowledge that such an undertaking was impossible without a huge loss of life, but the last thought lay the lightest, our chief worry being that the stunt might end in hot air and all of us be sent back to the Fleet. However, no time was wasted, for on April 11th we weighed anchor and proceeded out to sea in company with other ships of the expedition.

Our send-off lacked nothing in heartiness as the crew of the *Hindustan* cheered us on our way, and what with our responding cheers, the huge harbour sounded for all the world like some cup-tie arena; the momentary sadness that inevitably follows these partings (for your bluejacket is not totally callous) soon gave way to the thoughts that we were at last on the way for our objective.

The land left behind, our fleet took up some semblance of order, but proper order among such a strange assortment of craft was impossible. In the centre steamed the *Vindictive* with the *Iris* and *Daffodil* in tow, astern of these came the *Thetis*, *Intrepid*, *Iphegenia*, *Sirius*, and *Brilliant*, whilst surrounding these disreputable looking ships were destroyers, motor-launches, C.M.B.s, and a sturdy little picket boat could be seen towing a submarine, whilst far away monitors were taking up position to cover the attack.

As the final hour approached, the finishing touches were put to a well-organized ship, ammunition was fused and placed in readiness, hoses run out and all preparations made prior to going into action.

The night was dark, and far away could be seen the British aircraft making a bombing attack on Zeebrugge, and further still the dull red flashes of the artillery in Flanders. The ship slowed down and stopped whilst the heads of departments conferred, until slowly the whole significance dawned on the troops; the wind had changed and we could not carry out our plans, and it was a disappointed ship that sailed for England that night.

The following day another attempt was made, but this again was unsuccessful, as the wind, this time in the right direction, was too fresh and made it impossible for the smaller craft to proceed, and these were needed to ensure the success of the operation.

Another shift was our portion, for on account of the. congestion of the living accommodation, the battleship *Dominion* was sent out to act as an overflow ship, and we duly found ourselves aboard her. The days were spent now in keeping fit, but I think most of the time was spent in sleep and, on the whole, we had a fairly easy time.

The time was approaching when, if the next attempt failed, the whole stunt was likely to be postponed, as after this period the necessary flood tides would not occur at the times required. April was nearing its end when we embarked on the *Vindictive* again. This was on the morning of Monday, April 22nd, and once all the troops were assembled we lost no time in breaking our moorings, taking the *Iris* and *Daffodil* in tow, and proceeding to sea in the exact formation of the previous attempts.

The trip across the Channel was uneventful and most of the time was passed with impromptu concerts and dances and I doubt if any there thought of the serious mission of this strangely assorted fleet. After supper had been served, practically everybody snatched an hour or two's sleep before the fateful zero hour; how anyone could sleep with an adventure like the one before us speaks volumes for the mental and physical fitness of the party. Our slumbers were disturbed by a bugle call, and a ration of hot chicken-broth was served out, supplemented by a ration of grog, the latter ration being left practically untouched, it being thought that a clear head and steady eye were more beneficial. Word was passed round then, and the men assembled at their stations for the attack as leisurely as if going to a football-match.

A cheerless scene greeted one's arrival on the upper deck. It was a black night, everything was wrapped in fog, while behind, the ships were unnaturally quiet, the only sounds being those of the engine going slow, the lap of the water against the ship's sides and the subdued murmur from the bridge, with now and again the rattle of the helm; nothing could be seen.

Suddenly the quietness of the night was shattered by a single rifle-shot; this was followed almost immediately by a dull red flash over the fo'c'sle and the angry crack of a bursting shell, a few yells and an isolated call of 'Mother.' The game was on, and Jerry had drawn first blood.

The wind had now changed and was blowing the smoke screen and artificial fog back over us, leaving us the target for the shore batteries, but ahead of us loomed the Mole, 200 yards away, and for this we raced.

Following the burst of the first shell the night had turned into day by searchlights and star-shells, and all the venom and hatred of the shore batteries seemed concentrated on us, salvo after salvo struck the ship, doing indescribable damage in the packed starboard battery where all the storming party were awaiting to land; the foremost howitzer's crew were wiped out with the exception of the voice pipeman, who was a couple of yards away.

The strangest part of this was that the trench mortar battery, not more than 4 feet away, did not receive injury at that time. Within the space of a few seconds the leading seaman in charge of our battery had been hit in the back of the head, whilst half a dozen of our battery had received superficial scratches.

We were now alongside the Mole and sheltered a little from the murderous hail of shell from the forts, which continued to keep up a burst of shrapnel around our funnels, which showed up and made excellent targets. Every gun in the *Vindictive* that could bear had now given tongue and the night was made hideous by the nerve-racking shatter of the pom-poms, the deep bell-like boom of the howitzers and trench mortars, and all-pervading rattle of musketry and machine-gun fire; it was hell with a vengeance and it seemed well-nigh miraculous that human beings could live in such an inferno.

Meanwhile, down on the quarter-deck the ship was being secured by means of the large grappling irons fitted on wire pennants, which had continually been thrown back from the wall by a few Germans whose bravery was eclipsed by none, until they were driven off by rifle-fire. After what seemed an eternity, the anchor rattled down and the all-fast signal was given. Of our sixteen specially constructed gangways only two remained, but these were already in position and up into the night went one huge yell, all the pent-up feeling of the years of war and hatred and the lust for killing, and the seamen's storming party landed, followed by the Royal Marines.

To many, that yell was their last earthly sound, as the Germans kept up a concentrated machine-gun fire on the gangways, and the dead and wounded were piled up three or four deep, but the remnants of the platoon staggered through, reorganized, and carried on as though still in the peaceful heart of Kent. To see these men, the cream of the youth of England, laughing, cheering, and swearing, rushing into what seemed certain death, was not inspiring; it was heart-breaking to think that in these enlightened days the youth of the country was being butchered in the cause of civilization, and St. Peter must have wiped his eye as he greeted most of them home.

Once on the top of the Mole one was assailed by the overwhelming feeling of nakedness and maddening desire to go forward at all costs and stop the hail of death that swept the upper Mole; sense and reason were replaced by insane fury and the events that followed cannot be remembered coherently; it was a horrible nightmare of sweating and cursing men, thirsty for blood, the sickening 'sog' of bayonets and of shots at close quarters. Of the individual deeds of heroism that were enacted that night there are hundreds that never will be told, they are kept a jealously guarded secret in the hearts of the survivors.

At last, through the din and uproar, rose the wailing of a siren, the signal that the job had been done, telling the storming parties to retire and the remnants of the platoons, by now sadly depleted, to fall back to the ship, bringing wherever possible their wounded. But what of the *Vindictive*? Whilst the landing-party was on the Mole, she had been subjected to a galling bombardment of shrapnel, and her upper-deck was a veritable shambles, while the superstructure presented a sorry appearance. Willing hands had ventured forth under heavy machine-gun fire and cleared the wounded below and given help to the returning parties from the Mole.

After the safety limit of time had been reached in allowing the parties to return orders were given to slip the cable, while the guns that were still serviceable put up a barrage to prevent a counter-attack, and the wind, now favourable, again carried down the artificial fog and blotted out the ship from the shore batteries whilst we steamed all out for England and home.

W. Wainwright joined the Royal Navy in 1915, at the age of 16, and served in H.M.S. Monarch *(Grand Fleet) in the North Sea, taking part in the Battle of Jutland. Was drafted to H.M.S.* Superb *in 1917, and served in her until volunteering to take part in raid against Zeebrugge (April 23rd, 1918). Returning to depot was sent to H.M.S.* Gardenia, *engaged on anti-submarine warfare and convoying duties in the Irish Sea and North Atlantic, and later in the Mediterranean. Was in Tripoli (Syria) when Armistice was signed and proceeded to Constantinople with the occupying Fleet. Engaged in 1919 in operations against Russia, around the Crimea and Black Sea ports, and on repatriation duties in Turkey-in-Asia. In April 1920 left H.M.S.* Gardenia *with the Engeli Expedition (a party of 31 men) in an attempt to reach Engeli (North Persia) via Batoum and Baku, to reorganize the volunteer Fleet on the Caspian Sea. The party arrived in Baku (Azerberzium) the day that state turned Bolshevik, was surrounded by the 11th Red Army and forced to surrender. The whole party, along with a few other Britishers, being confined first at the Checka and then in cells in the Bieloff*

Prison, on the outskirts of Baku. Exchanged, in November 1920, reaching England December 1920.

Served later in H.M.S.s Bruce, Malaya, *and* Serapis, *and was finally discharged in June 1928.*

TORPEDOED IN THE AEGEAN SEA

Reginald Cecil Huggins

The early part of April 1917 found H.M. Transport *Arcadian*, as she then was, with a full complement of 'cannon-fodder' pushing her nose through the grey seas in the direction of the Eastern theatres of War, Salonika and Palestine.

At that time the submarine blockade, which was intended to bring Great Britain to her knees, was in full swing, and the constant fear of the ocean traveller was the making of the unwelcome acquaintance of a torpedo, or 'tin fish,' as that death-dealer was familiarly known.

Apart from one or two scares, no untoward incident occurred this side of Malta, and reaching that stage of the journey, one of the two Japanese destroyers that, so far, had afforded us protection, remained in harbour, leaving the *Arcadian* for the remainder of the journey with only one destroyer zigzagging at a respectful distance across our bows. The Japanese destroyer brought us, after days and nights of steaming, within sight of the African coast. This was the scene of our first brush with the enemy.

A submarine had been spotted, and with the destroyer circling around at full speed, belching out the while a thick black smoke screen, we raced as fast as the engines would turn over, to a place of comparative safety, that being a small river on the north coast of Africa. There we were literally bottled-up for three days together with another crowded transport, while our underwater foe patrolled the river's mouth waiting and watching for us to come out.

Upon the morning of the third day, the other transport set out only to return in the early afternoon in a sinking condition.

After that, we were not too optimistic as to our chances, but in the early evening the *Arcadian* directed her nose seawards once more, steaming out into the open without mishap. Our Japanese friends, of course, still playing the part of protector.

Arrived at Salonika, the troops intended for that front disembarked, and, under cover of darkness, we of the Egyptian contingent put forth to sea bound for Alexandria. Three hundred souls of us, however, were destined not to reach that objective.

Through the night we sped on our way down the Aegean Archipelago, and the following evening, a Sunday, saw our real encounter with the U-boat that had dogged us so relentlessly. Without one moment's warning, a terrific explosion occurred, made hideous by the splintering into matchwood of great timbers, the crash of falling glass and the groaning of steel girders wrenched asunder, followed by the hissing rush of escaping steam from the ship's boilers.

Nobody needed enlightening as to the fact that the old *Arcadian*, which had so often completed the Eastern trip, had received a 'Blighty' one, and was shortly due for Davey Jones's locker. If doubts existed, these were soon dispelled; since, having given one convulsive shudder from end to end, the great ship began to settle down on her port side with the loose deck paraphernalia slithering about in all directions and dropping into the sea.

To get away easier, I discarded my military boots, and donned a life-belt. On reaching the side of the ship and peering over, one of the two small boats which had survived the explosion was to be seen putting away full to overflowing with men. Nothing else remained but to make the descent into the sea by a rope conveniently to hand, and this I attempted. Unfortunately, my equilibrium on the ship's rail was disturbed by someone in great haste to be among the rescued, and, falling, my arm became jammed at the wrist between two steel uprights employed as supports.

For moments that seemed long years, I was dangling from the side of the rapidly sinking *Arcadian*, but was rescued just in time from that perilous position by two comrades, one easing my weight from underneath the shoulders while the other wrenched the caught arm from the fixture. I do not know the identity of my rescuers to this day.

Seizing the means of escape, I shinned quickly down into the sea – my hands suffering badly from rope-burns, and was surprised to find the water comfortably warm. My attire consisted of trousers, shirt and socks. The lifebelt, I found, supported my body so that my head from the chin was above water, and I looked about me, taking in the seascape. Being a non-swimmer at that time, I was unable to get clear of the ship, and her enormous bulk seemed likely to topple over upon me at any moment, supposing I was not sucked down one of the huge funnels by the inrush of water. That actually did happen to our Chaplain. He was, subsequently, vomited out again like a rocket and suffered no ill effects, when the water charging up against the heated boilers caused an explosion.

Having read about the vortex a sinking vessel will make, I was ruminating on my chances as a survivor. The suspense, fortunately, was brief. For a moment or two the *Arcadian* partly righted on her keel and then with much hissing of escaping steam and explosions from the boiler rooms, she slid for ever out of sight of human eyes, carrying with her hundreds of troops and her own crew caught like rats on the lower decks.

Within three minutes (official Admiralty time) from the time that she was struck an that remained of the ship was bits of floating wreckage.

It is difficult to describe my sensations during the minute or so following. Down and still further down, I was dragged by the suction till it seemed that I must soon touch bottom. I was spun round with great rapidity and swirled about in an alarming manner. I held my breath and closed tightly both eyes and mouth, until forced by bursting lungs to take in air, I opened my mouth, getting a large helping of Aegean Sea.

My mind was functioning normally. I can recollect that I had quite decided that H.M. Army was about to lose one live cavalryman. And though I cannot justly claim to being more courageous than my neighbour, it is curious that having made up my mind that my name would shortly appear in the casualty lists, I was not the least bit afraid. I can give no reason. I was young, eighteen at that time, having declared a false age on enlistment, and naturally I had no overwhelming desire to provide provender for the denizens of the deep.

At last, however, I came with a rush to the surface, and was violently ill for some time. Glancing at my wristlet watch, I found it had stopped. The time was 5.45 p.m.

Large numbers of drowned, the survivors, and a quantity of wreckage were close by me. After desperate efforts to propel myself through the water, I gave up in despair, finding that no headway was being made. That fact, however, was of no importance, as only miles of ocean waste stretched around. The sun now was lowered on the horizon: the sea became chilly and turbulent. The heads of the survivors by this time were dotted about with great distances between, they having drifted with the wind and the currents.

After some hours, I was brought by the same means within reach of a small raft, which was clutched with considerable gusto, and found myself in the excellent company of five officers, three Navy and two Army. Only an occasional word was spoken. Darkness descended quickly, and the sea was bitterly cold.

Wafted across the waters, our ears received the words of the hymn 'Nearer my God to Thee.' Apparently every poor devil – more than three-quarters drowned – was doing his level best to swell the chorus on that awful night. The incident has imprinted itself indelibly on my memory.

The combined weight of our six bodies completely submerged the slender support, but, nevertheless, by arrangement we each of us managed in turn to scramble on to the raft's surface, and to get for a short spell as much of our numbed bodies above sea-level as was possible in the circumstances. This we continued to do, helping each other as best we could.

Towards midnight a small white light was plainly visible in the far distance, and later another, and some time after, another. Through the ingenuity of one of the Navy officers we were shortly located. In his possession was an electric torch – quite unaffected, apparently, by its prolonged immersion – and with the instrument he proceeded to signal in the Morse code. We watched intently. The beam of a searchlight shot into the sky from the rescuing ships. It swung from side to side, missing our little group again and again. Eventually, however, it found its mark.

Then quickly the lantern shut down to allow of a message to be flashed out. Slowly this was read to us by our friend with the torch. 'Will pick you up soon as possible with other survivors.'

Utter blackness again and another long waiting; this time, however, with a hope. At last there came stealing upon us the tall black bows of a ship. The 'Q' ship *Redbreast* she was. Voices hailed us from the deck. She drew swiftly alongside, and dropped a rope ladder. Down this came a couple of men, who heaved us up. A basin of piping hot grog, a belabouring with rough towels, a berth with an abundant supply of blankets and to bed.

Trooper Reginald C. Huggins enlisted in March 1915 in the City of London (Rough-riders) Yeomanry. Underwent period of cavalry training in Ireland (Curragh and Dublin) and drafted the East Riding of Yorkshire Imperial Yeomanry for service on the Palestine Front. From there in early part of 1918 to France in the 102nd Machine Gun Corps. Wounded in the fighting before Valenciennes on October 28th, 1918, and discharged from hospital in May 1921.

FIRST DAYS OF IMPRISONMENT

Reginald Morris

It was at a time when in England the blackthorn begins to break into beauty, when fairies flit over the hedges, leaving traces of gleaming whiteness; it was at a time when the pale-scented cowslip shows the joy of life... It was the first day of spring.

The much-discussed possibility of a great enemy offensive had become a reality. Overnight we had been moved up to the supports on that sector of the line facing the little village of La Fontaine, south-east of Arras.

It had rained heavily during the night and the trenches were filled with water. Dawn broke with a dense mist, which did not lift until noon. The enemy barrage started in earnest between two and three in the morning and continued with hardly a moment's lull for many hours. Mixed with the deluge of shrapnel and high explosive were irregular spasms of gas shells. The barrages were mostly of the creeping variety, returning again and again in deadly waves.

Although the enemy had surrounded us early in the day, it was not until the evening that we had any inkling of our real position. We discovered then that we were being enfiladed from behind by machine guns, as well as from above by enemy planes. Acting as a regimental stretcher bearer – the only one alive with what was left of our company – my work was not very easy, especially as a gas mask had to be worn most of the time. The mud and water were above our knees, and so many dead and dying lay around me that I was bewildered.

Without boasting, I can say that I led a charmed life. I would attend to an urgent case at a machine-gun post and deal with it just before the post was blown up...and from that post to another and so on. Being a big fellow, I carried some of the smaller ones on my back to a dug-out. The dug-out soon got full up...and I got so exhausted that I carried on in a mechanical sort of way. In the end my headquarters was a narrow bit of trench containing the captain of my company, my platoon officer, a sergeant, another private and myself. We seemed to be the only people left capable of standing up.

I remember my captain saying, 'Stay here, we shall need you soon.' It was not long before he partly collapsed against the parapet with a good sniff of gas. I broke half a dozen of those small anti-gas containers under his nose and in his mouth, which brought him round.

Friends credit me with iron nerves, but by this time I was nearing the end of my tether. I moved like one in a trance. My stock of field and shell dressings had long since given out and I was tearing up puttees, shirts, socks, anything that would make a bandage. I was hungry, worn rout, wet through to the skin, and covered in mud and blood. I had had nothing to eat since tea-time the day before. The few biscuits I did have I gave to my platoon officer in exchange for his last cigarette and a drop of rum. A few minutes after, he was dead with a lump of shrapnel in his brain.

At the moment of my capture, I was working on a fellow with his ribs smashed, kneeling down and bending over him, trying to stem the rush of blood. I happened to glance up, looking for someone who could assist me, when I found the fair face of a Saxon looking down intently at me. Pre-occupied with my work, I had not noticed him before. With his rifle slung across his back, he pushed a long-nosed field revolver almost down my throat. His sudden appearance completely surprised me. Glancing round quickly, I found myself surrounded. The trench and parapets swarmed with German infantrymen.

I got up slowly from my kneeling position, the revolver still pointing at me, and put up my hands. My captor stripped my pockets, but gave me back some photographs and, smiling, pointed up the trench. Moving up it was a string of wounded, guarded by the enemy.

I followed them. We threaded our way across No Man's Land in batches of about six, two or three guards watching each group. The artillery reply to the enemy's fire was not very heavy and it fell short, else some of us might have been spared the journey across. We had been deprived of our gas masks, hence it was no joke trying to avoid the gas-infected areas. In and out of the smashed wires, shell-holes, and dead we filed, the guards stopping now and again to examine the bodies of the dead. Some of us had to pick up German wounded. A series of long marches from station to station followed, until finally we arrived at a field hospital. This was a three-walled store tent, open to the inclemency of the weather. Inside, the dead and dying were heaped one upon another, the dying shivering with cold. We thought to find food here, but none was forthcoming.

It was quite dark by now, and the inside of the tent could be seen only when a shell burst near enough to light up the interior with its flashes. Walking through the wires with a mud-soaked greatcoat was well-nigh an impossibility, so I had discarded it. At nightfall, however, it got very cold and I began to shiver. Seeing a dead man at my feet wrapped up in a cloak, I quietly robbed him.

After standing about for a while, we filed off again. The guards leading us were in a hurry. They rushed away, but I was too tired to hurry and keep pace with them. I had a slight surface wound on my right heel. I could not help lagging behind until at last I was alone, lost in the dark. Early the next morning some German transport men found me wandering about and took me to an officer. He sent me to a barbed-wire enclosure.

In this cage I found many others, perhaps about 500 prisoners. We stopped there, exposed to the weather, all that day and the following night, and with nothing whatever to eat or drink. Here we were searched by an interpreter who tried to frighten us. He warned us we should be shot at sight if we attempted to escape. We were not to communicate with the inhabitants of the occupied area, or to receive food from them.

Next morning a weary crowd stumbled out of the cage headed by two Uhlans mounted with all their gorgeous martial trappings. This display made the procession dramatic and spectacular. The night had been cold and had left a heavy dew on the grass. In the morning the sun rose, and its warmth put more heart into me and a little more strength into my legs. As we passed through the billets of soldiers, resting or waiting to be moved up in an emergency, they came out in crowds and lined the route. Some ran from great distances to see us. They eyed us with stolid, unemotional faces. Their minds seemed to have been ground down to a soulless state by their circumstances. Once we passed a transport-driver who had half a black loaf in his hand – that is to say, a piece of coarse bread measuring about 5 inches by 4 inches by 4 inches. He offered it to a fellow prisoner in front of me in exchange for a leather jerkin. The exchange made, the prisoner tore the bread into pieces and gulped it down. Such an incident cannot easily be forgotten; it is stamped into the memory.

A week of tramping about behind the lines followed. We moved like a herd of cattle about to be slaughtered, from one barbed-wire cage to another. Sometimes we were nearly bombed by our own airmen. We seemed to be on exhibition, and forced to march in fours and keep in step. In our weak condition, marching was a necessary agony, but to keep in step was more; it was an imposition. To suffer under restraint is deadly. It is like chaining a man to the scaffold on which he is to be hanged. The clothes I stood in and my tin helmet were all I possessed.

Day by day, I became weaker until at last it got difficult for me to walk any distance. My feet began to blister; my socks were dirty and began to rot. In time the blisters became open sores and my socks fell off my feet. My slight wound complicated matters. I just dragged myself from place to place. The guards paid no attention to my painful state. They just pushed me along or hit me with the butt-end of their rifles when my legs began to give way or the pain of walking became too great.

There were many other prisoners like me. Sometimes, even my 'tin-hat' became heavy and sat on me like that great burden which Bunyan's famous Pilgrim carried in his illustrious Progress. I did not throw it away, however, because it was the only kind of hat I possessed. I thought it might become useful later on.

About the end of March we reached Marchiennes.

Here, I first tasted *sauerkraut*. We were supposed to line up for this, but the fellows were in such a state that the sight and smell of anything like food sent them mad. The first taste made me sick. With this delicacy we were given a morsel of bread about three inches cubic once a day.

Unfortunately, our prison was placed next to a field bakehouse. Hour after hour, fascinated, we would watch groups of Russian prisoners stack hundreds of freshly-baked loaves on wagons to be sent away. In our eagerness to smell the bread, our faces were pressed right up to the barbed wire. It was a horrible torture to which we helplessly submitted ourselves. The temptation was irresistible. In this case pain itself became a pleasure. Every few minutes, a guard came along and slashed with his bayonet to keep us away from the wires. French children native to the place watched the guard, and when the way was clear, approached the wire and threw in pieces of bread, lumps of swede, sugar-beet, and carrot. These were given to us at first out of merciful good-nature, but some of the prisoners, eager to get more, began to barter with anything of value that they were still fortunate enough to possess, such as money, gold rings, and boots. The original good intentions of the children were corrupted and the only extra source of life then available cut off from all but a very small minority. In course of time even this minority undercut itself, because in the circumstances the most opulent of prisoners could not go on producing money or gold rings or whatever was necessary to carry on their self-inflated and self-imposed system of trafficking. When one of these fellows got a little bit of food, he gulped it down before his comrades had had time to snatch at it. My chief amusement consisted in watching the children playing about and in wondering when I should have the joy of being free again. Every act of their freedom was followed with hungry, envious eyes.

There were a few hundreds of us at this camp at Marchiennes. It was a cheerless place...designed to break the best of hearts. We had to sleep on a stone floor. If a small quantity of straw could be got, and what is more important, kept, the coldness of this floor could be modified. Straw could only be kept by sitting on it; as soon as your back was turned, it was taken by your neighbouring bedmates, At night, if the air was very cold we lay and froze until, becoming numbed, we were forced to get up and walk about the yard for an hour or so to try and keep warm. It can be imagined how utterly miserable I felt. I had to squeeze between rows of other sleepers. It was always a tight fit. We were compelled to preserve the same position all through the night, unless, as I have already stated, we were forced to move for sheer lack of warmth. Then you were fortunate, indeed, if the bed place could be found upon returning.

Lice, also, began to appear and became a continual source of irritation. They remained from this time onwards my constant and faithful companions until my release. Water for washing purposes was unobtainable. We had no blankets.

Now and again, small parties were made up and sent away. They never came back. Some said they had gone to Germany. It was discovered a long time afterwards that they had been sent to work behind the German lines in the occupied areas of France and Belgium.

The wheels of time turned slowly but surely and the hour came at last when I found myself in an outgoing party. I hoped it was going to be my fortune to find better conditions. I expected to say good-bye to the cold, lice, and starvation, Marchiennes once left behind. During the following march it poured with rain and, my feet still being bad, I staggered along all day in the mud.

It was evening when we arrived at Douai. We were shut up here in a cold, very dark, dirty dungeon of a brick-kiln. As far as billets were concerned, we had gone from bad to worse. The food was a little better. We only had *sauerkraut* at odd times. The same amount of bread was given, but the monotony of the diet was relieved by a meal of horse-beans and sometimes a small piece of black sausage about an inch cube or a teaspoonful of turnip-saccharine jam. All these came under the heading of dinner. Breakfast, served to us between 4 and 5 in the morning, consisted of a drop of some liquid, invariably hot, and seriously called coffee by the guards. It was compounded of a roasted mixture of acorns, sugar-beet, and other vegetable substances.

We were made to work, and were sent out in large working parties. After breakfast, we set out before it was light, and seemed to walk miles through deserted and shell-smashed villages. Although these villages had the appearance of being deserted, they were actually alive with German infantrymen, who lived underground.

Our work consisted of remaking the railroad along which was once the main French line from Douai to Arras. Some days we 'packed' under the sleepers with heavy hammering tools or helped to straighten the lines with great iron crowbars. Other days, we laid down the rails ourselves and fixed them. Sometimes we had to carry on under fire from our own guns. It was heavy and heart-breaking work on the little food we were given. The tramp to the neighbourhood of our work was in itself a task. Work was begun as soon as we arrived and continued until about 2 or 3 in the afternoon. There was no fixed hour for ceasing work. We were forced to wait until relieved by a mixed party of German and Austrian labour parties.

When relieved we tramped home, it being generally dark when we arrived at our brick-kiln abode. Then we had our dinner. Dinner! Let those two syllables sink in. Dinner! All the whole day between 5 in the morning and 5 in the evening, we had nothing whatever to eat.

It was curious to tramp along the old French line, past the broken-down stations, with all their glittering grandeur of glass smashed to dust. We sometimes came across some old wayside sign still hanging, a forlorn and tragic indication of the civilization that was once. I often wondered how many pretty damsels in neat dresses, or dapper, bearded, well-groomed gentlemen had waited for the train on those refuse-covered, grass-grown platforms.

The attitude of my mind during those unusual days reviewed in the light of to-day excites my wonder. Forcing myself to smile, I never gave up hope. Some fellows lost heart from the first. Their spirits gradually sank, their bodies with them until to live became too great a burden. They just passed away.

From this time on to the Armistice is a bitter story of months of the agony of demoralizing starvation, of sickness, of ever-present death, of escapes and recaptures, of hard work, of the great retreat, of the stupefaction of sudden freedom – a bitter story with one or two bright moments.

Private Reginald Morris joined the Artists' Rifles in June 1915, at the age of 19, but was recalled to the Civil Service, enlisting again in January 1916. In June 1916 he was in France with R.A. Ordnance Corps, having a hectic few months dodging explosions on bombed and shelled ammunition dumps. In April 1917 he was transferred to Infantry Training Corps, joining the 25th Northumberland Fusiliers in May 1917. He served at Ypres, Cambrai, and Scarpe Salient, and various points on the Arras front. In March 1918 he was captured opposite La Fontaine.

CAPTIVITY IN THE ARDENNES

Victor Denham

I shall never forget the morning of March 28th, 1918, when I watched our trenches and the familiar landmarks disappear under the intense bombardment of hundreds of minenwerfers – those earthquakes in miniature. I watched and waited in a state of mental numbness or apathy, and at last the bit reserved for me hit me in the head. When I took a further interest in matters I was a prisoner.

Yet the memory of that morning and of the months in France that preceded it are not so vivid as the memories of my captivity.

After spending a few hours in a prisoners' cage I was given a bag containing some biscuits, and a German soldier, no doubt pitying my bandaged head and my youthfulness, gave me his ration of 'coffee.' This action impressed me very favourably at the time, as we were conjecturing on the treatment we were going to receive.

Then we started to march. A Uhlan, complete with lance, rode at the head of the column and another at the rear. We marched without a single halt all through the afternoon, and reached our destination – Douai – about eleven o'clock. That march became a very tragic procession towards the end, and I have no doubt that it would have been more tragic if any of us had fallen out.

At Douai we spent a nightmare of a night. We were herded into a long, low building once used for storing coal. This place was already packed with English prisoners, and someone had lit two huge fires, one at each end. All through the night we stood there – it was only with difficulty that I could turn round – and the red glare of the fires, the pitch blackness of the shadows, and the groans, cursings and stench of perspiring humanity gave me a good impression of the ancient idea of Hell.

At last the door was unlocked and we stumbled into the blessed rain-laden air. We resembled coal-men. Although my head was throbbing painfully, I considered myself lucky, as all the wounded were sent to a large, clean building with wire beds. Here I made my first acquaintance with German black bread, and after drawing two wisps of straw from my portion I decided I did not want it. Later on I was not so particular.

After Douai, Denain, where we realized the full meaning of captivity. There were days of idleness divided by 'meals' of bad black bread and 'soup' made from dried mangel-wurzels. This horrible stuff was the cause of daily cases of dysentery.

We travelled from place to place until a party of us arrived at some saw mills near Tannay, in the Ardennes. We were arranged in groups according to our civil occupations. I was a clerk, but having heard good things about working on a farm I decided I was a farmer's boy – only to find that my job was to load trucks with heavy planks of wood.

The country around was beautiful, the weather glorious, and if we had had sufficient food we might have been to some degree reconciled to our lot, but every day our plight appeared more hopeless: every day we became a little weaker. How we managed to work at all surprises me now. Our rations were a slice of black bread every evening with sometimes a small herring, and soup at midday, consisting of horse beans and a few small cubes of meat. There was 'coffee' in the morning.

The sleeping quarters were of wood and so old that the beams and roofs were alive with wood lice and bugs, which dropped on our faces as we tried to sleep, and gave out a horrible smell when squashed. When we complained, our guards thought it a huge joke.

At last most of us slept out of doors. If only we could have stopped dreaming about food! Food! That was all we thought and talked about. We mentally prepared and partook of most elaborate banquets. I used to sleep with a fellow of my own age and we told each other of our favourite dishes. What feasts we spread as we lay together beneath the stars! Every evening with great will power I managed to save a portion of my bread ration for the morning, putting it inside the straw mattress on which

I lay to make sure of it. Yet in the morning it was always gone. I thought that I must have eaten it during my sleep. It was only after some weeks that I learned that my bed-fellow had been caught in hospital taking other men's rations. I had never suspected him.

A man who was a lay preacher held services, which I attended. The Germans laughed and mocked at us from the other side of the wire. Yet that man, though urging us to pray for strength to endure and play the game, was caught stealing his fellow prisoners' food.

One man made a bowl of soup which he placed by an open window to cool. He turned his back for a few seconds and when he turned round again it was gone.

Hunger at last made me part with my wrist-watch – the only article of value I had besides my boots. It was a great moment of decision when I took it to the Italian cook. He gave me a small sack of dried crusts of bread, kept back from our rations, no doubt. I put one or two crusts in my pockets and smuggled the sack under my greatcoat into my sleeping box. But many pairs of eyes must have noticed my sudden stoutness. I left the place for about half-a-minute and when I returned not even the sack remained. And still those eyes looked at me, blandly and innocently.

It was a true saying in those days that 'An Englishman was an Englishman's worst friend.' If a German was in charge of the food store we were sure of obtaining our fair ration, but a fellow prisoner in charge would soon grow fat at our expense. Still we were all mad for food, and madmen cannot be made responsible for their actions.

The most dreadful thing about captivity is the loss of that spirit of comradeship which on the other side of the line kept men decent in the most trying circumstances. I sensed this change in relation to one another soon after I was captured, and before very long it was every man for himself at any cost. No pity or kindness was to be found behind barbed wire enclosures, and the weakest went first. Hunger made hatred universal. For this reason I was glad I had become separated from those with whom I had been captured. Often I wondered how men of the same race could be such beasts to one another.

In charge of us was a huge bearded German sergeant-major whom we called 'Bluebeard.' He was a typical German bully, with a hatred for us that one only found in those who had never been to the Front. There was also a sergeant under him who was just the opposite, but this sergeant had lost an eye in the trenches.

At roll-call one evening I overslept myself, and after half-an-hour's search this sergeant discovered me – a very small portion of humanity curled up in my box blissfully unaware of the uproar in the camp over my disappearance. I was greeted by my fellow prisoners with howls and curses for making them wait so long. Out of the corner of my eye I could see 'Bluebeard' getting his big stick ready for me, but the sergeant had seen him as well and putting himself between me and 'Bluebeard' he pushed me into the back rank of the crowd. I was placed in a cell as punishment and was anticipating a pleasant night's sleep – for the cell was the only clean place in the camp – when about ten o'clock old 'One-eye' came along to release me with a fatherly pat on the head.

There was another unpleasant person at this place; a white-haired, blue-eyed German in charge of our working party. With my head still plastered he gave me the job of loading coal with a huge shovel. I could only manage a quarter of a shovelful at a time, but mistaking my weakness for laziness, he caught hold of me by the throat and nearly choked me. He learnt my name, and whenever I heard him say with a grin, 'Come here, Mr. Victor Denham,' I knew I was 'for it.'

By now our numbers had rapidly decreased. Illness and mutilation in the machine shops took toll each day. It is still a mystery to me how a weak, insignificant boy as I was came through it when fine, strong men went to pieces and disappeared every week.

At last we became too weak to work in the mills any longer, so were drafted off in small numbers to various villages and given the work of hoeing mangel-wurzels – which seemed to be the staple food at the time. We were not trusted with the potato fields.

About this time I became something of a fatalist and considered that every change I made was for the best, so I volunteered for different working parties and was always moving about. At one place the French inhabitants were quite friendly to us, and at one cottage which we used to pass every day the occupants, with the acquiescence of our guards, allowed us to raid their potato store. What a feast we had that night! But the authority in charge heard of it and the inhabitants were warned that drastic punishment would follow the giving of food to the English prisoners. The villagers resorted to putting potatoes and apples along the roads we had to travel. No one could punish us for finding a potato or apple.

Another move. More mangel-wurzels needed hoeing. Our party numbered about a dozen. And what a party we were! So prematurely aged and weak that our hoes were a necessary aid to getting to work.

At this village a Scotsman was our cook – as we knew to our cost. He soon got fat on what he kept back from our rations and very soon collected hundreds of marks by selling as supper food he had kept back from our dinner. But he was paid in his own coin, for one day all his marks were missing. His suspicions immediately fell on us and, appealing to our guards – all decent fellows – he made us strip, and then searched our clothes. But he never found his money. The German sergeant who watched the proceedings was much amused; we found out that it was he who had taken the money.

With his plausible tongue, this Scotsman won the sympathy of the French woman who lived next door (we were lodged in a house), and she gave him some good dinners which he carried past our very noses with such unctuous remarks as 'God bless her!' How I hated him!

I was becoming very weak now and it was evident that the guards noticed it, for they would enter our room every night with the remains of their suppers and, after searching round, would discover me in my corner and put what they had brought in my basin.

A German infantry regiment passed us one day. They seemed very dispirited. In front of the column was a scarecrow of a horse. We were told that it was the regiment's meat ration. And so it turned out to be. The inhabitants of the village also had their share and, thanks to them, we were given the head and a few ribs.

The sight of an officer passing along the road by which we were working would act on our guards magically. We would be peacefully working when they would suddenly seize us round the throats and shake us like dogs, calling us all kinds of names. This was the kind of treatment the officers delighted to see us subjected to. When they had gone normal relations were resumed by our guards.

It was whilst in this part that I commenced to suffer from a form of dropsy. I would be working in the fields and would suddenly discover that my legs seemed rooted to the ground. I then found that they had swollen to twice their normal size.

One day a German commandant visited us and asked if we had any complaints! We were surprised into silence. Any complaints! One of us ventured to say that we should like to write home, and after a few days we were each given a field card to satisfy us. These cards never reached home.

Home! I tried not to think of it. I did not even know if it still existed. It might have been bombed out of existence for all I knew. Things were bad enough as they were, but to think of home and all it meant made one feel absolutely hopeless.

One day, as I was hoeing, one of the guards came over to me and gently led me away, I did not worry about what was going to happen to me as I was getting past caring for anything, but I was rather surprised when he made me lie down in the shadow of a hedge and told me I was to work no more. All that day I rested in the warm sun and compared the country with the English country and thought how happy I could have been if only I were strong again and not hungry. The next day I could not get up in the morning. I did not want to eat. I only wanted to be let alone, and I had my wish. During the day it seemed as if I had been completely forgotten.

The next day was my birthday. What a birthday! I well remember praying that I might die. Utterly hopeless I had no desire to live. My very body seemed a burden to me.

I did not undress at night, but lay in a kind of stupor, not caring for anything or anybody. But I overheard the others discussing me. A little ginger-haired man whom I disliked for no other reason than that he had a head-wound alive with lice remarked: –

'He won't last much longer. He doesn't wash. He doesn't undress. He doesn't do anything. He just lays there. I know what that means.'

I knew what it meant too – and had been hoping for the end, but hearing myself discussed in such a manner awoke what little self-respect and pride I had left. I thought to myself, 'I'll show them if I'm done for or not.'

The next morning, although I had eaten nothing for several days, I managed to stumble downstairs and out to the working party. The guards seemed delighted to see me again. Perhaps they did not want to be bothered with the trouble of a funeral. I did not do any work, but the fresh air and the sunshine helped me to regain a little strength.

But it did not last long. Soon I was in hospital in Sedan, so weak that I could not walk; so thin that I could not sit down.

Rifleman Victor Denham joined the London Rifle Brigade at eighteen, and went to France in August 1917. Took part in the battle for Cambrai in November 1917. Shot in the head during the German offensive at Arras, March 1918, and made prisoner of war. Repatriated from Lamsdorf Camp (an unofficial War Prisoners' Camp), December 1918. Discharged, September 1919.